Successful Adoption

Successful Adoption

A Guide for Christian Families

NATALIE NICHOLS GILLESPIE

INTEGRITY®
PUBLISHERS
family

Nashville

SUCCESSFUL ADOPTION: A GUIDE FOR CHRISTIAN FAMILIES

Published by Integrity Publishers, a division of Integrity Media, Inc.
660 Baker's Bridge Ave., Suite 200, Franklin, TN 37067

HELPING PEOPLE WORLDWIDE EXPERIENCE THE MANIFEST PRESENCE OF GOD.

Published in association with Yates & Yates, LLP, Literary Agents, Orange, California.

Scripture references are used by permission from the following sources: The King James Version of the Bible (KJV).The Message (MSG), copyright 1993, 1994, 1995, 1996, 2000, 2001, 2002, by Eugene H. Peterson, NavPress Publishing Group. The New American Standard Bible® (NASB), copyright © 1960, 1962, 1963, 1968, 1971, 1972, 1973, 1975, 1977, 1995 by The Lockman Foundation. Used by permission. The Holy Bible, New International Version® (NIV), Copyright © 1973, 1978, 1984 by New York International Bible Society, Zondervan Bible Publishers. The New King James Version (NKJV). Copyright © 1982 by Thomas Nelson, Inc. Used by permission. All rights reserved. The Holy Bible, New Living Translation (NLT) copyright © 1996 by Tyndale Charitable Trust, Tyndale House Publishers. The New Revised Standard Version (NRSV) (Anglicized Edition), copyright 1989, 1995 by the Division of Christian Education of the National Council of the Churches of Christ in the United States of America. The New Century Version® (NCV®). Copyright © 1987, 1988, 1991 by Thomas Nelson, Inc. Used by permission. All rights reserved.

The information in this book is believed to be accurate and reliable. However, the information contained in this book is for educational and research purposes only and should not be construed as legal, medical, or financial advice for any specific situation. You should seek legal, medical, financial, or other similar advice from licensed professionals who can advise you after considering all of the facts and circumstances of your situation as well as the applicable rules, laws, and regulations of the appropriate city, state, and country. We do not necessarily endorse the adoption agencies mentioned in this book and can not vouch for their quality of services.

ISBN 13: 9-781-59145-412-0
ISBN 10: 1-59145-412-3

Cover Design: Christopher Tobias; Tobias' Outwear for Books
Interior Design: Teresa Billingsley

Library of Congress Cataloging-in-Publication Data (to come)

Printed in the United States of America
06 07 08 09 LBM 9 8 7 6 5 4 3 2 1

Dedication

This book is dedicated to the millions of children around the world who wish for nothing more than the love of a family to call their own—and to the families reading this who will bring them home.

Contents

Part One:
Opt to Adopt! You're Interested, but Where Do You Start?

Start at the Very Beginning: Yes, There Are Kids Who Need You!
What God Wants for His Kids
Love One Another ♦ The Chance to Be Part of God's Big Picture ♦ Adoption in the Scriptures
How God Uses Adoptive Families
Adoptive Families Touch Others with Their Stories ♦ Adoptees May Influence Their Birth Countries ♦ Adoption Is an Example of His Love for Us
What Adoption Is and What It Means
Who Thinks About Adopting?
Forever Families ♦ Relative Adoption ♦ Simple Adoption ♦ Stepparent Adoption ♦ Nonrelative Adoption
Where and Who Are the Adoptable Children?
Infant Adoptions in the U.S. ♦ Children in the Foster-Care System ♦ Fostering vs. Adopting ♦ International Children
Kinds of Families Who Adopt
Families Without Children ♦ Families with Children ♦ Older Couples ♦ Singles Who Want to Be Parents
We Could Never Afford It
A Matter of Trust ♦ It Does Not Have to Cost a Fortune
We're Not Perfect—Can We Adopt?
Age Considerations ♦ Background Issues ♦ Newlyweds ♦ Children Already in the Home ♦ Divorced
Adoption: The Family of God
My Adoption Miracle
I Was Adopted! (by Mark Schultz, Christian Singer-Songwriter)

Part Three:
The Paperwork Is Finished and the Wait Begins

People You Need to Tell

Counselors ♦ Caregivers ♦ Other Adoptive Families

Preparing Your Answers

My Adoption Miracle

The Right Max for Us (by Nicole C. Mullen, award-winning singer)

The Wait Is Over!

A Birthmother Picks You ♦ Moving Forward Together ♦ Learning About Relinquishment ♦ Gifts for a Birthmother

You've Found Your Child!

Preparing for Children from State Care ♦ Getting to Know Your Child

Your Referral Is Here!

International Adoption Referrals ♦ Posing with the FedEx Driver

International Travel—Getting Ready to Go

Immunizations and Other Health Considerations ♦ Preparing for the Unknown ♦ Suitcase Restrictions ♦ Baby Supplies You Might Need ♦ Packing Lists ♦ Funds You Need on Your Trip ♦ Speaking Your Child's Language ♦ Bringing Home Memories ♦ Calling Home

My Adoption Miracle

The Miracle of Two Sisters (by Cory and Marlene Barron, Children's Hope International)

Part Four:
Gotcha! A Forever Family Is Born

We Gotcha! Now What?

Being at the Hospital ♦ What to Take with You

The International Child

Gotcha Day! In Your Child's Country ♦ Your Child Cries at the Sight of You ♦ Keep Your Child Close ♦ Helping Your Child Sleep ♦ Addressing Medical Issues ♦ Before You Come Home

After International Travel

Give Yourself and Your Baby a Break ♦ See the Pediatrician ASAP

Bringing Home the Hurt Child

This Is Too Easy! ♦ This Is Too Hard! ♦ Fighting Your Fears ♦ Lift Your Spirits with Christian Fellowship ♦ Can Someone Take Away My Child?

Post-Placement Blues

Are You Depressed? ♦ Everything's Out of Control! ♦ Why Am I Not Falling in Love? ♦ Our Other Children Are Acting Up ♦ It's Not What I Expected

My Adoption Miracle

Love Never Fails (by Robin and Paul Pennington, FamilyLife's Hope for Orphans)

The First Days Together

Document Every Moment ♦ Prepare Meals Ahead ♦ Keep Visitors to a Minimum ♦ Take Plenty of Time Off ♦ Take Care of Yourself

During Childhood

You Can't Hold Your Child Too Much ♦ Good Character Is More Important than Good Grades ♦ Some Hurts Take a Long Time to Heal ♦ Preserve Memories

During the Teen Years

Teens Need Hugs ♦ Grace Is More Important than Authority ♦ Remember Unconditional Love ♦ Questioning Identity and Authority Is Normal ♦ Recognize What Is Not Normal

The Blessings

God Really Is Faithful ♦ You Can Trust Him with All Your Children ♦ Adoption Blessed Us More than We Blessed a Child ♦ Adoption Opened Our Eyes to Others' Needs

My Adoption Miracle

Our Precious Jem (by Traci DePree, Christian fiction author)

Part Five: Adoption as a Ministry: How Can You Help?

Share Your Story ♦ Adoption Workshops

We Are Not Adopting—How Can We Help?
Volunteer, Volunteer, Volunteer!

Volunteer at Local Children's Homes ♦ Give Financially ♦ Join Mission Trips ♦ Become a Guardian ad Litem ♦ Become a Foster Parent ♦ Start Listening ♦ Throw a Shower

Helping Birth Families Heal

Volunteer at a Crisis Pregnancy Center

Mentoring Adoptive Families
My Adoption Miracle

Mothering the Motherless (by Rita Springer, modern worship leader)

Discover Local Needs ♦ Offer Classes ♦ National Adoption Awareness Month ♦ Support an Orphanage ♦ Partner with Adoptive Families ♦ Become Respite Caregivers

How to Get Going

Meet with Your Pastor ♦ Establish Your Bookkeeping ♦ Create a Committee ♦ Write Letters of Reference ♦ Organize Fund-Raisers

Churches Making a Difference for Orphans
Brenham First Baptist, Brenham, Texas ♦ West Angeles Church of God in Christ, Los Angeles, California ♦ Irving Bible Church, Irving, Texas ♦ Just Get Involved

My Adoption Miracle
A New Home, a Grateful Heart (by Robert and Jennifer Marks, international adoption)

Part Six
Where to Go from Here: Continuing the Journey

Foreword

Bracing against the winter cold of a Kentucky night after the warmth of the Steven Curtis Chapman and MercyMe Christmas concert, a little girl called out to her mother, "Mommy, do you think those foster children who were onstage will get adopted?" Her mother replied, "I don't know, honey." The girl was silent for a few moments, then answered resolutely, "We'll take them all, won't we, Mom!"

The greatest need of orphans can even be recognized by a child—the love and security of a family. God sets the lonely into families, and he does this by speaking to the hearts of his people with a still, small voice . . . and it begins with a simple call . . . the call to adopt. God is calling his church to reach out and care for orphans in their need.

Yet many prospective adoptive parents who hear the call to adopt soon find themselves lost, overwhelmed, and afraid. If you are one who has heard this call and you have already begun to delve into the murky waters of adoption through Web research and the like, I am sure you have quickly discovered that the amount of information available is overwhelming—and it is nearly impossible to separate the wheat from the chaff, the secular views from the Christ-centered. You may be feeling at a loss when you begin to consider the practical details of all that adoption entails for you personally.

My wife, Kerry, and I have been working in the field of orphan care and adoption for nearly twenty years combined and have encountered countless people who are interested in adoption but at a loss for proper guidance. According to a recent study, nearly half the people in the United States who consider adoption turn to their house of worship first for information, yet few churches are equipped with the necessary resources and experience to help.

In February 2003, during a promotional tour for Steven Curtis Chapman's album *All About Love*, my wife, Kerry, Steven, and I took the opportunity to meet with a few senior pastors out West to discuss the role of adoption in the church and specifically what is hindering more couples from adopting. We met with pastors representing various facets of Christendom, including John MacArthur, Chuck Smith, and John Piper. Each had his own personal encounters with adoption: Chuck's wife, Kay, was adopted as a child, while John Piper and Steven Curtis are adoptive dads themselves. As you can probably imagine, their views on the subject were varied; however, on two points all were in complete agreement. The first point was that and caring for orphans adoption are important to God. The second point was their perception of the many barriers to adoption that exist. There seems to be a veritable chasm between those who long to adopt and those who are in desperate need of loving, godly families. The great chasm needs to be spanned—bridges need to be built to link waiting children with wanting and willing parents.

The book you are reading by Natalie Nichols Gillespie is perhaps the best bridge-building guide for Christians to successfully adopt that has ever been penned. She has created a power tool for pastors to share with those in their congregations interested in adopting but in need of a guide to maneuver through the thick forest of information.

This book is a good balance of heart, mind, and spirit. It is a tremendously honest and comprehensive resource that covers all the major nuts and bolts of adoption including domestic, international, infant, older child, and foster-adopting. It also touches on a wide variety of peripheral yet critical topics such as orphan care, post-adoption services, and foster care. It is practical and informative yet spiritual and inspiring. Herein, Gillespie not only identifies potential struggles for adopters but illustrates ways to overcome from a biblical point of view. It is rare in the world of child welfare to find such an unbiased resource that encourages the reader to fully submit to God's leading for him or her personally, not to media biases or daunting fears and myths. Gillespie removes the guesswork from the adoption process and eliminates the many anxieties that often hinder families from stepping out in the first place.

The most unique and refreshing aspect of this book is the way Gillespie always brings the reader back to the heavenly perspective as she artfully weaves the Word of God throughout its pages. She talks of those things that are essential in adopting but rarely addressed, such as being patient in the process and waiting on God, trusting and believing God in the midst of setbacks, seeking what is truly best in God's sight, honoring the laws of man, glorifying God in your adoption, being thankful in all things, and honoring and respecting all parties involved: the child, birthparents, adoptive parents, and adoption professionals.

This work is honest, balanced, biblical, practical, informative, and full of wisdom. After reading this book, one cannot help but become inspired, equipped, and involved. Natalie's work will compel people to experience and hear God's heart for orphans.

My wife, Kerry, and I agree that if we could give only one resource to a friend considering adoption, this book would be what we would choose over all others.

Gillespie writes, "Adoption is synonymous with [God's] love," and that sums it up.

Scott A. Hasenbalg
Executive Director
Shaohannah's Hope

Kerry Marks Hasenbalg
Founding Director
Congressional Coalition on
Adoption Institue

Acknowledgments

The dream of this book began when my family started the process of adopting our daughter Amberlie Joy from China. Along the way, many people helped us through the adoption and the preparations for this book, and I would like to thank them.

Thanks to Steven Curtis and Mary Beth Chapman for impacting families and orphaned children around the world through their adoption ministry, Shaohannah's Hope; and to Emily Chapman for first sowing the seeds of adoption in her parents' hearts and for generously telling her story in this book.

Thanks to Shaohannah's Hope executive director Scott Hasenbalg and especially his wife, Kerry, for their willingness to read through the manuscript and provide invaluable advice. Kerry, your words of encouragement were precious to me. Thanks to Mark Schultz, Senator Sam and Mary Brownback, John Fuller, Robin and Paul Pennington, Nicole C. Mullen, Rita Springer, Karen Kingsbury, Sandi Patty, Traci DePree, Robert and Jennifer Marks, Brad and Caprice Payne, Dave Bartlett, Cory Barron, Bob Zaloba, Susan Fremer, Sheena Nesbitt, and those who asked to remain anonymous for their children's sake but were willing to share their personal adoption stories and advice. You touched my heart, and your stories will encourage others.

A huge thanks to Integrity Publishers, especially Laura Minchew, who caught the vision for this book immediately and knew it would help give children around the world forever families to call their own; to Byron Williamson for taking on this project; to first-class editor June Ford for working long hours to make this book better; and to my agents Sealy Yates and Jeana Ledbetter. Thanks for believing in me and working hard to make this happen.

Thanks to Children's Hope International, the agency who helped us bring home Amberlie Joy and who provided answers to some of my international questions; Kristine Faasse at Bethany Christian Services; adoption attorney Linda Barnby; and the National Adoption Information Clearinghouse. They were valuable sources of research and insight.

Finally, thanks to my forever family—my husband, Adam, who stands beside me in everything I do, encouraging me to reach for the stars, cooking and cleaning when I run off to hotels to write, and working hard to be the world's best dad. To Lorra, Leigha, and Lydia, the beautiful stepdaughters God placed in my life. It hasn't been easy for any of us, but I wouldn't trade it for the world. To my sweet Jessica, Joshua, and Justin, thanks for letting your mom sit for hours at her computer and for loving me, faults and all. And to Amberlie Joy, our precious girl from across the world. Your middle name never lets us forget that the only way to have true JOY in our lives is to put Jesus first, Others second, and Yourself last. You bring joy to all those you meet, and I know God has amazing things in store for you.

Introduction

In 2004, my husband and I began to feel like God was calling us to adopt a little girl. It was a call that came out of the blue, and we really couldn't believe it. At first, we thought we must have misunderstood, because we already had six children in our wonderful, chaotic, beautiful stepfamily. But the call wouldn't go away. Soon, we began to see, hear, and meet stories of adoptions, adoptive families, and adopted children everywhere. We met them in our community, heard them on the radio, and even ran into them in line for the monorail at Walt Disney World! We began to pray in earnest for God's clear direction, and in early 2005 began our journey to adoption.

At first, we were afraid—like many of you—that it would be too overwhelming or too expensive. We didn't know anything about adoption agencies or fund-raising. We had heard the adoption horror stories and wanted to find people we could trust to work with. We didn't know where to turn, and there were no practical resources from a Christian perspective in the bookstores.

We got educated by reading, searching the Internet, attending agency presentations, and asking adoptive families all the questions we could. As we got our paperwork started, we realized that if we could do it, anyone could. We are two self-employed adults with six children. We certainly aren't rolling in the dough! But God was faithful to see us through the paperwork and provide every cent we needed to bring our precious Amberlie Joy home to us from China. (You can find our whole adoption story and pictures of our family on the Web site: www.successfuladoption.com.)

Since you have picked up this book, you obviously have an interest in adoption—and you are already ahead of the game, because you hold in your hand a Christian resource to help walk you through your adoption journey. Inside *Successful Adoption* you will find the tools you need to help you become more educated about adoption options, the paperwork involved, and the finances required, as well as discover what to expect from adoption agencies and attorneys.

I can tell you without hesitation that adoption has opened our eyes to more miracles of God than we had ever witnessed before. God was indeed faithful to provide the finances, the stamina, and the grace we needed for Amberlie Joy to travel all the way across the world from China to join her forever family in Florida. I have no doubt that he will be just as faithful to your family on your journey to successful adoption.

Keys to Help You Get the Most Out of
Successful Adoption

Every good map has a legend or key to help you interpret the symbols that indicate important places, topographic features, and roads for getting where you need to go. *Successful Adoption* has been written and organized in much the same manner.

Easily recognized symbols will help guide you on your journey to learn more about adoption.

There are six parts:

- **Part One** takes you through the very basic understanding of what adoption is, what it entails, how God views it, and what Christian families should consider before beginning the process.
- **Part Two** is the "meat and potatoes" of the actual process of adoption—from sorting through the choice of domestic or international adoption to getting the paperwork started and finances organized.
- **Part Three** includes chapters on issues adoptive families might face with relatives and friends, with their adopted child, with their other children, and with their own emotions as they wait for the adoption to come through. It offers suggestions on preparing for the new arrival and on using the wait time most effectively.
- **Part Four** provides helpful hints for you on your adoption journey such as packing lists for international adoptions, suggested gifts for the birthmother or children's home caregivers. It covers making a birth plan in domestic adoptions and what to do in the first weeks at home, and focuses on helping children heal and forge loving bonds with their forever families. It covers adoption's long-term effects, including when and how to talk to your child about adoption.
- **Part Five** helps you get involved in adoption ministry. It shows you how to help orphans worldwide by volunteering at hospitals, orphanages, crisis pregnancy centers, and missions organizations. It outlines ways to start an adoption ministry in the local church and how to minister to birthparents.
- **Part Six** offers a variety of appendices that include actual sample documents from real-life adoptions, a glossary of adoption terms, and a wealth of resources to continue your adoption education, including Web sites, books, movies, children's books, and selected adoption agencies and attorneys. (*Note:* While you can find lists of adoption agencies and attorneys in many places, the ones chosen for this book were picked because they

have the reputation of operating under solid biblical principles, with a proven track record of serving Christ. This does not mean the agencies or attorneys will be infallible or that you can't look elsewhere and find a reputable adoption arranger. It just means that these are people and agencies with a track record over time of handling adoptions in an upright, forthright, moral manner with Judeo-Christian principles as their foundation.)

Near the end of each chapter there are heartwarming personal stories of adoption from Christian celebrities, including Focus on the Family radio co-host John Fuller (who has an adopted son from Russia), singer Mark Schultz (who is adopted and proud of it), Republican Senator Sam Brownback and his wife, Mary (who have an adopted son from Guatemala and a daughter from China), award-winning singer Nicole C. Mullen (whose son Max was adopted domestically), and best-selling fiction author Karen Kingsbury (who adopted three boys from Haiti), along with people just like you who have chosen to adopt or whose lives were changed through an adoption experience. Read these stories and look forward to the great miracle story God will unfold in your own life as you become involved in the world of adoption.

To help you use this book more effectively, look for the following symbols:

I DIDN'T KNOW THAT!
Fun and interesting pieces of adoption trivia, statistics, or technical information to enhance your knowledge about adoption.

MY ADOPTION MIRACLE
Heartwarming personal adoption stories to encourage you on your adoption journey.

WORDS OF WISDOM
Bible verses or passages of scripture that help provide a deeper understanding of God's heart for the adoption experience.

BEST PRACTICES OF FOREVER FAMILIES
Ideas from adoptive families about how to help make your adoption journey the most wonderful experience possible.

RED LIGHT, STOP!
Questions to consider, ask yourself, and pray about before taking action.

GREEN LIGHT, GO!
Action points for you to apply in your adoption journey.

Part One

Opt to Adopt:
You're Interested,
but Where Do You Start?

And whoever welcomes a little child like this in my name welcomes me.
—Jesus Christ (Matthew 18:5 NIV)

Time and experience have taught me a priceless lesson: Any child you take for your own becomes your own if you give of yourself to that child. I have borne two children and had seven others by adoption, and they are all my children, equally beloved and precious.
—Dale Evans Rogers

Chapter One

Start at the Very Beginning:
Yes, There Are Kids Who Need You!

As little girls, most women I know dreamed of adopting a baby someday. I did, but as I grew up, married, and began my own family, those dreams of adoption faded. When they were rekindled a couple of years ago and I began sharing with friends, family, and total strangers that our family was going to adopt, almost everyone I spoke with had one of two replies: "I have thought about adopting, but I wouldn't know where to start," or "We would love to do that, but we'd never be able to afford it." Those statements kept haunting me as my family went through the adoption process. I couldn't help thinking about all the children who might never have a loving home and family just because the adoption process seemed too difficult and too costly.

When my family decided to adopt, we, too, did not know where to start, and my husband and I had no idea where we would get the money. We had heard that an international adoption cost $30,000 or more, and that newborn domestic adoption could run anywhere from $25,000 to $100,000! We knew there was no way we could accomplish an adoption under our own power. However, my husband and I also felt that God was calling us to bring home a child, and to spread the word to other Christians that there are millions of children who desperately need people to be involved in their lives. Without families willing to take care of them or take them in, these children might die, fail to thrive, or grow up with no one to love them and point them to Jesus.

According to the United Nations Children's Fund (UNICEF), and other humanitarian organizations, around the world there are as many as 143 million orphaned children (meaning that a child has one parent who has died) and at least 16.2 million of those are "double-orphaned," meaning that both parents have died. With the Acquired Immune Deficiency Syndrome (AIDS) crisis in

Africa and recent world disasters, the number is expected to increase. It is obviously that no one family, church, or community can bring home tens of millions of children, and many orphans are not available for adoption due to their laws or other legal reasons. But if everyone who thought about adoption actually followed through and adopted one child, far fewer children would lie sick, neglected, exploited, dying, and forgotten. Together, Christians can make a difference in the lives of children in need. In fact, we are called by God to do so.

I DIDN'T KNOW THAT!

Many celebrities are also adoptive parents. Check out these adoptive parents past and present: actor Kirk Cameron and his actress wife, Chelsea Noble; singer Toby McKeehan (tobyMac); singer Sandi Patty; fiction author Karen Kingsbury; journalist Connie Chung and her talk-show-host husband, Maury Povich; actress Calista Flockhart; President Ronald Reagan; football-player-turned-commentator Dan Marino; film director George Lucas; actress Jamie Lee Curtis; actress Meg Ryan; and singer Steven Curtis Chapman and his author wife, Mary Beth Chapman.

Studies show that, like those who responded to my adoption news, many people think about adoption but not many actually adopt. According to data from the 1995 National Survey of Family Growth (NSFG), which was conducted by researchers for the divisions of health and vital statistics for the Centers for Disease Control and Prevention, ten million married or previously married American women ages eighteen to forty-four had ever considered adoption, but only 487,000 women—or not quite 5 percent of those who had thought about it—had ever completed an adoption. To break it down even further, more than one-fourth of all women in America in that age range who had ever been or were currently married had considered adoption, yet only 1.3 percent of all women in that demographic actually adopted.[1] If a higher percentage of women who considered adoption actually made the decision with their husbands to adopt, and if more people who had never considered adoption were introduced to enough information that they might consider it, the number of orphans in the U.S. and in other countries waiting for a family to love them could be reduced considerably.

Christians are lovingly commanded by God to love others, particularly the innocent, the young, and the poor. If you have ever felt even the smallest pang of curiosity about adoption, the merest flicker of interest in an orphaned child, ask God if he wants to fan it into a flame. Then trust him to take care of the details. As you consider adoption, focus on the resources you do have and let God take care of what you don't.

12/'09/'09

What God Wants for His Kids

So how *does* God feel about adoption? A look at the Scriptures paints a clear picture.

LOVE ONE ANOTHER

The main message that Jesus preached throughout the Gospels was for people to love God with all they have, then love one another with abandon. Look at Christ's attitude toward children. Whenever children approached him, he lovingly gathered them to him. In Mark 10:13–14, the disciples tried to keep the children away from Jesus, and Jesus was not happy about it. The passage states:

> People were bringing little children to Jesus to have him touch them, but the disciples rebuked them. When Jesus saw this, he was indignant. He said to them, "Let the little children come to me, and do not hinder them, for the kingdom of God belongs to such as these." (NIV)

If the kingdom of God belongs to "such as these," then the care of hurting children is not the world's problem; it is the responsibility of God's people, who are royal members of his kingdom. Kerry Hasenbalg, former executive director of the Congressional Coalition on Adoption Institute, tells this story of God's revelation to her about the role orphans play in God's plan:

> I vividly remember when God first spoke to me about his royal family, the orphans. I had invited special friends of ours, two young ladies who became orphaned during the 1994 Rwandan genocide, to spend the holidays with us. And I was furiously preparing my house and decorating it like I had never done before. I can remember standing at my kitchen island and beginning to laugh at myself, thinking, *Why in the world am I cleaning like this—as if the Queen of England is coming to stay?* and immediately, I heard that still, small voice of God gently say to my heart, *Because members of my royal family are coming to stay with you.* And so it was, at that moment, I understood, that he—the King of kings—is serious about being the Father of the fatherless—so they are the royal family of God.[2]

THE CHANCE TO BE PART OF GOD'S BIG PICTURE

Adopting and caring for orphans give believers the opportunity to be God's hands and feet, to practice serving another human being. What those who have adopted soon discover is that their efforts to become a servant by adopting and ministering to orphans bless them as much as they bless the child or children they bring home. Caring for orphans is mandated by God throughout the Bible—not because he can't care for them himself—but because it is part of God's plan for his people to show others what he looks like by their willingness to help those in need. In ancient times, when Rome ruled the world, infanticide ran rampant—with sick, disabled, or orphaned infants literally cast aside, sometimes sacrificed. The first Christians believed in the sanctity of life and demonstrated that by taking in the unwanted children and caring for them, even Roman children. The Romans took note of this, and it began to change society. Christians today can change the world by putting their faith into action and showing the world that every human being is wanted and loved. Until we care about orphans around the world as much as God does—enough to surrender our plans in exchange for his call to care for the unwanted and unloved—we miss an opportunity to play a hugely significant role in God's "big picture," his plan for drawing the unreached to him.

ADOPTION IN THE SCRIPTURES

In the King James Version of the New Testament, the word *adoption* is used six times. In each instance, adoption is the term by which Jesus Christ has reconciled human beings to God. It is through adoption that God becomes our *Abba*, our *Daddy*, according to Romans. Adoption is synonymous with his love. Galatians 4:4–5 states:

> But when the fullness of the time was come, God sent forth his Son, made of a woman, made under the law, to redeem them that were under the law, that we might receive the *adoption* of sons. (KJV, italics added)

This kind of spiritual adoption is mentioned again in Ephesians 1:5. Adoption means that God loves us enough to bring us into his forever family.

But what about actual, physical adoption of one human being by another? Does God have an opinion about this? Does he care one way or the other? Christians can see by looking through scripture that the answer to these questions is a resounding *Yes!* God shows that he is concerned about the way orphans are treated not only by commanding his followers to care for widows and orphans, but he also demonstrates the importance of adoptive relationships by placing key adopted characters throughout the Bible.

How God Uses Adoptive Families

Adoptive relationships are obviously special in God's eyes. He sent his own Son to earth to have an adoptive father, Joseph. Jesus knew what it was like to have half-siblings. He must have known exactly what it felt like to be different, to share the love of Joseph and his name but not his blood or his genes. Joseph played the role of a foster father, knowing that Jesus really belonged to another dad and that he was the earthly stand-in, a significant part of God's plan for his Son's human experience.

ADOPTIVE FAMILIES TOUCH OTHERS WITH THEIR STORIES

Adoptees play key roles throughout the Bible. Many important figures in Bible stories were adopted, and *all* were used to save God's chosen people from destruction. These key characters were the turning point whenever God's chosen were on the brink of disaster. Adoptees have an incredible call by God on their lives to make a difference in this world. What a privilege it is to be the adoptive parents called to love, guide, and accept one of these special chosen ones. The stories of adoption, in both Bible times and today, touch and change lives. They demonstrate God on the move, at work, and in control. The saving grace in these stories of redeemed lives often inspires people to seek their own redemption.

For example, Moses was placed by his mother in a basket made of reeds and left to float down the Nile River in order to save his life after Pharaoh ordered that the infant Hebrew boys be killed. Pharaoh's daughter adopted Moses as her own son and raised him in the palace. As an adult, God called Moses to lead the nation of Israel out of captivity from Egypt and toward the Promised Land—all because Moses' adoptive relationship put him in a position of influence (see the Book of Exodus).

I DIDN'T KNOW THAT!

Throughout the Bible, God uses adoptees to save his people. As you consider adoption, read the stories of Moses, Joseph, Samuel, Esther, and Jesus. Each was adopted; each was used powerfully by God. Adoptees who follow Christ will be used by him in a special way.

ADOPTEES MAY INFLUENCE THEIR BIRTH COUNTRIES

The Old Testament figure of Joseph was another prominent adoptee. As a teen, he was sold into slavery by his jealous brothers. He ended up with a position of power in Egypt and was used by God to save a nation and his own family from starving to death during a famine (see Genesis 37, 39–50). The prophet Samuel was taken as a small boy by his mother and given to the high priest Eli to raise (see 1 Samuel 1:24–28); and Esther, the queen who saved the Jews, was adopted by her cousin Mordecai after her parents died (see Esther 2:7, 15).

The biblical message seems clear that not only has God deemed adoption acceptable, but also that he uses adoptees in great ways to preserve his kingdom. God is still using adoptees today. Some adopted children from nations where their lives were not valued will return to their birth countries to help change laws. Some adopted children may go on to also adopt children. Many are bringing their adoptive families a better understanding of God's great love for them, and some will even lead family members to Christ.

ADOPTION IS AN EXAMPLE OF HIS LOVE FOR US

Perhaps there is no better correlation on earth for the way God draws us into his family than adoption. When you choose to bring a child home who was not born into your family and make the decision to love that child unconditionally, you experience how God calls each of us to become part of his family. When people reconcile their relationship with God by accepting the sacrifice of his Son, Jesus, he embraces them as full-fledged members of his family. In fact, the Bible states in Titus 3:7 that those who accept Christ are justified by his grace so that "we might become heirs having the hope of eternal life" (NIV).

When someone dies, who are the heirs to that person's estate? Family members, first and foremost. God loves us enough to make us his heirs, his children. Adoption provides an earthly picture of that heavenly kind of love.

WORDS OF WISDOM

For ye have not received the spirit of bondage again to fear; but ye have received the Spirit of adoption, whereby we cry, Abba, Father. The Spirit itself beareth witness with our spirit, that we are the children of God.
—Romans 8:15–16 (KJV)

What Adoption Is and What It Means

Exactly what is adoption? *Adoption* means to take a person into a family by legal means, entitling them to full rights as a member of that family in the eyes of the law. It is a complete transfer of rights from birthparents to the adoptive parents (sometimes by way of an agency or the state). It can be accomplished in a variety of ways, which will be discussed further in the following chapters.

Who Thinks About Adopting?

Adoptions can be completed by married couples and singles, by families who have never had children, and by families who already have several (even many) children. The children who are eligible to be adopted must be *orphans*, which means that their parents have died, relinquished their parental rights, or had their parental rights legally terminated.

Adoption terminology is fairly simple for the most part. An *adoptive family* is a family who adds at least one member through the adoption process. The *adoptee, adopted child,* or *adopted adult* is the person who was added to the family through the adoption process. Adoptees can be infants, children, or adults who are adopted by relatives, stepparents, or nonrelatives. (Adult adoption is unusual, but there are some countries that classify young teens as adults, and some adults who choose to legalize an adoption after they reach majority as a way of legally recognizing that they belong to a family.) *Birthmother, birthfather,* and *birth parents* are terms used to refer to the biological parents of a child who is being relinquished for adoption.

The parties involved in an adoption are sometimes called the *adoption triad,* which refers to the three "sides" or parties involved in an adoption: the birthmother and birthfather, the adoptive parent(s), and the child. In recent adoption language, the adoption triad is being replaced with *adoption circle,* as researchers and those involved in all areas of adoption are concluding that there are other parties beyond the triangle who are closely connected to any adoption, including social workers, foster-care parents, grandparents, siblings, and others.

FOREVER FAMILIES

A *forever family* is created when an adopted child is permanently united with a parent or parents.

RELATIVE ADOPTION

A *relative adoption* or "kinship placement" occurs when there is formal recognition of a child being adopted by a blood relative such as an aunt, grandparents, or older sibling.

SIMPLE ADOPTION

Simple adoption takes place when there is a nonjudicial type of adoption that is still considered legal. This occurs in some African cultures.

STEPPARENT ADOPTION

A *stepparent adoption* takes place when a stepparent legalizes his or her relationship with a stepchild by taking the steps to adopt the child with a court decree.

NONRELATIVE ADOPTION

A *nonrelative adoption* is the kind of placement most people think of when they hear the word *adopt.* It simply means that a child has been adopted by people who are not biologically related to the child.

Most nonrelative adoptions are coordinated through an *adoption agency*, a state-licensed business that connects children with adoptive families. Agencies specialize in different areas. Some arrange domestic adoptions throughout the country; some help match only children and parents within their state of residency and licensure. Some agencies are geared toward only international adoptions, and some handle both domestic and international adoption arrangements. An *agency adoption* means that workers at a licensed adoption agency have arranged a domestic or an international adoption. This term usually refers to private adoptions, not public or state agency adoptions.

I DIDN'T KNOW THAT!
In the United States, November is National Adoption Awareness Month. It first became official in 1990 for the purpose of focusing attention on the increasing number of children in the child-welfare system waiting to be adopted. Each year, the president proclaims November as a month when Americans should be aware of adoption as a way to build a family. Visit www.nationaladoptionday.org for more information.

Where and Who Are the Adoptable Children?

According to data from the United States Census Bureau, in the year 2000 there were 1.6 million adopted children under the age of eighteen living in the U.S., and about 100,000 of those were age one and younger. Also, 473,000 adults responded that they were adopted. That's a total of about 2.1 million adopted Americans.[3] Each of those adoptees has parents and other family members and friends, making the number of people touched by adoption much, much larger.

Despite the fact that many people think there are no babies to adopt, there are actually tens of thousands of babies who are placed for adoption each year. Some are relinquished to loving families by birthmothers in the United States who are unprepared or unable to raise them. Others are infants adopted internationally who are relinquished or abandoned. A smaller group includes infants in the United States who are abandoned or taken into foster care and whose parents' rights have been terminated.

INFANT ADOPTIONS IN THE U.S.

More than twenty-five thousand domestic infant adoptions take place each year. These adoptions are arranged by adoption agencies, adoption attorneys, birthmothers, and birth parents directly, or through some combination of the above. At least half of all domestic infant adoptions take place independently, not through an adoption agency.

Adopting an infant domestically can be a longer and more difficult process than accepting a waiting child or pursuing an international adoption. However, it can and is still being done every day. (Chapter 3 discusses the domestic adoption process of newborns and children in state care.)

CHILDREN IN THE FOSTER-CARE SYSTEM

Every day, children are removed from the care of their biological parents due to neglect, abuse, or abandonment and placed in each state's foster-care system. When the parental rights are legally terminated, these children become *waiting children* and are eligible for adoption. According to the latest data, approximately 119,000 children were waiting in the foster-care system in 2003 for a permanent family. Heartbreakingly, these children had been in the foster-care system for an average of more than three years![4]

A qualified single or couple who has completed a successful home study can apply to adopt one or more of these children in their state. The parents rarely pay adoption fees, and various state and federal subsidies and tax credits are often available to help with ongoing medical and emotional needs.

Waiting children are often considered hard to place because they are older, because they might have siblings (and they want to be adopted together), or because of their special needs. In the last several years, states have stepped up their efforts to find homes for these children, and the numbers of adoptions are on the rise. However, there are still thousands of children in each state every year waiting for their forever families. Most are classified as having *special needs*, a broad term that refers to disabilities and challenges that can be mental, social, physical, emotional, or educational. It also refers to placement factors such as race or age that can make finding an adoptive home challenging. These needs can range from severe physical and mental disabilities to the mild condition of a correctable birthmark.

I DIDN'T KNOW THAT!

If just 1 in 500 American adults who said that they had considered adoption actually adopted, all of the more than 119,000 children in foster care waiting for adoption would have permanent, loving families.
—2002 National Adoption Attitudes Survey.[5]

FOSTERING VS. ADOPTING

Children whose parental rights have been legally terminated and are eligible for adoption differ from foster children in that a *foster child* is placed in a licensed caregiver's home temporarily for days, weeks, months, or even years, until that child is returned to his biological parents or until the parents' legal rights to the child are terminated, leaving him eligible to be adopted.

While adoption is a vitally important calling, the need is also great for foster parents in every state. Many children who are removed from their homes do not become eligible for adoption because the legal steps to terminate parental rights are so involved, or the children's special needs keep them from being chosen for adoption. Foster-parenting provides these fragile children with some stability and love while they are waiting for a forever family. If you cannot adopt but want to help children in need, consider taking the steps to become a licensed foster parent in your state.

Experienced foster parents admit that it is often difficult to let their foster children go, but they are encouraged by the knowledge that many times the children are receiving permanent placements, or adoptions, or they are being reunited with a family that is better able to care for them. While the parting is sad, the knowledge that they have given a child love and made a positive difference in a traumatized child's life brings great satisfaction.

INTERNATIONAL CHILDREN

International or *intercountry adoption* simply means adopting a child from another country. International adoptions are on the rise, in part because more foreign governments are finally putting the political mechanisms in place for their governments to allow them, and in part because more people are recognizing the needs of orphaned children worldwide.

Countries that allow international adoptions vary depending on their political climate and relations with the U.S. Countries that have received the most recognition in the past ten years include Russia, Korea, and China, but children are also adopted each year from countries such as Vietnam, Colombia, Guatemala, Haiti, Ethiopia, Liberia, Bulgaria, Ukraine, Kazakhstan, and the Philippines. Most international adoptions are arranged by adoption agencies that have established formal relationships with the countries. Some adoptions occur independently, usually through a ministry or individual who has worked within that country and has found a way to make adoptions happen. (For more information on the international process, see chapter 4.)

Kinds of Families Who Adopt

There are all kinds of families who choose adoption. At one time, the most common scenario was a young couple, unable to have children, who decided to pursue the adoption of a newborn infant. Today, however, the picture is changing dramatically.

FAMILIES WITHOUT CHILDREN

Many couples without children still turn to adoption as a means of fulfilling their dream to have a family. These couples adopt domestically and internationally. Often, they try to adopt domestically first, as they desire to raise a child from birth.

FAMILIES WITH CHILDREN

There are many reasons families with children pursue adoptions domestically and internationally: Families might choose adoption as a means of enlarging their family due to secondary infertility (meaning that they have had a biological child or children but can't biologically have a child now); or because their faith leads them to make that decision. Stepfamilies might choose to adopt a child as part of their newly formed family unit; or others may have started their family by adoption and are so blessed that they opt to adopt again.

OLDER COUPLES

Adoption agencies report that couples in their forties and fifties also have a variety of motivations for choosing to adopt. Sometimes they adopt because their children are grown and gone, and they still feel they have the time, money, and energy to devote to raising children; others adopt because they are unable to conceive; and still others because it is their second marriage or beyond, and they want to raise a child together.

SINGLES WHO WANT TO BE PARENTS

Today, single men and women are adopting children as a way to fulfill their dream to parent when marriage is not on the horizon. This is due partly to the fact that there is far less cultural stigma in the U.S. today than there was even twenty years ago about being a single parent. The number of Christian singles who feel called to adopt is rising, as some men and women feel that God wants them to use what they have been given to bless a child's life. The number of homosexual or same-sex couples who adopt is also on the rise.

Adoption agencies usually consider a healthy, married couple between the ages of thirty and forty-five to be "ideal," but that, too, is changing. Some adoptions can take place when the prospective adoptive parents are younger than thirty. Many international countries accept parents who are older. Some are willing to accept parents with disabilities, as long as the potential parent can show evidence that the disability will not interfere with his ability to parent. The "colors" of adoption are also changing. Whereas adoptions used to occur almost exclusively within racial lines, today's adopting families are very willing to become transracial, which means adopting children of various races, ethnicities, and skin tones.

We Could Never Afford It

If God places adoption on your heart, the first thing that probably comes to mind is the question: "How can we afford it?"

Finding the finances to adopt is possible for anyone called and determined to do it. Adoptions can cost very little (if you adopt waiting children from foster care) to a whole lot (at least $25,000 for most domestic and international adoptions). Before you become discouraged, consider that there are adoption grants, low-interest loans, tax credits, employer credits, and other means available to help you put your adoption finances together (see chapter 5).

A MATTER OF TRUST

If you are being called to adopt and do not have the finances, it comes down to a matter of trust. If God is leading you to get educated about adoption and build your family by helping an orphaned child, then he is asking you to trust him to provide the means to make it happen. After all, God loves that child and wants him or her to find love and support in your family.

IT DOES NOT HAVE TO COST A FORTUNE

There are many ways to ensure that adoption does not cost a fortune. Choosing a reputable agency, planning prudent travel options, considering a waiting child, and finding experienced people to help can get you through the process efficiently and help you reduce the cost of adoption.

We're Not Perfect—Can We Adopt?

Contrary to popular belief, you do not have to be the perfect couple to adopt.

AGE CONSIDERATIONS

While many agencies prefer couples between the ages of thirty and forty-five, there are some agencies that will accept applications from adults as young as twenty-one. (For a domestic infant adoption, birthmothers usually choose the couple who will adopt their babies, and most birthmoms prefer couples who are at least twenty-five but not older than forty.) However, potential adoptive parents can be older and still adopt successfully, especially internationally. Some countries even prefer parents with more life experience and allow adoptions by parents who are up to sixty years old—if the couple will adopt a toddler or older child.

I DIDN'T KNOW THAT!
The breakdown of people who adopt in the United States looks like this:

67%   Married Couples
28%   Single Females
3%   Single Males
2%   Unmarried Couples
—National Adoption Day: Adoption Statistics[6]

BACKGROUND ISSUES

Adoptive parents should not have a history of criminal activity, but a minor offense in a parent's background will probably not prevent an adoption from going through. The key to overcoming any potential background issues (divorces, arrests, or a criminal record) is to be completely honest with your agency, attorney, and social worker from the beginning. They should be able to tell you before you spend a lot of time and money whether or not your special case will prevent you from successfully completing an adoption.

NEWLYWEDS

Couples are usually asked to wait at least a year after they marry before applying to adopt. This is not always the case, as some unmarried couples do adopt; however, many agencies like to see that a marriage has had an adjustment period of one year before placing a child in the home for adoption.

CHILDREN ALREADY IN THE HOME

There can be limits on the number of children already at home. For example, China allows adoption if there are no more than four children still living at home, with some exceptions for special-needs adoptions. Domestic adoptions are not usually limited, but birthmothers often prefer couples without children. If you already have children, check out the restrictions for the country you are interested in before you get too far into the process.

If you have a stepfamily, you are still eligible to adopt in most cases.

DIVORCED

If you have been divorced, you are still eligible to adopt in most cases. Most countries have a limit of one divorce per spouse, and copies of divorce decrees will be needed as part of your adoption paperwork. (For more on paperwork, see chapter 6.)

Adoption: The Family of God

Some people never think about adoption as an option for expanding their family because it doesn't fit their idea of the perfect family. Others have heard scary stories about adopted children who were taken from their adoptive parents and given back to their birth families, stories of couples who spent tens of thousands of dollars in adoption fees only to have the birthmother change her mind, and tales of adopted children who had problems their adoptive families could not handle. Are these stories true? Some are, yes. But Christians who feel God has led them to adopt experience a peace and reassurance about being part of his plan, even when they do not get a textbook happy ending. Also, most people who set out to adopt *do* finalize adoptions.

When you begin telling people that you are learning more about adoption, you might be surprised to see how many people you know have happy connections with adoptions. Either they were adopted, a sibling or parent or cousin was adopted, or they are adopting or have adopted. Soon, you will begin to hear about the blessings of adoption far more often than you will come across a story that had an unhappy outcome. Adoptive families are quick to tell you that adoption is not a second-best option for creating a family. In God's eyes, we are all the same family, and adoption adds a new layer of understanding to the wonderful mystery of being part of the family of God.

RED LIGHT, STOP!

Questions to consider at this point in your adoption journey:

____ Have you prayed about whether you are to adopt?

____ (If married) Are you and your spouse in agreement about adoption? Have you prayed about it together?

____ (If single) Have you received wise counsel from a mentor, family member, or pastor about your desire to adopt?

____ What are your feelings about raising a child you did not conceive or give birth to?

____ Have you considered how the decision to adopt will affect the rest of your family and extended family?

____ Do you have some or all of the financial resources needed to adopt, or do you have the willingness to trust God and to work on a plan for raising them?

____ Have you read what the Scriptures say about adoption?

____ Are you willing to wait the time it takes to adopt?

____ Can and will you devote the time necessary to become educated about the right adoption process for your family?

____ Do you think you can truly love an adopted child as your own?

GREEN LIGHT, GO!

Action points for your adoption journey:

____ Consider adoption as a possibility for building or expanding your family.

____ Submit your picture of the perfect family to the Lord and ask him what his will is for you.

____ Start praying regularly about whether God is calling you to pursue adoption.

____ Talk to your spouse about whether he or she is also feeling called to adopt.

____ Begin getting educated about adoption by visiting Internet sites, talking to adoptive families, and reading books.

____ Pray together for orphans around the world, and ask God how you are supposed to help them.

____ Examine your age, backgrounds, family size, and financial picture to get a better feel for whether adoption is right for you.

____ Consider becoming foster parents to help children in need of love and support, if adoption is not the right fit for you.

____ Read about adoptees in the Bible, such as the stories of Moses, Joseph, Samuel, Esther, and Jesus.

____ Search the Scriptures to see how you are supposed to respond to children in need.

My Adoption Miracle
I Was Adopted!
by Mark Schultz, Christian singer-songwriter

When I was a little boy and my sister and I were thumbing through the pages of our photo albums or baby books, I noticed that my book was different from hers. It had other documents or something, so I called my mom in from the other room and asked her why mine had different documents and such. That was when she explained to me that while they did not have a choice in what they were getting when they had my sister Susan, they got to pick me out special. Basically, they made it seem like they got a raw deal with my sister.

I don't remember being adopted as traumatic or anything. My mom always made me feel like being adopted was something to be proud of, and I really feel like it was. Especially when I think about the fact that my birthmother could have chosen to abort me or keep me in a situation that was not healthy. I think it made me the kind of person who doesn't take life for granted. I am grateful for the one I got.

When I think about God's grace and the way he adopts us in much the same way into his family, it's pretty cool. I remember when I was a sophomore in high school, I got the opportunity to go to the state basketball

16

tournament. I wasn't supposed to be one of the ones to go, but one of the players broke his leg or something, so they called me the night before the tournament and asked if I could go. I got to go with the team, and that was huge for me. I'm sure everybody enjoyed it, but not to the extent I did, because I knew I wasn't good enough to go, had not been chosen to go, but still I was invited—just like God invites us. I am just in awe all the time that I get to be included in his family.

I think being adopted actually helps me live life more freely. I don't get embarrassed easily; I love to hug people. I'm definitely a hugger. I can't say that being adopted is something I really focus on a lot. I don't really even remember that I am adopted unless someone in the room asks how many people are adopted. Then I look around for a minute at the hands before realizing I need to put mine up too.

I have never searched for my birth family, because I really have not felt like anything was missing in my life. If anything, I am just grateful for the choice my birthmother made. She could have said, "Gee, my life would be a whole lot easier if I had an abortion." The easy way out for a birthmother would be to have an abortion or to selfishly keep the child, knowing she would not be able to give it a good home. The hardest thing to do after nine months of carrying a child inside is to say, "You could give them a better life than I can."

I really think God matched me with just the right family. I think he knows what he is doing when it comes to adoption. My dad is an athlete and a coach, and I played football, college baseball, and ran track. I have never felt as though I am not complete. The percentages of my even being here at all are smaller than most people's, and I am grateful for every minute of it.

You can find out more about Mark at www.markschultzmusic.com.

Sorting Through the Adoption Options

If you feel that God is calling you to consider adoption, it is natural to have concerns. Anything unknown can be scary, and fear is one of the main reasons those who consider adopting do not follow through. This chapter addresses some of the more common myths and fears along with the realities of the adoption process. While adoption comes with its unique difficulties, it also offers great rewards.

Debunking the Myths

MYTH #1: ADOPTION TAKES FOREVER

It is true that the adoption process can be tedious. Certain steps must be followed, paperwork must be gathered, and then there is the waiting. It is not true, however, that adoption has to take years and years. Adoption is a journey of faith that can be completed in the relatively short time of a few weeks (although this is not typical), or the journey may take as long as several years. The thing to keep in mind is that most people who set out to adopt, and who meet the criteria to adopt, do finalize adoptions. The time required to adopt a child depends largely on how assertive those who want to adopt are, how quickly they get their paperwork and home study done, and whether or not they want to adopt only a non-special-needs, nonminority newborn. Most agencies estimate that the average adoption process takes ten to eighteen months to complete and can vary greatly from domestic to international and from country to country.

"When you view adoption as fulfilling God's plan, the time becomes less important," says Kristine Faasse, licensed social worker and national adoption consultant for Bethany Christian Services. "I just talked to a family not long ago who waited a long time. I ran into them at an event and asked how it was going. The mom said, 'You know, you told us there was a reason why we waited and waited. Now we know what you meant—because this is the child who was meant to be ours.' I could tell you hundreds of those stories, and they all give me goose bumps. God has the right child for adoptive families in the right time."

For adoptive parents who do their part quickly and efficiently and who are open to different options, adoption can take place very quickly. Some friends in Texas experienced infertility and decided to go through the adoption process to create their forever family. They adopted a baby boy domestically after a wait of nearly a year, and when he was three they decided to try to adopt again. Within days of putting their profile on the agency's Web site, the couple was matched with a birthmother. They brought home their daughter just a couple of weeks later.

For other couples who adopt domestically, the wait can be longer. A couple in Florida had no difficulty adopting their first son seven years ago using an adoption attorney and agency. However, when they tried to expand their family five years later, it took two and a half years and several disappointments before they brought home their second son. As they gaze at their infant son, this couple is quick to say that the wait was worth it.

Adopting internationally varies in wait time, with the average adoption taking six to eighteen months for Eastern European countries, Russia, and Asian countries and sometimes fewer than six months for some South American adoptions. If couples are willing to take an international child with special needs, the wait can be shortened to just a few months from the time they first fill out an agency application to their Gotcha Day, the day they are united with their child.

If adopting parents choose to adopt from foster care and are willing to become licensed as foster-care parents, a child can be placed with them almost immediately after the several-week licensing process is completed, with plans under way for adoption to make the placement permanent if the child becomes legally available.

Although the adoption process might not be as quick as you would like, be assured that God will lead you to just the right child in just the right time.

WORDS OF WISDOM
The one who calls you is faithful and he will do it.
—1 Thessalonians 5:24 (NIV)

MYTH #2: YOU MIGHT LOSE YOUR MONEY AND YOUR HEARTS
Adoption is a costly process, and all or a portion of the money is usually non-refundable—*even if an adoption is not completed*. If that thought frightens you

enough that you want to close this book right now, please be patient. Losing money in an adoption attempt is a possibility, but a relatively slim one. For every adoption that goes awry, there are thousands of other adoptions completed every year. Trust that God will lead you in the right direction if you plan to adopt, and do your homework and use reputable agencies and attorneys.

Of course, some adopting parents have invested more money than they anticipated. Costs vary greatly among the types of adoption available.

U.S. domestic adoption laws lean in favor of the birthmother so that she is not coerced to give up her child. Adoptive parents pay her and the baby's medical expenses (usually covered at least in part by their own health insurance policy—see chapter 5 for more on the costs of adoption), as well as any agency, attorney, and filing and court fees. In most cases, they pay her living expenses—if they are paired with a birthmother during her pregnancy. So the cost of domestic adoption varies widely. Before the birth and for a short amount of time afterward (which varies by state—see chapter 3), birthmothers have the option of changing their minds and keeping their babies; however, most do not. Before you contract with an agency or attorney, make sure that you know what happens to your money if the adoption falls through. In a case where the birthmother does keep the baby, the agency and attorney fees paid to that point are usually applied to the next attempt to contract with a willing birthmother, but make sure you have that in writing in your initial contract.

International adoption costs should be explained up front and should not vary much, with the exception of travel expenses. The financial risk with international adoption is that a government can close its doors to international adoption unexpectedly, as more than one thousand families discovered when Romania banned international adoptions in 2001. In this case, most agencies would then apply fees toward adoption from another country; but make sure you thoroughly investigate the policies of any agency you consider before signing on the dotted line, and be sure your contract covers what happens to the fees if for some reason the adoption can't take place. (Adopting parents would incur additional expenses, if the new country's fees are higher.)

Foster-care adopters have little up-front, out-of-pocket expense. The costs they might incur include, other than a successful home study, any costs associated with becoming licensed foster parents in their state and other smaller fees. Costs for foster adoptions sometimes come in later, such as in the case where the child has ongoing special needs medically or psychologically that subsidies do not fully cover.

As far as losing your heart, no child and no adoption comes with guarantees. If a birthmother decides to raise her child herself or if an international or foster-care adoption falls through, the heartache will come. But those who have experienced it know that God sees every one of their tears and does not waste their pain. Psalm 30:5 states, "Weeping may go on all night, but joy comes with the morning" (NLT). Only by experiencing trials does anyone have a testimony to share with others and the empathy to feel others' pain.

MYTH #3: ADOPTED KIDS DO NOT ADJUST

Ideally, infants begin bonding in the first few minutes after birth and will continue to form loving attachments as they grow in healthy, stable homes. In the best-case adoption scenarios, an adopted child goes home from the hospital with his adopting family twenty-four to forty-eight hours after birth, or is placed in a foster home or an orphanage where the caregivers are loving and attentive just days after birth. Unfortunately, many adopted children have experienced some kind of trauma—ranging from the loss of their birthmothers' attention in the first days after birth to overcrowded orphanages without enough caregivers or sustenance to abusive or neglectful birth families or foster homes. All or any of these experiences can result in a child's trust in adults being broken, which in turn can cause some difficulty in bonding with the adoptive parents, especially at first. By educating themselves about ways children bond (see chapter 11), most adoptive parents are able to encourage a loving bond with their child. In some cases, there is regression in the early elementary years and again in adolescence and teen years—a time when most teens pull away from their parents, not just adopted teens. Wise adoptive families pray for their children daily, asking God to help their children trust, to erase their children's fears, and to help their children embrace the love of their adoptive families.

I DIDN'T KNOW THAT!

You will easily recognize the names of many people who were adopted. Included on the list of famous adoptees are the ancient philosopher Aristotle, comedian Art Linkletter, country singer Faith Hill, blues legend Bo Diddley, inventor George Washington Carver, actress Melissa Gilbert, author James Michener, singer Debbie "Blondie" Harry, and singer Sarah McLachlan.

MYTH #4: YOU MIGHT NOT LOVE YOUR ADOPTED CHILD

Author and adoptive parent Karen Kingsbury (see "My Adoption Miracle" section, chapter 4) admits that she did not know what she would feel when she adopted three young boys from Haiti.

"At first, with the boys, we knew we loved them, but we didn't know them yet. It was more of a Christlike, take-you-as-you-are, servant kind of love," Kingsbury shared with *mtl* magazine.[7] "Now it feels funny to look at pictures of our family before them. Now we love them because of who they are."

Kingsbury, like many adoptive parents interviewed for this book, said she and her husband Don gave themselves permission not to be *in love* with each of their adopted children from the moment they received them. Loving is what Christians are called to do, but it is often an action more than a feeling. The feelings will come, and adoptive families say they cannot imagine life without the blessing of their adopted members. Kingsbury suggests that couples and families who are adopting pledge to be honest with one another before, during, and after the process so that they can work through their feelings and concerns together.

WORDS OF WISDOM
Do not worry about anything, but pray and ask God for everything you need, always giving thanks.
—Philippians 4:6 (NCV)

MYTH #5: ADOPTION ISN'T AS GOOD AS GIVING BIRTH

The pain associated with infertility may cause a couple to question whether or not they would love an adopted child with the same passion they would feel for one of their own. Adoptive families who have been in the same situation give a resounding "YES!" Many say, if they had to choose, they would choose adoption *over* having a biological child.

Brian Luwis, who with his wife, Renée, founded America World Adoption Association after adopting their daughter Fei in 1994, admits he was scared at first that he would never feel as close to an adopted child as he would a biological one, even in the days after they brought Fei home.

I was in our home experiencing the newness of fatherhood and suddenly realized that this child, because of some ink on paper (or so I thought), was now my daughter. As I carried my daughter, Fei, slowly to her crib she gently patted my back (which was also my way of showing her affection). With that gentle touch, she spoke a thousand words into my heart and showed me what love is all about. Fei would soon call me Papa and with her smile fill my heart with a joy that brings tears to my eyes. Through Fei, God would show Renée and me the incredible joys of parenthood. Ultimately, it was through a new understanding of God's Spirit of adoption that we would learn that God truly had the best plan imaginable for our lives and that our children by adoption were a part of that plan.[8]

While anxieties and fears creep in before and during the adoption process, these end when your beautiful adopted child comes home. There is nothing about adoption that makes it second-best to having a child by birth. In fact, God made it his first choice for his Son, Jesus, who was conceived by the Holy Spirit and raised by a human carpenter, Joseph, who adopted Jesus as his own.

Above all, do not be anxious that you will not *feel* the same way about your adopted child that you would a birthchild, even if you later have a birthchild. The collected wisdom of hundreds of thousands of adoptive parents shows this fear is unfounded. Renée Luwis later did give birth to a daughter, Sophia, after the family had adopted two girls. Yet the bond between each child and her parents was unbreakable.

> When Renée gave birth to Sophia we likewise questioned if God considered her to be more "ours" than Fei or Gwenn were "ours." We read in 1 Corinthians 6:19, "Do you not know that your body is the temple of the Holy Spirit who is in you, whom you have from God, and you are not your own?" (NKJV).
>
> If we are not our own and God owns us, then He must own our children too, for it is by His grace that we move, live, and have our being. We have children by His grace, adopted or by birth. God entrusts them to us. He is their true Father in heaven. We are their earthly parents. This seems like such a logical conclusion, but I think when we hear "That's my boy," more attention is often placed on the "my" than the "boy." That child is God's boy, and God entrusts him to us.[9]

Talking It Through

It is important when considering adoption to have conversations about it with your spouse. If you are approaching adoption as a Christian single, you need someone with wisdom to be your sounding board as you walk through the process. This may sound like a no-brainer, but it is vitally important that adopters discuss what they are facing and put all their questions and fears on the table for discussion.

COUPLES: GETTING ON THE SAME PAGE

Before a couple begins the process of adoption, someone has to bring up the subject. Usually, one spouse will begin thinking about adoption, learning about adoption, and feeling a heart tug whenever they hear a story about adoption. When the husband or wife broaches the subject, the real work begins. Both spouses must be fully committed for a truly successful adoption to take place. If a spouse is initially resistant to the idea of adoption, the one feeling the call should ask their spouse if he or she would be willing to pray about it—together and individually. Give the reluctant spouse time to listen for God's response and to see if his or her heart is being moved to adopt. Remember that planted seeds take time to grow, so do not bring up the subject too often. Let God do the heart preparation, and make sure you are on the same page as a couple before moving forward. If both of you feel ready, the adoption process will flow more smoothly, and any bumps in the road can be handled together.

SINGLES: SEEKING WISE COUNSEL

If you are a single Christian and you want to adopt, you have to be prepared for the challenges, and even the controversy, your decision will bring. It is vital for singles who are considering adoption to seek wise counsel from those who really know and understand them, whether family, friends, a pastor, or a counselor. Discuss with them the motivation for wanting to adopt, and figure out whether there is a strong support system. Ask them to be open and honest about what they see as your strengths and weaknesses, and accept both the positive and the negative from them (without hurt feelings). Being a single parent is tough and will present challenges for you and your adopted child. Be very sure that you are ready and equipped to be the primary support for a child for the long haul, if marriage does not ever enter the picture.

As a prospective single parent, you need to make sure you can parent effectively while still providing for your family and making time for your child's needs. Also, get to know other adoptive parents and single parents who can share your experiences. Making connections with new people and groups before the child comes home will make it easier to adjust when the child is home. So take the waiting time to get connected with baby-sitters, a Bible study or small group, child-care programs, and places that offer fellowship. That way, you have support systems in place that will enable you to take respites of a few hours at a time from parenting.

SHARING WITH FAMILY AND FRIENDS

As you take steps down the road toward an adoption, the news will undoubtedly be shared with family and friends. Extend grace if their reactions are not instantly favorable, especially if you plan to adopt from another country or race. Remember that you have had time to process your desire to adopt. In most cases, for those you are telling, it is the first they have heard of it. They may be afraid that you have not thought the decision through, that adoption will be too hard and financially draining, or that a child from another country or race may not fit in with your family. Their concerns probably stem from the fact that they love you and think they are looking out for you. So if an initial reaction is not favorable, try not to take it personally or react with anger. Give friends and family time, and be quick to forgive any comments that hurt. Ultimately, the decision of how to expand your family is yours to make. If you feel called to adopt, most family members will come around when your precious child comes home. (For more on telling others about your decision, see chapter 8.)

CONSIDERING THE IMPACT ON OTHER CHILDREN

If you already have children, make sure you consider the impact an adopted child will have on each of them. Be sure that you have the time, resources, and patience to handle the new addition without neglecting the needs of your other kids. Each child in the family will go through an adjustment period when the newcomer arrives. If your children are very small, prepare them for the new infant or child just as you would if experiencing a pregnancy. If children are older, ask them how they would feel about an adopted brother or sister. Take time to answer their questions, and reassure them if they have concerns. If any of your children have a severely adverse reaction to the idea of adoption, give that child time and take his or her anger or fears seriously. Pray about whether you should move forward with the adoption process if your child refuses to come around. Most children will eventually embrace the idea of a new brother or sister and joyfully anticipate the new arrival, especially if you engage your children in conversation about their reasons for being against adoption. Children may have fears that are unfounded and based on what they have heard or seen on TV or in movies. They may fear you will not love them anymore or that you will not have time for them. Take time to address their concerns, and that will help them come around.

COUNTING THE COST IN TIME AND MONEY

Two of the biggest factors that always come with raising a family are time and money. Before you adopt, make sure you have a working budget of money *and* time in place. The last thing you want to do is adopt a child only to have to leave him or her with caregivers all the time. On the other hand, everyone in the family needs to eat, and you cannot neglect your work to devote every moment to parenting. If you are undisciplined in the area of money or time, now is the time to get organized. If you have no budget, gather receipts for every penny you spend for at least one month, then track where your money goes and create a budget that keeps you from going into debt once your child arrives. (For help with finances, visit Crown Financial Ministries at www.crown.org for resources and, in some areas, free sessions with a finance counselor.)

As far as your time, make sure that you are prepared for interrupted sleep, jet lag if you travel internationally, less solitude, and fewer hours of free time. Your child will require lots of attention, cuddling, reassurance, and care. Whereas you used to spend Friday nights out at the movies, once the baby arrives you will probably spend them at home with a video. If you are a procrastinator, you may need to create a *time* budget. Write down everything you do over a week's or month's time, and determine where time could be saved or where you could be more productive. Start organizing your time in a calendar, planner, or PDA; and schedule your quiet time with God, romantic time with your spouse, playtime with your child, work you need to accomplish, and all the other items on your to-do list. Pray that God will help you order your days so that you can put him first, your marriage second, and your child's needs next.

BEST PRACTICES OF FOREVER FAMILIES

Often, like in the middle of the nights when the baby's crying and you don't know why and they can't tell you, it hits you again that love is not a game of convenience. It does what is needed for the other person's gain. Love goes out of its way, and the one loving ultimately benefits more than the one they have loved.
—Nicole C. Mullen

Baby or Older: Which Age Is Right for You?

Once you decide to adopt, you must then decide whether you want a baby or a child who is past the infant stage. Maybe you would be happy with either one, but both come with different needs that should be considered.

WANTING A BABY

An infant requires expensive formula, bottles to be given regularly around the clock, diapers to be purchased and changed, and lots of sleepless nights. Adopting an infant is special, however, because the adoptive parents get to be part of all or many of the child's firsts—first tooth, first steps, first word, first smile. An infant's sheer dependence captures parents' hearts.

TODDLERS AND BEYOND

On the other hand, a toddler or older child offers adoptive families the opportunity to be the facilitators of God's healing in an abused, abandoned, orphaned, or neglected life. Adoptive parents of older children get to experience the joy of seeing a child make loving connections, be lifted out of poverty, or receive help emotionally, physically, and spiritually.

When deciding on the age of the child you will adopt, consider the needs each age will have, where your time and talents lie, and also take your own age into consideration. If you are older parents, you may be better suited to adopting an older child, and many international adopting countries do ask older parents (forty-five and up) to adopt a toddler or older child.

Sibling Groups

If you have room in your heart, home, and budget for more than one child, there are thousands of sibling groups waiting in the public foster-care system who would like to be adopted together. Often, these children feel the only love and connection they have is with their siblings and half siblings. Older siblings tend to be very protective of their younger brothers and/or sisters and might give up an adoption opportunity if it means being separated from them. Sibling groups pose unique challenges in that parents will have to adjust to more than one child at once, and if there are other children in the home, it means more adjustments for everyone. The benefits of adopting a sibling group include that they have someone to play with and they can help each other make adjustments.

I DIDN'T KNOW THAT!

Every November on National Adoption Day, courts set aside time to finalize adoptions from foster care that might otherwise be delayed for months, and communities celebrate adoption with retreats, proclamations, and other events. National Adoption Day was started in 2000 and has grown each year. In 2004, courts and community organizations finalized the adoptions of more than 3,400 children from foster care as part of 200 National Adoption Day events in 37 states.[10]

Adopting an Adolescent

The older a child is when he or she is adopted, the more trauma the child might have experienced. That is why so many children remain in foster care until they are adults. When a child reaches the age of ten (in some cases even younger), he or she is considered by many to be "unadoptable." The window of opportunity is likely to be gone. However, most of these children still long to be loved, to find a permanent family and have parents they can call their own. Even teens as old as seventeen—knowing that they are almost legal adults—can be seen on waiting-child Web sites, asking to be adopted and loved. Some adults who grow up in foster care still long to be adopted. The desire to belong is intense, and these young adults often want to have someone to walk them down the aisle, be the grandparents of their children, and share a last name.

It takes a special kind of single adult or couple to step into parenthood when many of the child's formative years are already gone. However, helping a child or teen learn to form permanent bonds with others, <u>love unselfishly,</u> develop <u>skills and talents, and live for God</u> can be a gift that returns great rewards to the parent and child.

Different Kinds of Adoptions

When considering adoption, adoptive parents, especially in domestic adoptions, need to make a decision on what kind of adoption they want to have. There are three classifications of adoptions today: *closed*, *semi-open*, and *open*.

Closed or *confidential adoptions* are now considered somewhat old-fashioned in the United States, but are still common in international adoptions. Today, most adoptions domestically are *cooperative adoptions* or *adoptions with contact*, also called *semi-open* or *open adoptions*.

CLOSED OR CONFIDENTIAL

In a closed adoption, no personal information is exchanged between the birth family and adoptive family. In international adoptions, there may be no information about the birth family, especially if the child was abandoned or if records were not accurately kept. In closed domestic adoptions in the United States, the agency keeps the records, and there is no contact between the birthmother and the adoptive parents. If any information is shared, it is usually basic, nondescriptive information.

The general view in the adoption community today is that it is better for the child, the adoptive family, and the birthparents to share at least some information and have some type of ongoing contact.

SEMI-OPEN

In a *semi-open* or *mediated adoption*, the parties agree that letters and photos will be exchanged after the child's birth and adoption, but they are sent through a third party, usually the adoption agency. Some families send and receive letters once or twice a year. Some exchange these more frequently. One benefit to the birthmother is that she is reassured that her child is healthy and doing well. A benefit to the adoptive family and adoptee is that the photos and letters provide reassurance for the child that she or he was loved by the birthmother and answers questions about what the child's birth family looks like. The reason for the semi-open label is that the birthmother and adoptive family do not meet and still do not exchange identifying information such as each other's last names, whereabouts, or contact information.

OPEN

Open adoptions are becoming more popular today, although for each family this definition varies widely. In an open adoption, some or all identifying and contact information is exchanged, and adoptive parents agree to have ongoing contact with the birthmother through e-mails, phone calls, letters, visits, or some combination of these methods of keeping in touch. Open adoption proponents say this helps minimize the child's loss of relationships and allows the child to know the truth and deal with the loss, rather than being left to fantasize about what their birth family might be like.

If you feel that you will be chosen as an adoptive family by a birthmother only if you choose an open adoption, think again. Some birthmothers still prefer a closed adoption, especially if the pregnancy has been traumatic for them or was the result of an act of violence. Open adoptions need to have full commitment by both parental sides of the adoptive triad to work over the long-term.

Adoptive couples need to seek the Lord's will and pray about what kinds of ongoing contact they would be willing to have, the frequency of the contact, and the positives and negatives it might bring to their family in the upcoming years. Things to consider include how you will handle it if one adopted child's mother visits and another adopted child's does not, how a long-distance move could impact an agreement, how you might feel about visits and contact if a birthmother is in constant crisis or has an unhealthy lifestyle, how she might feel if you decide contact is no longer right for you, and other considerations.

Some open adoptions work well, with birthmothers becoming friends with the adoptive parents and spending time with the family and child. In the book *The Story of David: How We Created a Family Through Open Adoption*, by Dion Howells with Karen Wilson Pritchard, the Howells family not only got in touch with the teen birthmother of their son David, but were present at the hospital during his birth, brought her into their home for weekend visits after the birth, and took family pictures that included the birthmother, the Howells, and David.

Christian adoptive couple Brad and Caprice Payne have completed two domestic adoptions and have worked hard to foster good relations with the birthmothers of their children and even some extended birth-family members.

"We send e-mails, pictures, and letters," Caprice says, "and we have had our son's and daughter's birthmothers to our home. We want our children to know their heritage, and we really care about our birthmoms." (See the Paynes' "My Adoption Miracle" story in chapter 3.)

When parties cannot agree on the amount of time spent together or the methods of contact, some open-adoption arrangements do fall apart. If in a semi-open or open adoption a birthparent or the adoptive family wants to break off contact or does not uphold the agreement to exchange letters and photos, there is little or no legal basis in most states to fall back on to get either party to comply, according to the National Adoption Information Clearinghouse (NAIC). Only a few states have legal recourse available to either party if a post-adoption contract is not kept. The NAIC shows that in 2003, eighteen states (Arizona, California, Connecticut, Florida, Indiana, Louisiana, Massachusetts, Minnesota, Montana, Nebraska, New Mexico, New York, Oregon, Rhode Island, South Dakota, Vermont, Washington, and West Virginia) had legislation allowing written and enforceable adoption with contact agreements.

In most of these States, an agreement for adoption with contact can potentially be permitted for any adoptive child as long as the type and frequency of contact is deemed to be in the child's best interests. Some States, such as Connecticut, Nebraska, and New York, limit the application of agreements to children in foster care. Indiana limits enforceable contact agreements to children ages two and older. For children under age two, non-enforceable agreements are permitted as long as the type of contact does not include visitation.

Most statutes permit post-adoption contact for birthparents; however, some States also allow other birth relatives, including grandparents, aunts, uncles or siblings, who have significant emotional ties to the child, to be included in the agreement. Minnesota permits foster parents to petition for contact privileges; for Indian children, members of the child's tribe are included among the eligible birth relatives. California, Indiana, Maryland, and Massachusetts have separate provisions for sibling visitation.
—NAIC 2003 report[11]

According to the statutes in these states, all parties who want to be included in the agreements must agree in writing to all of the terms, and any who wish to modify an agreement must attempt to do so through legal action in the court of jurisdiction. In the remaining thirty-two states, either there are no laws on the books to enforce post-adoption contact, or the states acknowledge agreements but will not uphold them.

INTERNATIONAL

For international adoptions, obtaining information about birth families can be difficult to impossible for reasons including language barriers, abandonment, the orphaned status of children, or orphanage workers who do not tell adoptive families the truth (sometimes for fear that a birth family would get in trouble for abandoning a child). A child growing up in a foreign closed adoption can still connect to his or her biological background and culture if the adoptive family is faithful to help. Most adoptive families create scrapbooks, Web sites, or other records of their journey to adopt their child and take the child back to visit his or her native country when he or she reaches an appropriate age.

Not all international adoptions are closed. In some countries, the policies are changing and birth families are permitted to have semi-open or open adoptions with adoptive families. Some adoptive families send cards and letters to their child's orphanage to be passed on to birthparents. Check with your agency to see what the policies are for the country you want to adopt from, and ask others about their experiences before deciding on the type of adoption that is right for you.

Racial Considerations

Until recent years, American adoptions occurred largely within the same race. That is, Caucasian adoptive parents adopted Caucasian children, African-American adoptive parents adopted African-American children, and so on. It was believed that there would be less stigma attached to the adoption, and the child would fit in better with his or her own race.

TRANSRACIAL ADOPTIONS

Today, transracial adoptions—meaning adoptions that cross racial lines, with the adoptive parents being of a race different from the adopted child's—take place every day. Thousands of children from China, Korea, Vietnam, India, Africa, Haiti, and other countries have been adopted by parents of another race. In domestic adoptions, parents are adopting children of other races and mixed-race children. The families say that while other people might notice a difference in race, they might also just be noticing how cute the kids are or how happy their family looks. If family members become very comfortable with it, they can educate others and help them understand the joys that can be found in diversity.

At some point, most adoptees who are of a different race or ethnic background from their adoptive parents' will wonder why they look different. They may feel disconnected or that something is missing. Adoptive parents can help their child overcome these feelings by making friends with other transracial families, by giving the international child a sense of his or her native culture, and by reassuring their child that God loves families of all races and cultures.

ANSWERING OTHERS' QUESTIONS

One of the biggest challenges for transracial families may be answering other people's questions. People are naturally curious, and adoptive parents might be asked questions such as, "Is he yours?" or "Are you foster parents?" because the skin tone of the child differs from theirs. Smiling graciously and simply answering, "Yes, he is mine," or "No, we are not foster parents" is enough. Common courtesy is required, not long explanations—unless you enjoy telling your family's adoption story and see it as the opportunity to share one of God's miracles!

ONE FAMILY, DIFFERENT RACES

Families with members who are of differing races sometimes still attract attention. Parents who adopt these children should be prepared to sometimes be stared at in some places because their family members are of more than one race. Remember, however, not to be overly sensitive. People tend to notice cute little children, so they might be looking at your pretty baby just because she's a beauty!

God will use your differences to attract people to him. You are privileged to be entrusted with learning about a whole new race and culture and to show the world how you value the beautiful shades of color with which God gifted people. Becoming a transracial family encourages others to set aside their prejudices and step out of their comfort zones to see the beauty of his children everywhere. You may be different races, but you are one family.

Special-Needs Adoptions

There are many special-needs children waiting to be adopted. *Special-needs* is a broad term that refers to an adoptee's disabilities or challenges in mental, social, physical, emotional, or educational areas. The term may also be used in reference to some placement factors, including the child's age, race, or the fact that he or she is part of a sibling group. In other words, a special-needs label does not necessarily mean that a child has mental or physical disabilities. It may mean that the child is over the age of ten, has difficulty reading, or would like to be adopted along with a brother or sister.

MEDICAL SPECIAL NEEDS

Medical special needs can range from something as small as a birthmark on the face or an extra toe on one foot to severe diseases or birth defects. If a child wears glasses, needs a hearing aid, has a stutter, or has a cleft lip, the child will most likely be classified as special needs and generally will be considered less adoptable to the adoption community domestically and internationally.

Many of these small "imperfections" are easily correctable or manageable, and adoptive families who accept a special-needs child experience great joy. Even children with more severe medical challenges need a forever family to love and care for them. Children with severe special needs might have AIDS or another terminal illness, have severe mental or physical incapacitation, or suffer from other disabilities.

EMOTIONAL SPECIAL NEEDS

Some children are classified in the special-needs category because they have emotional special needs. This means that the child has experienced trauma, physical and/or verbal abuse, sexual abuse, or neglect that has affected emotional growth. Some children act out in anger, others exhibit symptoms of depression, and still others may act out sexually in inappropriate ways. Emotional special needs also range from mild to severe, and many children learn emotional healing through the love and acceptance of their forever family and the knowledge that God loves them and cares for them (a message they may have never heard before). Many adoptees benefit from ongoing sessions with a trained counselor, but make sure you find one who specializes in adoption and is a Christian. Special therapies and medicines also can help them manage their feelings.

EDUCATIONAL SPECIAL NEEDS

Some waiting children have educational special needs perhaps because they missed a lot of school, were too hungry to concentrate in school, or were so traumatized that they could not focus on academics. Others have learning disabilities such as an auditory processing disorder or dyslexia. A child with educational special needs is not working academically up to his age or grade level and will need extra one-on-one attention, tutoring, and patient love to help him recognize that he can excel.

CAN YOU HANDLE THE CHALLENGES?

As you look at the overall picture of adoption and decide to proceed, the decision of whether or not to accept a child with special needs is a big one. Not only must you choose the age, race, gender, and nationality of the child you hope will join your family, but also you must seriously consider your talents and strengths when deciding whether a special-needs child is right for you. Each special-needs child deserves to have parents, but that does not necessarily mean you are equipped to be that parent.

Parents of special-needs children need to be gifted with an extra dose of patience to deal with bureaucracy's red tape in order to help their child be enrolled in special classes at school, get the appropriate therapies, or receive necessary insurance coverage. Parents should be gifted with an ability to overlook flaws and faults—ranging from failed tests at school to regular temper tantrums in the grocery store—and see their child through God's eyes as a unique and beautiful person. The challenges can be great, but the rewards are even greater.

Anyone considering accepting a special-needs child should think through and discuss all the different types of special needs, and decide which ones they truly feel they can handle. There can be guilt attached to this process as you look at a list of "imperfections" and decide that you may be able to take a child with a cleft lip but cannot handle a child with heart disease or AIDS. It is better to be realistic than to say that you will accept any child regardless of his or her special needs and then, after the adoption process is nearly finished or already finalized, find that you cannot cope with the child's special needs.

If God does call you to parent a special-needs child, he will not forsake you to do it alone. Do not worry that you will not bond with or love your child, because soon you will look past the imperfections to see the loveliness of the gift God gives you. He will give you the extra strength, support, and grace needed to do your very best for the child he places in your forever family.

WORDS OF WISDOM
For He Himself has said, "I will never leave you nor forsake you."
—Hebrews 13:5 (NKJV)

Changing the Family Dynamic
Adopting a child will change the dynamics of your family. If you are single, the adoption will impact all areas of your life and may affect your parents, siblings, and friends as they are enlisted to be your support system in loving and raising this child. As a couple, entering parenthood for the first time through the adoption process will change the amount of time you spend together. You will transition from focusing only on each other to focusing much of your time, attention, and resources on the new child in your home. For families with children already in the home, adding another child impacts every family member as you adjust the time, energy, and resources spent on each member.

REALISTIC EXPECTATIONS
As you talk about adopting, examine your expectations together. Does one of you expect your adopted child to become the president of the United States and nothing less? Does the other just hope the child will make it through elementary school? Do you think the adoption process will be a piece of cake, while your spouse is afraid it will bankrupt you and leave your hearts broken? Create a list

of your expectations and look for the commonalities and differences. Compare your approaches to the adoption process and your feelings about it. Decide where you will compromise and in what areas you feel you must stand firm. Imagine worst-case scenarios and plan for how you would handle them. Singles should discuss these issues with their support network.

For example, in a rare and extreme scenario, consider that you invest $30,000 in the birthmother's living expenses, medical expenses, and agency and attorney fees, but the birthmother ultimately changes her mind and does not relinquish her child to you. How will you react? (Remember, you should not lose the entire $30,000 if this situation occurs—only the portion that went to the birthmother. See chapter 5.) It is common for one spouse to feel extreme sadness while the other reacts with anger. With differing emotions, couples sometimes find themselves pulling apart instead of together. Will one of you be unwilling to try again while the other will want to keep pursuing adopting a child no matter what the cost?

Another scenario: you bring home a healthy child only to discover that he or she needs a costly surgery or has an impairment that was not discovered or disclosed. Will both of you be able to work together for your child, or will one of you pull away?

There is no predicting what kinds of challenges, illnesses, and difficulties any child—birthchild or adopted child—will face during his or her lifetime. Adoptive parents, like birthparents, must be willing to take the journey with their adopted child wherever it leads.

FACING YOUR OWN FEARS

At this point in considering adoption or beginning the process, it is completely normal to have fears and questions. In fact, it would be rare if you didn't. Be honest and open with your spouse, your family or other advisers, and yourself about your fears. Also, talking with families who have adopted is one of the best ways to alleviate the fears of what can go wrong with adoption. Most adoption agencies have online forums, chat groups, or other means of helping families connect and share their stories. Talk to those who have been there and ask to hear their personal adoption stories. Ask them how long it took, how they made their decisions, and what became their biggest obstacles. Get their insider tips on how to help your adoption process go smoothly, and invite their best advice for handling the first days at home.

If you have not chosen an agency and want to learn more before you commit, ask friends and extended family if they know people who have adopted or who are adoptees. You will be amazed at how many people you already know whose lives have been touched by adoption. In addition, there are many chat groups, forums, blogs, and personal story Web sites on the subject of adoption. Be aware that not all are in favor of adoption. There are some Web sites dedicated to eliminating adoption. Some of these have been established by organizations who feel that birthmothers have been coerced into placing their children for adoption; others are run by people who have experienced the trauma of failed or disrupted adoptions and do not believe that adoption is beneficial or that it works. The majority of sites share positive stories of adoption, and most adoptive families will tell you that God gave them the blessing of a child who was just right for their family.

Adoption as a Calling

For a truly successful adoption, Christians need to feel called by God to pursue this method of building their family. In order to be called, you have to be listening and willing to follow his lead.

The best advice for any Christian who begins to consider adoption is to get on your knees—literally. Spend time in prayer. Do it often. Ask God if he is the one awakening in you a desire to adopt.

If the idea of adoption takes root and changes from fleeting thoughts to persistent reminders and the desire to research, ask God to continue to make his will clear. If he wants you to adopt, he will be faithful to lead you every step of the way. He will take the seed planted in your heart and grow it into new branches of your family tree, but before he does, it is important to learn all you can about the adventure you are considering.

How Are You Being Called?

Now that you have learned what adoption is, who the players are, and what the process entails, it's time to decide what role God is calling you to play in his miracle stories of adoptions. Do you feel called to become an adoptive parent? Have you learned enough now to commit to becoming a foster parent, or do you want to get involved in adoption by helping another family or working in adoption and orphan-care ministry? With millions of orphans around the world waiting for someone to love them, care for them, or bring them home, there is plenty of work to be done.

After looking at adoption from many angles, if you do not feel called to adopt, this book is still for you. Reading about the process can help you empathize with and assist friends and family who do walk through the adoption process, and in part 5 (chapters 14 and 15), you will find ways to heed God's call to care for orphans in practical ways. You may be called to develop an adoption ministry, work with birth families, or even volunteer at an orphanage. Your calling might be to make a positive difference in many children's lives. Not everyone is called by God to adopt a child, but everyone is called to love and serve his children—including you.

RED LIGHT, STOP!

Questions to consider at this point in your adoption journey:

____ What are you and your spouse's fears and concerns?

____ Have you decided which type of adoption you want to pursue—closed, semi-open, or open?

____ How committed are you to adoption?

____ Have you discussed some "worst-case" scenarios so that you are prepared to pull together in a crisis?

____ Are you ready to begin the adoption process?

____ If you do not feel called to adopt, are you ready to learn other ways you can get involved in adoption ministry?

GREEN LIGHT, GO!

Action points for your adoption journey:

____ Continue talking about adoption with your spouse, family, friends, a pastor, or a counselor. Ask about your strengths and weaknesses. What do others see as your positive and negative attributes?

____ Decide what kind of child you feel called to adopt. Discuss your preferences for the child's gender and age, and whether you would consider a sibling group or special-needs child.

____ Plan for the type of adoption you would want to pursue: confidential, semi-open, or open. Decide what kinds of contact you could be comfortable with for a period of up to eighteen-plus years, including letter and photo exchanges, e-mails, phone calls, and visits from birth-family members.

____ Discuss the positives and negatives for you of transracial or international adoption.

____ Figure out which spouse would be the best one to work with school officials and which one should work with insurance agencies, who will be most available to take your child to everything from fun extracurricular activities to physical therapy sessions, counseling sessions, and medical appointments as needed. If you are single, figure out who will help you when you can't be everywhere at once.

____ Address the way adoption will change your family dynamic, including the importance of continuing to have time as a couple and meeting the needs of other children in your home.

____ Talk about the feelings you might have or might not have at first for your adopted child.

♥ *My Adoption Miracle*
The Little Sister I Prayed For
by Emily Chapman, daughter of singer Steven Curtis Chapman

Compassion International in Haiti sparked my love and made me aware of the abandoned and forgotten youth of the world. I was eleven. It would be a couple of years later before my family's adoption journey would begin, but the seed had been planted.

I have always loved kids, but I just didn't realize the extreme poverty most of the world lives in, until our trip to Haiti. It just pulled a pretty big heartstring inside me because these kids just had so much joy no matter their circumstances. When I returned home, one of my best friend's family was adopting their second child. They already had four biological kids, and that got me thinking. My parents told me we helped orphans by supporting them financially, but I wanted to know why we couldn't take the next step and bring a baby home.

I had two little brothers, and I started asking for a little sister. At first, my motives were more for me. I wanted to bake cookies and have tea parties instead of playing ninjas. So I started writing "baby sister" at the top of my Christmas and birthday lists. My mother said there was no way that our family was adopting. I was obnoxious in my pursuit. I wrote petitions and had my brothers sign them and left them on my parents' bed. I even wrote them a note that said they were disobeying God by not adopting. I spent my own money one time and bought a book on adoption that I would keep in the car and read to my mother when we were driving. I was making her crazy.

Finally, after more than a year of praying and trying to persuade my parents, I went to visit our pastor. I asked him, since the Bible says that God will give us the desires of our heart if we ask him, why I wasn't getting a baby sister when I really had been praying and believing. My pastor asked me if I was praying for Emily's will or if I was praying for God's will. So I started praying, "Lord, if this is your will, you're going to have to work a miracle in my mom's heart."

Once I left it in God's hands and stopped bringing it up so much, that's when things started changing. The Lord did begin to work in my mom's heart, and in March 2000, we traveled as a family to China to bring home Shaohannah, my little sister. Little did I know that when my mom's heart was finally filled with a desire to adopt, God would over-fix her! In 2003, we brought home Stevey Joy. Then my dad got over-fixed, and in 2004 we brought home Maria. My family also created Shaohannah's Hope, an organization to help other families financially so that they can bring their adopted children home.

While my parents do not plan to adopt any more kids, I am the next one in line. I am still in college, so it won't be for a while, but I definitely plan to adopt someday. It's funny, because most siblings sit around and talk about how many kids they'll have one day. My brothers and I sit around and talk about what countries our kids will come from. That's our adoption miracle.

Part Two

Saying "Yes!": Starting Your Amazing Adoption Journey

Be strong and courageous. Do not be terrified; do not be discouraged, for the LORD your God will be with you wherever you go.
—Joshua 1:9 (NIV)

WANTED

Loving, happily married christian couple seeks to adopt a child. Will provide a stable home, college, and all the tools for a successful future. Will pay living and medical expenses. Call our attorney at 888-555-1212.

Chapter Three

Adopting in the United States

If you have decided to pursue an adoption here in the United States, congratulations! You are on your way not only to creating the forever family God designed for you, but also to providing a loving family for a child who needs one.

Domestic Adoption of a Newborn

Domestic adoption of newborn infants can be thrilling, exhilarating, challenging, and exhausting. The way to achieve the best outcome in domestic adoption is to seek the Lord's guidance on this adoption option, talk to everyone you know about their experiences with domestic adoption, and become as educated as possible about the process.

Because many potential adopters are anxious to begin a family and in many cases weary from the frustration, grief, and expense of infertility treatments, the tendency for those pursuing domestic adoption can be to jump at the first opportunity offered. However, the first agency you hear about, the first adoption attorney you meet, or even the first birthmother you are connected with may not be the right fit for you. That's where trust comes in once again. If you trust the Lord with your future and truly believe that any child you will ever have belongs to him and is merely entrusted to you, you will have the patience and wisdom to select the best people to help you in the adoption process, and you are more likely to be matched with the right birthmother.

I DIDN'T KNOW THAT!

Most private adoptions in the United States are of newborns. Typically, a pregnant woman who does not feel she can raise her child makes a plan for adoption sometime during her pregnancy, and the transfer of the child to the adoptive parents takes place shortly after birth. Older children who are adoptable in the United States are typically in state foster care.

THE HOME STUDY

One of the first and most important steps to accomplish in any adoption, including domestic adoption, is a successful home study. A *home study* is a series of interviews with the prospective parents, their children, and anyone else who lives in their household. Couples are interviewed together and separately, and each prospective parent is required to fill out an extensive questionnaire about childhood, extended family, the marital relationship, discipline style, and other background information.

The home study must be completed by a social worker who is licensed to conduct home studies within your state. Some adoption agencies have social workers on staff to conduct home studies; others will ask you to select an independent social worker. In the latter case, the agency should have recommendations for you. Also, ask other families who have gone through the process which social worker did their home studies. Finally, Christian agencies may require independent home studies to be done by a social worker who has set up a nonprofit practice.

Interviews for the home study will usually take place within the adopters' home, and social workers will expect to receive a brief tour of the house, including the space that is allotted for the adopted child. The adopters must also provide letters of reference from relatives and nonrelatives, and contact information for these references. Other items needed for the home study include a state criminal background check, a local background check, a state department of human services (or children and family services) background check for any child-abuse investigations, financial information, and a medical clearance from your local physician.

After you provide this information and undergo a series of three to five interviews, the social worker will write a several-page report that describes your home and family life and, ideally, states that you are capable and worthy of adopting a child. This home study report must then be given to your agency or attorney as part of the process to legally adopt a child domestically or internationally. The average home study takes thirty to sixty days to complete.

While home studies can feel somewhat uncomfortable, they are designed to protect adopted children from being placed in homes where they would be neglected or mistreated. Social workers should be thorough in their questioning, but also kind. Most social workers conduct home studies to help children be adopted, not to prevent people from adopting. In addition to interviewing you, the best social workers also allow you to ask questions and will provide resource lists for you to learn more about the adoption you are undertaking. Some social workers have adopted children themselves, and some were adopted as children. Most work in this field because they have a love for children and desire to see them placed in forever families. They can be a wealth of information about adoption, so feel free to ask them all your adoption questions.

"I am not here to look under the beds or scare anyone away from adoption; as long as they are qualified, I am here to help people get their babies," says Donna Bradley, licensed social worker and adoptive mom in Florida. "I want to help them through the process."

I DIDN'T KNOW THAT!

The wait time for a domestic infant adoption placement in Massachusetts in 2002, following a completed home study:
The shortest time—less than one month
The longest time—sixty-six months
—Survey by the Center for Adoption Research at the University of Massachusetts

If you contact a social worker to conduct your home study, ask the following questions before you sign a contract:

- How long have you been licensed to do home studies?
- How many home studies have you done in the past year?
- Have you interviewed any families in the past year whom you could not recommend to adopt? If so, what factors disqualified them?
- If I hire you, when will you conduct the first interview?
- How far apart will the interviews be spaced?
- How long after the interviews will I receive my completed home study?
- Do you offer a reduction or a partial refund of fees if my report is not completed by the date promised?
- Are you operating as a nonprofit company?
- How much do you charge? Does this include post-placement visits?
- What is your personal experience with adoption?
- What adoption resources can you point me to in the local community?
- What three things would you say every adoptive family should know?

A successful home study should result in not only a good report but also a rapport between the social worker and the family. Most social workers will conduct the pre-adoption home study and later return to do the required post-placement reports to make sure that the adopted child and family are settling in well together after the adoption.

Be gracious, greet your social worker with a smile, take an interest in his or her life, offer refreshments, and make sure your house is presentable. (It does not have to be spotless!) Overall, your home study should seem a little bit probing but not an overly unpleasant experience.

If your social worker is concerned about anything in your background, discuss the issue openly and talk about ways it can be resolved.

However, if you contact a social worker and

- do not feel your questions are being answered forthrightly,
- the social worker seems overworked or distracted,
- the social worker is not giving you his or her full attention,
- the social worker is unfriendly or overly particular, or
- the social worker makes you feel uncomfortable,

consider interviewing another social worker. If the worker was provided by your agency, speak to his or her supervisor. If the social worker is provided by the state for a public adoption, try to resolve your differences with him or her. If you are working with an independent social worker, consider switching to another one.

In any private adoption, you are paying for this service, and it is a very important one. A good working relationship with your social worker is vital to a successful adoption. You have the right to have a social worker who works for you, not against you.

FINDING AN AGENCY, ATTORNEY, OR BOTH

Finding an adoption agency or attorney to work with can be tricky business. You want to make an informed decision, but the choices all sound good. There are no comprehensive, comparative studies that indicate which agencies adhere to which standards, although some research in that area is now being undertaken. In 2004 and 2006, the Christian organization Hope for Orphans surveyed thirty adoption agencies and asked them a number of questions about their operating policies. Eighteen of the agencies identified themselves as Christian, while twelve said they were not. Of the eighteen Christian agencies, fifteen would not allow homosexuals to adopt; three would. Twenty-Four of the thirty agencies allowed single parents to adopt, while six of the Christian agencies would not. Half of the Christian agencies said they do not require potential adoptive parents to be Christians.[12]

With so many differing standards, how do you know which one could be right for you? You won't unless you know what to look for first. That means knowing which questions to ask and being bold enough to ask them. One consideration for Christians is the financial accountability of any agency. It is important to find out not only if the agency is charging an appropriate amount for an adoption but also in what ways they're using the monies they raise. This

45

can be difficult to determine, as there are few umbrella organizations that track fiscal responsibility. One organization that does provide accountability measures for nonprofit organizations is the Evangelical Council for Financial Accountability (ECFA), an accreditation agency based on annual renewal that sets standards charities must meet to become members. It currently represents more than twelve hundred organizations that collectively receive nearly $15 billion annually.[13] Find out if the agency you want to use is a member of ECFA. If they are, you can be assured the agency has taken extra measures to show that they are fiscally above reproach.

The following are other important questions to ask any adoption agency you consider:

- Are you a nonprofit agency with 501(c)(3) status?
- Are you a member of the ECFA or pursuing accreditation?
- How long have you been in business?
- Who founded your agency, and why did they start an adoption agency?
- What is your mission statement?
- Where can I acquire a copy of your annual report and financial statement?
- What do you do with the adoption fees paid to the agency? Do you have humanitarian projects?
- How many babies did you place in the last year?
- What were the demographics of the parents who received babies (age, race, single or married, etc.)?
- Do you allow people to adopt who believe in spanking as a means of discipline? (Many secular agencies and some Christian ones require adoptive parents to sign statements that they will not use corporal punishment.)
- Do you allow adoptive parents to homeschool their adopted children?
- How long is the average wait for placement through your agency?
- How many adoptions have failed, been interrupted, or fallen through within the last year?
- How much are your fees, and when are they due? (See chapter 5.)
- How do you find your birthmothers?
- Will you locate a birthmother for me, and if so, by what means, or am I responsible for advertising or finding one myself?
- How many prospective parents are you currently working with? How many birthmothers?
- What is your process for locating birthfathers?
- What happens to the baby between the time of birth and signed consent for adoption?

If you choose to use an adoption attorney, the questions remain largely the same, although most lawyers will not have a 501(c)(3) corporation. The best kind of attorney to handle an adoption is generally one who specializes in adoption. The lawyer who drew up your will or settled your divorce might be legally qualified to handle your adoption, but chances are he or she might not be as effective as one who has made adoption his or her specialty. Some adoptive families choose to work with an agency *and* an attorney to cover all the bases.

Many adoptions today are taking place across state lines. An agency may be in one state, the adoptive family in another, and the birthparents in yet another. Make sure your agency or attorney is well versed in interstate adoption and the laws that will have to be followed in both states, since state laws governing adoption vary.

INDEPENDENT ADOPTIONS

Linda Barnby is an adoption attorney in Florida who adopted her daughter domestically and decided to devote her law practice to handling adoptions for other families. She encourages potential adoptive families to learn all they can about their options before signing on any dotted line.

"Meet with the agencies and attorneys if you can," Barnby urges. "For example, I offer an adoption seminar with no expectation that attendees will adopt at all or work with me. I encourage people everywhere to look for as much unbiased information as they can. Look for the specifics for your state, because each one varies widely on the availability of birthmoms and how you can look for them, the living expenses that can be paid, and those kinds of things."

The differences between agencies and attorneys also vary. Agencies primarily are private and operate under policies set by the executive or the board of directors. A law firm that handles adoptions also has a certain set of policies it follows, based on the personalities of the attorneys heading the firm.

"What adoption boils down to is trust, and ultimately the adoptive parents and birthmother need to trust each other," Barnby says. "But before you get to that point, the adoptive parents need to trust an agency or a law firm they choose for their adoption."

She says most prospective adopters who come to her seminars have a healthy dose of skepticism, and they fear that an adoption will not work and they will lose a lot of money. The first thing she does is calm their fears.

"Families come to adoption seminars full of questions and outright fear that they will be lost in the maze or taken advantage of. So it is important to talk through all the scenarios and answer all the questions about younger children versus older children, who birthmothers and birthfathers are and why they place children for adoption, and dealing with mixed races."

After the seminars, Barnby reviews applications prospective parents have filled out with an eye toward eliminating families with whom she does not believe she could place a child within a "reasonable amount of time."

Things that can eliminate prospective parents from working with an agency or attorney or make them less likely to be chosen by a birthmother include the following:

- They already have a child or children. Many birthmothers want to make a family out of a couple.
- Single status. Many birthmoms want their child in a married, two-parent home.
- Criminal background or a background that includes child-abuse findings. This may cause an attorney or agency to decline to work with you.
- Age (too old or too young). Most birthmothers choose adoptive parents who are at least twenty-five but not older than forty.
- Medical conditions that could interfere with parenting. Serious medical issues can cause an agency or attorney to decline to work with you.
- An obviously unstable marriage can also cause an agency or attorney to decline to work with you.
- Recent death of a spouse or a child, or being a newlywed. Many agencies ask that couples be married at least one year and that they wait one year after any major loss or crisis before applying to adopt.

Once an application has been reviewed by an agency or attorney, the adopters are told whether the agency or attorney will be working with them or not. If so, the new clients will be asked to begin their home study—if they do not have a successful one already—and to create a profile of themselves for their birthmother. The agency representative or attorney will also ask the adoptive parents all about the child they envision having and what their preferences are. Adopters who are willing to accept a child of either gender, of mixed race, or with special needs will generally adopt sooner than those who insist on a specific gender, race, or background.

I DIDN'T KNOW THAT!

National adoption consultant Kristine Faasse of Bethany Christian Services says some birthmothers will not choose adoptive families who insist on a specific gender, even if an ultrasound indicates their child is the preferred gender. Birthmothers bond to some degree with their chosen adoptive parents during the process and want to be assured that the adoptive family they choose will not reject their child because of gender when born.

"The adoptive family has to really do some hard work and some soul-searching about what they are open to and what they are not open to," says Kristine Faasse, national adoption consultant for Bethany Christian Services. "We all know that no child is born perfect, but if a family only wants the closest to perfect that we can guarantee, they have to be very honest about that and be prepared for a very long wait."

A Christian Agency, Attorney, or Both

For Christians looking to adopt a newborn baby, a Christian agency or attorney who upholds the same standards you believe in, has a good reputation, and comes with a personal recommendation from a family member or friend is your best choice for a domestic newborn adoption. An agency or attorney who offers full birthmother services, including prenatal and postnatal counseling and referrals to services, is also preferred. While the ultimate goal of the adoptive parents is to bring home a baby, the birthmother should not be forgotten in the process. Her decision, which will affect the lives of everyone involved, requires much soul-searching on her part without pressure from the agency or adoptive family. Professional counseling should be made available to help her process her emotions. (Preferably, it should be made available to the birthfather as well.) When these factors are in place, the long-term adoption plan has the best chances for success, not just in placement but also throughout childhood for the birthparents, the adoptive parents, and the adopted child.

As Christians who want to adopt a newborn, it is important to pray for the birthparents. It may feel natural to pray for your future child, but you should include his or her birthmother and birthfather as well. A wanted pregnancy is filled with such joy and anticipation, while an unplanned crisis pregnancy brings with it heartache and turmoil. It is typically the birthmother who loves her child so dearly that she is able to put aside her desire to parent the child she cannot provide for and let someone else become his or her mom and dad. Pray for her health, safety, and emotional stability. Pray for wisdom in making your post-adoption plans, and for healing for your birthmother's emotions.

Finding a Birthmother

There are many companies today who offer to facilitate adoptions of newborns by promising to locate birthmothers. Some are legitimate; some are not. They may charge a few thousand dollars or much more. A facilitator's role is to find a birthmother for you and arrange for you to meet by phone or in person. You will still pay the birthmother's expenses, still need a home study, and still need to hire an attorney to finalize the adoption.

Sometimes using a facilitator works well, but most states do not license them, and they are not regulated by any government agency at this time. This should be a warning to most adoptive parents to stick with an agency or attorney who has some built-in safeguards and accountability, instead of jumping at promises from a facilitator that might be too good to be true. If you are content with waiting for the child God has picked out for you, an adoption agency or attorney is usually a wiser choice than a facilitator.

Some adoptive parents facilitate their own adoptions by making it known that they are looking for a birthmother—through word of mouth, advertising in publications (if permitted in their state), or other creative means. Sometimes, birthmothers are matched with adoptive parents through someone in their church, someone at their office, or other people they know. Occasionally, doctors still connect a birthmother with a waiting couple directly, although privacy laws prohibit that to some degree.

Once you've found the birthmother you want to work with, it is wise for everyone's sake to seek the help of trained agency professionals or an adoption attorney.

CREATING YOUR PROFILE

After you have located an agency or attorney and they have agreed to work with you, it's time to get busy creating your profile. You will probably need to keep on hand several identical copies of your profile. Some birthmothers will want to take a copy of your profile home, and the agency or attorney may send your profile to several birthmothers simultaneously. Ask before you start, so you'll know how many copies of paperwork, photographs, etc., you'll need. Be sure to keep a master profile for yourself.

Your profile includes pictures, the story of your marriage, information about any other children, and your family background. It contains a letter from you to the birthmother. Profiles should be personal, warm, friendly, and detailed. The profile is usually a notebook, and the style can vary widely. Some profiles are created by scrapbook experts who dress up the information with borders and stickers; others are much plainer. The important thing is that your profile contains all the information needed.

The adoption agency or attorney you choose should have outlines available for you to follow in creating your profile. You can also look at other adoptive families' birthmom letters and profiles online.

Generally, your profile should include pictures of

- your home,
- your recreational activities,
- your family members, including any other children (if desired),

- your pets, and
- you and your spouse in a variety of settings.

Include with the pictures a description of the people and places in each shot.

In your birthmother letter, you should begin by showing concern for her and appreciation for the difficult road she is traveling. Other tips for creating your profile include the following:

- Write in your own style, using a conversational tone.
- Include information you would want to know about adoptive parents if you were in her place.
- Describe you, your spouse, and the rest of your household.
- Mention your age, education, parenting style, occupation, hobbies, and Christian beliefs.
- Tell how you met your spouse and what your relationship is like.
- If you are single, describe what having a child would mean in your life and why you feel equipped as a single to adopt.

Stating outright that you are a Christian might be an advantage if you are using a Christian adoption agency. In fact, most birthmothers want their child raised in a Christian home.

Finally, keep your entire profile detailed but not too long or bulky. You don't want to lose your birthmother's interest by including five pages on the bubblegum-that-got-stuck-to-your-shoe incident in third grade. Instead, paint a picture of yourself and the people, education, spirituality, and values that led you to where you are today.

I DIDN'T KNOW THAT!

A *dossier* is a collection of official papers that adoption agencies—domestically and abroad—examine to decide whether prospective parents are qualified to adopt. It includes things like the home study report, criminal background clearances, and financial affidavits.

A profile is a scrapbook-like collection of photographs, letters, and biographical information that prospective domestic newborn adopters create for birthmothers to look through when making their placement decision.

If you are still not sure what a birthmother letter should look like, in chapter 6 and appendix H you can find examples of letters actually written by successful adoptive families.

ABOUT BIRTHMOTHERS

Obviously, in order to adopt a newborn domestically, you must be matched with a birthmother. A *birthmother* is a woman who places her child for adoption or a pregnant woman who is making plans to legally relinquish her child for adoption after birth. (Legally, before the child's birth, she is simply the *mother* of the child, although the term *birthmother* is commonly used before and after the baby is born.) Birthmothers who consider adoption often start early in the pregnancy and choose to place their child for adoption for a wide variety of reasons. Most of their pregnancies were unplanned, and the birthmother might feel unprepared to properly care for a child. Some mothers are addicted to drugs or alcohol, some suffer from mental illness, and others are teens who do not feel capable of taking on the burdens of motherhood. Some birthmothers relinquish children with severe illnesses or birth defects, and some place their child because the child is the product of rape.

Some birthmothers do not fall in these categories at all. The typical birthmother of the past might have been in her teens, but since the stigma of illegitimate birth has lessened and abortion has become legal, many teen mothers today either keep their babies or abort them. According to a 1999 report by the National Center for Health Statistics, U.S. Department of Health and Human Services: "Between 1989 and 1995, 1.7 percent of children born to never-married white women were placed for adoption, compared to 19.3 percent before 1973. Among never-married black women, relinquishment rates have ranged from .2 percent to 1.5 percent."

Kristine Faasse says that many of the birthmothers she has seen in recent years are in their twenties, and are often single parents of one or more children already. They feel they do not have the resources of time and money needed to raise another child.

Birthmothers usually place their children for adoption today after thinking long and hard about whether they can let go of their own desires to keep the child they have carried and cared about for nine months. When they do place a child for adoption, their goal is that he or she be raised in a better situation or lifestyle by loving parents. The choice to experience pregnancy and relinquish a child is an unselfish act of sacrifice that birthmothers make.

If the birthmother decides that adoption is the best answer, she may obtain a referral from her doctor or crisis pregnancy center to an adoption agency, she may find one online or in the phone book, or she may ask a friend for a recommendation. Some birthmothers respond directly to prospective adopters through the finding ads they place. The birthmother, or both parties, should then contact an adoption agency or attorney. While you may be excited when a birthmother contacts you, it is usually wise to involve your attorney or agency right after the initial contact. If a birthmother or couple pressures you not to involve an attorney but to send them money directly, there is cause for concern. Adoptive couples have found themselves the unwitting victims of birthparents who seemed to offer significant savings by working together directly, only to find that they were being swindled.

When an agency or attorney is in contact with a birthmother, they will try to obtain as much background information and family history as possible:

- They will talk extensively to the birthmother about her financial, physical, medical, and emotional needs.
- They will ask for identifying information such as her Social Security number, address, birth date, and phone number.
- They will ask about her education, her current circumstances, and her medical history.
- They will ask her about the birthfather—who he is, where he is, and whether he has shown any interest in parenting the child.
- They will want to know her reasons for wanting to relinquish her child for adoption.

In a closed adoption, some of the non-identifying answers to these questions will be the only information you will have on your child's history. If the adoption is open or semi-open, you might receive more information as you go through the process and meet or exchange information with the birthmother or birthparents.

The attorney or agency will let the birthmother know if they feel comfortable in working with her to place her child in an adoptive home. They will usually ask the birthmother to come in and meet them in order to better assess her intentions. If there is some reason the birthmother cannot come in, they will ask for proof of her pregnancy or proof that she has a baby she wants to place.

If she decides to work with a particular agency or attorney and they agree to work with her, they will then ask her to review profiles of people who want to adopt. Some birthmothers choose an agency because they have already read online the information about specific prospective parents working with that agency. Others will choose a family from the scrapbooks and profiles at the agency.

WORDS OF WISDOM

Since the day we heard about you, we have not stopped praying for you and asking God to fill you with the knowledge of his will through all spiritual wisdom and understanding.
—Colossians 1:9 (NIV)

When an agency or attorney is actively working with a birthmother, they will give her the scrapbooks and "Dear Birthmother" letters from prospective parents. Once a birthmother has chosen a couple or an individual to consider, depending on the agency's policies and all the parents' preferences, the agency might request permission to give the birthmother more information or arrange a face-to-face meeting between prospective parents and the birthmother.

Meet adoptive parents say that the first meeting with a birthmother can be absolutely nerve-racking. Hopes are riding high on being found acceptable by this pregnant woman, yet most adopters have no idea what she is looking for. For Christian adopters, when the call comes to meet a birthmother, take a deep breath and get on your knees in prayer. When God is orchestrating something, it usually inspires a sense of inner peace. Butterflies are normal; a sense of deep foreboding is not. Ask God to guide you through your birthmother meeting, to keep your expectations under control, and to give you clear signs of whether this is the right match for your family.

"A birthmother may pick a family because they drive the same kind of car her dad drove when she was growing up, or something else that seems totally random," shares adoptive mother Caprice Payne. "It is not usually about what stuff you can provide for their child but that you remind them of someone or something. There is just something there that connects."

Adoption coordinators warn prospective parents not to get too excited when they first hear that a birthmother is looking at their profile or to place too many hopes on the first meeting. The initial meeting with the birthmother, if arranged by your agency or attorney, will usually take place in their offices. If you have located a birthmother yourself, it is wise to suggest meeting at your agency's or attorney's office or to pick a neutral location, rather than your home.

Not all meetings result in a match. The Payne family felt that their first birthmother meeting went very well. In fact, it went a little too well, as the birthmother felt they were more her peers than a potential set of parents for her child. At first, the Paynes felt a keen sense of rejection. Later, when they met the birthmother of their son, they understood why God allowed them to be disappointed the first time.

Before you meet with a birthmother or birthparents, pray about it. Ask God to help you love the birthparents and feel concerned for their well-being, not just for the child the birthmother is carrying. Ask him to help you see past any stereotypes or prejudices you might have and see this birthmother as a beloved child of God. Before you meet with the birthmother, ask your agency or attorney what suggestions they have for you to make your birthmother meeting fruitful?

If you meet with a birthmother in the presence of your agency worker or attorney, ask for feedback after the meeting. You may want to ask the following:

- Were we too eager or too withdrawn?
- Did we make our birthmother comfortable?
- How could we better answer her questions?
- What suggestions do you have for us to make our future birthmother meetings more fruitful?

It is important to note that until the birth and relinquishment of the baby, the birthmother is considered to be in the driver's seat in the adoption process. She generally has control over choosing an adoptive family for her child, how much contact she wants to have with them, and whether she wants them to be at the hospital for the birth.

The law gives her time to consider her decision to place her baby for adoption not only before the birth but also for a short time after the birth—usually from one day to two months. The birthmother must first sign a consent form (or relinquishment form) to relinquish the baby for adoption. This can be done in most states between forty-eight to seventy-two hours after the birth. Other states allow the signing to take place anytime after birth, and others allow a period longer than seventy-two hours. (For example, Louisiana and South Dakota laws call for five days.) After the consent has been signed, some states consider this placement irrevocable; others allow another window of time for the birthmother to reconsider—usually three to fourteen days, but in some cases longer.

Because adoption law is governed differently in each state and because laws change frequently, those who wish to adopt need to become familiar with the current laws of their state. The U.S. Department of Health and Human Services, Administration for Children and Families, operates the National Adoption Information Clearinghouse. On its Web site, www.naic.acf.hhs.gov, those interested in adoption issues and laws can look up information and guidelines for each state.

ABOUT BIRTHFATHERS

A *birthfather* is a man who has a legal claim to a child who is relinquished for adoption. In past decades, birthfathers did not have much legal say in whether or not they had a right to parent a child they fathered outside marriage. Today, there are a wide variety of ways the birthfather plays into the adoption process. However, unlike the birthmother, in some cases the birthfather does not have to be the biological father of the child.

For instance, the legal father of a child is the man who was married to the mother at the time of the child's birth. Period. Even if he did not physically conceive the child with the birthmother, in the eyes of the law the birthmother's husband at the time of the birth is the legal father and has the support obligations and responsibilities of a father. The legal father's rights can be lost, and the child placed for adoption, if the husband can't be located and has not made any effort to parent (such as bonding or spending time with the child, paying child support, or giving presents to the child). The legal father's rights can also be terminated if a judge determines that he should not have custody, or if he claims parental rights and DNA testing proves that he did not actually father the child.

A biological father can claim rights to a child being placed for adoption. If he wants to challenge an adoption plan for a child he believes he physically fathered and DNA tests prove his claim, he can be given the same parenting rights as the biological mother and the same legal standing. He must then agree to an adoption by consent, or his rights must be terminated by the courts.

Other terms used when talking about birthfathers include *adjudicated fathers, alleged* or *putative fathers*, and *presumed fathers*. An adjudicated father is a man the courts have ruled to be the father of a child, usually based on a paternity suit or DNA test results. If a man is trying to win custody of a child and is waiting for DNA test results, any adoption process will usually be put on hold. Alleged or putative dads are men who might or might not have fathered a child with a woman who was not their wife, according to the best of their knowledge or the mother's statements. A putative father must come forward and file suit to preserve his parental rights if he opposes the adoption of a child he believes he fathered.

Every state differs as to how each type of birthfather must be notified of any impending adoption and when his rights to the child can be terminated. Your agency or attorney can advise you of your state's requirements and what steps are being taken to track down and notify any potential birthfather who could have cause to come forward in your adoption. Be wary of anyone who tells you that looking for the birthfather is not necessary or does not matter. That is simply not true. He matters on a legal basis, because a birthfather who comes forward and says he was not notified of the impending adoption can file a motion to stop the adoption. He can try to gain custody of the child himself.

He also matters on an emotional level, because some day your adopted child might want to know about his or her biological dad. Also, if the birthfather is included in the adoption, the child's family history will be more complete. Birthfathers who are part of the process may also have an easier time giving their consent to adoption, knowing that their children will be well cared for and safe.

Most states have a putative father registry, usually kept by the health department, where men who think they may have fathered a child can register their identifying and contact information and thus be notified if a child who might be theirs is being placed for adoption. This registry places the burden on the alleged father to step forward, rather than trying to make adoption agencies or attorneys track down alleged fathers. The time frame for registering is limited and usually ends thirty days after the birth of the child or within thirty days of an adoption petition being filed, although judges have some leeway in this area.

Putative fathers who put their names on the registry may also be held responsible for helping pay medical bills and paying child support. For more information on registries, ask your adoption agency or attorney about the laws in your state and what rights birthfathers have.

If a birthfather is unknown or has not been named by the birthmother, an adoption can be risky if the birthfather's rights are not terminated. If it can't be determined who the party is or where he is located, states have ways to terminate his rights without his permission. Some of those ways may include searching the putative father registries for his name and publishing adoption notices in newspapers in the known or suspected location of the birthfathers. If the birthfather does not come forward or take action within a specified time frame, his rights can be legally terminated.

While it may seem complicated to have to obtain consent for an adoption from a birthmother *and* a birthfather, it is usually better to have both birthparents in the picture during the process. In that way, both parents are available to give legal consent to the adoption, both are available to receive counseling, and both are available to provide information about your child's family and medical history. Most agencies and attorneys welcome the participation of the birthfathers in the adoption process, because it actually makes things less complicated by eliminating the risk of an unknown or nonparticipating birthfather suddenly coming forward and demanding his parental rights.

Christians who are adopting should be faithful to include birthfathers, even absent ones, in their adoption plans. Try to find specific information on who the birthfather is, and welcome him into the process if he wants to be part of it. Pray for him, too, and see if you can ensure that he also has access to counseling and support services. If your adoption is open or semi-open, include the birthfather when you send pictures and letters or if you are going to allow birthparent visits.

COUNTING ALL THE COSTS

Prospective adoptive parents need to be prepared for many situations as they go into an adoption. Aside from the actual dollars spent, there are nonmonetary costs to be counted and sacrifices to make, especially in the case of an open adoption.

WORDS OF WISDOM
Many proclaim themselves loyal, but who can find one worthy of trust?
—Proverbs 20:6 (NRSV)

Going into a truly open adoption is a lot like becoming a stepfamily. Not only are you adopting the child, but you are also gaining a permanent connection to total strangers (the birthparents and birth family) who might have drastically different lifestyles and values from yours. Most adoptive parents think only about the baby and rarely become educated on how close to a blended family they are about to become. Yet the same issues that occur in stepfamilies can pop up in families involved in open adoption, such as jealousy, loyalty to one family over another, the longing to be with absent family members, and the chaos that comes with sometimes dysfunctional people becoming part of the family unit. Talk to some stepfamilies about the struggles they face and consider whether those scenarios might apply to you.

Finally, don't feel pressured to agree to the arrangement unless you are positive you can abide by it over the long-term. Even if a post-adoption agreement to have contact is not legally enforceable, keeping one's word is the honorable thing to do.

WHAT HAPPENS AFTER PLACEMENT?

Depending on the degree of openness in your adoption, you might go to the hospital for the birth or receive a phone call before your birthmother leaves for the hospital and after the baby is born, or you might not be notified that anything is happening until after the baby is born and consent has been signed. Many birthmothers tell the adoptive parents that they want them at the hospital or that they will call when they go into labor, but lots of them do not call. They might be in too much pain or too embarrassed; they might suddenly feel pressured or uncomfortable. Other family members might urge them not to have you there. Try not to let your feelings be hurt if you are not called to go to the hospital for the birth. At this point, labor needs to proceed as calmly as possible for both the birthmother and the baby.

Once you get the call that the baby is born, most states will allow the baby to go home with you from the hospital upon his or her discharge. In some states, you must be licensed as foster parents to take the baby home during the period of time when consent has not yet been signed or the waiting period for revocation is still in effect. Other states allow the baby to go home directly with the adoptive family. Find out what the laws are in your state so you are prepared to pick up your baby. Also, make sure you have a properly installed car seat. Ask your agency or attorney what the exact process is and what items you will need in your state.

The birthmother will be contacted by the agency or attorney to sign the consent form. Adoptive parents are usually not present for this, so they could not be construed as unduly influencing or pressuring the birthmother's decision. Agencies and attorneys have their own consent forms, but all have some of the same elements, including the statement that the birthmother is giving away her rights voluntarily, that she is not under the influence of any drugs or alcohol that might impair her judgment, and that she has read the consent form and understands it. As a general rule, consent to adopt cannot be given by the birthmother before the baby is born. Only two states, Alabama and Hawaii, currently allow birthmothers to consent before the birth. However, the decision to consent must be reaffirmed after the child's birth. In twenty-eight states, consent can be executed by a written form that is signed, witnessed, and/or notarized. Other states require the filing in court of a petition or an appearance before a judge.

Once consent is given and relinquishment forms completed, the waiting period before finalization begins. Most domestic adoptions are finalized by the time the baby is about six months old. However, remember that the opportunity for a birthmother to attempt to revoke her consent in most states is much shorter. The time frame during which a birthmother can withdraw her consent and the legally accepted reasons for her to be able to do so vary widely from state to state. Some states will consider revocation only for cases of proven fraud, coercion, or duress. Some allow a birthparent to withdraw consent without cause within a specified period of time (usually a few days).

After the baby is home, you will be very busy adjusting to parenthood and helping your baby adjust to you. Your social worker will schedule several post-placement visits according to the laws of your state and the agency's policies. These visits are usually short and include the social worker's observing that the child is well cared for and healthy. The social worker then writes a post-placement report outlining the progress and status of the child. This supervisory period usually lasts the first few months.

While you are waiting for the adoption to be finalized, and if you do not have a Social Security number for your child, you can apply to the Internal Revenue Service for an Adoption Taxpayer Identification Number. This program was started by the IRS in 1998, and it assigns a temporary number to your child while you are waiting for his adoption to be finalized. You can use the ATIN on your tax forms in order to claim the child as a dependent and take advantage of any child tax credits to which you are entitled.

You should apply for an ATIN only if you meet all of the following qualifications:

- The adoption is a domestic adoption.
- The child is legally placed in your home for adoption by an authorized adoption agency or agent.
- The adoption is not yet final, and you are unable to obtain the child's existing Social Security number or you are unable to apply for a new SSN for the child pending the finalization of the adoption.
- You qualify to claim the child as a dependent.[14]

(See chapter 9 for more information on your first days home with your adopted child.)

HEADING TO COURT—YOU DID IT!

The final step in a domestic adoption is to legalize it. Receiving the adoption decree signed by a judge declares that this child is now your child forever. The birth certificate is reissued with your names on it, and the baby now has the same rights as any birthchildren you might have. Some people are nervous at the thought of having to go to a courthouse and face a judge, but this is a joyous occasion that should not be feared. It is the end of your long journey to become a forever family.

If you did not use an attorney for your adoption, you will need one for this last step. The attorney prepares the necessary motions and requests of the court to finalize your adoption, and the judge asks you to promise that you will care for this child and give him the same rights as a biological child. When you answer yes, he can sign the adoption decree.

Once the adoption ceremony at the courthouse is complete, many families choose to have a party with friends and family to celebrate. Some choose to send out adoption announcements at this point to let people know the adoption is official.

Find a way to mark this special day in your child's life in his or her baby book, and don't forget to stop and give thanks to the Lord for this miracle he brought into your lives. Celebrate not only this precious child but also the God who gave him to you.

WORDS OF WISDOM
Sing and make music in your heart to the Lord, always giving thanks to God the Father for everything, in the name of our Lord Jesus Christ.
—Ephesians 5:19-20 (NIV)

Waiting Children in the United States

The other available children who can be adopted domestically are the waiting children in foster care. There are more than a half million children currently in state care, and about 120,000 of them are already eligible to be adopted. This means that the rights of their parents to raise them have been legally terminated, and they are waiting for a family.

CHILDREN MOST LIKELY TO BE AVAILABLE

Children in foster care have usually experienced some trauma in their lives. Their parents might have been neglectful or abusive, addicted to drugs or alcohol, or maintained a lifestyle in which the children could not thrive. Foster-care children are typically four years old or older, although some infants and toddlers do become available, and many are minorities. There are typically more boys available than girls. Some have physical disabilities, mental disabilities, or emotional disabilities. Some are part of a sibling group. They are children who might be more of a challenge to raise, but they are also children who desperately need families to call their own.

Children who grow up never knowing the love of a permanent, healthy family will not have a model of working relationships to follow in adulthood. They will not know what it is like to belong to a family, to maintain a marriage, or to have someone care about their achievements, successes, and failures. Christians who consider adoption from foster care can change that for their child.

"Our perspective on the adoption process is different, because in other kinds of adoptions, agencies are looking for a *child* to place in a specific family. In our case, we are looking for a *family* in which to place a specific child," says Sharen Ford, manager of permanency services for the Colorado Department of Human Services, Child Welfare Services. "We have to consider all eligible people who apply. So would I like to see the church step up to the plate more? Absolutely."

I DIDN'T KNOW THAT!

Each year, approximately 20,000 children in foster care will age out of the system without ever being placed with a permanent family.
—Child Welfare League of America, 2005

WHY HAVEN'T THEY BEEN ADOPTED?

There are a variety of reasons why waiting children have not already been adopted: their parental rights might have just been terminated, and now they are available for adoption; they have been rejected because of their race, physical disabilities, or behavioral issues; they are part of a sibling group and want to be adopted together; or, they might have just slipped through the bureaucratic cracks. The main reason why so many children remain in foster care without ever being eligible to be adopted is that their parental rights are not legally terminated. If parents do not voluntarily terminate the rights to their children placed in foster care, the state must take action to involuntarily terminate parental rights. This is not a quick or easy process. Termination can take years, or it might never occur.

If adopting a child with these additional challenges scares you, consider this: How many challenges did you have when God adopted you into his forever family? Did he expect you to be perfect, or did he accept you just as you were? Waiting children in the foster-care system are keenly aware of what it feels like to be "not good enough" to be wanted. What they need are families who will look past their difficulties and bring out their potential. There are many tremendous testimonies of families who have adopted children from foster care and discovered the blessings as they saw their adopted children fight to overcome special challenges and blossom as children of God.

ADOPTING FROM FOSTER CARE: THE PROCESS

If you feel called to give a waiting child a forever family, the first step is to contact your state's department of human services or child and family services department. You can find the telephone number in the government pages of the phone book. Ask for the adoption specialist, and the specialist should be able to direct you to the licensed adoption agencies that are contracted to handle public adoptions in your state. (See appendix C, Public Adoption Agencies by State.)

You can also obtain information about waiting children in your state via the Internet. Many states have photo listings of waiting children on their Web sites, as well as contact information and criteria for the approval of adoptive parents. When you are looking for an adoption agency to adopt publicly, your choices might be more limited. However, the North American Council on Adoptable Children recommends that you ask any agency you consider the following questions:

- What are the criteria for adopting from the agency?
- What are the ages, backgrounds, and other factors of the children the agency generally places?
- From where does the agency receive the children, and how many of the children are legally free for adoption?
- What is the average wait time for a child? How much time does it take between the application and the placement?
- What are the agency's policies regarding forms, classes, fees, and visits?
- How much does a completed adoption cost, and will the agency help find sources of financial aid, including adoption subsidies?
- What are the home study requirements?
- Have any of the agency's adoptions fallen through in the past five years? What does the agency do to make sure that adoptions don't disintegrate after placement?
- What is the agency's policy toward applicants who do not accept the first child offered to them?
- What services—such as parenting classes, support-group activities, access to therapy and counseling, and respite care—will the agency provide before and after a child is placed in your home?
- Can references be provided from parents who recently adopted through the agency? (Your state's adoption specialist may also know if complaints have been filed against the agency.)[15]

BENEFITS AND RISKS OF ADOPTING A FOSTER CHILD

Once you have chosen an agency and identified a child, the agency and the child's assigned caseworker should guide you through the process of adoption. Because you are working with a governmental system, you can expect that the process may seem slow at times. You will need to keep on top of your own case and work closely with your agency worker and the child's caseworker to keep it moving. You will need to have a successful home study, which may be done privately or may be paid for by your state. The home study officially says you are qualified to offer a healthy home to an adopted child.

Each state has its own laws regarding the children in its care, and you will need to find out exactly what you are required to do to complete an adoption and bring your child home permanently. Some states might require you to take foster parenting classes to become a licensed foster home in order to have your child for overnight visits before his or her permanent placement. Some states require that specific parenting classes be attended. Even if parenting classes are not required, take full advantage of them if they are offered. If you are adopting a child from foster care, your child comes with a history and issues. Classes help prospective parents consider situations that might arise from their child's unique special needs and past experiences. Classes also help parents handle interactions with new siblings, classmates, teachers, doctors, and others. Issues related to disability, culture, early abuse, and a child's birth family should all be discussed before a child is placed in an adoptive home.

When you are adopting from foster care, you will receive your child's file. It should contain the background information on your child, his identifying information, the reasons why he was removed from his biological family, the placements he has had since being removed, and all medical, psychological, school, and behavioral reports that have been done while he has been in state care. This information can be valuable in determining the level of special care your child will need.

There are some children who can be placed in your care who are not legally eligible to be adopted yet, but state termination of parental rights is planned. If you agree to adopt and accept placement of a child whose birthparents' rights have not been voluntarily surrendered or have not yet been involuntarily terminated, this is called a legal-risk placement. It means you know and accept that there is a chance the child will be returned to his birthparents. Until birthparents' rights are terminated, the child cannot legally become a member of your family and must instead stay in your home as a foster child. It also means that you might be required to facilitate or participate in visitation of your foster child with his birthparents. This can be emotionally challenging if the birthparents have been neglectful or abusive. As licensed foster parents, you will receive a monthly foster-parent stipend from your state before adoption is finalized.

Whatever route you choose to adopt a child from foster care, you will need to work closely with your agency and caseworker to make sure you are eligible to receive the full range of services and subsidies your child might need. These can include medical assistance, transportation, therapies, counseling, and monthly financial assistance. Because each state offers different things, you will need to work with knowledgeable people for assistance in these areas. You may want to consult with an adoption attorney, other families who have adopted through the foster-care system, or the local adoption specialist to make sure that your child receives the services your state can provide.

As you prepare for the adoption of your child from foster care, you should gather all the information and personal effects you can find that belong to your child. If you can, get a copy of the original birth certificate and keep it, as once the adoption is finalized the record may become sealed by the court. With the original birth certificate, adoptees have a head start later in life if they want to search for their birth families. Also, it can help to have it for passport applications. Prepare to get a new Social Security card and birth certificate that has your child's new name and legal status as your child. You should also try hard to get any personal items, photographs, school papers, and anything else that ties your child to his family history. Ask for the "Life Book" of your child if your state has one. It contains the history of your child and will be important for them. Even when a child's past is full of pain, the personal items are still good to have.

Although it can vary from state to state, children who are placed for adoption through public agencies may move in with an adoptive family as soon as the parents complete required preplacement visits and are approved to adopt. The adoptive parents will then have temporary legal custody while the agency monitors the adjustment of the child. After the adjustment period and postplacement visits are completed, typically in six months to a year, the agency will recommend to the court that the adoption be finalized. However, before the adoption is finalized, make sure you know the legal restrictions in your state. Foster-care programs come with strict rules as to whether children can be taken out of state or out of the country, who can baby-sit them, and other limitations.

The adoption hearing process for a waiting child is the same as for a newborn adoption. An adoption petition is filed with the court by an attorney, and the adoptive parents promise to care for the child always. Before the hearing, contact your caseworker to make sure that all the necessary paperwork, such as your financial statement and the child's parental rights termination papers, has been filed properly. Missing paperwork could result in a delay of the final hearing. Adoption hearings often take place in the judge's chambers, and the 1994 Uniform Adoption Act requires the informed consent of anyone between the ages of twelve and eighteen to be adopted, unless the court waives the consent requirement by finding that the adoption is in the child's best interests.

"With an older child, you are not only choosing this child, but the child is also choosing you," Sharen Ford says. "It is wonderful, because both parties are agreeing that they can bring something valuable to the other."

When the hearing is finished and the adoption decree is signed, the child is legally a member of the family.

RED LIGHT, STOP!

Questions to consider at this point in your adoption journey:

____ Do you understand what you will need to successfully complete a home study?

____ How will you prepare for the long wait you could experience if you choose to adopt a newborn domestically?

____ Are you willing to accept any child, or do you want to wait for a specific background and gender?

____ Have you done your homework in searching for the right agency for you?

____ Are you ready to be proactive in the search for a birthmother?

____ Are you educated about the rights of birthmothers and birthfathers?

____ Are you prepared for your adoptive family to have a lot of the same issues as a stepfamily, especially if you have an open adoption arrangement?

____ Have you considered adopting a waiting child from foster care? Could your family be the right home for a child already in the system?

____ Do you understand the process of working with a public agency rather than adopting privately?

____ Are you ready to work hard to get your waiting child the services and subsidies he needs and is entitled to?

GREEN LIGHT, GO!

Action points for your adoption journey:

____ Decide whether you want to adopt a newborn domestically or pursue the public adoption of a waiting child in foster care.

____ Choose a private agency, an adoption attorney, or a public agency to work with.

____ Begin to gather the necessary documentation for your home study, and choose a social worker to conduct it or line up the home study with your public agency.

____ Ask your private agency or attorney how you can help locate a birthmother. Decide whether you think it would be more beneficial to utilize professional services or facilitators to help you find one.

____ Learn about the rights of birthmothers and birthfathers in your state. Find out about waiting periods for consent, state registries for putative fathers, and the revocation period after placement.

____ Take parenting classes, especially if you will be bringing home a child from foster care. Take into account that every adoptive family is connected to another family (the child's biological family) and will face some of the same issues stepfamilies face. Ask stepfamilies and other adoptive families about their interactions with branches of their extended family trees.

____ Prepare your hearts for the long wait you may have before a child is placed with you or a birthmother chooses you. On the flip side, be ready for anything, as some families are chosen right away or a waiting child is placed with them as soon as they qualify.

____ Prepare a plan to receive your child, either a birth plan with your agency and the birthmother or a transfer plan for a child from state care. If you are adopting a waiting child, make your preplacement visits fun but real.

____ Pray for your child, his birth family, his caseworkers, and any others involved in his care. Ask God to help you love them and see them as the unique people he loves, rather than as those who are just helping you get a child. If your child has been abused by his biological family, ask God to help you forgive them.

____ Make sure you stay on top of the paperwork you will need in all stages of the adoption, from home study documents to adoption hearing documents to obtaining a birth certificate.

♥ My Adoption Miracle
God Started Our Family Through Adoption
by Brad and Caprice Payne

My husband, Brad, and I tried to have a baby for seven years after we were married, but it just didn't happen for us. At first, we didn't worry about it and just thought it would happen eventually. After four years, we began to seek medical help. We tried fertility treatments and visited specialists, but we did not get pregnant. No one knew exactly why. Our specialist told us he fully expected to see us get pregnant someday, but after years it just had not happened. Because we are Christians, I was reluctant to try in vitro fertilization because I did not want to create embryos that either would not be used or would be destroyed. When we discovered that we could choose the exact number of eggs to be fertilized and would not have to create embryos that would eventually be destroyed, we did an in vitro attempt. It did not work.

At the beginning of our marriage, we thought we might adopt a child someday—but now it was becoming apparent that adoption was going to be God's way for us to create our family.

My husband agreed, and we chose a Christian adoption agency. We wanted an agency that really focused on the needs of the birthmoms during their pregnancy and after. We decided not to specify the gender of the child we wanted, and it didn't matter to us if he or she had a higher risk of special needs because of a birthmother's background. We knew we wouldn't be able to ask for a boy or a girl if we were pregnant—and we figured that the more specifics we chose, the longer our wait would be. We decided to trust God to send us the right child for our family.

We made scrapbooks and completed our home study. Then we waited. After a meeting with our first birthmother did not result in a match, we were disappointed, but we still trusted God that he had the right child for us. We had no idea what was in store for us next.

In a conversation with a friend from church, she mentioned that a family she knew had a fourteen-year-old daughter who was pregnant. She knew we wanted to adopt and said how funny it would be if we ended up adopting this family's baby. However, the family was planning to keep the baby, and our conversation ended. A couple of weeks later, we got a call that the teenager now wanted to place her baby for adoption, and she wanted to talk to us. Our friend connected us by phone, and we had several conversations about adopting this child. When things seemed to be getting serious, we met in the local IHOP and had a great getting-to-know-you meeting. Then, we got our respective agencies involved. Our birthmother was already working through another agency she was comfortable with, and, although it was unusual, our agency agreed to work with them to complete our adoption.

I didn't know what to expect when it came to open adoption and writing out a visitation agreement. Brad and I thought it was important for the birthmother and for the baby to maintain contact, but I was afraid, too, because I couldn't imagine what it would be like. When our son Darrin was born and we brought him home, I found out that I needn't have worried. God had everything under control, and the visits we had with Darrin's mother after his birth were an important part of her healing process and Darrin's life story. We would now be able to tell him all about her and help him feel connected to his roots.

Three years after Darrin came home, we decided to try to adopt again. We completed the paperwork with our agency, and they posted our profile online. We expected a wait of at least a year, as we knew that many birthmoms want to place their babies with couples who have no children. However, just a few weeks later we got a call that our profile had been chosen by another birthmother. This time, the baby had already been born, and in just a few short weeks, Abigail came home with us. God had given us our forever family, and we truly felt complete. However, God wasn't finished with us yet.

When Abbi was two, I began feeling sick and overly exhausted and could not determine what was wrong. I went to the doctor for a series of tests to pinpoint the problem. We then went away to visit family, and when I called home to check the answering machine, there were a couple of messages from the doctor's office. Fearing something was wrong, I called and asked for my test results. To my complete and utter surprise, they told me I was three months pregnant!

When Brad and I adopted our children, in each case we told our families we were going to adopt and showed them the pictures of our new child. This time, we made a videotape to tell them we were going to add to our family *again and we wanted to introduce them to the birthmother. They were used to that, because that's the way children came into our family. Then I walked onto the screen and said, "Surprise! I am the new birthmother!"*

God has shown us so much through our adoptions, and we have now learned through having a biological child that we love them all for who they are, not how God brought them to us. He has made us a forever family.

Chapter Four

Adopting Internationally: Is It for You?

If you think you want to adopt internationally, congratulations! There are millions of children throughout the world in need of a forever family. Not all countries are open to international adoptions, and the United States does not permit adoptions from all countries, but many countries are revising and updating their adoption policies to make intercountry adoptions possible.

So where exactly are the kids? They're on islands such as the Philippines and Haiti, in big countries like Russia and China, and in small countries like Jamaica and Belarus. Most are in desperately poor countries like Ethiopia and Vietnam. Adoptable infants and children are available in Europe (although mostly Eastern Europe), Asia, North America, Central America, South America, Australia (although it is extremely rare for an American to be able to adopt from Australia), and Africa.

INTERNATIONAL ADOPTION NUMBERS ARE GROWING

Throughout the 1990s, the number of immigration visas issued for foreign children being adopted by American citizens gradually increased, with the totals falling between ten thousand and seventeen thousand per year. Since 2000, the number of visas issued per year has risen from approximately eighteen thousand to more than twenty-two thousand (see table that follows). While that barely scratches the surface of the number of orphans around the world in need of forever families, it does show that the number of adoptions is increasing. Those who work with the least fortunate children hope the numbers will rise even more dramatically as more governments allow international adoptions and as more Americans and others make decisions to adopt internationally. Those who work in orphan-care ministry pray that it will be Christians who inflate adoption numbers dramatically, as more heed the call to care and raise a generation for God.

HAGUE CONVENTION ON INTERCOUNTRY ADOPTION

To protect children, birthparents, and adoptive parents involved in inter-country adoptions and to prevent child trafficking (black market sales of children), the Hague Convention on Intercountry Adoption was approved by sixty-six nations on May 29, 1993, in The Hague. By 2006, sixty-eight countries had joined the convention. The convention covers adoptions between countries that become parties to it and sets certain internationally agreed-upon minimum norms and procedures.

The United States signed the convention on March 31, 1994, and it is expected to affect international adoptions by citizens of the United States by 2007. The U.S. State Department will be the regulating agency of the Hague Convention in the United States, and many adoption workers hope the ratification will open the doors for more intercountry adoptions.

I DIDN'T KNOW THAT!

The Chinese believe that some people have an invisible *red thread* connection, which means that those people—if connected by the red thread—will meet during their lifetime. Many families adopting from China refer to the red thread connection that brought them together.

WHERE THE CHILDREN ARE FROM

The U.S. Department of State, which oversees foreign travel and inter-country adoptions, reported that fifty or more visas were issued in 2005 for children in the following native countries (from the greatest number of visas to the least): China, Russia, Guatemala, South Korea, Ukraine, Kazakhstan, India, Colombia, Philippines, Haiti, Liberia, Ethiopia, Poland, Thailand, Brazil, Nigeria, Jamaica, Nepal, Moldova, and Mexico.

These numbers and countries have fluctuated a little over the past several years, with China holding the top spot since 2000, a few countries closing their doors to foreign adoptions or adoptions by Americans, and a few others opening their doors to foreign adoptions.

In international adoptions, the kinds of children who need forever families vary as greatly as the countries from which they come. In many countries, infants are available, although newborns are usually not. Regardless of the country, before infants are placed for international adoption, procedures must be followed to verify that the child has been willingly relinquished by his or her birthparents and that no relatives want to step forward and adopt the child. This process, along with the paperwork that must be collected and approved before an adoption can take place, usually takes at least a couple of months.

TABLE 1-1 IMMIGRANT VISAS ISSUED TO ORPHANS COMING TO THE U.S.

Country	2005	2004	2003	2002	2001	2000	1999	1998
China (Mainland)	7,906	7,044	6,859	5,053	4,681	5,053	4,101	4,206
Russia	4,639	5,865	5,209	4,939	4,279	4,269	4,348	4,491
Guatemala	3,783	3,264	2,328	2,219	1,609	1,518	1,002	911
South Korea	1,630	1,716	1,790	1,779	1,870	1,794	2,008	1,829
Ukraine	821	723	702	1,106	1,246	659	323	180
Kazakhstan	755	826	825	819	672	399	113	-
Vietnam	-	-	382	766	737	724	709	603
India	323	406	472	466	543	503	500	478
Romania	-	57	200	168	782	1,122	895	406
Colombia	291	287	272	334	407	246	231	351
Bulgaria	-	110	198	260	297	214	221	151
Cambodia	-	-	124	254	266	402	248	249
Philippines	271	196	214	221	219	173	195	200
Haiti	231	356	250	187	192	131	96	121
Liberia	182	86	-	-	51	25	14	7
Belarus	-	202	191	169	129	46	-	-
Ethiopia	441	289	135	105	158	95	103	96
Poland	73	102	97	101	86	83	97	77
Thailand	73	69	72	67	74	88	77	84
Brazil	66	69	30	26	32	-	-	103
Nigeria	65	71	47	45	33	4	0	-
Jamaica	63	51	56	39	51	39	-	-
Nepal	62	73	42	12	5	13	-	-
Moldova	54	-	12	7	46	79	63	-
Peru	-	-	-	65	-	-	-	-
Mexico	98	89	61	61	73	106	137	168
Totals	22,728	22,884	21,616	20,099	19,237	17,718	16,363	15,774

(-indicates that numbers were not obtainable for that year)

U.S. Department of State. Top countries since 1998 from which international children were adopted.[16]

In China, the country that currently participates in the greatest number of annual intercountry adoptions, the babies are at least six months old but usually around a year when they are united with their adoptive families. Toddlers and older children are also available in China. In some South American countries, such as Guatemala and Colombia, infants can be adopted who are just a couple of months old, and there are also some infants under six months old available in Russia. However, the majority of babies placed around the world are at least six months old at the time of their adoption.

I DIDN'T KNOW THAT!

There are more than four million orphans and homeless children in Russia. Officially, there are 700,000 orphans living in 2,000 state-run orphanages. Statistics show that only one out of ten Russian orphans become functional members of society. The others are lost to drugs, crime, and suicide.
—Ascent Russian Orphan Aid Foundation, 2005

THE CHILDREN WHO NEED YOU

As a whole, children who need forever families possess any number of skin tones, hair and eye colors, shapes, and sizes. They also have a wide variety of special needs. According to the Web site Orphan Doctor, www.orphan-doctor.com, and other medical sources, children who come from foreign countries where there is extreme poverty had mothers who often received no prenatal care, and the children have most likely not received proper nutrition. They are often malnourished (this can range from mild to severe), small for their age, and underweight. In some countries, there is a high percentage of orphans born with fetal alcohol syndrome, and some are born to mothers with drug addictions. Most children adopted from foreign poverty-stricken countries—even the ones whose paperwork states they are healthy or non-special-needs—might show some signs of developmental delays, many of which can be overcome.

International adoptive parents Jean Nelson-Erichsen and Heino Erichsen, who have worked with international adoption for the past three decades and are the authors of *How to Adopt Internationally*, share the following observations about a parent's first meeting with his or her new international child:

> Many people feel rather let down when they first see the child they were assigned. Orphanage children often look too small for their ages, may have a runny nose or bad skin rash or both. On top of that, they are usually dressed in worn out, ill-fitting orphanage clothes, and often have shaved heads as a treatment for insects or lice. Babies may have bald spots on heads that are flattened in the back from too much time lying down. . . . After all the work and all the waiting, the child does not match the dream child the parents have been carrying around in their heads for so long.[17]

The Erichsens say that for parents who don't let their expectations run too high and for those who can set aside their disappointment over the lack of "love at first sight," the feelings of emotional attachment to their adopted child come quickly and powerfully. Soon, parents are able to see the unique beauty of the child God has placed in their family, not his or her flaws. Young children can often catch up quickly once they are placed in an environment where they are given nutritious foods and loving care, progressing at an average rate of two months' "catch-up" per month. (Also see chapter 11.)

In an article by Dr. Dana Johnson, director of the International Adoption Clinic at the University of Minnesota, Johnson states that children from foreign orphanages will generally make good progress when placed in a home, but that eradication of developmental delays can take years:

> Most children make tremendous gains in growth and development during the first years with their adoptive families. Unless a child is truly neurologically impaired, gross and fine motor skills as well as strength respond well to improved nutrition and a stimulating environment. However, many children, especially those who spent considerable time within institutional care settings, continue to show delays in language and social skills, behavioral problems, and abnormalities in attachment behavior even after several years in their adoptive home. In most situations, areas of delay respond to appropriate treatment, but resolution of the problem may take time and expert guidance. In some situations, therapy will improve but cannot correct the fundamental problem; e.g., fetal alcohol exposure. In these situations, the challenges will be life-long.[18]

WORDS OF WISDOM
In you the fatherless find compassion.
—Hosea 14:3 (NIV)

RISKS AND BENEFITS

There are risks and benefits that come with choosing to adopt internationally. The risks include the fact that you do not know what your child experienced while he was institutionalized. *Institutionalization* is the placement of children in hospitals, orphanages, and institutions, which, if done during early critical developmental periods and for lengthy periods of time, is often associated with developmental delays due to environmental deprivation, poor staff-to-child ratios, or lack of early stimulation. It simply means that kids who do not have the love and nurture of parents who can provide for their needs do not fare as well as those who do.

There is also the risk, especially in a parent-initiated, facilitated, or independent adoption, that a *wrongful adoption* could occur. A *wrongful adoption* occurs when an adoption arranger fails to disclose important information about a child or his background to the adoptive parents. This can include the fact that the child is seriously ill or even that the child is not really an orphan and should not have been eligible for adoption. Wrongful adoptions can be disrupted or overturned by governmental authorities in some cases, or parents might have to deal with the unexpected heartache and medical bills connected with a serious illness.

Still, keep in mind that these extreme circumstances are rare, and that most foreign adoptions are completed successfully. Prospective adopters should become fully informed of all the adoption options and risks, but should not let fear drive them away from a call to adopt. God loves your future child more than you do, and he has plans "to prosper you and not to harm you," and to give you "hope and a future" (Jeremiah 29:11 NIV).

I DIDN'T KNOW THAT!
Nearly 10,000 children are abandoned annually at Romanian hospitals.
—UNICEF

When you choose to adopt internationally, you are often given limited information about your child's background and medical history, either because of language barriers, because adoption workers in some countries might not fully disclose the information they have for fear you will not adopt the child, or because the child was abandoned and the background is not known. Because most international adoptions are closed, your child might never be able to track down his or her biological roots, and you may never know your child's *genetic predispositions* (i.e., traits, attributes, or the likelihood of developing certain diseases the child may have inherited from his or her birthparents).

Another risk of international adoption is that you are at the mercy of foreign governments whose policies on intercountry adoption could change at any time. While many foreign adoption programs have been in place for years and have remained fairly stable, there is always a risk that governments may change the procedures or close their doors to foreign adoptions, even while you are in the middle of an adoption.

For example: This happened to prospective adoptive parents who in 2002 were in the process of adopting from Cambodia. The Cambodian Foreign Ministry verbally notified the U.S. State Department that it would suspend the issuance of adoption documentation to American families in acknowledgment of trafficking concerns and other problems in the adoption process in Cambodia. All adoptions ceased.

Then there are countries with whom the U.S. government does not allow international adoptions—often because the risk of child trafficking is high in those nations, and a system for governing the adoption process is not in place.

The U.S. State Department makes it clear that international adoption is essentially a private legal matter between a private individual (or couple) who wishes to adopt, and a foreign court, which operates under that country's laws and regulations. U.S. authorities cannot intervene on behalf of prospective parents with the courts in the country where the adoption takes place.[19]

If you have a problem with an international adoption, the State Department *can* make inquiries of the U.S. consular section abroad regarding the status of a specific adoption case and clarify documentation or other requirements. And it can ensure that U.S. citizens are not discriminated against by foreign authorities or courts in accordance with local laws on adoptions. The State Department *cannot*

- become directly involved in the adoption process in another country,
- act as an attorney or represent adoptive parents in court,
- order that an adoption take place, or
- require that a visa be issued.

The benefits of international adoption are that families are blessed with an experience like no other, according to the thousands of forever families created through international adoption. Many admit that God took them out of their comfort zones through the international adoption experience, and he stretched them in ways that were at times uncomfortable, but the rewards of loving their children are beyond compare. International adoption affords Christians the opportunity to examine their racial prejudices and be a testimony to others, to gain a new perspective on the depth of God's love "for the least of these" and for them, and to create a deeper walk of faith with him as he walks beside them through the process.

The vice president of Focus on the Family broadcasting, John Fuller, his wife, Dena, and their five children adopted a baby boy with special needs from Russia in 2004. While Zane has brought joy to his new family, he has also brought unexpected difficulties and trials. While the challenges have not been easy, they have birthed in John a zeal for orphan care that he never would have imagined.

"When you go into these waters, you have to be prepared for a struggle," John shares. "But through the process of adoption I've seen God's heart for the fatherless and the orphan, and it's become a passion." (See the Fullers' "My Adoption Miracle" story in chapter 5.)

I DIDN'T KNOW THAT!

The Department of State provides extensive information about the adoption processes in various countries and the U.S. legal requirements to bring a child adopted abroad to the United States. (See appendix D, Country-Specific Adoption Information.) A Web site is offered, www.travel.state.gov, and in addition the Office of Children's Issues in the Bureau of Consular Affairs provides brochures describing the adoption process in numerous countries. The State Department also provides recorded information on international adoption for several countries on a twenty-four-hour basis (call toll-free 1–888–407–4747).

Agency Adoption Abroad

The most recommended option for prospective parents is to choose an adoption agency in the United States that is licensed or approved to work with and facilitate adoptions in specific countries. Names of U.S. adoption agencies can be found under each country on the U.S. Department of State Web site, or on the many adoption information Web sites. Most agencies have their own sites, as well as toll-free phone numbers through which you can obtain information on their history, fees, adoption time frame, numbers of children placed, and their accreditations. Appendix B of this book contains a list of selected nonprofit adoption agencies who profess to operate under biblically based Christian principles. This does not mean that any agency will be perfect or will be exempt from unscrupulous practices; however, these agencies have, in most cases, taken extra steps to state their beliefs and show their accountability, such as meeting accreditation standards and/or openly posting their annual reports and tax reports.

FINDING AN AGENCY

The best way to choose the right agency for you is to choose which country or countries you are most interested in, then make a list of the agencies that place children from those countries.

INVESTIGATING THE AGENCY

Thoroughly investigate any agency you consider using, especially an international agency. Much of your research can be done through e-mail, which will also provide you a written record of the agencies you've researched. Also, when corresponding or talking to groups that work with complaints against adoption agencies, always ask: is there another resource through which I should check out this agency?

Here are some ways to investigate an agency:

- Read everything on the agency's Web site.
- Contact the National Better Business Bureau, the state social services department, the Joint Council on International Children's Services, the NAIC, and other groups that work with complaints lodged against an international adoption agency.
- Check out similar sources within the foreign country—even if it means having a translator help you write and interpret correspondence.
- Search the Internet for anything concerning the agency.
- Locate a library with a searchable database resource of media, including newspapers, magazines, and radio and television shows, and search for any information concerning the agency.

If after all your research, the agency is still on your list—attend a seminar held by the agency, if possible. Take note of whether former adopters through that agency attend the presentations—if they don't, request a list of former adopters you may contact. Ask other adoptive families what they know about that agency's reputation and what their experience was like.

Finally, it's time to interview the agency. The agency representatives should be forthcoming—not defensive—in answering your questions, and you should take lots of thorough, legible notes or ask if you can record the session.

Following are some questions to ask:

- Which countries do they work with? Do they have their own offices in that country, or do they work with other programs?
- How many children did they place in the last year, and from which countries? What is the average wait time?
- Do they place mostly infants or older children?
- How long has the agency been in business?
- Who started the agency and why?
- Are the staff workers adoptive parents themselves?
- How many people are on staff to handle the adoption applicants?
- Is the agency nonprofit, and does it have a board of directors?
- Can you see the agency's latest annual report? Does it have a business director or accountant who handles its finances?
- Can you see a copy of the agency contract adoptive families are asked to sign?

- How often does the agency send completed dossiers to the countries?
- How does the agency define *special needs*?
- What does the agency do if a newly adopted child turns out to have unexpected problems? How does the agency work with the family in this circumstance?
- Does the agency have its own translators for dossiers, and are the dossiers translated before being sent to the country or after they arrive?
- Does the agency include dossier preparation services or consultation, or does this cost extra?
- How long does the process typically take from the signing of the application to the placement of the child?
- What are the fees for the country you are interested in, and what do the fees include?
- What portions of the fees are nonrefundable if you change your mind? If your home study is not successful? If the country closes its doors to international adoption and you do not want to choose another country? If you get pregnant and cannot complete or choose not to complete an adoption?
- Will the agency provide you with names of families they have worked with as references for the agency?
- How does the agency obtain background information on the children it is placing?
- Is there additional information (brochures, pamphlets, videos—anything not available on the Web site) that can be sent to you?
- How does this agency help benefit orphans outside of adoptions? Are any outreach programs or other philanthropic projects sponsored by a portion of their fees?

WHAT DOES THE PROCESS LOOK LIKE?

What the process looks like for international adoption varies widely by country, but every intercountry adoption requires the home study (see chapter 3), a dossier of documents that are certified and authenticated or apostilled, adoption dossier processing in the foreign country (usually after it has been translated), a wait time, and travel (usually for the parents, but sometimes for the child). While some detailed country information for the most available countries will be provided in this chapter, more complete information for every country can be found in appendix D, Country-Specific Adoption Information, which was compiled from public information found on the U.S. Department of State Web site.

How Long Does It Take?

When you are considering adoption, two of the biggest questions are, "How much does it cost?" and "How long is it going to take?" Let's look at the time frame.

The paperwork or dossier-gathering phase can take as little time as two months to as long as six months or a year, depending on how aggressively you pursue the documents (or if you pay a documentation service to complete the forms for you); how quickly your state departments, USCIS office, and foreign consulates turn paperwork around; and how long it takes your social worker to complete your home study.

Once the dossier is complete, the time frame is up to the foreign country from which you are adopting. For Korea, the referral of a child is received somewhere between five and eight months after the dossier is sent. For some South American countries, a match may be made in a couple of months. If you choose a special-needs child from an international waiting-child list, your paperwork can begin being processed immediately, and your wait time will generally be shortened by a few months. The consensus among adoption workers is that most non-special-needs international adoptions, including the home study process, take between nine and eighteen months from home study to finalization.

WORDS OF WISDOM
I will not leave you as orphans; I will come to you.
—John 14:18 (NIV)

To Travel or Not to Travel

Another factor to consider in international adoption is whether or not you want to travel to the foreign country where the child is located. Most countries require that one parent travel to the country at least once, but some require more trips and sometimes both parents. For example: Russia and Ukraine require one parent to make two trips. South Korea does not require parents to travel. Instead, parents can choose whether to travel or to have an escort deliver the child, and the child is met at the airport.

If you do not want to travel to a foreign country, the costs are usually lower for one escort to deliver a child than it is for two to travel and stay in-country. The drawbacks with the escort service are that adoptive parents are handed a child sight-unseen, without the opportunity to ask questions of the orphanage workers or foster family, or to handle a problem if it is obvious that there is one. Also, the trip abroad helps adoptive families understand their transracial child's culture, background, and native roots. This can be valuable information to your child.

Independent Adoption Abroad

If you do not want to use an adoption agency, there are ways to locate orphans in other countries and try to adopt them. These are called parent-initiated adoptions. However, most adoption experts and the U.S. Department of State strongly recommend using an agency in order to best safeguard yourselves, the child, and your money.

The U.S. Department of State issues the following warning to prospective adoptive parents:

International adoptions have become a lucrative business because of the huge demand for adoptable children. The combination of people motivated by personal gain and parents desperate to adopt a child under any circumstances, creates the potential for fraudulent adoptions. Take care to avoid these adoption scams.

You can avoid the heartache of losing a potentially adoptable child by using only reputable agencies, attorneys, and facilitators. If the answers to your questions appear to be contradictory, vague, or unrealistic, be wary. The consular section in the U.S. Embassy or Consulate in the country of planned adoption can provide accurate information concerning local legal practices. If you have problems with agencies or intermediaries in the United States, you should report these concerns immediately to the appropriate state authorities, i.e., your state social services office, District Attorney, Better Business Bureau, or state Attorney General's office. The BCIS should be notified of these concerns as well.

The lack of state regulatory requirements for international adoption agencies in some states has permitted some individuals, inexperienced in the area of foreign adoptions, to set up businesses. Some prospective adoptive parents are charged exorbitant fees. Two common abuses are 1) knowingly offering a supposedly healthy child for adoption who is later found to be seriously ill, and 2) obtaining prepayment for adoption of a nonexistent or ineligible child. In some countries, it is advisable to have the child examined by a physician before completing adoption procedures. This examination is separate from the routine medical examination required after completion of the adoption for visa purposes. Some states have moved to revoke licenses or prosecute the individuals connected with these fraudulent activities after receiving complaints. However, it should be noted that most adoption practitioners in the United States are legitimate professionals with experience in domestic and international adoptions.

In the international area, the Department of State consistently takes a strong stand against fraudulent adoption procedures. This policy flows from our general obligation to respect host country laws, to discourage any illegal activities and to avoid the possibility that a country may prohibit international adoptions entirely. The Department of State has unfailingly expressed its support for measures taken by foreign states to reduce adoption abuses.

FINDING FOREIGN ADOPTION ARRANGERS

There are reputable adoption arrangers or adoption facilitators in some countries where there are no recognized adoption agencies. An adoption facilitator or arranger works to locate an orphan in a foreign country and help prospective adopters arrange the adoption with the proper authorities. This can be very risky business if the adoptive parents do not personally know the facilitator and have never visited the country.

Thoroughly investigate any independent party, even foreign attorneys, who are willing to arrange an adoption. Be sure to ask for references, and ask these arrangers the same questions you would ask an agency or adoption attorney in the United States. Check out their backgrounds and motivation for helping. Are the fees exorbitant? Do they make promises they are unlikely to be able to keep? Are you educated enough about the adoption laws in the country you are considering to be sure that adoption is even legal and possible, and that the United States will even grant an entry visa if the adoption is complete in the foreign country?

If you choose to try to go the independent route, you must still obtain a home study and prepare the proper dossier documents. After that, you are on your own to locate a child by visiting the country yourselves, letting others know that you are looking, or contacting foreign orphanages, attorneys, and arrangers. If your agent in the foreign country says he has found a child you can adopt, again you are on your own to make the arrangements, including travel, what monies to bring, guides and translators needed, flights and accommodations to arrange, and the adoption procedure to follow once you get there. Be sure you know how long you will need to stay in the country and what offices to visit to file paperwork and complete the adoption. Locate a knowledgeable physician to give the child a medical exam. You will also have to take responsibility for making sure you obtain your child's passport and visa.

In *How to Adopt Internationally*, Nelson-Erichsen and Erichsen write:

Over the years, we have heard of many sad cases in which a missionary or foreign lawyer, rather than an international agency abroad, assigned a couple a child but was unable to obtain the birth documents needed for a legal international adoption. The prospective adoptive parents send money overseas for years in the hope that the child can be legally freed for adoption. We usually meet them when they have given up hope and want to start over with an agency-initiated adoption." [20]

Not all independent attempts fail. If you are living or working overseas and identify a child, it is possible in some cases to arrange for the child's adoption independently. It can take time and extra effort, and you have to make sure that you know all the procedures for that country. Some missionaries and Christian humanitarian workers run orphanages in foreign countries where international adoption is permitted, and they may connect Christian prospective adopters with an adoptable child. This works well for some families. Overall, however, arranged adoptions generally carry a higher risk. Even when an arranger's motives are pure and a child has been identified, there might be a lack of political expertise in completing the right paperwork and having it approved.

If you are able to utilize a foreign attorney or even a foreign missionary to arrange an independent adoption, you can save the agency portion of the fees. However, the in-country fees and travel costs will remain much the same. If your arranger charges a fee, you might end up with costs comparable to using an agency. If not, you probably look at a savings of $3,000–$10,000.

Some intercountry adoptions are completed in the child's native country, while other countries grant custody or guardianship for the child to leave the country, and the adoptive parents finalize the adoption in their home country. For the adoptions that take place in other countries, adoptive American parents used to have to readopt their child in the United States for the child to become a U.S. Citizen. However, in 2001, the Child Citizenship Act of 2000 became effective, automatically granting citizenship to certain foreign-born children—including adopted children—currently residing permanently in the United States.

Before 2004, adoptive parents received a permanent "green card" for their child, which they could use to apply for the child's certificate of citizenship. In 2004 when the U.S. Citizenship and Immigration Services streamlined the process, adoptive parents began automatically receiving their child's citizenship certificate in the mail within forty-five days of their arrival. Note that some states still require international adoptions to be finalized or the child to be readopted in their home state. Ask your agency, attorney, or Department of State what the laws are that govern adoption in your state.

RED LIGHT, STOP!

Questions to consider at this point in your adoption journey:

____ What country or countries are you interested in adopting from?

____ Are you comfortable enough with an agency to proceed?

____ Are you prepared for the risks involved in that country?

____ Do you know exactly what your agency's fees cover, and what additional expenses you will need to cover?

____ Do you understand all the elements of the process of international adoption from the country you are choosing?

____ Are you considering using a foreign attorney or facilitator to arrange an independent adoption? If so, are you prepared for the additional work and risks?

GREEN LIGHT, GO!

Action points for your adoption journey:

____ Decide which country or countries you are most interested in adopting from and educate yourself about their adoption policies and procedures, number of visas issued annually for that country to adoptees, and which agencies work in that country.

____ Talk about the benefits and risks of adopting internationally. Consider all the possibilities of developmental delays and other ill effects of a child's unknown background or his or her institutionalization.

____ Once you know where you want to adopt internationally, make a list of three to five agencies and begin researching their backgrounds, services, and fees. Attend agency seminars if possible, and ask friends for recommendations.

____ Interview the top two or three agencies with your checklist of questions and choose the one that best fits you. If you are adopting independently, get recommendations for an attorney or facilitator and use the same list of questions to interview that person.

____ Compare the fees of the agencies you are interviewing. Crunch the numbers, create a time line of when the fees are due for each, and add in the extras not covered.

____ Choose an agency and fill out the application. When they agree to work with you, begin preparing your dossier.

____ If you are working independently, become educated about the paperwork requirements and prepare all the needed documents. Be sure to have them translated into the language of the country from which you are adopting.

____ Arrange your home study and send in your I-600A, Application for Advance Processing of Orphan Petition, and fingerprinting application and fees.

____ Send your completed dossier after certification and authentication back to your agency to be sent to the foreign country for processing.

____ If adopting independently, send the dossier to your facilitator or attorney or take it to the proper authorities in the foreign country.

My Adoption Miracle
My Boys from Haiti
by Karen Kingsbury, Best-selling Fiction Author

I was on the Internet late one night in my office when I came across a Web site that had pictures of orphans available for adoption in Haiti. I just saw those faces and felt an instant connection to a five-year-old boy named EJ.

"EJ is a charmer," the accompanying description said. "He is the first to hug the workers at the orphanage each day and is easily one of the fastest learners in our classroom."

I asked my husband, Don, if we could adopt this child. He felt the same connection. There was no hesitation. I printed EJ's picture, and the next morning we asked our kids how they would feel about having a brother from Haiti. They agreed that we should try to bring EJ home. We contacted the workers at his orphanage and began putting our dossier together. While we were accumulating the paperwork, I noticed another face among those pictures—the face of a six-year-old boy named Joshua. I asked Don if we could bring home two boys. He agreed, and the kids did too.

We contacted the orphanage and said we wanted to adopt both boys, but a worker told us that Joshua's information on the Web site was wrong and that he was a difficult child who would not blend well with the other children in our family. Reluctantly, we put aside the idea of adopting Joshua and decided on a different six-year-old boy named Sean.

Six months later, it was time for me to bring the boys home. I traveled to Haiti to pick up EJ and Sean and bring them home. I went to the orphanage and met EJ and Sean. They did not speak English, and I did not speak Creole; but we smiled at one another, they sat shyly on my lap, and our first meeting was a lot like I had expected it would be. Except for one thing.

As I sat there, a little boy walked up, brushed some hair from my forehead, said, "Hello, Mommy" in English, and began singing for me the popular praise chorus, "Lord, I give you my heart. I give you my soul. I live for you alone."

I asked him his name, and he said, "Joshua." This was Joshua, the same Joshua that I had been told was too "difficult" to adopt. The worker had given me wrong information, and this was the boy I decided not to adopt and instead had chosen Sean. To make matters worse, Sean, EJ, and Joshua were best buddies. The three of them were inseparable at the orphanage. Now I was here to take Sean and EJ away and leave Joshua behind.

I called my husband that night weeping. He said, "Two, three, what's the difference? Bring him home."

It was not quite that easy. We did not have paperwork completed for Joshua, so he did remain behind while Sean, EJ, and I returned to the United States. I frantically began the paperwork process again, and six months later, Joshua joined us too.

Today, the boys are young men, soccer stars in our community, and loved by all. It is hard to remember what our family was like without them.

Our first days with the boys were such an experience. I'll never forget how delighted they were the first time they felt running warm water or the way their eyes grew wide the first time they entered a grocery store and saw all the aisles of food. Our boys had lost parents to starvation or illness, and had gone without food for days at a time. They customarily ate something called "dirt cakes," which looked like cheap pottery made from clay, dirt, and water. Village women mixed this recipe, baked it, and gave it to the children to ease the pain in their empty tummies.

Adopting has made me more compassionate in my writing. That much is evidenced by my mention of adoption topics and the intense emotion in several of my novels, including _Even Now_ and _A Treasury of Adoption Miracles_. Another blessing has been realizing the depth of faith these children have. They had nothing in Haiti, not even a chance to live. But they had a deep love for Jesus and prayed and sang throughout the day. Even now, the children love singing for God, and sometimes cry during worship time at church.

"Are you sad, honey?" my husband will sometimes ask.

"No, Daddy. I'm just so happy when I think of everything Jesus has done for me."

The statistics on homeless children in our world remain daunting, but our family has seen this truth at work: adoption makes a difference.

Just ask our three sons. EJ, Sean, and Joshua.

(Find out more about Karen, her books, and her family at www.karenkingsbury.com.)

Chapter Five

Adoption Is More Affordable
than You Might Think

Nearly everyone has heard or read stories about how outrageously expensive adoption is. When figures like $15,000, $25,000, or more, are tossed into adoption conversations, people feel they can't afford to adopt and they quit considering it at all. That's it. Game over. Not gonna happen. Not many people can whip out the checkbook and write a check in the five-digit range without watching it bounce like a rubber ball. Few people have that kind of cash just sitting around, especially those who have been trying to become pregnant and have often undergone costly infertility treatments.

Yes, adoption can cost thousands and even tens of thousands of dollars, but here's a little secret: *you don't pay it all at once, and the IRS actually gives you some of your money back!* Plus, adoption agencies sometimes offer sliding scales, the costs of adoption vary widely, and there are many ways to raise the funds needed.

AVERAGE DOMESTIC ADOPTION COSTS
The average private domestic adoption of a newborn costs anywhere between $5,000 and $40,000. The reason the cost varies so much depends on a number of factors, including the fees charged by the agency, the attorney's fees, the advertising fees, the home study, and an extra telephone line (to protect your identity, if you are trying to locate a birthmother yourself and do not want your home number to be known). How far along in the pregnancy a birthmother is when you agree to work together toward adoption also varies the cost. Birthmothers who have months to go before delivery are also entitled to reasonable living expenses to be paid by the adoptive family, as well as her medical expenses and the baby's medical expenses.

AVERAGE DOMESTIC ADOPTION COSTS, WAITING CHILD

If you choose a child who has already been placed in state care and is waiting in the foster-care system, usually there are no agency fees involved. As when dealing with any bureaucratic entity, there will be a lot of paperwork to complete, requirements to fulfill, and some inevitable red tape; but the costs involved are minimal, usually only a few hundred dollars, and families adopting from foster care can actually come out ahead financially after receiving state subsidies, medical care, and the federal income tax credit.

WORDS OF WISDOM
You won't let them down: orphans won't be orphans forever.
—Psalm 10:14 (MSG)

AVERAGE INTERNATIONAL ADOPTION COSTS

International adoption costs generally range from $8,000 to $40,000, depending on which country the adoptive parents choose, the travel costs involved, and whether an adoptive family uses an agency or independent facilitator. In some international adoptions, attorney's fees and court costs must be paid to finalize an international child's adoption in the United States.

How Christians with Average Incomes Afford Adoption

In a study of all adoptions that took place in 2002 in the state of Massachusetts, the Center for Adoption Research found that public adoptions from the state foster-care system cost nothing, while the highest cost was $36,000 for a domestic infant adoption with agency resources, meaning that an adoption agency handled the entire adoption from filling out an application through the finalization of the adoption. In between were several other adoption options, including domestic adoption with the agency networking with other programs (high: $35,000), international agency networking with other programs (high: $35,000), international adoptions using agency programs (high: $29,000, which might or might not include travel costs and dossier fees), and domestic infant adoptions where the prospective parents already identified a birthmother and used an agency to finalize the adoption $15,000. (But this does not include the costs associated with locating the birthmother or possible attorney's fees.)[21]

While these are large amounts of money for average-income families, Christians who want to adopt absolutely can find ways to afford it. They do so by trusting God to provide, giving back to him, creating an adoption budget, using their imagination, and choosing a method of adoption they can realistically make work.

WORDS OF WISDOM
You shall remember the LORD your God, for it is He who is giving you power to make wealth.
—Deuteronomy 8:18 (NASB)

IT'S NOT ONE LUMP SUM

The first thing to note is that you do not have to hand over payment of the total adoption costs in one lump sum. The high figures you have just read encompass the entire adoption process from start to finish, but the fees are not paid in total up-front. When you first decide to adopt and choose an agency, an attorney, or a facilitator, there will be an initial cost to contract their services. That up front cost can range from just a couple of hundred dollars sent in with the agency application to a few thousand dollars in retainer fees to an adoption attorney. The other costs are spread out over the entire adoption process.

CREATING AN ADOPTION BUDGET

To estimate what you will be spending to adopt, you will need to learn all you can about the costs of the type of adoption you choose. Then, create an adoption budget by listing all of the costs associated with adoption that you can find, including long-distance and cell-phone bills, postage and overnight delivery services, paper and ink, notary fees, passport fees, medical checkups, background-check fees, birth certificate and marriage license certified copy fees, agency fees, travel costs, gas and tolls, baby furniture, and other assorted baby paraphernalia. Once you have listed all the possible expenses, you can begin to map out a time frame of when these costs will be incurred.

To let you in on how it worked in our family's case, my husband and I filled out an agency application and sent it in with a $100 application fee in the month of January. As soon as the adoption agency read our application and agreed to work with us, another $300 was due. Also in January, I spent time talking to the agency long-distance, overnighted some papers to various governmental agencies, and ordered new copies of birth certificates and our marriage license. The total cost of these items was about $150. In February, my husband and I applied with immigration for approval to bring a foreign child home as our adopted child and had our fingerprints taken for the FBI clearance. The cost of those things was $645. (By 2006, the charge totaled $685 for the I-600A and two fingerprinting services.) So in the first two months, I spent $1,195. In March, our home study was conducted at a cost of $1,200. In April, various documents were mailed back and forth to the state capital to be certified and in early May were sent to be authenticated at the Chinese consulate in Houston. The total cost for all the express deliveries, a courier service, and the state and consulate fees was around $500. Our total was up to $2,895.

In mid-May, our dossier, which included about forty pages and seven photographs (at a cost of less than $5 to photocopy and print on our home printer), was complete and ready to be sent to China. The agency required an agency fee of $2,900, plus $510 for legal fees to be paid in China to be sent with the dossier. Over a five-and-a-half-month period, we spent $6,305, or a little over $1,000 a month. Then it was time to sit back and wait. No more fees would be due until we received a referral of the child matched with us, an estimated wait of six to eight months—plenty of time to raise and save funds for the rest of our adoption adventure.

I DIDN'T KNOW THAT!

Be a wise steward and search for ways to save money on the adoption process. For example, many banks offer free notary services to account holders, as well as certified checks or money orders at reduced rates. Does yours?

For domestic adoption, the time frame to pull your finances together might be shorter if you are matched with an infant right away or if your adoption attorney requires a large amount of funds early in the process.

Where the Money Goes, Domestic Adoption

Different kinds of adoptions have different kinds of expenses. In domestic adoptions of newborns in the United States, expenses range from advertising to find a birthmother and contracting with an agency or attorney to picking up the medical and hospital expenses of the birthmom and your new baby.

HOME STUDY FEES

One expense that all types of adoption have in common is the home study. This is the first piece to the adoption puzzle that every prospective adopter must have. A home study costs anywhere from $750 to $2,500, depending on which state you live in. The average is around $1,500.

ADOPTION AGENCY FEES

When choosing a social worker to conduct your home study, ask around to see who other adopters in your area used, what the social worker charged, whether the social worker seemed friendly and helpful, and how long it took to complete the home study and get it to the adopters. Because a lot is riding on this report, you want to choose a social worker who wants to see you achieve an adoption as much as you want to adopt. Also, if you are in a hurry to get the report back, be aware that most social workers charge extra for an expedited report. It should probably take no longer than a month to get your home study report. If you pay the additional fee for an expedited report, the home study should be received in as little as three days after all information is supplied.

Some agencies conduct the home study using the social workers they employ and include the cost in their total fees. If this is the case with your agency, make sure the agency itemizes their total fee for you. If they do not, you may discover after it is too late that their fee for the home study was more than you could have had it done for yourself.

Because agency fees can vary so widely, and because there are unscrupulous agencies in existence who scam desperate couples out of thousands of dollars, make sure that you do lots of homework before choosing an adoption agency. Do not make the mistake of choosing an agency because it promises lightning-fast results, guarantees quick placement, or even because it sounds good, or has "Christian" in its name. Most agencies do not make promises that a newborn adoption will occur quickly. Some adoptions will take place in a short amount of time, but most reputable agencies do not promise that.

I DIDN'T KNOW THAT!

Adoption agencies who promise they can have a baby to you in a very short amount of time are likely to be a scam. No agency can know for sure how many birthmothers they will have, or promise any prospective adopter a baby before a home study is successfully completed and other criteria is met. Do not let your impatience cause you to fall for something fraudulent.

Agencies all differ in the services they provide, the amount of staff they have, and the fees they charge. Find people who have adopted and ask them detailed questions about what they were happy with and unhappy with in working through their agency. Decide whether it is important to you to work with an agency that is local, so that you can meet people face-to-face. Your best option is to interview several agencies about what they offer, how many adoptions they handle annually, and exactly what their fees cover.

Some important questions to ask about money include:

- Does your fee include the home study?
- Does your fee include advertising and locating a birthmother?
- How much less are your fees if I locate the birthmother?
- Does your fee include counseling for the birthparents?
- Does your fee include post-placement visits and counseling?

- Does your fee include the medical expenses of the birthmother or baby?
- Does your fee cover hospitalization of the birthmother and baby?
- Is your fee the same even if the birthmother has medical insurance?
- Do you use a sliding scale based on income?
- What else does your fee include?
- What extras might occur that your fee does not cover?
- Where does my fee go? Do you have any ministry or orphan-support organizations that you run or donate to?

It is also important to make sure that your agency is a nonprofit organization (although that does not guarantee they are operating honestly and fiscally responsibly). Check into the background of your agency to make sure they are a reputable company and not in financial trouble that could lead them to pack up (with your money) and leave overnight or go out of business before your adoption is completed. Ask any agency if it is accredited with ECFA or has other affiliations or accountability measures in place that you can verify. You can also call the Better Business Bureau and ask if there have been any complaints lodged against the agency you are considering.

ADOPTION ATTORNEY FEES

If you are using an adoption attorney to adopt independently, you can expect to pay attorney's fees of at least $5,000 to $9,000, plus $2,000 for the birthparents' legal representation. Even if you do not use an attorney to help you locate a birthmother, you will almost certainly need one to help you finalize your adoption in the appropriate court of law. Motions will need to be filed and court appearances made, and most people utilize the services of an attorney to complete these steps. Depending on where you live and how many adoption attorneys are available in your area, fees can vary widely. They can start at as little as $1,000 for a finalization only but go up rapidly from there. Again, ask around to find out who the attorneys are in your area who can do a good job at a reasonable price for you. You can also check with the bar association in your state to find out if the attorney has had any complaints lodged against him or her or the firm.

When you interview attorneys, ask if they offer a free consultation. Find out their hourly rate, how many adoptions they have finalized in the last year, and the average cost. Keep in mind that your attorney charges for phone calls, letters sent, and drop-in visits. Do not stop by to say "hi" if you do not want to be billed for it. If you have a valid concern or need to contact your attorney, by all means, do so. But if you start using your attorney as a "listening ear," your costs will run higher. Try to choose an attorney who is sensitive to your financial limitations and who seems willing to work with you. Some attorneys insist on handling every aspect of an adoption themselves. Others will let you track down needed documents and make some phone calls, saving you his hourly billing rate.

If an attorney expects an up-front payment of more than $5,000 as a retainer before he has done anything, you may want to keep looking. Also, do not pay for someone who only looks for a birthmother and offers no other services, or someone who charges just to put your name on a waiting list. Look for an attorney who specializes in adoptions and ask him what percentage of his business adoptions really are. A family attorney who is a friend but who handles only divorces might not be equipped to handle the complexities of your adoption and may end up costing more. Other important questions to ask include whether or not he escrows your money in the bank until a birthmother is found, if he obtains receipts for a birthmother's living and other expenses, and what happens to your money if a birthmother changes her mind.

THE EXPENSE OF LOCATING A BIRTHMOTHER

In order to adopt domestically, a birthmother must be located who wants to work with you. The top three ways of finding a birthmother are the following:

- having an adoption agency match you,
- hiring an adoption attorney to locate a birthmother for you, and
- independently locating a birthmother through word of mouth or advertising.

Locating a birthmother independently can cost fewer dollars but lots more in time and frustration. It all depends on who you know, how much time you have to devote, how patient you are, how bold you are, and how savvy you can be at deciding where to place affordable ads.

Phone calls to high school and college counselors, local adoption support groups, doctors' offices, and newspaper ads sometimes yield results. Make sure to find out what the laws in your state prohibit before trying to place an ad or otherwise "advertise" for a birthmother. Ads can also be expensive, depending on the circulation size of the paper and whether it is in a large or small city. Adoptive parents-to-be who place their own ads generally spend $250–$500 per month to keep the ads running.

I DIDN'T KNOW THAT!
There are reports of all kinds of creative ways prospective adopters have gotten the word out that they are looking for a birthmother. One woman created a T-shirt that read "I'm expecting" on the front and "to adopt soon" on the back. Another woman saw her wearing the shirt and actually knew someone who wanted to place her baby for adoption. Thanks to the shirt, an adoption was successfully arranged.
—From a networking article on www.adopting.org [22]

If you know that you want to adopt a newborn through domestic adoption, start putting the word out to everyone you know and let them know that you are looking for a birthmother. Tell your church friends, your extended family members, local crisis pregnancy centers, and coworkers. Ask them to keep you informed if they know of someone in a crisis pregnancy who wants to place her baby for adoption. Some people create a one-page résumé that includes a photograph and mail it to friends and family. Others have purchased mailing lists of those in their profession and mailed out their résumé and a plea for help in locating a birthmother. Some creative prospective adopters have made T-shirts, buttons, and business cards asking for help in locating a birthmother. If you want to make up business cards, you can leave them on tables when you go out to eat, drop them in envelopes with your bills, and hand them out wherever you go.

But be careful. There are some birthmother scams out there, so it is always best to hire an attorney or contract with an agency (or both) before you pay any money to a birthmother. They can help you discern at that point if the birthmother is legitimately interested in relinquishing her baby to you for adoption. Unfortunately, there are still some scams that occur. Some birthmothers have actually made "agreements" with more than one couple during a pregnancy and received support from all parties, when they had no intention of actually placing their babies. While this type of fraud is against the law, it is difficult to prove that a birthmother never intended to place her baby for adoption. State laws do not allow contracts signed before a birth to be legally valid and do allow a period of time for a birthmother to change her mind about adoption, even after placement, without returning the monies spent (except for Idaho!). Remember that while some birthmother arrangements fall through, most people who commit to the adoption process end up finalizing an adoption.

I DIDN'T KNOW THAT!
If you feel that you have been scammed, there are places to report your trouble so that others do not end up in the same boat. If you have a problem with an adoption agency, report it to the state licensing bureau, the state adoption coordinator's office, the attorney general, local adoptive support groups, and the Better Business Bureau (www.bbb.org). If an attorney gives you trouble, report the difficulty to the state bar association, the attorney general, local adoption groups, and the American Academy of Adoption Attorneys in Washington, D.C.

THE BIRTHMOTHER'S EXPENSES

As far as the birthmother's expenses, adoptive parents can expect to pay somewhere in the vicinity of $7,500 to $10,000 for the birthmother's prenatal care and hospitalization, if she has no insurance and is ineligible for Medicaid and if there are no extraordinary complications. Most states also allow adoptive parents to pay for the birthmother's reasonable living expenses or maternity-related expenses, if she and the couple meet during her pregnancy and agree on placement. These can include rent, food, utilities, counseling, and even lost income for the birthmother's time off work. (Check your medical insurance to see what portions of the birthmother's medical expenses and leave, if any, are covered by your policy.) Expenses that are specifically excluded by some states include cars, vacations, permanent housing, and other monetary payments that might be construed to look as if couples are buying babies. Find out what the laws are in your state, and be aware that of all fifty states, only Idaho requires that a birthmother reimburse the adoptive parents if she decides not to relinquish her child for adoption.[23]

THE BABY'S MEDICAL EXPENSES

Domestic adoption expenses include the medical expenses and care of the baby at birth and after birth until the child is placed with the adoptive parents. This includes the bills from the hospital for the birth, the pediatrician who visits the newborn during his or her hospital stay, and medical tests and supplies.

Other expenses for the baby can include guardian ad litem fees, court filing expenses, and paperwork fees.

DOMESTIC PAPERWORK EXPENSES

Most paperwork for domestic expenses will be handled by the agency or attorney facilitating the placement, but there are still some paperwork hurdles that prospective parents will have to cross. You will need photocopies of your driver's licenses, Social Security cards, birth certificates, and marriage license.

If you do not have the originals of these official documents on hand, you will need to order them. Submitting a request to your state for a criminal background check costs in the neighborhood of $25 each, and if your agency is in another state or you need to get paperwork there by certain dates, you will incur express delivery charges.

Where the Money Goes: International Adoption

International adoption costs are generally more predictable than domestic newborn adoption fees, if prospective parents use an adoption agency and choose a country that has an ongoing adoption program in place.

IMMIGRATION APPLICATION AND FINGERPRINTING FEES

When adopting from a foreign country, adoptive parents must establish with the federal government that they are acceptable adoptive parents for a foreign child by submitting to fingerprinting, which is run through the FBI database for clearance. This costs $70 for each person living in the prospective adoptive household who is age eighteen or older. This fingerprinting fee is sent in with the U.S. Citizenship and Immigration Service's "Petition to Classify Orphan as an Immediate Relative," which costs $545 to process. For the typical household with no adult children or other adult relatives living in the home, the fee submitted to USCIS is a certified check or money order in the amount of $685 ($545 for the petition, plus fingerprinting fees of $70 each for two adults).

HOME STUDY FEES

The home study fee for an adoption, whether it is for domestic, foster care, or international adoption, generally runs the same. In our case, the average fee in Florida at the time of our home study was $1,200. Fees can range from $750 to $2,000 on average.

AGENCY FEES

When an adoption agency is chosen, the initial agency fees required with an application usually run between $100 and $500. After that, the total fees an agency charges for international adoption can vary widely, depending on the services they include. If not already available, ask your agency to break down its total fee, specifying what is included and what you will be responsible for outside the agency fees.

Questions to ask your agency about fees in an international adoption should include the following:

- Does your fee include the home study?
- Does your fee include payments, court costs, and other fees charged by the foreign government of the country in which I am adopting?
- Does your fee include post-placement visits?
- Does your fee include the medical checkup of the baby before he or she leaves the country?
- Does your fee cover dossier preparation services?
- Does your fee cover translation of the dossier?
- Does your fee cover an interpreter and guide in the foreign country when we travel, or does it cover the travel expenses of the escort who brings the baby to the United States?
- Does your fee include in-country travel, accommodations, and food?
- Does your fee include travel expenses from the United States to the country?
- What adoption-related expenses can we expect to incur when we travel?
- Does the foreign government require any "donations" in order for us to adopt?
- Do you use a sliding scale based on income?
- What else does your fee include?
- What "extras" might occur that your fee does not cover?
- Where does my fee go? Do you have any ministry or orphan-support organizations that you run or donate to?

PAPERWORK COSTS

In an international adoption, adoptive parents will spend time and money on paperwork and lots of it. Some adopters will opt to use a *dossier preparation service*. These "paperwork people" are usually adoptive mothers who have walked through the process themselves, know what needs to be done, and want to work at home to provide their family with some additional income while helping other adopting families. For a few hundred dollars (typically ranging from $75 for consultations to "walk" people through the process to $1,000 for full dossier preparation), adoptive parents can hand over the paperwork to a service who will order birth certificates and marriage licenses, state and local background checks, and gather your medical reports and home study for certification and authentication. Dossier preparers check over each document to make sure that all the correct signatures, wording, stamps, and notarizations are in place before sending the completed dossier back to you or directly to your agency.

For those handling the paperwork themselves, the costs include any notary fees for notarizing each required document for the dossier; fees to order new birth certificates and a marriage license, as many countries will not accept documents dated more than twelve months past (new copies typically range from $7.50 to $20 each); the fee for a state background check, which is usually under $25 (in Florida, it is $23); and the fees attached to getting each of the dossier documents certified, then authenticated or apostilled.

Certification is handled by each state and runs an average of $10 per document, plus a small mailing fee of around $5. Certification by foreign consulates in the United States generally costs $10 to $20 per document—it can cost more than twice that per document, if the adoptive parents want expedited service. Consulates generally do not accept documents for certification that are sent via regular mail, and only some accept documents sent via an express delivery service. Most adoptive parents utilize the services of a courier in the area of the consulate that handles their documents or makes a trip to the consulate to personally deliver their documents and wait for them to be processed. Documents sent via an express delivery service will pay the delivery service fee (around $20) to get the documents there, and will include a prepaid delivery service envelope for the consulate to use to mail them back (another $20).

Those who hand deliver their documents may incur the cost of a flight and hotel or a several-hour drive and lodging, or two driving trips to the consulate to carry in and retrieve their documents. If you choose to use a courier service to hand deliver your documents and retrieve them when they are finished, fees are around $15 per document for the first 10 documents, dropping to $10 per document for twenty documents or more.

FOREIGN GOVERNMENT FEES

International adoptions also come with fees that must be paid to the country in which you are adopting. These foreign government fees include dossier processing, visas, "donations" to the orphanage, and court costs, if the adoption is finalized in the foreign country.

For example:

- Guatemala in-country fees range between $15,000 and $19,000, including all legal fees and attorney costs, permits, registration, foster care, medical exams, DNA testing, translation, and other fees.
- In Russia, in-country fees run anywhere from around $7,000 to $14,000

and include a minimum orphanage donation of $1,500, legal fees, the agency and government liaison fees, and a background investigation of the child, liaison with the government, and the agency presentation.

Make sure whichever agency you choose clearly outlines the fees required, whether they could vary and by what amount they could fluctuate, and which countries are least likely to change the process during your adoption period. Although there are no guarantees that a foreign government will not be overthrown, the laws will not change, or fees will not be raised, there are countries that have had a tried-and-true adoption process in place for some time with no major variations. Those are the countries that should contain the least unpleasant surprises during the adoption process.

MISCELLANEOUS EXPENSES

In addition to the expenses already outlined, international adoptions require that the prospective parents undergo a medical checkup and blood work, and that post-placement reports be filed by a social worker. Medical exams can cost $50–$400, with lab fees running $50–$150 more. The Centers for Disease Control and Prevention recommend that travelers get immunizations based on the foreign country they are visiting. These might cost a couple hundred dollars, depending on your health insurance coverage or whether you visit your local health department.

Post-placement visits must be done three or four times, on average, over the course of the first year or eighteen months after the child is placed in your home and should run $250–$800 total.

TRAVEL COSTS

Finally, adoptive parents can expect to pay travel expenses—either theirs or the expenses of the person who will be bringing the child to the United States and the child's. In most cases, one or both parents will travel to pick up the child. Airfare to these countries can cost from $800 to $2,500 for coach class, or several thousand dollars per ticket for first class.

Depending on how long you have to remain in the country, lodging and food can cost hundreds to thousands of dollars. Some countries require that one or both parents travel to the country twice before the adoption is finalized—the first time to meet and spend time with their child and file necessary paperwork, and the second time to finalize the adoption in court. Make sure you find out from your agency how much travel costs run on average and ask other adoptive families from your agency if those numbers were accurate in their case.

COMPARING COSTS: APPLES TO APPLES

Adoption fees for domestic and international adoption can vary thousands or even tens of thousands of dollars between attorneys, agencies, and countries; so it is wise to do your homework. To find out what an agency charges for adoption, start by looking at the Web site. Some agencies' Web sites require a password to see in detail what the adoption process entails. Ask for temporary access, or ask them to mail you information so you can compare your options before making a decision. Many agencies post a fee range per country on their main site. The key in comparing the true cost of adoption from agency to agency is to make sure you add in all of the same elements in each adoption total. In the Hope for Orphans agency survey, fee structures for adopting from Korea, Guatemala, Kazakhstan, Russia, and China were investigated and compared side by side to determine the range and average costs of adoption in each country from the reporting agencies. The results varied by thousands of dollars:[24]

	Range	Mean
China	$18,805–$24,860	$22,984
Guatemala	$26,030–$35,665	$29,207
Kazakhstan	$24,420–$32,274	$28,298
Korea	$19,695–$21,065	$20,525
Russia	$21,450–$36,935	$29,298
U.S.	$16,100–$25,680	$21,646

The most surprising discovery, researcher Corkydawn Mason said, was that Christian agencies generally underreported the actual total cost of adoption by an average of $3,000. These figures were in line with what I found, doing some quick calculations of five well-established Christian agencies' posted fees for their China programs in 2005:

AGENCY #1

The approximate program fees (meaning the money that goes to the agency) stated by this agency total $6,000–$10,000. The agency states that this fee includes their application fee, assistance with dossier preparation, telephone calls, some mailing costs, adoption workshops, background checks, and coordination with the foreign country. For China, the country fees (fees paid to China or in China) are $5,910, plus travel and accommodation expenses.

Total cost to adoptive parents: $11,910–$15,910, *not* including travel to China, the home study, and other additional expenses.

AGENCY #2

This agency provides more specifics on what it costs overall to adopt from China through its program and includes travel. Their breakdown looks like this: application fee: $250; program (agency) fee: $5,600; immigration fee: $685; dossier authentication fee: $500; home study and post-placement fees: $1,900; visas for two adults: $100; dossier translation fee: $695; foreign fees, which include orphanage donation and government fees in China: $5,000; round-trip airfare to China for two adults: $1,800–$3,000; airfare lap pass for infant: $200–$250; in-country expenses of accommodations, meals, transportation, and guides: $3,000. *Total cost to adoptive parents: $19,730–$20,980.*

AGENCY #3

The third agency also offers a breakdown of fees that looks like this: application fee: $200; dossier fee: $2,795; program fee: $9,360; home study fee if done by the agency: $1,682–$3,066; post-placement services fee if done by the agency: $801–$1,512; optional document processing fee (similar to a dossier preparation service): $500. This agency does not include the cost of immigration or travel.

Total cost to adoptive parents: $12,355 (without home study, post-placement, or document processing fees) to $17,433 (if you include the high end of the home study and post-placement range and the document processing fees). This agency points out that there will be additional costs including fingerprinting, visa filing fee, medical exams, and other miscellaneous expenses.

AGENCY #4

The fourth agency charges: application fee: total $350 in two payments of $175; program fee: $4,400; document processing fee: $250; express delivery fees: $200; international fees: $565; legal fees: $1,400 (in China); document translation fee: $200; maintenance support fee (orphanage donation): $3,000; and travel costs (based on two people): $5,800.

Total cost to adoptive parents: $16,165, with additional costs to include $685 for the immigration petition and fingerprinting, the home study or post-placement report fee, plus miscellaneous expenses such as medical exams, postage, phone calls, and the child's visa to enter the United States.

AGENCY #5

The last agency examined gives a ballpark total for fees on its main China page, with more details given if requested by e-mail, phone call, or snail mail.

Total cost to adoptive parents: The estimated total cost of a China adoption for one parent, not including travel, is $11,315; and the estimated total cost of a China adoption and travel for two is $16,820. This does not include the INS application fee, the local home study fee, fees for certification and authentication from the Chinese Embassy, or post-placement report fees.

Looking at these agencies side by side, what does it all boil down to? How do you really know what the entire adoption would cost? You can do the math based on two adults traveling to China and the fees that China adoptions have in common:

1. A home study and post-placement report. Average cost: $2,000 for both.
2. Fingerprinting and immigration petition I–600 or I–600A. Cost: $685.
3. Orphanage donation of $3,000 and in-country fees of roughly $1,900.
4. Dossier of documents that have to be ordered, certified, and authenticated. Cost: approximately $500.
5. Miscellaneous fees including phone calls, paper, ink, gas, express delivery services, and the like. Cost: $200.
6. A recent (not more than six months old) medical exam and certain blood tests for parents. Cost: $400–$1,000.
7. Travel. Approximate cost: $5,000–$6,000 for two.
8. Application and program fees for handling the adoption. These five agencies' application and program fees ranged from $4,400 to $10,000.

Looking at these requirements and adding a midrange figure for medical exams and blood work of $600 and travel of $5,500, the five agencies' total figures for adoption with all of the above requirements added in would look something like this:

Agency #1: $25,395–$29,395 (with the addition of home study and post-placement report, medical exams, immigration petition and fingerprinting, travel for two, dossier documents, and miscellaneous expenses)
Agency #2: $20,130–$21,980 (with medical exams and blood tests added)
Agency #3: $21,840–$24,418 (with the addition of the home study and post-placement report on the lower figure, plus immigration petition and fingerprints, medical exam, miscellaneous expenses, and travel added for both)
Agency #4: $19,900 (with the addition of medical exam, immigration petition and fingerprinting, the home study and post-placement report, and miscellaneous expenses)
Agency #5: $20,805 (with the addition of medical exam, immigration petition and fingerprinting, dossier documents, miscellaneous expenses, and home study and post-placement report)

Now comparing the agencies side to side, it is easy to see that the range falls between Agency #4's low of $19,900 to Agency #1's high end of $29,395, a difference of $9,495. This does not mean you should automatically choose #4 or rule out #1. It just means that it is easy to see how the numbers can look vastly different, depending on what fees are included in the price or left out.

When choosing an agency, do your own number-crunching of all the factors, and keep in mind your checklist of questions before signing on the dotted line. Be suspicious of figures that are too low (the agency's estimates might not reflect the current costs) or too high (where is all that money going?). Remember that most agencies do not refund the application fee or their program (agency) fee once you start the process.

Subsidies and Credits

The federal government, state government, and some employers cover some adoption expenses through special programs, subsidies, and tax credits.

THE BIG INCOME TAX CREDIT

Now for the exciting part: there is a federal *adoption tax credit* that is widely known among people who have already adopted or are well into the adoption process but little known to people who have not considered adoption because they think the costs are too astronomically high. It's a tax credit the federal government provides of *up* to $10,630 for tax year 2005 for qualifying expenses paid to adopt an eligible child (including a child with special needs). So, if you pay more than $10,630 in qualifying adoption expenses and finalize an adoption, you can get up to $10,630 of tax money you owe or have already paid back in your own pocket. If you finalize two adoptions, you may be eligible for a credit of $21,260. If you adopt a child who meets the definition of a special-needs child from foster care and have no adoption expenses, you also qualify for the tax credit.

Here's how it works: The adoption credit is an amount subtracted not from your gross or adjusted gross income, but from the actual taxes you owe. Even better, you are not limited to claiming it all in one year but can take it over a five-year period. That means that if you paid $2,000 in federal income taxes in the year your adoption was finalized, you can apply to get that back. The following year if you owe $3,000 in taxes, you can apply to get that back. And so on, up to five years and $10,630. Another bonus: your new child can be claimed as an additional dependent on your returns. (I can hear you now, saying, "Gee, honey, this adoption thing is getting so affordable that we should bring home two!")

The IRS publication "Topic 607–Adoption Credit" uses the following terms and conditions for qualifying for the tax credit:

For both the credit and the exclusion, qualifying expenses include reasonable and necessary adoption fees, court costs, attorney fees, traveling expenses (including amounts spent for meals and lodging while away from home), and other expenses directly related to and for which the principal purpose is the legal adoption of an eligible child. An eligible child must be under 18 years old, or be physically or mentally incapable of caring for himself or herself. The adoption credit or exclusion cannot be taken for a child who is not a United States citizen or resident unless the adoption becomes final. An eligible child is a child with special needs if he or she is a United States citizen or resident and a state determines that the child cannot or should not be returned to his or her parent's home and probably will not be adopted unless assistance is provided.

The credit and exclusion for qualifying adoption expenses are each subject to a dollar limit and an income limit. Under the dollar limit the amount of your adoption credit or exclusion is limited to $10,630 for each effort to adopt an eligible child. If you can take both a credit and an exclusion, this dollar amount applies separately to each. For example, if you paid $9,000 in qualifying adoption expenses for a final adoption, and your employer paid $4,000 of additional qualifying adoption expenses, you may be able to claim a credit of up to $9,000 and also exclude up to $4,000.

The $10,630 amount is the maximum amount of qualifying expenses taken into account over all taxable years. Therefore, it must be reduced by the amount of qualifying expenses taken into account in previous years for the same adoption effort, including an unsuccessful effort to adopt a different child.

The income limit on the adoption credit or exclusion is based on your modified adjusted gross income (modified AGI). If your modified AGI is $155,860 or less, the income limit will not affect your credit or exclusion. If your modified AGI is more than $155,860, your credit or exclusion will be reduced. If your modified AGI is $195,860 or more, your credit or exclusion will be eliminated.

If you are married, generally you must file a joint return to take the adoption credit or exclusion. If your filing status is married filing separately, you can take the credit or exclusion only if you meet special requirements. The other important thing to note is that the adoption credit is scheduled to be phased out in 2010 (so adopt now!). Additional information can be found in the IRS Topic 907 at www.irs.gov.[25]

BEST PRACTICES OF FOREVER FAMILIES
Keep receipts for everything. Keep a record of your phone bills, gas, tolls, travel expenses, postage, express delivery, courier services, document fees, agency fees, attorney fees, and anything else adoption-related. You might need them to prove what you spent in order to receive your tax credit.

EMPLOYER CONTRIBUTIONS
To make the adoption deal from the IRS even sweeter and to encourage businesses to help people adopt, the federal government offers *adoption tax exclusions* of up to $10,630 in qualifying *employer assistance* for your adoption expenses, meaning those adoption costs were paid or reimbursed by your employer, to be excludable from your gross income, further lowering your tax burden. So make sure your boss knows that his help toward your adoption will go a long way.

MILITARY CONTRIBUTIONS
Since 1991, every active-duty member of the military services has been eligible for a $2,000 adoption reimbursement per child (maximum: $5,000 in any calendar year) of qualifying adoption-related expenses after the adoption is finalized. The child must be adopted through a licensed, nonprofit agency and may not be the biological child of the adoptive parent. The reimbursement must be applied for no later than one year after the finalization of the adoption. The reimbursement can apply to domestic and international adoptions, and married and single parents may apply.[26]

STATE ADOPTION CREDITS
While the federal government offers the big tax credit, many states also offer tax credits for adoption of up to $10,000. See a qualified tax preparer in your state to find out what you might be eligible to receive. Most states also offer one-time payments of up to $2,000 for qualifying adoption expenses of a special-needs child from the foster-care system.

WAITING CHILD ADOPTION SUBSIDIES
When adopting a special-needs waiting child from the state foster-care system, there are a variety of subsidies and ongoing programs you and your child may be entitled to under the federal government's Title IV-E *adoption assistance* program, which administers funds for disbursement by the state to qualifying

adoptive families. These waiting child *adoption subsidies* include monthly cash assistance, in which the amount may not exceed the amount that would have been paid for maintenance if the child had remained in a foster home in that state. Payments can continue until the child reaches age eighteen (or until age twenty-one where the state determines that the child has a physical, mental, or emotional disability), and these payments continue even if the family moves to another state. Eligibility for these payments is based in part on the resources of the adoptive parents, and partly on the circumstances of the family and the needs of the child.

I DIDN'T KNOW THAT!

If you adopt a child from foster care, you are generally still eligible for the $10,630 tax credit, even if you had no expenses to adopt your child.

Adopted children eligible for the Title IV–E adoption assistance also qualify for medical benefits under the Medicaid program (called Title XXI), and states may offer additional services that include counseling, legal aid, respite care, information, referral, and transportation services under Title XX. Families should check with their state agency to determine what services are available to meet their child's ongoing special needs. In addition to these programs that are paid for with federal dollars given to the states, there are state programs in place to provide assistance to children with special needs who do not meet the Title IV–E requirements. Eligibility criteria varies by state, but programs include medical assistance to cover some or all of the costs of medical expenses not covered by a family's health insurance (most states dub this "Medicaid" also), direct payments to the family for a child's special physical, mental, or emotional needs, and supplemental adoption assistance, which is designed to cover a child's emergency or extraordinary needs and consists of payments over three or six months for services not covered by other programs.

Most waiting children are already set up in the system to receive these benefits upon their adoption, but oftentimes some things fall through the cracks. Wise adoptive parents will take the time to learn what benefits are available to their child in their state and will make sure that the paperwork is in place properly to receive them.[27]

WORDS OF WISDOM

We know what real love is because Christ gave up his life for us. And so we also ought to give up our lives for our Christian brothers and sisters. But if anyone has enough money to live well and sees a brother or sister in need and refuses to help—how can God's love be in that person?
—1 John 3:16-17 (NLT)

Raising Your Adoption Funds

Even though the tax credit can be a big help, if you plan to adopt internationally or domestically, there are still funds to be raised and several means to raise them. The key to raising your adoption funds rather than using your savings, borrowing the money, or maxing out your credit cards is to be creative. Use your imagination to come up with fun, intriguing ideas that will raise the money you need.

BEST PRACTICES OF FOREVER FAMILIES

Most express delivery-companies charge an extra pickup fee and, with the higher cost of gas, have begun charging a fuel charge. So, to save money, take your documents to the overnight delivery services store (like UPS or Federal Express), instead of having their drivers pick them up from your home.

FUND-RAISING THROUGH SUPPORT LETTERS

One way you can raise funds for your adoption is through letters asking family, friends, local businesses, civic organizations, and churches for donations to your adoption fund. A support letter should explain your adoption process and give an idea of what it costs and what you need to raise. One example of a support letter might look like this:

Bill and Jane Smith
123 Liberty Lane
Tampa, FL 37653

Dear Friends, Family, and Colleagues,

We are writing you today with a special request on our hearts. We are in the process of adopting a precious baby girl from China to add to our wonderful forever family. The adoption costs are quite high, in the neighborhood of $25,000, and we are humbly asking if you would prayerfully consider helping us bring our little girl home.

Adopting a little girl from China means that her life may literally be saved, as girls are often abandoned due to the government's limit of one child per family. At the very least, this little one will have opportunities for education, nutrition, and most of all, spiritual growth that she would not be afforded in her native country.

We are working with a Christian adoption agency, (insert your agency name here), to bring our daughter home, and we expect to travel to China when our funds are raised. If you can help us financially and with your prayer support, we would be so grateful. Please make your checks out to_____, and we will keep you informed as to when we will be bringing her home.

Thank you for loving and helping us!
Bill and Jane Smith

The letter of support should be kept to one page, and checks should ideally be made out directly to your agency or to a special account you have set up for your adoption fund. The agency should send you a list of names (not necessarily donation amounts) of anyone who sends a donation, so you can thank them. This way they'll know their donation was received and credited to your account. (With the exception of close family members, many potential donors will not feel comfortable giving money directly to you.)

There are some Christian organizations that will accept donated funds for your adoption under their nonprofit umbrella, thereby offering your donors a tax deduction. Life International, www.lifeintl.org, is one organization whose mission is to help Christian couples afford adoption by providing matching grants, offering no-interest loans, and receiving adoption donations on your behalf.

Fund-raising letters may be distributed in person or through the mail. If you are mailing them, you will get a better response if you include a stamped, self-addressed envelope inside. Letters can be sent to close and extended family members, old friends from school, coworkers, neighbors, church friends, local businesses, and civic organizations such as Kiwanis, Rotary, or Civitan. Try to make them personal, rather than form letters, and be sensitive to the fact that some people might take offense at this type of fund-raising. If you have a picture of your waiting child or the referral picture of your international child, show them around as you explain the letters you hand deliver. Be gracious to those who turn you down, and do not approach businesses that clearly post a "No Solicitation" sign.

BEST PRACTICES OF FOREVER FAMILIES
My husband was a big change collector, and we counted all of that and used it toward our adoption!
—Kimberly Evans, adoptive mother of a Chinese daughter

FUND-RAISING THROUGH YOUR CHURCH
With your pastor's permission, you could raise money a number of ways through your church. The support letter in the example above can be tweaked

just a little to be addressed directly to your fellow congregants. Some pastors will post the letter in the weekly bulletin or include it as a special insert and announce it from the pulpit. Others may allow you to enlist the help of the youth group and hold a car wash, bake sale, mom's day, or couple's night out (where you and the teens offer baby-sitting services for donations or a set fee), or a fund-raising dinner. You can also ask for donations of airline frequent-flier miles to be donated to your accounts. Do your homework first and figure out which airline you want to fly, what their frequent-flier availability is, and whether or not they charge a fee to transfer miles.

Make sure that you tithe 10 percent of the monies raised back to the church and give an offering above that, if the Lord calls you to do so. Perhaps with the funds donated back to the church, you will be able to create an ongoing ministry of support for other adopting families.

BEST PRACTICES OF FOREVER FAMILIES
When you create adoption documents, fund-raising letters, etc., be sure to back them up on a disk or portable hard drive. That way, you still have what you need if your computer malfunctions or gets hit by a virus.

CREATIVE FUND-RAISING
There are a ton of creative ways to fund-raise beyond support letters and your church. If you still need to raise some serious adoption funds, it's time to use your imagination. Think about items you can clear out and sell on eBay, clean the closets and have a garage sale, or ask the local convenience store, fitness center, or any other mom-and-pop businesses in your area if they will let you set up a jar on the counter near the cash register and leave it for people to drop their donations into.

Try calling local Christian radio stations and see if you can make your plea over the air. You may even try writing up a press release and sending it to the local newspapers, family magazines, radio stations, and TV stations to see if they find your story interesting enough to cover. If you live in a small town or it is a slow news day, you may get some free publicity and the opportunity to ask for donations. A press release is somewhat similar to a support letter, except that it needs to sound like a good story that readers, listeners, and viewers will want to read, hear, and see. Try to keep your press release to only one page, make it sound like an article, include a photo if you have it, and make sure your contact information is included.

The following is an example of a press release that could be used as an article:

FOR IMMEDIATE RELEASE
Contact: Jane Smith
(777) 555-1111
janesmith@aol.com

LOCAL FAMILY SETS OUT TO EXPAND THEIR BORDERS

Just ask the Smiths what they want for Christmas this year, and it isn't their two front teeth. *(Start with a clever opening line that makes the reader want to know more.)*

This local couple wants nothing more than to bring home their little girl from China. *(Emphasize the fact that you are local residents, and tell the main point in a nutshell.)*

Bill and Jane have tried for more than five years to start a family, with no success. Finally, the couple began to look into adoption and realized it would be the perfect way to create a forever family. *(Appeal to the sympathies of readers.)*

They began the adoption process almost a year ago, and now they are waiting to receive pictures of their new daughter. Once they are matched with a child, they will travel to China for two weeks to finalize her adoption and bring her home. *(Provide more background information for your story.)*

"Infant girls are abandoned by the thousands in China, and many never have parents to call their own," says Bill. "The little girl who is waiting for us deserves to have a daddy." *(Include a personal quote within the press release.)*

The Smiths are almost ready to go except for the $12,000 they still need to raise in order to pay for the adoption trip, agency fees, and adoption fees in China. If you would like to help this couple fulfill their dream, donations can be made to a special account that has been established at Century Bank, 1234 Jones Ave., Tampa, FL 32323. *(Include the plea for assistance and the special account information.)*

For more information on this story or to contact the Smiths, call Jane Smith at 777-555-1111 or e-mail her at janesmith@aol.com. *(Always include a contact name and information at the top and bottom of the press release.)*

END

If writing letters and asking for donations is just something you feel you cannot do, how about fund-raising by selling products? There are several online companies that have been established especially to help adoptive families raise monies by selling goods. The programs work a lot like any school fund-raiser for candles, magazines, candy, or home décor items. The companies send you the catalogs, you go door-to-door or to friends and family and take orders, you mail the orders and the money to the company, and they send back the products and the profit check. (For examples of these companies and their contact information, see appendix E–Selected Adoption Financial Resources Web Sites.)

Of course, you don't have to go through a middleman to find products to sell. If you want to try your hand at raising some funds, consider a home-party company like Southern Living at Home, PartyLite candles, or Discovery Kids toys. You can even buy boxes of candy bars or cases of soda at a discount retailer, as long as they can legally be sold individually and without a permit, and ask your local shopping center if they will provide you a place where you may sell them to their customers.

If you want to fund-raise by holding a garage sale, see if you can get friends and neighbors to donate their unwanted items to your sale. Publish a classified ad to draw shoppers, and make it clear in the ad and on signs that you are raising funds for an adoption. Many people will donate beyond the price of the used item they are purchasing, if they know it is to help a child.

If your adoption decision is impacted by your finances, look carefully at the different countries that are open to international adoption. Some countries cost far less in accommodations, souvenirs, food, and air travel than others. Also, travel packages vary widely in price. When it is time to arrange your travel, make sure you compare different classes of fares if booking your flights directly with the airline. (Northwest, for example, has an "adoption fare." It is often higher than some published fares that can be found online, but it allows more flexibility in changing travel dates.) Try travel agencies, Priceline.com, Expedia.com, and other travel services to compare prices. Finally, consider whether an upgrade to first class for the long flight home with a baby or child would be worth the additional fees.

BEST PRACTICES OF FOREVER FAMILIES

My friend had a huge garage sale to raise money for her adoption. Her friends and family all brought items to sell, and they sold snacks, water bottles, and drinks. They made sure they had signs posted stating that the money was going toward their adoption, and in one weekend they raised more than $2,000.

—Adoptive mother of three daughters

APPLYING FOR ADOPTION GRANTS

There are a few organizations that offer adoption grants, but there is an increasing amount of competition for them. Most adoption grants are awarded based on financial need and are given by organizations who rely on donations. Some organizations are quite small and award only one grant a quarter or even per year. Some grants are given by adoption agencies themselves to families who are contracted to adopt a waiting child with them and have great financial need. (In cases of financial need, some agencies may offer a reduction of fees or rates based on a sliding scale.) As adoption becomes more visible within the church, hopefully there will be more grants given by local church-based adoption ministries.

One organization that has provided a substantial number of grants is Shaohannah's Hope, www.shaohannahshope.org. In 2001, singer Steven Curtis Chapman launched this foundation, which is named after his first adopted daughter from China and is dedicated to helping connect children and their forever families around the world through grants to adoptive families, a Web guide on how to adopt, efforts to assist orphans in foreign countries and at home, and programs to help churches begin their own adoption ministries.

In 2005, Shaohannah's Hope helped more than 275 families with their adoption finances through grants that averaged $3,000. The organization also made an impact worldwide, as it donated $10,000 to the "Tomorrow Plan," a project to help orphans in need of corrective surgeries; began work on rebuilding an orphanage in Kitgum, Uganda; agreed to help sponsor and oversee a committee of El Salvador officials as they modify their child-welfare placement system; and provided more than $50,000 to hurricane relief efforts in the affected Gulf Coast region to help reconstruct damaged orphan-care facilities.

In order to be considered for an adoption grant from any organization or foundation, prospective adoptive parents must go through an application process that often requires pulling together documents and letters of reference. Most organizations will not allow you to apply until you have successfully completed your home study. Once your home study is finished, you can begin the grant application process. Each application will require your name and contact information, but many will also require a letter explaining why you are applying for the grant and what your needs are, letters of reference, and financial documents such as the previous year's tax returns. Since you have already gathered most of this information for your home study and adoption paperwork, it should be easily accessible.

The easiest way to apply for grants is to first locate all the possibilities, then find out the deadlines for paperwork, when the awards are actually given, and if you are eligible. Finally, plan a day to fill out all the applications at once, since many require the same information. Look over each grant's requirements thoroughly to find out what items you will need to include. Make copies of the items that you need, including the multiple copies of your home study, financial statement, background checks, and reference letters. Then, write a letter on your home computer explaining your family's adoption story, why a grant is needed, and how much it would mean to your family. Include ways that you would help the grant-giving agency, such as telling people of their assistance, donating back to the agency if there is a time when you are able, volunteering to help the agency, or other ways that you would "pass along" the kindness given you. If letter writing is not your strong suit, do an Internet search for examples, ask other adoptive families if they would share their letters, or enlist a friend's help to create one. (See example letter #11.) Keep the letter on a personal computer or disk, so that you can change the organization name and address but use basically the same plea with each application.

If requesting assistance feels "wrong," ask yourself the following questions:

- Can we do this on our own and leave assistance monies for those who would not be able to adopt without them?
- Will we be able to adopt without financial assistance?

If you know that it would be next to impossible to adopt without help, there is nothing wrong with asking for it. The grant-giving organizations are designed for that purpose—to help children be united with forever families and to help loving families be able to bring their child home. This is an example of why God has asked Christians to live in fellowship with one another, so that needs can be met through community when they are too big for an individual to manage on his own. Is it humbling to tell others that you have a need? Of course it is, but pride should not be the barrier between your child and his or her forever family.

APPLYING FOR ADOPTION LOANS

On the other hand, if you are financially comfortable enough that although adoption would be a strain, you could manage it from your own funds, it might be better to leave grants for those who truly would not be able to adopt without them.

Applying for adoption loans is somewhat like applying for adoption grants, but there are generally fewer questions about your family and your adoption and more about your debts, assets, credit rating, and tax returns. Loans can be no-interest or low-interest from private organizations, or you can apply for a home-equity loan or other loan from your bank or another financial institution. For a list of some places to try for adoption loans, see appendix E.

Most grant and loan sources will want to know that you have already exhausted other funding options, and may ask that you apply to your bank for a loan or use existing savings such as an IRA or other retirement account before they will give you a grant or loan. Private grants may also require a cosigner to help ensure that monies will be repaid, even if you have outstanding credit.

BEING A GOOD STEWARD WITH YOUR ADOPTION FUNDS

Remember that in your adoption, as in every area of your life, you want to be a good steward of the blessings God has given you. Be fiscally responsible in your adoption process, so that you can have the best experience with the least financial worries. Be honest and make sure you keep up your tithes and offerings. Also keep in mind that the less money you already have to work with, the more room there is for God to really show you the way he works.

RED LIGHT, STOP!

Questions to consider at this point in your adoption journey:

____ Do you feel comfortable enough after reading this chapter to know for sure that you can make the right financial decisions for your adoption?

____ Have you asked your agency for a list of all fees, what they include, and how they are broken down?

____ Are you prepared to pay a birthmother's expenses? What if you meet her early in her pregnancy and she does not have health insurance?

____ Are you prepared to be on the lookout and protect yourselves from potential scams?

GREEN LIGHT, GO!

Action points for your adoption journey:

____ Ask God to show you the right avenues through which to raise the funds.

____ Create your adoption budget and figure out how much of it you already have, might need to borrow, might need to raise through grants and fund-raising, or will be able to come up with over the next year.

____ Make a list of fund-raising ideas that you are comfortable doing.

____ Talk to an accountant and your employer to see what tax credits and employer assistance you qualify for.

____ Pull all the documents together that you will need for grant and loan applications and make several copies of each of the following: last year's tax returns, your criminal background checks, your home study, your letters of reference, your financial statements, and your letter asking for assistance.

____ Begin mailing, faxing, or e-mailing your grant applications after your home study is completed, your agency is chosen, and you know what your adoption expenses will be.

____ Decide whether you can afford to work with a birthmother who has no medical insurance and who needs living expenses for several months. Do not jump at the first possibility of a baby if you know that you will not be able to afford it without considerable strain on your finances.

____ Research the best travel deals and options for your flights and accommodations if you are traveling internationally.

♥ *My Adoption Miracle*
I Wouldn't Change a Thing
by John Fuller, Vice President of Focus on the Family Broadcasting

One Sunday, our family was heading to church, and as the kids climbed into the van I did a mental head count to make sure no one got left behind. I counted five, but it felt like somebody was missing. I shared that with my wife, Dena, but we didn't think anything more of it. Call it a "senior moment"?

Then, a short time later, my wife had an encounter with the Lord. In her prayer time she was asking him, "Why don't you do something about all these children who don't have a home and somebody to love them? There are so many children being abandoned and abused. Why don't you do something, Lord?" He gently told her, "Why don't *you* do something?"

Dena came to me and said, "I think the Lord wants me to go hold babies in an orphanage."

I fully supported her, telling her we could get her to Romania or somewhere else with needy children to heed that call. I thought that'd be the answer to her heart's cry to reach out to the fatherless.

Dena prayed for several months to be sure it was the Lord's voice she was hearing, and eventually she admitted to me, "It's not going away. God talked to me about this a bit more. I told him, 'I just wish I could give them all a home.' He replied, 'You can give one a home.'"

About a month later, she came up to me and said, "I think the Lord wants us to do more. I think he wants us to adopt."

I was not against adoption. I had no sense of "We can't do that," just a real intrigue about the possibilities and ways that it might change our family.

We then remembered my feeling that day at the van that we were missing someone. So we started praying. After several months of asking God for guidance, we decided to put in an application with an agency in January 2003. We anxiously awaited what God might do, and whom he might bring us to adopt.

As most adoptive families have learned, however, the journey to open your heart and home usually takes some unexpected turns. So, a year later, when Romania had not opened its doors back up to international adoption, we were looking at a referral packet from Russia. This little guy, Zane, had been born prematurely, at just twenty-six weeks, and weighed only two pounds at birth, according to that country's medical records. He came with the possibility of fetal alcohol syndrome, something that affects far too many babies in the former Soviet states. I think we had talked to enough people that we had some pretty realistic expectations about the possibility of health challenges. And we were comfortable with God's sovereignty, and his grace to carry us through whatever he called us to do.

We prayed for a long time about the right child. Our kids prayed for the right little one. And then we did feel called, certain that Zane was that child. In March 2004 we traveled to Russia to eventually bring Zane home.

For a variety of reasons, it hasn't been easy bringing this little fellow into our lives, but because we prayed and the kids prayed with us for this child—and because God delayed the process for a long time—our family has done really well, even with the difficulties. Our other children have responded exceptionally well—even though Zane has special needs and pulls Dena's time and attention away from them. They usually respond with love and understanding, even when Zane behaves in ways that are difficult—even more difficult than most two-year-old boys. Less than a handful of times have I heard complaints from our other children, because they know this is who God led to us.

I've become passionate about adoption and orphan care. Becoming an adoptive parent has given me a newfound tenderness in my heart for special-needs kids. I didn't ask for one, but I gladly accept this assignment, this child. As we are discovering and working with Zane's special needs, there has been some dying to self. We've been challenged in unexpected ways, nearly every day. I'll be sixty-two years old when he leaves the nest, if he can leave the nest. It's not that I had grandiose plans for my son, but I did enter this process with some expectations and hopes. Hopes of, "Oh, I can take my son hunting some day." Well, I may not be able to take Zane hunting. And you know what? That's okay. This is not about me, not about my comfort and my plans. This is about God's leading, his work in our lives, his eternal plan and unfathomable ways.

Because of this boy's premature birth and circumstances surrounding his first nine months, we feel he is a survivor for a purpose. His purpose might be to affect us and a few other people, or God may be planning to use Zane to change the lives of lots of other people. We absolutely believe that God makes no mistakes. With this adoption, he has rocked our world, and that's a hard thing—but it's not a bad thing. It has stretched us way beyond what we thought we could handle. Zane will leave an indelible mark on us for the rest of our lives. And I wouldn't change a thing.

Chapter Six

The Great Paper Chase

If you've made it this far, you can see that completing any adoption is an exercise in prayer, paperwork, persistence, and patience. Whether you are adopting from the foster-care system, adopting a newborn domestically, or adopting a child internationally, any adoptive family can tell you that the adoption process will be a roller-coaster ride of frustration and exhilaration, tediousness and accomplishment, as you make your way through the months of collecting documents, filling out reams of paperwork, and waiting for the day when your child will be in your arms.

WORDS OF WISDOM
Better a patient man than a warrior.
—Proverbs 16:32 (NIV)

Paperwork, Persistence, and Patience

The first piece of adoption paperwork you will fill out is the application, but it certainly won't be your last. Every agency, attorney, and even facilitators have an application form. They use it to get to know you, to collect your identifying and contact information, and to get your thoughts on the journey you are about to embark on.

FILLING OUT THE INITIAL APPLICATION

Your initial application will look a lot like a job application. It is usually just a few pages that ask for your name, address, phone numbers, e-mail, Social Security numbers, employment information, educational background, and other identifying information. Many ask personal questions such as whether you have ever had counseling, a mental illness, or a history of substance abuse and ask about other adoptions and other children in your home. Your agency's application will probably ask if you already have a completed home study, are in the process of completing one, or have contacted a social worker for a home study yet. (It's okay to answer no to all of these if you haven't started yet.) Applications from Christian agencies might ask about your personal commitment to Christ and church involvement.

The application needs to be accompanied by the application fee, and signed (by both parties, if a married couple is applying). Filling out the application should be pretty painless and can be accomplished quickly if you have your Social Security numbers and other identifying information on hand.

TOOLS TO ORGANIZATION

As you begin the actual process of assembling the needed paperwork for an adoption and especially if you are handling the paperwork yourself (as opposed to hiring a dossier preparation service), it is vitally important that you start and stay organized. Buy an accordion file, empty a filing cabinet drawer, or choose whatever method will keep your paperwork together, organized, and accessible. Heavy plastic accordion files and manila file folders work well together because you can keep your paperwork in one place but separated into categories. You can also carry it with you in order to make copies, put in receipts, and have forms with you when you need them. The big drawback to a portable file is the possibility that it could get lost. If you choose this method of organization, carry it out of the house as little as possible, and make sure the folder is clearly labeled with your contact information in case it is misplaced. (Permanent markers write well on these folders.) It is also a good idea to keep a second set of copies of everything in the file in a permanent drawer at home. If you choose a file cabinet, note that there are times when you will need to have papers with you that might be back at home.

I DIDN'T KNOW THAT!

Always carry a blue ink pen with you, in case you need a signature (like a doctor's) on paperwork. Why blue? Some countries require that all signatures be in blue ink, because today's printers are so good at making photocopies that it is difficult to distinguish originals from copies when signatures are in black ink.

You can label your manila folders in whatever way feels comfortable. You might have folders labeled Agency Application and Agreement, Home Study, Immigration, Birthmother Info, Attorney, Background Checks, Finances, Receipts, Dossier, Birth Certificates, Medical Reports, Passports, and more. This file should be treated like a precious possession, because it will soon contain all the documents required to bring your child home.

Other items you will need to have on hand include the following:
- printer (or an easily accessible store that makes inexpensive copies)
- paper
- ink
- paper clips
- blue ballpoint pens (some countries require signatures to be in blue)
- staples and a stapler
- personal computer and access to the Internet (for researching and typing letters)
- calculator
- calendar, preferably an 18-month to two-year version
- notepads or spiral notebook
- stamps
- envelopes
- express-delivery service accounts and mailing supplies
- a place to get money orders or certified checks
- access to a notary public whose commission does not expire for at least a full calendar year

THE IMPORTANCE OF ACCURACY

Accuracy is all-important in the paperwork stage, especially if a foreign government will be scrutinizing papers. Dates by the signatures and notary dates should match on each document, and for some states the notary wording must be in a specific format. If you fill out an application by hand, such as the I-600A for immigration, make sure your handwriting is neat and legible. If you make mistakes, it is probably better to start over than to send in a marked-up form. Check and double-check your answers for mistakes, typos, or other inaccuracies. (Ask a friend to proofread it for you.)

Honesty is also important, especially with your agency, attorney, and social worker. They are working with you to help you adopt; don't make their job harder by withholding information or not telling the truth.

WORDS OF WISDOM
My God shall supply all your need according to His riches in glory by Christ Jesus.
—Philippians 4:19 (NKJV)

MAKING YOUR LIST, CHECKING IT THRICE
Create and keep a to-do list with you. On it you'll track phone calls you make,

contacts, documents you mail, and things you still need to do. Tuck the list into your file folder or drawer and consult it often.

Most agencies and attorneys who handle adoptions also provide you with lists of things that need to be done and the order in which they should be done. If you do not fully understand something on the list, even if you have already had it explained more than once, ask for the explanation again. You have never done this before, so no one expects you to be an expert. It is better to ask all your questions than to make mistakes that could cost time and money later.

Create a log of all documents, forms, or letters you send, the date each was mailed, and proof of mailing (such as registered mail, certified mail, return receipt, overnight). Also, keep a running log in a spiral notebook or on a notepad of phone calls you have made, including the date, time, subject matter, contact name, and phone number.

Writing the Right Letters

Letters are an important part of the adoption process. As explained in greater detail in chapter 3, the letter, photo album, scrapbook, or résumé you create for your child's birthparents will be what initially draws them to choose your family. Hopefully, your letter and pictures will be a cherished keepsake for the birthmother and birthfather to treasure when they think about the baby they are relinquishing to you.

LETTER TO BIRTHPARENTS

Do not agonize too much over putting the "perfect" words into your letter; just be yourself. Your letter should not be designed to catch the eye of every birthparent. It is being created for the right birthparents who will walk through the adoption journey with you. Your words should be honest and from the heart. Birthparents know that most of the people who qualify to adopt have the resources to raise their child. What they are looking for is a feeling of connection to you and—this is the most important part—the reassurance that you will remember their connection to the son or daughter you will in some ways share.

Following is a real-life letter to a birthparent created by the adoptive parents of two boys through domestic adoption:

EXAMPLE

Dear Birthparents:

We are Dwayne and Shelly, and we would like to share with you about us and our family. Hopefully this will help you in making the difficult decision that you are facing.

120

We have been married for fifteen years and have lived in central Florida since before we met. As newlyweds, we thought about having a large family, but we encountered infertility problems. After a couple of years of seeking treatment, we were told we could not conceive a child. In 1998 we adopted our son, Nicholas. We couldn't love him any more if he were our biological son. His adoption has been a very positive experience for us. We continue to exchange letters and pictures with Nicholas's birthmother.

A few years ago we felt ready for another child. Realizing there have been many advances in infertility medicine in the last few years, we decided to take one last shot at treatment. We were again told we could not conceive a child, so we knew immediately that we wanted to adopt again.

Dwayne enjoys working from home as a media consultant. In addition to assisting Dwayne, Shelly volunteers at the elementary school where Nicholas attends kindergarten. Shelly plans to stay home until the baby is older, and then may work part-time outside the home.

Running is one of Dwayne's favorite hobbies, and we all go to the gym regularly. Dwayne and Nicholas also like bike riding, and Shelly and Nicholas are learning to Rollerblade. Nicholas is also learning to play basketball.

Our house is a four-bedroom, 2½–bath home on a quiet street. Nicholas loves to play outside with his friends in the neighborhood. We plan to convert our play room / guest room into the baby's room. We also have a sweet little cocker spaniel named Casey.

After reading about us and looking at our photo album, we hope you feel better equipped to make your decision. We would love to meet you and answer any questions you may have.

Love,

*Shelly and Dwayne**

* Names have been changed

LETTER TO A FOREIGN COUNTRY

When you are adopting from a foreign country, most countries require that you write a letter asking to adopt a child and specifying what kind of child you would like to adopt. These letters are different from the personal letters to birthparents, as they are going to a government agency that will coordinate an international placement. The letter should give the adoptive parents' names and dates of birth, ask for permission to adopt a child, and state the child's preferred gender, age, and any special needs you will consider accepting. The letter should also state that the child will be loved, will never be abused or abandoned, and will be given the same rights as a birthchild in every area, including inheritance. Not all countries require this letter of petition, but many do. Following is an actual letter of petition to the country of China (the names have been changed):

EXAMPLE OF PETITION TO CHINA

January 27, 2005
To: The Officials of the China Center for Adoption Affairs
From: Alan and Nancy Williams

Dear Officials of the China Center for Adoption Affairs,
My name is Alan Williams, and I was born on (birth date here) in (city, state). My wife's name is Nancy Williams, and she was born on (birth date) in (city, state). We are both citizens of the United States.

It is our intention to adopt a child from China. We respectfully wish to adopt a healthy, female infant between the ages of 0 and 12 months. We have thought for years about adopting a child, especially one from the beautiful country of China. Our family has much love to share with a little girl who will help make our home and family complete.

After researching, we discovered that babies from China are very healthy due to the excellent care they receive. We have also talked and visited with other families who have adopted from China and have had a positive experience with your well-organized process.

We promise never to abuse or abandon this child. She will always enjoy the same rights as a biological child. We promise to raise her with lots of love and educate her to be a healthy adult.

Thank you so much for your consideration. We appreciate you!
Sincerely,
Alan D. Williams
Nancy K. Williams

THANK-YOU LETTER TO YOUR CHILD'S BIRTH FAMILY OR CAREGIVER(S)

As you travel the road to adoption, you may also want to place some personal letters into your file that you can give later in the adoption process. For domestic adoptions of infants, you may want to write a more personal letter to your child's birthmother, birthfather, or birth family, thanking them for the gift they have given and reassuring them that you will give your child the knowledge that he was loved and that the birthparents will be remembered. If your child was in the foster-care system or is being adopted internationally, you may feel led to write a letter to your child's caregivers. Foster families often like to hear the hearts of the adoptive families. In international adoption, it would be an extra special touch to write your letter in English and have it translated before you leave for your adoption, so that your son or daughter's caregivers can have something to remember you by. One letter might look like this:

EXAMPLE

Dear Foster Family,

We just wanted to thank you from the bottom of our hearts for taking such wonderful care of our son until the day he could be united with us and become part of our family. We appreciate the way God has used you in our child's life, and we will remember your compassion always. You took the time and opportunity to bless a child who needed you, and our family will be forever grateful.

We have been and will continue to pray for God's blessings on you!
(Insert child's name here)'s *adoptive family*

PERSONAL LETTERS TO YOUR CHILD

You may even want to write letters to your adopted child, telling him or her about your feelings during this process and how much you are looking forward to being his or her parents. For example, your letter might look like this:

EXAMPLE

Dear Daughter,

Although I do not yet know what you look like, how you will feel in my arms, or what adventures God has in store for us as a family, I can't wait to participate in the miracle of adoption he has for us. Your daddy and I have waited so long for you, and we know God chose you from the beginning of time to play a special role in our hearts and family.

God has great plans for you, my sweet daughter, and he loves you forever—just like we do. We can't wait to run and play together, to sing and laugh, and to teach you about how much Jesus loves you.

Hang in there, baby. Mommy and Daddy are coming soon.

Love,
Your Forever Family

BEST PRACTICES OF FOREVER FAMILIES

Many adoptive parents keep a detailed journal, scrapbook, videos, or online blog of their adoption experience. (Some do all of the above!) It not only allows them to share their feelings about their upcoming adoption with others, but also creates a legacy or life book for their adopted child to know his beginnings with your family. Choose the method you prefer, and make it prayerful, personal, and fun. It will be a treasure to you and your child!

COVER LETTERS FOR YOUR DOCUMENTS

Other letters that will need to be created include cover letters for various documents, such as documents sent for certification in the international paperwork process. All cover letters should be in standard business-letter format, including the date, the name and address of the party the documents are going to, your name and address, a short description of what you need to have done, and your signature. Remember that once you have created a letterhead (your name and address) and signature, you can keep saving the same file in your computer by giving it a different name and then altering the contents to fit the new purpose. For sample fund-raising letters and other documents, see appendix H: Sample Letters and Documents.

Documents Needed Domestically

The biggest job you will have in the beginning months of the adoption process is to collect paperwork. Lots and lots of paperwork. So much paperwork that you will wonder if you will ever get it all done, then you will wonder what to do with yourself when it is all turned in and the waiting begins.

Although these documents have been mentioned before, following is a handy checklist of paperwork you will need to complete or collect if you are adopting a newborn domestically or adopting from the foster-care system:

___ Favorable home study
___ Letter to the birthmother or birthparents (sometimes called a résumé or profile)
___ Financial statement
___ Most recent tax returns
___ Three to five letters of reference or reference contacts
___ A recent medical clearance
___ Photographs, photo album, or scrapbook
Criminal background checks:
___ local ___ child abuse
___ state

___ Copies of birth certificates
___ Copy of marriage license
___ Profile questionnaire

PROFILE QUESTIONNAIRE

The profile questionnaire is common for adoption agencies, social workers, and adoption attorneys to use. The purpose is to really get to know your motivations, the solidity of your relationships, and what kind of adoptive parent you will make. It digs deeper into your childhood experiences, relationships with siblings, marital relationship, parenting style, discipline style, personal accomplishments, and other items. They may also ask about pets and about whether you own any firearms (and, if so, where you keep them). A sample profile questionnaire is included in appendix H at the back of the book.

BIRTHMOTHER AD

If you will be searching for a birthmother yourself and your state allows classified advertising, you will need to write ad copy for your classified ad letting a birthmother know that you want to work with her. Ads are short (because newspapers charge by the word), sometimes contain abbreviations, and include a contact number for you or your attorney. Following is an example of an ad:

Thank you for giving your baby life. We would love to give your baby a family.
If you want to place your baby in a loving, Christian home, please call Melissa
and Brad at 1-XXX-XXX-XXXX.

Documents Needed for International Dossiers

The great paper chase can be even more detailed when it comes to international adoptions. Not only do the same documents need to be collected, but each document must be certified and authenticated, as explained later in this chapter. There also are extra documents that domestic adoptions don't require, like letters to foreign governments and the I-600A. Your dossier must be sent to the foreign government for them to approve your adoption.

Your checklist of documents usually needed in a dossier for international adoption will most likely include the following:

___ Home study
___ Letter of petition to adopt or other letter to the appropriate foreign adoption authority
___ New copies of birth certificates

___ New copy of marriage license
Criminal background checks:
    ___ local ___ child abuse
    ___ state
___ USCIS I–171H Approval
___ Financial statement
___ Federal income tax return
___ Medical clearance
___ Letters from employers
___ Letters of reference
___ Photos of the adoptive parents, family, and home
___ Passports (copies of the photo page)

MAKING YOUR DOSSIER OFFICIAL

International adoption paper chasing begins as soon as the agency application is accepted or a facilitator is contracted. You will order new copies of your birth certificates, as well as state and local criminal background checks. You will need to send in the I–600A "Application for Advance Processing of Orphan Petition" and be fingerprinted.

Your agency should provide you with the I–600A or have the link available on their Web site. If you need a copy of the form, you can read the instructions for filling it out and download it from http://uscis.gov/graphics/formsfee/forms/i-600a.htm. Some offices allow you to hand carry in your form and payment. Others require that the form and payment be mailed in. It is safest to mail all of your adoption documents in a way that can be traced, either through an express-delivery service such as Federal Express or DHL or through the Express Mail via the United States Post Office. Most agencies recommend using an express-delivery service, not the USPS (claiming that more forms have been lost through the U.S. Mail than through the other companies).

I DIDN'T KNOW THAT!

Warning: *Never* remove the certification pages or authentication pages from any document for any reason, including to make photocopying them easier. No staples should be removed from the documents, or it might invalidate the certification and authentication, and you would have to start all over.

After receiving your payment and form, the immigration office will send you a notice of when your fingerprint date has been scheduled. If you cannot make that date, alternate dates are usually included. The fingerprinting process requires going to the assigned authorized fingerprint site, which is either a USCIS office, Application Support Center (ASCs), or U.S. consular offices and military installations (abroad), and having your fingerprints taken. At your scheduled appointment time, take your appointment paper with you and go to the office. You may have to take a number and wait for a time. Then, a worker takes your fingerprints, usually digitally (black ink fingerprints are going the way of the dinosaur!), and you are finished. Take your spouse, a friend, or yourself to lunch or dinner after your appointment to celebrate this big step!

In the midst of this initial paperwork, you should be gathering the other documents for your dossier listed in the checklist. These are many of the same items that will also be needed by your social worker for a favorable home study.

I DIDN'T KNOW THAT!

In many countries your adoption documents may expire. New copies of birth certificates and marriage licenses usually have to be ordered from the state of birth or marriage or from VitalChek Network, Inc., www.vitalchek.com. Obviously, your birth certificate probably hasn't changed, but many country requirements still state that any dossier document's date of issuance must not be older than six months, a year, or eighteen months, depending on the country. Check with your agency to find out exactly what needs to be in your dossier and how old it can be.

As soon as these documents have been gathered and your home study is completed, your social worker will send a home study report to the USCIS office. The USCIS will review the home study and your FBI background check (conducted from your fingerprints), discuss with your social worker any possible issues in your background, and, if satisfied, issue an I-171H form, "Notice of Favorable Determination Concerning Applications for Advance Processing of Orphan Petition," which is sent through the mail. If you join any adoption chat groups or forums, you will soon notice that there is much rejoicing whenever an I-171H is received. It is usually the last piece of the dossier puzzle that needs to be assembled before the dossier is complete and ready to be sent to the adoption officials in the foreign country.

Before the dossier is sent off, however, each required document must be notarized (with specific wording as prescribed in your state's statutes) by a notary public whose commission does not expire for at least a year, then sent to the Department of State in the adopters' home state for certification, the process by which the Department of State verifies that the documents have been notarized by a currently licensed notary public in that state. When the documents have been sent back by the Department of State, they should be taken to the adoptive country's foreign consulate that handles documents from your state to be authenticated or apostilled. Documents can also be express-delivered to the appropriate consulate for the adoptive country to be authenticated or apostilled or sent to a courier who can hand carry them to the consulate for processing.

Authentication is the process of verifying the original paperwork as authentic by attaching a letter of authentication (usually in the language of the adoptive country). For countries that participate in the Hague Convention, the apostille process is the form of authentication required for each dossier document. The apostille services are also rendered at the foreign consulates. Once all documents, including the I–171H, have been certified and authenticated or apostilled, they are ready to be translated and sent (or sent and then translated) by your agency to the adoptive country. It is very important to make copies of each of your documents, including the certification and authentication pages, to keep in your records.

RED LIGHT, STOP!

Questions to consider at this point in your adoption journey:

____ Do you feel confident that you can pull the paperwork together?

____ Do you want to hire a dossier preparation service, or will your agency consult with you and help you with the paperwork?

____ Do you know whom to ask specific questions about documents that need to be collected?

____ Have you chosen a method of organization and assembled your tools?

____ (For international adoption) Have you sent in your I–600A, gone to the fingerprinting appointment, and received the I–171H?

____ (For domestic newborn adoption) Are you responsible for creating and placing ads in order to find a birthmother? If so, have you written and placed them?

GREEN LIGHT, GO!

Action points for your adoption journey:

____ Check and double-check each document as you receive it for the correct dates, wording, and signatures.

____ Fill out your profile questionnaire. (Husbands and wives must each fill out their own.)

____ Ask those you trust to write letters of reference and set a deadline for when they need to get them to you.

___ Send off the requests for background checks, new birth certificates, and marriage license copy.

___ Apply for a passport, if needed.

♥ *My Adoption Miracle*
I Always Wanted Four; God Gave Us Five
By Mary Brownback, wife of Republican senator Sam Brownback, KS

I always wanted four children. We had three, and then I had two miscarriages, so we looked into adoption to complete our family. Sam looked into Chinese adoption first, but I was really intent on a boy. We had two girls, Abby and Liz, and with Sam being in Washington so much, I really wanted another boy to be our son Andy's little brother.

In 1998, we sent our information to an agency in Kansas that worked with an orphanage run by Baptist missionaries in Guatemala. The missionaries care for the children and only place children from that orphanage. We sent our paperwork in May, and in November we got a referral for a little boy. We thought, "Wow! This will be quick." Little did we know.

Several more months went by while the legal paperwork was being gathered in Guatemala. Evidently, there was some confusion as to whether our son's birthfather was living. When it was discovered that he was deceased, paperwork had to be redone. Finally, in March 1999, I gave up. I decided that the paperwork was simply not going to be straightened out, and this little boy would not become ours. Sam and I decided to go ahead and submit paperwork to another agency to adopt from China. We sent our paperwork to China in April, and the first week of May we got a call from the original agency saying, "Okay. Come get your baby in Guatemala."

In mid-May, before school was out for our other three, we all went to Guatemala. Once we got down there, it went very fast. We arrived late on a Sunday evening and went to the embassy, where we met Mark. Monday we went to the home of the birthmother, who had relinquished him just after birth, for the required DNA testing. Early Tuesday morning, we were on our way home again with eighteen-month-old Mark in tow. We spent the summer adjusting to being a family of six with a toddler in the house again.

In September, we got another call. This time, it was from the agency handling our paperwork to China. They had a referral for us of a little girl! While we had not forgotten about our paperwork with the second agency and had decided to leave it in their hands, we never expected a second referral so soon. Both of us, Liz, and a nephew traveled to China in December, returning home with twenty-month-old Jenna the week before Christmas.

Those first days home were chaotic. I remember a day or two after I got home, Andy had basketball practice after school and I forgot to pick him up. He called, and as soon as I heard his voice I knew what I had done. When I got to school, Andy had told the coach that I had just gotten back from China—completing our second adoption in a year.

The coach said, "Is your mom crazy?" Andy's response was, "No, my dad is. My mom just goes along with it."

Seriously, though, Sam and I thought about pulling our second set of paperwork back, but then we thought, "Why not?" I'm sort of a jump-in-the-deep-end-before-you-think-about-it kind of person, so we jumped. We knew they would be close in age and would have each other to play with. We had the means to provide for them and the love to give them. We did think it would take longer, but then the picture came, and how can you say no?

Mark and Jenna are now in elementary school, and I don't remember what life was like without them. Looking back, I think it was a good thing that we had to wait so long for Mark's paperwork to get straightened out because our daughter Liz was having a hard time with the idea of us adopting. She was twelve, and she wasn't at all sure we should do it. Now she and Mark are really close.

Probably the hardest thing in our adoption was meeting Mark's nanny in Guatemala. He had been in the orphanage since shortly after birth, and she had cared for him since he arrived. He cried for her when they parted. It was sad, and our kids wondered if we were doing the right thing. We explained that his mother had given him up at birth and could not care for him and that an orphanage, even with wonderful caregivers, is not a family. After hearing that and seeing the conditions down there, it really brought home to our kids that adoption is a good thing—that we could give Mark a home, running water, education. We could love him and provide for him.

I can see as I look back how God put us all together, and I really believe that Mark and Jenna were meant for our family.

Part Three

The Paperwork Is Finished and the Wait Begins

But they that wait upon the LORD shall renew their strength; they shall mount up with wings as eagles; they shall run, and not be weary; and they shall walk, and not faint.
—Isaiah 40:31 (KJV)

Today I Closed the Nursery Door
By Sheena Nesbitt
November 2005
(written while waiting to adopt)

Today I closed the nursery door,
Afraid of how I feel.
I have become attached to a child,
Who, as of yet, is not real.

Today I put away the toys,
That would belong to him.
The Tonka truck, the teddy bear,
The little chair he'd sit in.

Today I read the final book,
We would have read together.
Nursery rhymes and fairy tales,
And happily ever afters.

Today I finished his life book,
Of the life he could have had.
A warm home, lots of laughter,
A loving mom and dad.

Today I put that life book,
Up on the highest shelf.
I will not linger, I will no longer dream,
I refuse to delude myself.

Today it became clear to me,
That I do not have a son.
And I have absolutely no control,
Of if I'll ever have one.

My life, my future, my family, my child,
Are all in the hands of others.
They will decide what is best for me,
And whether or not I'm a mother.

So I closed the books, closed the door,
And put the toys away.
I am a mommy without a child,
I realized that today.

Chapter Seven

Praying for Patience

Probably the hardest thing to do in the whole adoption process, especially for adoptive moms-to-be, is to wait. Forget all the paperwork, personal questions, scrutiny, and trying to make the money work. All of that seems like a walk in the park compared to waiting for your child. In fact, those who are in the waiting stage often look back at the paper-chasing phase with fondness, because at least then their time was occupied accomplishing things that they knew would bring them closer and closer to their dream of becoming united with a child as a forever family.

Whether your wait is two weeks or two years, waiting is tough. However, waiting has a God-designed purpose. God does not always work immediately. In fact, he hardly ever does. He often places his people in the uncomfortable position of waiting, and he uses that time to grow your faith in him, to stretch you beyond your comfort zone into a new level of trusting and believing in him. The waiting time is a growing time, to be used to actively pursue the heart of God and his plan and purpose for you and your family. There are also lots of practical details to take care of in preparation for this new addition, like lining up child care, pediatricians, health insurance, and your support system.

Do not waste your wait time complaining about what you do not yet have (your child), but instead make it your goal to ask God, "Lord, what would you have me do during this wait time to draw me closer to you, to my spouse, and to the people you have placed in my life?" Ask him to help you get the focus off yourself and onto the work he would have you do in the meantime. He will honor these requests and make your wait time fruitful and satisfying.

Getting Ready for Life with a Little One
FIND A PEDIATRICIAN
One of the things every good parent needs is a pediatrician who is knowledgeable, caring, and taking on new patients. Before you get the call that you have

been chosen by a birthmother, that your foster child is ready to come home, or that your international referral is here, you should locate and meet with a pediatrician in your area who you feel will do a great job for your family.

Some things to consider when choosing a pediatrician:

- The distance to the office from your home
- The hours the doctor is open and available
- Whether or not the doctor is a Christian
- Whether or not the doctor is accepting new patients
- If this doctor is a preferred provider on your insurance plan
- If the doctor has other adopted patients or has a specialty in adoption

Most pediatricians who are accepting new patients will meet with you (for free) prior to the time when you bring home your child. Prepare a list of questions for the doctor, and get a feel for how comfortable you are with his answers and his demeanor. After all, this is a doctor who may play a prominent role in your family's life for years to come. You will be entrusting the health of your child to this man or woman. If you do not get a good feeling after your initial meeting, find another pediatrician.

When you schedule your meeting, arrive a few minutes early. Spend time in the waiting room observing. Take note of the following:

- Is the waiting room filled or overfilled?
- Does the doctor have a separate waiting area for sick children, or is everybody waiting in the same room?
- Is the waiting room clean?
- Does it have toys, books, or other ways to entertain children?
- Are the staff members friendly and knowledgeable?

If you already have a pediatrician, be sure to make an appointment (preferably before your child comes home) to fill him or her in on the details. It's important that your child's pediatrician knows where your child was adopted from and any history you can give. With this knowledge, the doctor can be more understanding and knowledgeable about developmental delays. If your adopted child suffered from fetal alcohol syndrome or had a birthmom who was a substance abuser, this information is vital for your child's doctor to know, so the doctor can give you advice on nutrition, care, bonding, and even referrals, among other things.

If you are adopting internationally, it is important to inform your pediatrician or find one who specializes in adopted children because they may be able to evaluate and test your child for illnesses or diseases they might have picked up in their country. They also might be able to run tests to determine a child's age (if it is uncertain), and to give you instructions on how to help your child catch up nutritionally and developmentally. Most international children will also have to have blood work done to see if they have had the immunizations they need.

The American Academy of Pediatrics has developed a list of pediatricians who specialize in adoption and foster care. The list is organized by state, although a few states have no doctors listed. If no doctor is listed, this does not necessarily mean that adoption specialists do not exist in particular states, just that their information has not been submitted to the AAP. Ask your agency and other adoptive families for their recommendations to find a pediatrician who will serve your family well. To find the directory, visit the "Parenting Corner" of the AAP's Web site at www.aap.org, then click on "Topics A–E" and drop down to "Adoption." The AAP site also includes a wealth of information about children's health, including growth charts, car-seat guides, and advice on everything from bed-wetting to bicycle riding.

FIGURE OUT YOUR INSURANCE

As you choose a pediatrician, it will be important to coordinate the doctor and your insurance. There are both federal and state laws that affect whether your adopted child is eligible for health insurance. If you have health insurance through your employer, these kinds of insurance plans are regulated federally. If you have an individual plan, your insurance is regulated by your state. If your plan is covered or regulated federally, federal law requires that adoptive children receive the same coverage as biological children.

The Health Insurance Portability and Accountability Act of 1996 (HIPAA) goes a step further. It states that insurers can't give you a waiting period or refuse to cover preexisting conditions of a child under eighteen who is adopted or placed for adoption and who is enrolled in a health benefit plan within thirty days of the date of adoption or placement for adoption. This provision applies equally to domestic and foreign adoptions.

In other words, your adopted child's preexisting conditions should be covered if you have a group plan—if (and it's a big *if*)—you enroll your child within thirty days of your adoption. So when you have jet lag after two weeks in China or have spent the last two months flying back and forth to Russia, do not neglect to cover all your insurance bases. In fact, the wait time before your child is placed with you is the perfect time to figure out what kind of coverage you have, if you need to change insurers, and what their requirements are for enrollment of your new child. Ask them to send you the enrollment forms, and get them filled out as completely as you can. Find out if you can send them to your benefits administrator before your child comes home.

If you have an individual plan, you will need to check the regulations of your state to see what coverage of your adopted child your insurer is obligated to provide. You can call your state's insurance commissioner consumer hot line to find out what you can expect from your insurer. Under the Child Citizenship Act of 2000, children who are adopted internationally are entitled to automatic citizenship and therefore may apply for Medicaid.

PREPARE FOR CHILDCARE

If you work outside the home, you will need to find reliable childcare that you can afford. There are a variety of options: a childcare provider who will come to your home to care for your child, a provider who keeps children in her or his home, or a day-care facility. Whichever method you choose, the time to make plans is now. Many childcare providers and day cares have waiting lists. You will want to inspect and interview the person (or people) who will be with your child many hours during the day. Ask for advice from other families who work, and check out the background and references of any provider you interview. Following are some of the questions you might want to ask:

- Are you a Christian?
- Are you licensed to provide childcare?
- What is the maximum number of children for whom you are licensed or are able to provide care?
- Do you provide the food for my child, or am I responsible for providing food?
- What vacation times do you take? Holidays?
- Can you offer a substitute when you are on vacation or ill?
- Do I pay for your vacation time?
- Do I pay for your time when I'm on vacation?
- Do I still pay for sick days?
- If my child becomes ill, what is your policy for notifying me and for pick-up?
- How much do you charge?
- How often do you raise your prices?
- What activities do you do with the children?
- Do you have a daily schedule I can see?
- Do the children play outside?
- How do you discipline?

- Can I drop in for a visit without notice? (If the answer is no, you might want to choose another caregiver.)
- What plan do you have for an emergency?
- How much notice do I need to give if I decide I no longer will need your services?
- Will my child only be in your home, or do you go places with children in your care? Would you notify me prior to taking my child anywhere?

If you choose in-home childcare, you will need to report the monies you pay on your federal income taxes and provide your caregiver with a 1099 at the end of the year. In all cases for the childcare provider, this is a job. Be sure to extend professional courtesies like calling if you are running late (and try not to be late), if your child is sick, or to schedule vacation days.

Do not bring a sick child to infect the other children (or the worker). And, if you take time off and want to keep your child with you, keep in mind that many workers expect to be paid anyway—unless you've worked this out in advance.

FIND LOCAL ADOPTION SUPPORT GROUPS

During the wait, find local adoption support groups so that you can share with other families what you are experiencing during the process and after your child comes home. Veteran adoptive families can be a treasure trove of good information and advice to make your transition easier. Just like some families stay friends for years with others who were in their childbirth classes, you want to develop a circle of friends who share in the unique aspects of adoption. If your child will be an international child or transracial adoption, find other families with children of their race or country so that your child doesn't always feel different because he or she looks different from the rest of your family. Local adoption support groups can be found through your agency, through the Internet, or through putting the word out that you are looking.

LOOK INTO EDUCATIONAL OPTIONS

If you adopt an older child, you will need to look into local schools and decide if you want to enroll your child in a public or private school, or if you want to homeschool. In some states if you are adopting a child from state care, the state expects the adopted child to be enrolled in public schools for a supervisory period following the adoption. Know the laws in your state, so that you can make the educational choices that best fit your family. Visit the local public and private schools, check out their requirements and curriculum, and talk to the staff. If your child has special needs, find out exactly what programs are available.

If you are interested in homeschooling, attend local homeschool support group meetings and find out the laws in your state that govern homeschooling.

Ask to meet your child's teacher ahead of time, because teachers can assist adopted children on many levels. They can help through assessing skills and education and then helping locate resources for you within the public school system that address your child's specific needs; they can place your child in a classroom buddy system with a peer to help him or her develop friends; they often have access to information and services offered within your community's private, public, and nonprofit sectors; they can also give you updates and insights into your child's behavior in the classroom and with his classmates.

DECIDE ON DISCIPLINE STYLES

The wait time is the time to decide what discipline styles you plan to use and how to be an effective, loving authority. There are many resources that can help you learn how to raise your child to be loving, obedient, and respectful of authority. Talk with your spouse now about different parenting situations and how you will handle them. It is never too early to think about whether or not you think spanking is an appropriate mode of discipline (especially if your child has experienced abuse in his or her past), if you can speak calmly or tend to yell, and how you will work together as a team. Decide whether or not you will allow your child to sleep in your bed with you to be comforted, or if you will go to him or her. You can even think ahead and talk about how you feel about TVs, phones, and computers in the bedroom, and at what age you feel dating is appropriate. Your conversations now will lay the groundwork for effective parenting throughout your child's life.

PRAYER PARTNERS

As you go through what might seem like an interminable wait, find a prayer partner to walk with you. This may be your spouse, a sibling, a parent, or a friend. It should be someone you can trust, meet with regularly, and share with openly. Make a habit of getting together with someone to pray on a regular basis, preferably at least weekly. This can be one of the best habits you have ever started, as you will be able to witness and recall together the way God is personally working in your lives.

Learning Opportunities During the Wait

A great way to use your wait time wisely is to learn. Absorb all the knowledge you can from others, from great literature, and from your Bible. Learn about parenting, about the heart of God, and about the gifts and talents he has given you. Make it your goal to learn at least one thing every day that you did not know. Maybe you will want to read about personality styles and temperaments and how these affect your thoughts, emotions, and decisions. Perhaps you will want to take a *spiritual gifts* test for the first time to see where your skills and talents lie that you can use to do the work God would have you do for him. If you are adopting internationally, take some time to learn about your child's native country so that you can be prepared when you visit it, and so that you can share with your child later about his country of origin.

WORDS OF WISDOM

The LORD himself goes before you and will be with you; he will never leave you nor forsake you. Do not be afraid; do not be discouraged.
—Deuteronomy 31:8 (NIV)

Become better educated about parenting. Read not only books about adoption but also great parenting books that can help you prepare for becoming a mom and a dad or continuing your parenthood journey. To help you get on the same page in this area and acquire some new skills, take some parenting classes during your wait. Many churches offer the Gary and Anne Marie Ezzo course "Growing Kids God's Way" or other series on parenting. Exchanging information and sharing with other families in your classes, who often become lifelong friends, can be as valuable as the course information itself.

PARENTING RESOURCES

If you are looking for some Christian parenting resources that can be good starting points for discussion, James Dobson's books are some of the most classic Christian parenting literature. Titles like *The Strong-Willed Child, Bringing Up Boys*, and *Dare to Discipline* line the shelves of hundreds of thousands of Christian homes. Dobson is the founder of Focus on the Family, which also offers a daily radio broadcast on family-oriented issues on Christian radio stations around the world. You can even listen to the broadcasts online. Focus also operates a Web site with many valuable parenting articles, links, and other resources. Visit Focus on the Family at www.family.org.

Dennis and Barbara Rainey are the parents of six children, and their FamilyLife ministry is another great resource for Christian families to tap into. The Raineys offer tips on parenting, keeping your marriage alive, and even adoption on their Web site, www.familylife.com. The organization has come up with some great products for families, including a "Simply Romantic Nights" kit for married couples to create their own steamy date nights.

In recent years, former television star Lisa Whelchel has become a prolific author of some wonderful family tools. Whelchel is a homeschooling mom of three, and her book *Creative Correction* gives parents new ideas for disciplining their children in a way that not only brings surface compliance but also reaches the heart. She also wrote *Taking Care of the "Me" in Mommy: Realistic Tips for Becoming a Better Mom—Spirit, Body & Soul*, which will help you save time for the more important things.

Another beautiful parenting book is *Sacred Parenting: How Raising Children Shapes Our Souls* by Gary L. Thomas. In this book, Thomas points out that parenting is as much a learning experience for adults as it is for the kids—perhaps more so. Parenting molds our character and draws us closer to the heart of God. *Sacred Parenting* affirms the spiritual value of being a parent, examining the holy aspect of the parent-child relationship.

For books to help you improve your marriage and gain knowledge of how you love and interact with others, read books such as Dr. Emerson Eggerich's *Love and Respect*, Gary Chapman's *The Five Love Languages*, and Stormie Omartian's *The Power of a Praying Wife*. Also, books on personality types and relationships by authors such as Florence Littauer and Gary Smalley are must-reads (and should keep you busy while you are waiting).

USING THE WAIT TO REACH OUT

campaign volunteer?

The waiting period is also a good time to reach out to others. Do not isolate yourself, as isolation lays the groundwork for self-pity and even depression. Make it your goal to do something for someone else—a random act of kindness—as often as you can. Offer to be a listening ear, a driver for someone without a car, or a volunteer. Maybe you can be the one to coordinate a food drive in your neighborhood, host a covered-dish dinner at church, or offer to man the phone lines of a crisis hot line. There are numerous ways that you can help someone who needs a hand—whether it is visiting an elderly neighbor who is often alone or singing in your church's choir. Ask the Lord to put people in your path who need you, and watch out for the results!

USING THE WAIT TO DRAW CLOSER TO GOD

One of the most important ways you can spend time during your waiting period is to focus on God. Develop a plan to start a quiet time or extend the one you have, going deeper into Bible study, prayer, and worship. It is difficult to find time for God when a little one comes home and demands your energy and attention. In fact, many parents enter a very dry time spiritually when their children are young because the time is so limited (and the sleep is too). Fill yourself with God's Word, and spend time listening for him closely, so that he can give you the strength for the tasks that lie ahead. If you do not have a Bible, now is the time to get one. Head for the nearest Christian bookstore and ask a staff member to help you find one that has the study aids you need. If you have a Bible but no study aids, it might be refreshing to pick up a new Bible study, concordance, or devotional to get you excited about your quiet time again. Appreciate this opportunity to go deeper with God, so that he can prepare you to be the mother and father he wants you to be, and you can guide your child toward a life with him.

USING THE WAIT TO PRAY FOR YOUR CHILD

As you are deepening your relationship with God, begin to pray for your child. Pray for him as often as you think of him (which means you will be learning how to pray continually). Pray that he is being nurtured and cared for, that he has food and shelter, and that his birth family will be comforted. Pray specifically for his birthmother and birthfather, that they will be protected and that in some way you can be a witness to them about Christ. Even if you know that you will never meet them, pray that this experience will send them seeking God and that he will meet their needs. Pray for your child's health and safety, and most of all pray that his heart will be tender toward the Lord and that he will grow up to love and follow him all the days of his life. There is no greater gift you can give your child than to intercede before the throne of God for him all the days of his life.

USING THE WAIT TO RAISE FUNDS

You can also use the wait time you have been given (and, yes, it really is a gift), to raise the funds you need to complete the adoption. Develop some creative fund-raisers or do something as simple as holding a car wash or bake sale. The wait time is a good time to write your letters asking for support and to make sure you keep a file of them with you in the car to hand out when you go to the bank, the grocery store, or the dry cleaners. You never know who God will use to help you bring home your child, and those who help you are joining in his work and his blessings. (See chapter 5 for more fund-raising ideas.)

USING THE WAIT TO WORK

Make sure your budget is in order for when your child comes home. Use the wait to pay off those credit cards and reserve funds for the extra monthly expenses of diapers, formula, and trips to the pediatrician. The last thing you want to have to do is work extra shifts at your job or go to work outside the home (if you plan to be a stay-at-home parent) because your finances dictate that you need more money to make ends meet. Do the number crunching and penny pinching now so that later you can spend time with your child instead of in the office. Yes, the $1,500 designer crib with Egyptian cotton cri... would be absolutely beautiful and perfect in your nursery, but the $50 one from the neighbor's garage sale might be the more fiscally sound choice. And if you have $1,500 that you could spend on a designer crib, pray about it first. You may still opt for the $50 one and give the other $1,450 to help another family adopt.

I DIDN'T KNOW THAT!

For the past 40 years, the United States Department of Agriculture (USDA) has estimated the annual costs of raising a child. In 2004, the American two-child, married-couple family in the middle-income group spends [spent] an average of $9,840 to $10,900 in child-rearing expenses annually per child.[28]
—Mark Lino, *Expenditures on Children by Families, 2004*

If you do need extra funds in order to have more time later, the wait time can be a good time to work. Work not only pays the bills and helps you develop savings, but it also helps occupy your time. Find out if you can work overtime, take on a second job, or find a job you can do at home if this will help you meet your long-term financial goals. Using the time to work can also mean working on projects you have been putting off. Maybe the outside of your home needs to be painted or the lawn weeded. Maybe you have been telling a friend for months that you would help her clean out her garage. The wait time is a good time to put yourself to work. You get the benefit of the extra finances, or the satisfaction of seeing at least *something* that is finished and accomplished (unlike your adoption, which you are still waiting for).

USING THE WAIT TO REST

Of course, work time also has to be balanced with rest time, and God may be calling you to use some of your wait to rest. If your schedule is overcommitted, how are you going to fit a child into it? If you claim that it is too full just because you are trying to fill the time while you are waiting, you may be too tired to enjoy your child once he or she gets here! Ask God if he wants you to slow down during this period of waiting. Maybe he is trying to teach you to stop and smell the roses, to enjoy a walk on the beach, or to be still and wait for him. Now is a good time to establish a Sabbath, a day of rest, and get into the habit of it. If you do not learn to rest, how will you teach your child to rest?

USING THE WAIT TO GRIEVE

For those who have lost children to miscarriages or failed pregnancies, been unable to conceive, or experienced adoptions that fell through, this wait time may be your time to grieve. Walking through the steps and stages of grief is an important part of healing. Without grieving and healing, hearts can become hardened and bitter, or they can be closed and unwilling to love again. Use some of your wait time to grieve your losses. Cry, talk to a counselor, or pour your heart out to your best friend. Get on your knees and beg God to take the pain, the anger, and the mistrust and to renew your heart and hope. Ask him to heal the wounds in your heart and spirit perfectly, so that they are not hardened and calloused with scar tissue, but soft and pliable and ready to love him and the child he gives you. Grieve the loss of your dream of a child growing in your own body, a child that looks like you or your husband. Ask God to help you see adoption as first choice, not second-best. He will bring healing and help you be prepared to love your adopted child fully.

WORDS OF WISDOM

I cried out to the LORD in my suffering, and he heard me. He set me free from all my fears.
—Psalm 34:6 (NLT)

Another way to use the time you are waiting (boy, with all these things to do, the wait should fly by now!) is to develop your talents. Once you have a child, time just for yourself is limited and sometimes nonexistent. Why not use the wait to further develop a talent you possess but have never had the chance to polish or brush up on? If you have always wanted to take voice lessons or learn to throw clay on a potter's wheel, sign up for lessons now. Have some fun, and use the gifts God has given you. Maybe for you it is piano lessons, and for your husband it is gourmet cooking. Take a fun class together, or try your hand at writing a novel. If you have a heart's desire that you have never fulfilled, the waiting period is a great time to go for it. You may never get another chance, and you will be a better mom or dad when you feel good about yourself and the unique talents God has gifted you with.

USING THE WAIT TO CREATE

You can also use the time to create something wonderful. Plant a garden that will bloom in the spring or give you vegetables in the summer. Create a life book for your child with a journal of your adoption experience, pictures of his native country, and mementos that you have picked up along the way. Paint a picture for the nursery, or put together a scrapbook of all those pictures you have been meaning to organize. Make a sculpture, or write a poem or a song. Give birth to something you create as you are waiting for the birth of your family. You are uniquely gifted, and what you make will be a one-of-a-kind legacy for your child.

Using the Wait to Spend Time with Others

While you are in this waiting period, spend time with others. Once your child is home, you will focus much of your time on him or her. For now, you can spend time developing relationships with those at church, in a Bible study, in your neighborhood, or at your office. Get connected now to local adoptive families and support groups, or join a small group fellowship. Spend extra time with your siblings and parents, and ask your parents what they would do differently if they had you to raise all over again. Plug in to your church's ministries, and spend time making friendships and deepening bonds with other families who can support you when your child comes home.

Using the Wait to Get Ready

Before you can bring your child home, you have to make a place for him in your house. This might mean he will be sharing a room with other siblings and needs a bed and space for his things in the closet, or it might mean he will have a nursery all to himself. Either way, you can occupy some of your waiting time by putting all the pieces in place. If you are adopting an infant, you will need a crib, a place to change the baby, a wardrobe or dresser for clothing and supplies, a car seat, a highchair, diapers, clothing, blankets, crib sheets, baby wipes, formula, and bottles. These are the bare necessities, but you can also have fun indulging in some cute baby clothes!

Other things you might want to have on hand include:

- An infant swing (Most babies do not use swings past about six to eight months of age.)
- A portable crib
- A mobile
- A baby monitor
- A CD player or something to play music
- Toys
- Stuffed animals
- Pictures for the walls
- Shelves
- Storybooks
- Stroller
- Shopping-cart padded protector

- Sippy cups
- Baby food
- Pacifiers
- Bibs

Yes, babies come with a full arsenal of equipment. (And your pristine home will never look the same!)

If your child is already mobile, you will also need to childproof your home. This means looking at your house from the eye-level perspective of a crawling or toddling child (some people actually crawl on the floor themselves to get that perspective) to see what corners they might bump into, electrical sockets they might poke things into (you can buy inexpensive plastic covers for them), cords they might pull on, glass figurines they might grab and break, and other dangers. If you want to be thrifty, many childproofing items can be found at thrift stores and garage sales. Friends and family might opt to give you a baby shower, and if you get the must-haves first you can always accumulate more when you get home.

If you are adopting a toddler or an older child, you will need to decide if you still need a crib or want to go with a toddler bed or adult-sized bed. You will also need to decorate the room and buy some special things that can belong to the child. Pick out a blanket, a stuffed toy, or an other object he or she can hang on to for security, and make the room comfortable and fun. Get your other kids in on the decorating act, and have a blast.

Let them paint a wall or help decorate the room. Help them invest and take ownership in this adventure the entire family is embarking on.

RED LIGHT, STOP!

Questions to consider at this point in your adoption journey:

____ What things do you want or need to learn before your child comes home?

____ Do you have the tools you need to go deeper in your relationship with God during this wait time?

____ Do you keep a Sabbath or other time of rest?

____ Are you working on a project that will help your finances?

____ Are you connecting with others who are also on the adoption journey?

____ Are you giving your time to help others?

____ Are you getting prepared to parent by finding a doctor, insurance, and parenting resources?

____ Are you praying for your child?

GREEN LIGHT, GO!

Action points for your adoption journey:

____ Develop or deepen your daily quiet time with God.

____ Pray for your child.

____ Find a pediatrician, and make sure your insurance coverage is in place.

____ Choose a parenting class, a good book, or a Bible study that you (or you and your spouse) can take or get involved in.

____ Get to know other adoptive families.

____ Find a prayer partner to pray with at least once a week.

♥ *My Adoption Miracle*
Blessings Through Loss
by Stormie Omartian, author

Diane and I were best friends from the moment we met each other in high school while acting in the school play. Diane was funny and smart, and we had a lot in common. We stayed close friends through college, career years, getting married to our respective husbands, and having children. My husband and I had two children, Christopher and Amanda, about four years apart. Diane and her husband, Jack, had one child, John David, born right in between our two. That meant when Christopher was ten, John was eight, and Amanda was six. Our families were close and spent every holiday together, and sometimes John went on vacation with our family.

When Diane was in her early forties, she was diagnosed with breast cancer. After a terrible fight for her life, she died a year later. John David was eight at the time, and he had lived with us for the six months prior to her death so that Jack could take care of Diane. After she died, John David lived with us for months so that Jack could get back on his feet. After he reunited with his dad, they moved to Oregon where his dad could retire and devote his time to taking care of him. We still spent every holiday together like one big family.

A few years later I got a call from the Oregon police department. The officer said, "John Kendrick was killed in a car accident." I thought he was talking about John David, the son, and I was devastated and shocked. But when I asked where his father was, they explained that it was his father who had been killed by a drunk driver who had run a red light. We had called his father "Jack" all these years, and I had forgotten that his legal name was actually John.

My daughter and I got on a plane as soon as we could and flew out to be with John and make funeral arrangements. On the plane I thought about how agonizing Diane's death was and what a relief it was when she died and didn't have to suffer anymore. But Jack's death being so sudden was extremely hard for all of us to get out arms around. John was fifteen at the time and needed his dad so much. I didn't know how he would handle this tragedy.

When John was born, Diane and Jack asked us to take John into our family if anything happened to them. Of course we agreed and he was left to us in their will. None of us ever thought anything like this would happen. John David had been part of our hearts and our family since he was born. Having him as a legal family member seemed natural to us. And he has continued to be such a blessing to all of us. He is smart and funny, just like his mom and dad. Looking back now I see that God knew we needed one normal person in our family, so he gave us John.

John David stayed in Oregon to finish high school with his friends and spent summers and vacations with us, just like always. He adjusted so well and is such a wonderful young man. Now he is married to the perfect girl for him and they are expecting a baby in a few months. He does social work for the homeless. We never formalized the adoption because we wanted John David to keep the legacy of his wonderful original family and my beautiful friend, Diane. I couldn't take any credit for how great he turned out. He was great from the start. We are his family on earth, and he has a family in heaven. Amanda and Christopher call him their brother, and he is in every way my son. I was there when he was born, and now he is my adoption miracle.

Chapter Eight

What Do You Tell Everybody?

For married couples who make plans to adopt, the decision usually comes after much discussion and prayer. One of you initially had the idea, thought about it, perhaps researched it, then shared your thoughts and feelings with your spouse. By the time the two of you decide to proceed, the adoption is old news to you. However, if you have kept this time of discussion to yourselves, it is good to be prepared for the reactions of others the first time you share it with them.

If you are married, discuss with each other whom you want to tell and what details you want to share. Usually, one spouse is more outgoing and talkative than the other. Remember that your spouse will have to respond to whatever you share as well. If he or she would like some things to remain private, it is important to know that before it is too late!

When you tell anyone about your plans to adopt, it's important to evaluate the situation before you speak. Ask yourself if this is a person who will react positively or negatively, so that you can be prepared for their reaction. Also, if someone does say something that hurts you or makes you angry, be careful that you do not lash out. Wise parents-to-be understand that people are naturally concerned, nosy, or apt to share the horror stories they have heard. Unkind words and comments can last a lifetime. Even if someone hurts you, you don't want to hurt them right back.

Once you start telling people, you will be barraged from that point forward with questions about how the process is going and when your child is going to come home. Be patient, and expect to answer the same questions again and again. Remember that people ask questions because they want to show you they care and are interested in your life, not because they are just trying to be nosy. After all, you are "expecting," and expectant parents answer many well-meaning questions. Prepare your family and friends for a long wait. That way, if it happens sooner, everyone will be pleasantly surprised.

TELLING YOUR PARENTS AND FAMILY

Telling your own family may be your most difficult task. These are the people who have known you all your life. They are the ones who love you the most and probably anger you the most. Telling your parents may be the toughest thing for you to do or the easiest, depending on your family and perhaps even the race and the age of the child you plan to adopt.

It takes time for new ideas to simmer and settle with people. If you are likely to get a negative reaction from your parents or siblings, first talk about it with your spouse or trusted friend before giving your folks the news. Talk about all the reactions you could get, the comments you might receive, and the advice that might be heaped upon you. Rehearse your responses, so that you are not caught off guard. Pray before you have the conversation that God will guide your tongue and give you grace and favor.

Why would anyone react negatively to your adoption news? Following are some reasons:

- They might be worried that you are not prepared for parenthood.
- They might be afraid that the adoption will not work out and you will be hurt. (Remember that you are *your parents'* baby, and no parents want their child to be hurt.)
- They might be nervous about the physical, mental, and emotional condition of the adopted child.
- They might be afraid of your traveling to a foreign country.
- They might worry that a child of another race will not fit into your family.
- They might worry that they could not love someone is not a blood relative.
- They might fear that you cannot afford an adoption, and that they will have to finance it.
- They might worry that a child will take you away from them, as you will not have as much time to spend with them.

If you have the kind of parents who are constant worriers or tend to be negative, try not to take their questions or criticisms to heart. They might hit a nerve, but keep in mind that this is nothing out of the ordinary, and that they will probably come around when they get their hands on that sweet baby or child. Most adopted children, like all grandchildren, have a way of working themselves firmly into Grandma's and Grandpa's hearts.

Even if you fear that telling your parents and other family members might not gain you the positive reaction you hope for, it is best to tell them anyway. They might want to be included in the adoption process, which could help them start feeling bonded with your baby or child-to-be before the child is chosen.

TELLING YOUR FRIENDS AND COWORKERS

Telling friends and coworkers about your decision to adopt is a private decision. If you are trying to locate a birthmother willing to work with you, telling as many people as possible increases your odds of finding one quickly. However, remember that there will be people who react negatively to your announcement. In the workplace, be circumspect about when and how you share your adoption plans. In the break room or at lunch is a great time to talk adoption to your heart's content. Holding an informal meeting in your office to tell everyone how your adoption plans are proceeding when everyone is supposed to be getting their work done will not win you any points with your boss.

The average positive or negative reactions should be easily manageable, but you might also come across someone who has an extreme reaction (positive or negative) that you do not know how to handle. Maybe you have just inadvertently shared your happy news with someone who had an adoption fall through or just suffered a miscarriage. Their grief at your good news may show through plainly. Consider this an opportunity to be a comfort. God places you in situations to show others his love for them. If this kind of reaction comes up, ask gently if you can provide a listening ear, give a helping hand, or pray for or with them. If they seem angry about your adoption, shift the subject to something else. Having noted their reaction, in the future try not to discuss your adoption around them unless they ask about it.

TELLING YOUR OTHER KIDS

If you already have children, preparing them for their new sibling is a vital part of the adoption process.

If your child or children are *toddlers and/or preschoolers*, preparing for a new child might not seem very real to them. They might not give you much of a reaction at first, because small children live in the concrete world of immediacy. They might be excited about a new brother or sister, or they might act very casual and nonchalant. Prepare them for a baby the same way you would if you were pregnant. Find out from your local hospital if you can attend a siblings class with them, where an instructor teaches children about the responsibilities of being a big brother or sister, how to handle and treat the baby, and even how to put on a diaper. Kids usually love this class, because it makes them feel like an important part of their sibling's impending arrival. Of course, you can also teach these things to your child on your own, showing where the baby will stay in your home, how you will feed and take care of her, and how your child can be a helper to you.

Children might express some anger or anxiety during the wait. They might even decide they do not want a brother or sister. These reactions stem from a fear of the unknown, a fear of having to share you, and a fear of being displaced or unloved if a newcomer comes along. Reassure your toddler or preschooler that they will always have their own special place in your hearts and lives that no one can take away. Let them know that God did not create us with a limited supply of love that gets all used up. Explain that the more love you give to people, the more love you have. It is normal for birthchildren to regress both before and after you bring a new baby home. Comfort your children, let them playact for a time if you feel they need it, but encourage them to be proud of their status as the big brother or sister.

There are many books on adoption geared to four to eight-year-olds, and some are written directly to the siblings of adopted children.

WORDS OF WISDOM
If your outcasts are at the ends of the earth, from there the LORD your God will gather you, and from there He will bring you back.
—Deuteronomy 30:4 (NASB)

Elementary-school-age children will need more conversation about what adoption is, what the differences are between adoption and giving birth to a child, what kinds of feelings your child might have about having a new sibling, and what the process involves.

Because elementary-school-age children are susceptible to peer pressure, you'll need to prepare them for their peers' reactions and questions, and the answers you would like them to share.

Encourage your child to ask questions, and reassure your child that his or her role in the family is very secure. Elementary children may not express their fears as readily, but they might become anxious when you leave the house, become easily angered, or even have bad dreams. If these start occurring, ask your child if he or she is worried about the adoption. Children might fear that you won't have enough time to spend with them, enough money for their allowance or the family's planned trip to Disney World, that they won't be able to love a new baby.

The best way to help your child open up about his or her feelings might be in casual conversations that you direct while doing things together, so your child does not feel as if you are interrogating him or her. Invite your son or daughter into the kitchen while you cook, and talk about the differences the baby will bring—emphasizing the positive but letting your child know you are open to discussing the negatives. Invite your child to go on a walk or a car ride so you can take time to talk without being confrontational.

When appropriate, take your child to a support group meeting or waiting meeting for families in the process of adoption, so he or she can get to know other families and meet their children. This can go a long way to allay a child's fears.

If you have *adolescents*, their reactions—or nonreactions—could hurt your feelings deeply. Their level of disengagement might exactly match your level of excitement and enthusiasm, leaving you at odds. Relax; it's normal. Teens are in a time of self-discovery (the reason they can be so selfish!) and inwardly focused. They will probably process the news in terms of how it will affect *them*, asking questions such as:

- Will I have to change diapers?
- Does this mean I will have to stay home and baby-sit?
- Will I have to share my room?
- Aren't you guys too old to be having a baby?

While you can help your child focus on the needs of others, try not to react to these questions with anger. Your teen is normal, and these questions can mask fears about changing family dynamics. Talk to your teen, write a letter, or take the teen away for some special dinners out and let the topic of adoption come up naturally. Ask about his or her feelings and if they have any advice. While your teen may never act outwardly enthusiastic, he or she is likely to develop a bond with his or her new sibling when the child comes home.

TELLING TOTAL STRANGERS

When it comes to telling strangers about your adoption, their reactions can run the gamut from disinterested to totally captivated, from skeptical to encouraging. If you are bubbling over and want to tell everyone in sight, prepare yourself to answer lots and lots of questions. People can be very bold in asking anything personal that they are curious about—from whether you are infertile to whether you could love a child of a different race. You might also hear some incredible stories of adoption miracles and tragic stories of adoptions that fell through. If you tell people early in the process, prepare yourself for the inevitable "When do you get your child?" question that you will get every time you see them after that, even if it takes years to bring your child home. If the process takes a long time or you have an adoption that does not go through, these questions may turn from exciting to painful. Pray about whom you should tell of the adoption and how you should handle their questions. If you are outgoing and do not mind sharing, your adoption story can be a wonderful testimony to others who might be curious—and who might adopt someday!

Handling Others' Reactions
DEFLECTING NEGATIVE COMMENTS

Negative comments about your impending adoption will sting. After all, this is your dream. It is precious to you. If you tell a close friend or family member about your adoption and they react hurtfully, think of ways you can deflect their negative comments without unleashing your anger on them. You might say things such as the following:

- Thank you for sharing, and I will pray about your suggestions.
- Well, I suppose we will just have to agree to disagree on this. (Then change the subject.)
- I hear what you are saying, and I will take it under advisement.
- Thank you for your concerns. We feel that we are making the right decision for us.

SOOTHING THEIR FEARS

If you suspect family members and friends may be reacting negatively out of the fears listed earlier, talk about them. Share with your family what you expect from them and what help you will need. Let them know you are prepared for a bumpy road ahead, and that you have faith you are being called to this family decision. Let your parents know that if they do not fall in love with their new grandchild right away, that is okay. Share with them the things you have researched and learned, and connect them with other adoptive families so they can see the joy in forever families.

ENCOURAGING COMMUNICATION

Encourage close friends and family to communicate with you openly, rather than cutting off communication if they have concerns about your adoption. On some issues, you might have to agree to have different opinions. Other concerns, however, might be laid to rest—if you are able to share the knowledge you have about adoption and the factors that led to your decision.

MOVING PAST DISAPPOINTMENT

Imagine that you are bursting to share your adoption news, but you tell someone who gives you a negative or even neutral reaction. One of your biggest challenges can be getting past your disappointment and remembering it is natural for others not to feel as enthusiastic as you feel. Extend others the same grace God gives you, and ask God to keep negative comments from deflating your sense of joy. If you harbor disappointment or resentment, it will drive a wedge between you and those you will need the most as you journey toward adoption. Pluck any roots of bitterness right out before they have a chance to grow. Extend forgiveness easily and keep moving forward.

Keep in mind that it is important not to constantly overwhelm people with news of your adoption plans. While every minute detail and development affects you, constant updates may become annoying to others. Just as it is tough to see a thousand pictures of someone's grandchild or sit through a home video when you know no one in it, it might be tough for others to be enthusiastic at your umpteenth retelling of the same story, with only a slightly new update.

People You Need to Tell

COUNSELORS

If your child ever needs counseling, it is important to share the adoption information with the counselor, so the counselor does not prescribe therapies that do not apply or confuse issues occurring in your child's life that could actually be attributed to the fact that he or she is adopted.

CAREGIVERS

Your child's caregivers will need to know that your child is adopted, whether that be a full-time day-care provider, an occasional baby-sitter, or the church nursery workers on Sundays. By sharing this knowledge, your caregiver is better prepared to reassure your child that you are coming back, to comfort your child, and to make you aware of any behaviors that might be of concern.

OTHER ADOPTIVE FAMILIES

Finally, it is important to share your adoption information (or at least the fact that you are an adoptive family) with other adoptive families. Sometimes having close friends who also have adopted gives a child a sense of commonality and a place to belong.

PREPARING YOUR ANSWERS

Many people have no problem asking very personal questions from start to finish during adoption. Following are some of the questions adopting families have heard:

- Couldn't you have children of your own?
- Why can't you have children naturally? (or why would you adopt if you can have your own?)
- What kinds of fertility treatments did you try?
- Aren't you afraid the baby will have something wrong with him or her?
- What if the mother takes the baby back?
- How could you adopt a child of another race?
- What if the birthmother used drugs or alcohol?
- Will you let the birthmother be part of your lives?

It is your decision what to tell, what not to tell, and when to tell—but knowing ahead of time what you might be asked gives you time to prepare the short version and long version of your responses. If you are asked by a total stranger in a restaurant what kinds of fertility treatments you have tried, you might want to let him or her know that you would like to keep that information private. If you are asked what kinds of fertility treatments you have tried by a friend who is also trying to start a family and having difficulty, you might choose to share all the details. Keep in mind that the stories you tell will follow your child when he or she comes into your family. If everyone knows that the child was an adopted embryo or that you are not her birthmother, she may hear things from others that you would have preferred to share with her first.

RED LIGHT, STOP!

Questions to consider at this point in your adoption journey:

____ Have you decided what you will share with family and friends?

____ Have you thought about whom you will tell and what their reactions might be?

____ Are you prepared for personal questions from strangers?

____ Do you have a plan for telling your other children and helping them understand the adoption?

____ Are you asking God to help you forgive those who hurt you with their negativity or lack of excitement?

GREEN LIGHT, GO!

Action points for your adoption journey:

___ Make a plan and time frame of whom you would like to tell and what details you feel comfortable sharing about your adoption.

___ Pray and ask God to protect you from hurt over negative comments or reactions, and to give you wisdom in allaying your family members' and friends' fears and concerns.

___ Come up with some conversational escape routes to get you out of sticky situations without offending or blowing your top.

___ Make a plan to walk your other kids through the adoption process with you and help them know what to share with friends.

___ Be aware that your story may strike a nerve in some, and ask God to prepare you to be a comfort.

___ Understand enough about your adoption process that you can share with others if God uses you to lead them toward adoption.

My Adoption Miracle
The Right Max for Us
by Nicole C. Mullen, Singer

Adoption is a family legacy for me. I have a sister and a brother who are adopted. My grandparents adopted children; my aunts and uncles adopted children. It used to be my fantasy when I was a little girl and in trouble that I was adopted and my real parents were going to come rescue me. So when I grew up and married David, we always talked about adopting.

We had our daughter Jasmine first; then a year later I had a miscarriage. The doctors told me I would probably have a premature birth if I had another baby, so that's when we knew we would adopt. We did our home study and applied to a couple of agencies. We met a birthmother who was really young and wanted us to adopt her baby. I was there at the hospital when he was born, and I cut the umbilical cord. He was the first Max, and we had him for three days. In Tennessee at that time, the birthmother had ten days to change her mind; and on day three, she decided she wanted to keep him.

I remember the trauma of us crying, and David and I prayed, "Lord, if this is the child for us, soften the biological mom's heart. But if not, protect this child to be raised to love and serve you and bring us the child you have for us at the right time."

We knew that God had the right child for us. It hurt, but at the same time, we had a peace. We had confidence that God was in control. We had to find out that every need is not a *call*. Wisdom is discerning which is and which isn't. We had other babies offered to us, but when we found out about the baby who is now *our* Max, I didn't know if David was going to say yes

155

or no. But we both had peace, and we drove twenty-two hours to bring the right Max home. We have told him this story since he was small, and he loves to hear how he was the right Max for us. We have told him that his sister Jasmine was born out of Mommy's tummy, but he was born out of Mommy's heart.

I am definitely an advocate of adoption, and I'd rather have my heart broken a thousand times to have the right child that we have now. Our Max was worth the pain of losing the first Max. I gave birth to my other two children, but Max is the only one who looks just like me. People say, "Oh my goodness, your son looks just like you," and I just laugh and say, "Yes, labor was so hard."

I hope that more godly people will stand up and adopt. You won't love your adopted child "like your own." Your child will be your own. Some friends at school said to Max, "So, you're adopted? So that means Miss Nicole is not your real mom?" Max said, "Yes, she is," and the boy protested, "No, she's not." When I heard the story, I said, "Where is that boy, so I can tell him a thing or two?" I asked Max, "Who does your laundry?" He said, "You do." I said, "Who takes care of you when you are sick?" He said, "You do." And I assured him that I am his real mom. He is my child. He is the son of my heart. He is wild and crazy and all boy, and I could not have had a more perfect person placed in my family. He is my adoption miracle.

Chapter Nine

The Wait Is Over!

Now comes the most exciting part in every adoption—the wait is over, and you have received a call telling you that a birthmother wants to work with you, the state social services is definitely going to place your chosen waiting child with you, or your international child's referral is here. Parenting is about to begin!

A BIRTHMOTHER PICKS YOU

In the domestic adoption of a newborn, when a birthmother chooses you it will probably put you on cloud nine—nervous, excited, trying not to let your hopes get too high, and usually failing miserably! It might be months and months after you place your profile, and it might happen right away. When you create your profile and scrapbook or photo album for birthmothers to see, some agencies will contact you only when a birthmother is seriously interested. Others will tell you every time a birthmother wants to see your book. Still others will allow you to choose when you want to be notified. Think carefully about this decision, as choosing to be contacted every time a birthmother looks at your profile might put you on an emotional roller coaster.

Once a birthmother wants to place her child with you, the next step is to exchange more information. You should learn about her background, her prenatal care, the birthfather's background, and other important considerations, such as any medical conditions or addictions the birthmother might have. Do not be afraid to ask questions, and do not let fear of scaring the birthmother away keep you from getting the information you need to make a wise decision as to whether or not to partner with the birthmother on the adoption journey.

If you get any danger signals or feel it is not the right fit, do not be afraid to turn down the opportunity to work with a birthmother. You are entering a relationship with this woman for the rest of your adopted child's life, and you need to be sure it is the right thing. Whether it is a closed or a fully open adoption, your child has ties to his or her birthmother for life.

MOVING FORWARD TOGETHER

When you mutually agree to travel together toward adoption, the level of direct communication you have with the birthmother will vary in accordance with the type of adoption the birthmother and you have chosen. If you plan to have a fully open adoption, then ongoing meetings and phone calls with the birthmother are likely. If you prefer semi-open, you might or might not meet your birthmother at all and might only exchange pictures, letters, and information. You might only meet the birthmother at the agency or in a neutral setting and with the safeguards in place that you will not disclose last names, addresses, or phone numbers. What your relationship looks like with your birthmother will be unique to your adoption journey.

LEARNING ABOUT RELINQUISHMENT

As you get closer to the time of delivery, prepare your heart for the possibility that your birthmother may decide to parent her child after all. Even if you have been working together for months, the birthmother has the right to decide to raise her own child if she decides at birth or shortly afterward that she cannot bear to relinquish the baby.

"The decision made in abstract in pregnancy has to be revisited when she is holding that child and seeing his face for the first time," says Kristine Faasse, a licensed social worker and national adoption consultant for Bethany Christian Services. "Now, that is a high danger point from the adoptive family's perspective for her to change her mind. But maybe it is not a danger point from God's perspective. The best thing you can do is pray that God's plan for that child will be fulfilled."

Faasse says that birthmothers who have had the right counseling throughout their pregnancy and who have truly made an informed decision do not change their minds as often as everyone thinks.

"You do the hard work up front so that decisions are not impulsive," Faasse says. "I have a real heart for birthmoms because of the courage and maturity and intense maternal instinct that it takes to place a child for adoption. The birthmoms who make adoption plans have been able to dig deep and say, 'What is going to be best for my baby?'"

GIFTS FOR A BIRTHMOTHER

Before you shower your birthmother with presents for giving you the gift of parenthood, check with your agency or attorney regarding the laws that govern your state. There is sometimes a fine line between paying for legitimate expenses and being seen as buying a baby. Some states have greater leeway than others, so be sure to know what is legal and appropriate in your situation. If it is permitted, ask the birthmother what you could do that would mean the most to her. Would she like one of the baby's hospital bracelets or a snippet of his or her hair? Would she like a copy of the fingerprints and footprints? Or would these mementos be too painful for her to keep? Most birthmothers would appreciate having copies of the first photos taken in the hospital, so be sure to order or print two sets. Ask your adoption professional how you can bless your birthmother after birth.

WORDS OF WISDOM
The fruit of the Spirit is love, joy, peace, patience, kindness, goodness, faithfulness, gentleness and self-control.
—Galatians 5:22-23 (NIV)

You've Found Your Child!

PREPARING FOR CHILDREN FROM STATE CARE

If you are adopting a waiting child from state care, the preparations are different from getting ready for a newborn. Before a waiting child is placed with you permanently, you will usually have several visits to get to know and interact with him or her. These might take place at the caseworker's office, at the child's foster home, and gradually in your home. The length of visits will probably increase to help you and your child transition. Partings at the end of a weekend or day together can feel traumatic for you and your child, especially as you begin to bond. Give lots of reassurances that you will see your child again soon and that you are not abandoning him or her. If you can, call the child to say you are still thinking about him or her.

GETTING TO KNOW YOUR CHILD

As you prepare to bring your child home to live with you permanently, you might need to arrange childcare, check out local schools, set up any medical appointments, interview local therapists, meet with any specialists who have been working with your child, and talk with the child's current teachers to gather information that will help make the transition smooth.

If you are licensed as a foster-care home or foster-to-adopt home, your child might be placed with you with little warning, and suddenly full-time parenting begins. If you are a foster home, your child might not legally be free for adoption yet. If the parental rights have not been terminated, you might be required to arrange visits between your child and his biological family. This can be difficult for you, your child, and the birth family.

Ask God to give you the grace to see past their problems and love this child as he does. Do not make disparaging comments to your child or within your child's hearing about the birthmother or birth family. This can plant seeds of anger that will grow roots of bitterness in your child and drive a wedge in your relationship for years to come.

Pray for your child's protection, bring up any concerns directly to his social worker, and put on a smile when visits occur. You want God's best for this child, even if the outcome is not what you so desperately desire.

If your child is legally free, the child might be old enough to clearly remember the birth family and pine for them. If your child has siblings, it can be crucial for them to maintain contact. As you are preparing for a child from state care, take into consideration the child's whole history—the good and the bad parts—and try to honor it for the child's sake. For the older child, it is important not to take away their things, even if an item of clothing is tattered or a teddy bear is falling apart. Make the repairs you can and let them cling to this remnant. They have experienced losses in life you might not be able to begin to understand. They do not need to lose anything more, even if it is an old corner of a blanket of which you don't understand the significance.

Your Referral Is Here!

For each country involved in international adoption, the process of finding out which child you are receiving and how you will meet your child is different. But no matter what the policies and procedures, whenever international adoption referrals come in, there is much rejoicing on chat boards, in adoption-support groups, and among the family and friends who have been waiting for so long.

INTERNATIONAL ADOPTION REFERRALS

International referrals for countries where children have not been previously identified by parents are sent directly to the adoption agencies. The agencies usually call the new "parents" right away and tell them, "It's a girl!" or "It's a boy!" and give them a small amount of pertinent information. The referral documents are sometimes faxed to families, and if there is a picture, it is little more than an indistinct dark form on the fax. The referrals are then overnighted via an express delivery service to the waiting families.

POSING WITH THE FEDEX DRIVER

Some document this long-awaited day by posing for pictures with the delivery driver or videotaping the momentous knock on the door and handover of the package. Most delivery drivers do not know they are providing stork service, and they might look confused at the level of excitement over this envelope. They are often very touched, if you feel like sharing the reason for your joy.

Referrals from China generally contain two or three pictures, the area of the country your son or daughter is living in, how much they weigh and how tall they are, whether they are healthy or what medical conditions they might have. The referral must be accepted or rejected quickly—usually within twenty-four hours. If for some reason you feel this child is not the one for you, the best advice is to say no, even if it means more waiting. God has a plan for your family, and if your referral really does not feel right, get advice on whether or not to keep waiting. This decision is one that will affect your family for the rest of your life and should not be made hastily or with reservations, for your sake and the child's.

Government regulations of countries such as Russia and Kazakhstan prohibit you from seeing your child until you meet on the initial trip. A child is referred to you, and you know about the child; but you do not receive pictures.

On the first "getting-to-know-you" trip, parents spend time visiting with the child for several days. Then they decide whether or not to accept the referral of that child. If the family says yes, usually they return to the United States to await their court date. When the call comes—several weeks or months later—that the court date has been set, one or both parents travel a second time to finalize the adoption in foreign court and bring their child home.

WORDS OF WISDOM

You made my whole being; you formed me in my mother's body. I praise you because you made me in an amazing and wonderful way. What you have done is wonderful. I know this very well.
—Psalm 139:13-14 (NCV)

In Colombia, the children most available for intercountry adoption are sibling groups. When an agency is notified that a sibling group is available, they sort through the families who have contracted with the agency, looking for a family who might be the right fit. The family is contacted, and a match can be made.

INTERNATIONAL TRAVEL—GETTING READY TO GO

Once you have accepted your referral, the agency contacts the foreign government and schedules a date for your appointment at their consulate or before their courts to finalize your adoption. When you have that date, the agency will tell you your dates of travel. For China, the travel dates are usually six weeks to three months after the referral. For Kazakhstan, it might be only a few weeks after your initial visit. For Russia, it can be several months after you meet your child. That means more waiting before your little one comes home, but you now have a picture or memories to go with your prayers, and you will have plenty to do to get ready to bring your child home.

IMMUNIZATIONS AND OTHER HEALTH CONSIDERATIONS

When your paperwork is finished and you are waiting for a referral, it's a good time to visit the Web site of the Centers for Disease Control, www.cdc.gov. There you will find travel information for your child's country, a list of contagious diseases, and the recommended immunizations you should get before you go. Some immunizations need to be given over a series of six months; others can be obtained shortly before you leave. Check with your agency and other adoptive families as well for immunizations they opted to have and medicines they took with them.

If you have health considerations, make sure you have your prescriptions up-to-date and enough of a supply for your trip—and some extra days' worth in case of a delay. Find out if you need to package them in a certain way in order to clear customs, and check to see if they will interact with any foreign foods you might eat. If you are prone to headaches, respiratory troubles, or upset stomachs, make sure you pack plenty of over-the-counter medicines that might not be readily available in the country you are traveling to. Also, if you are squeamish about trying new foods, make sure you pack some familiar snacks to keep you going. Nuts, trail mix, and protein bars can help keep your energy levels up.

PREPARING FOR THE UNKNOWN

"When you are getting ready to travel, our number one mantra around here is 'Expect the unexpected,'" says Cory Barron, director of public relations for Children's Hope International, a Christian adoption agency that has placed more than forty-five hundred children in forever families. "And our other motto is 'Be flexible.' When you are traveling to a foreign country where the language and customs are different, you are kind of like a baby. You are totally dependent on your agency's guides to take care of you. So you had better be able to trust your agency."

Cory and his wife, Marlene, learned about the unexpected firsthand when they adopted from China in 1999. (See the Barrons' story in the "My Adoption Miracle" section in this chapter.) When they had an emergency situation, their agency coordinator worked night and day to resolve it.

"It might be hard for you to put your faith in your guides, but remember that they have done this lots of times," Barron says. "They will help you get what you need and get you and your child home."

When preparing for international travel, there are many practicalities to consider.

- Do you want to buy flights directly from an airline or from a travel agency?
- Do you need to book hotel rooms, or does your agency arrange it all?

I DIDN'T KNOW THAT!

- If comfort on the plane is a priority to you, look online at the diagrams and seating arrangements of the plane before you book. Try www.seatguru.com to compare types of planes and seating.
- Locate enough frequent-flier miles or dollars to upgrade to business or first class.
- Find out if your child needs a ticket. (Depending on the airline, a child older than one or two needs a full-price ticket; an infant without a ticket means that on a full flight, you will be holding the baby on your lap all the way home.)
- Contact the airlines and ask which days and times your flights are typically the least filled—in order to have the best chance at comfort in coach class, and possibly a free return trip for an infant.

SUITCASE RESTRICTIONS

If you will be flying in-country, you need to know what the restrictions are for baggage, for example. If you are allowed to check two bags and have a purse and carry-on to fly from the United States to Russia, but then are allowed only one suitcase and a carry-on each for an in-country flight from Moscow to your child's region, what will you do with the other suitcase?

Ask your agency to link you to chat groups where those who have traveled to your child's country share their packing lists, baggage restrictions, customs recommendations, places to go, and sights to see.

BABY SUPPLIES YOU MIGHT NEED

Your agency should be able to help you with a list of which baby supplies you might need and which ones are available in your child's country. Do you need to take an umbrella stroller? Do you want to bring an infant wrap to be able to keep the baby close to you and still have your hands free? Some countries expect you to bring clothes to dress your child in just as you would to bring a baby home from the hospital. You might need diapers, wipes, bottles, and formula. Again, chat groups and local families who have adopted from your child's country can share what they wish they had taken and what they took that they really needed.

BEST PRACTICES OF FOREVER FAMILIES

Bringing small snacks or toys in your pockets or bag are a great way to engage your child the first time you meet him or her. Cheerios work great for babies, and small cars, coloring books, or snacks might grab an older child's attention or stop his or her sobs.

PACKING LISTS

Some people who are adopting internationally love the packing lists that can be found on many adoption sites and Web boards; others think they are overrated. Basically, the best rule is to find out the restrictions in detail—size, weight, and number of bags—and stick to it. There are many packing lists that can advise you on how to pack so that you can travel carry-on only and not have to worry about losing a suitcase somewhere along the way.

The best way to get the most mileage out of your packing is to pack just a few basic mix-and-match clothing items and find out if there will be places to do laundry or send laundry out during your travels. Take travel and sample sizes of health and beauty items, and take only the basic necessities. This is not a beauty contest, and no one will be taking notes on whether you wore the same outfit twice.

FUNDS YOU NEED ON YOUR TRIP

When traveling to complete an adoption in a foreign country, you need to be very sure of what funds you will need, what can be paid ahead of time, and in what form the funds can be paid. Will you need to exchange money? Where is the best exchange rate? If your country prefers American dollars, will they take used bills and any currency? Some countries prefer that money be new and with consecutive serial numbers, which means you might need to ask your bank ahead of time if they can provide it. You might need one-hundred-dollar bills only. ATMs might be available, and major credit cards might be accepted. Or they might not.

Do not assume you can pay with a credit card. Also, notify your credit card companies that you will be traveling, so they do not put a hold on your card for security measures. (Some credit companies also charge fees for each overseas transaction in addition to your regular interest.) Make sure you know what you will be paying before you get the bill.

SPEAKING YOUR CHILD'S LANGUAGE

When traveling to meet your new child, you might want to prepare by learning some common words and phrases in his or her language.

Some agencies provide a disk or booklet with common phrases; some do not. There are many resources available for learning foreign languages. At the very least, you will want to know the words for "mommy" and "Daddy," and phrases such as "I love you," "Are you hungry?" and "Do you need to go to the bathroom?"

Hearing their own language spoken by their new parents might comfort a child who does not know you. If you just can't manage to pronounce a word of Russian or Vietnamese, try developing some hand signals or learn enough sign language so that you can show your child ways to communicate with you until the language barrier comes down and your child learns English (which will happen faster than you think). If you are traveling with your adoption agency, they will provide a guide, but it can be helpful to have some common phrases written down as well.

BRINGING HOME MEMORIES

Get out those video cameras, digital cameras, laptops, or plain old pen and paper and keep a journal of your trip. It will go by in such a blur that you might not be able to recall important memories later. You will want to keep track of your child's reactions, experiences, and words in his or her first days in your forever family. It is a legacy for your child to know his or her beginnings and a connection to the country from which he or she came. Remember to get pictures that include both parents, rather than most of the video being of one parent only while the other one holds the camera.

BEST PRACTICES OF FOREVER FAMILIES

If you are traveling with a group of families with your agency, switch cameras once in a while with another family traveling with you in order to take pictures for each other. That way, both parents can be recorded with their new family member in these first precious days together.

CALLING HOME

Check out the technology available where you will be traveling.

- Does your cell phone work within that country, or will you need to have some international calling cards or rental phones?
- Is there Internet service available for uploading and e-mailing pictures and messages home?
- If Internet access is fairly reliable, are there areas you'll have access to the Internet, or do you need to bring a laptop?
- Will you need a dial-up modem, or any special modems or cords for the area?
- What's the electrical currency? Will you need to pack adapters?
- What type of cord will you need to charge your electrical equipment or upload pictures?

BEST PRACTICES OF FOREVER FAMILIES

If you are leaving other children behind while you travel, record some bedtime stories on a videotape or CD for them to watch or hear at night. For older children, read a devotional and Scripture. That way, they can see and/or hear you while you are gone. If you do not get around to taping something, write out notes to be opened each day while you are gone, and give your child a picture of his family that he can keep with him.

RED LIGHT, STOP!

Questions to consider at this point in your adoption journey:

____ Do you feel comfortable with this birthmother match, or do you feel the Lord is calling you to keep waiting?

____ Have you learned enough to pack properly for your international journey?

____ Do you know what funds you need and what form they can be in?

____ Do you have all the technological gadgets you need to take with you (cell phone, laptop, digital camera, video camera) and all the right cords, adapters, chargers, and batteries?

____ Do you have all the basic items necessary to bring your baby home?

____ Have you prepared your other children?

GREEN LIGHT, GO!

Action points for your adoption journey:

____ If you know this is to be your child, rejoice in your referral! Thank God that the waiting time is coming to an end, and praise him for your new child.

____ Make a post-adoption plan with your birthmother and the help of your agency or attorney. Pray over this long-term decision carefully.

____ Make plans with your caseworker to transition your child from state care into your home.

____ Get your travel plans together—if you are adopting international-ly—including airline tickets, immunizations, and currency.

____ Talk to your other children about the trip, their feelings, and their new sibling. Let them help with the process of getting ready to bring their new brother or sister home.

____ Leave a videotape, audio recording, or notes behind for your kids to have part of you while you are gone. Make sure their caregivers have insurance cards and medical release forms.

My Adoption Miracle
The Miracle of Two Sisters
by Cory and Marlene Barron

As my wife, Marlene, and I prepared to travel to China to adopt a baby girl, we had no idea of the miracles that lay ahead.

Our first week in China followed the adoption agency's itinerary right down the line. We toured Beijing, then flew to the central Chinese city of Wuhan to pick up our daughter Abbi. She was healthy and, after a fretful first night, generally happy. We would be spending seven days in Wuhan waiting for the official adoption papers and passports to be completed.

The next few days were also routine, but on the fifth day, we got the surprise of our lives. That morning, our group of adoptive families decided to cancel the scheduled tour of the Yellow Crane Tower because it was too cool and rainy. Instead, all of us gathered on the spiral staircase in the hotel lobby for a group photo. While one camera after another captured the moment, a Chinese family entered the hotel and watched. (This had become fairly common for the group, because the sight of Americans with Chinese babies brought many stares.) But soon this family was pointing and waving in the direction where I held Abbi. I realized that this was Abbi's foster family, for Abbi had spent her days in an orphanage and nights in a foster home. I recognized the father from the night we received Abbi.

This was a little confusing, for the orphanage didn't want us to have contact with the foster parents, yet the whole family was obviously here to see Abbi. That's when the surprise hit. As we looked closer, my wife turned white in shock. The baby in the father's arms looked just like our new daughter! Both of us were thinking, *It's her twin!* She was smaller and not as healthy looking, but had all the same features. We knew she must be Abbi's sister, and if that was true, we knew we could not separate them.

The foster family loved and cared for these girls for the first ten months of their lives. At great heartache and risk, this family had boarded a bus for the two-hour trip to Wuhan to find us and let us know that there was another baby who belonged with our Abbi. After a private meeting with the foster parents, our Children's Hope International adoption coordinator confirmed that the girls were probably twins. Because there was no governmental record of them being twins, however, we would have to opt for genetic testing if we wanted to prove it and try to adopt both girls.

We set up a DNA test for the following evening. The orphanage officials through the China Center of Adoption Affairs agreed to have the foster father and baby brought to a laboratory at the Wuhan University Hospital.

We still had no idea if the Chinese government would let us adopt both babies, even if they were twins, or how long we would have to remain in China to adopt this second baby if we were allowed. We also did not know where we would get the extra money for more adoption fees, visas, and even more baby supplies. We simply had faith that God would see us through.

When we entered the room where the DNA testing would be done, there was the foster dad smiling broadly as he held Abbi's sister. Abbi was laughing and smiling, enjoying yet another reunion with her Chinese family. After blood was drawn from both girls, they were separated yet again. The sister and her foster family went back to the family's home, while we were still on schedule to leave the following day with the other families for the southern China city of Guangzhou. There we would finish up the paperwork for Abbi and fly home.

As we packed our suitcases, our coordinator called with the DNA results.

"It's a match!" she said excitedly. The test proved the girls were not only twins, but probably identical twins. But could we bring Abbi's sister home?

We flew to Guangzhou with Abbi, while our Children's Hope staff in Beijing and back in the United States worked with the adoption officials in China to approve our adoption of Abbi's twin. We not only had to present the DNA evidence, but we also had to convince the government that we were qualified and willing to take home two girls. As the time neared for us to fly home to the United States, our agency called.

"Get your bags packed; you need to fly back to Wuhan," they told us. "They have approved the adoption."

What normally would have taken months to approve took only six additional days in Wuhan. Members of our traveling group gave us money, prayed with us, and even gave us an extra stroller. We received everything we needed to take care of our newest daughter. These were friends we had met only two weeks before. Now they were friends for life.

When we got back to Wuhan, the girls were reunited again. Abbi was giddy with delight, but her sister was sobbing, feverish, and covered with blistering sores. That first night, Marlene rode the elevator with a man she thought was one of the athletes from Iran who had been staying in our hotel. My wife asked him how he was doing. He told her he was not a competitor but the team's physician. Marlene told him about the baby's illness and asked if he could help her.

He reminded her that there isn't a very good relationship between Iran and the United States. Marlene said, "I'm just a mother with a sick child."

"I am just a doctor, so I will see your child," he responded.

He checked on the baby for the next several nights. She had impetigo, and with the right medicine was soon fine and ready for us to fly home. We returned to the United States with Abbi and her twin sister—whom we named Grace, for she is living proof of God's grace.

Part Four

Gotcha!
A Forever Family Is Born

I prayed for this child, and the LORD has granted me what I asked of him.
So now I give him to the LORD. For his whole life he will be given
over to the LORD.
—1 Samuel 1:27–28 (NIV)

FOREVER A FAMILY

We waited, and you waited.
We loved, and you wanted to be loved.
We prayed, and you longed to be heard.
God heard, and here you are.
Forever home, Forever a family.
—N. N. G., AUGUST 2005

Chapter Ten

We Gotcha! Now What?

Depending on what type of adoption you are pursuing, there are different ways in which your child may come home. In domestic adoption, every state has a waiting period after the birth of a child before the birthmother can sign relinquishment papers. This is to give the birthmother time to consider her decision before she places her child for adoption. Because of this waiting period, in some states the baby is allowed to go home with you directly, but in other states the baby is kept in the hospital (if medically necessary or if no foster family can be found) or placed in a licensed foster-care home in the interim. Some agencies have specific families contracted to foster only these babies (often called *baby care* or another name that sounds better than *foster care*).

Most adoptive couples and birthmothers do not like the thought of their child going into foster care, even for a day or two, and if their state requires it, the adoptive parents will complete the classes to become a licensed foster-to-adopt home. Then, the baby can go into their care immediately upon release from the hospital with the understanding that the birthmother has committed to sign the relinquishment papers but has every legal right during the waiting period to change her mind and decide to raise her child herself. If you are in this situation or if your state has direct placement after birth, you will get the call to come to the hospital and pick up your baby.

BEING AT THE HOSPITAL
At the hospital, adoptive couples report different types of reception from different hospital staff. Some are very kind and helpful; others might look at you as if you are a baby snatcher. Ask God to help you be a good witness to those around you, even if you feel you are receiving treatment that is not especially kind.

WHAT TO TAKE WITH YOU

When you are preparing to bring the baby home, make sure you have
- a car seat that is safe and is installed properly,
- the same type of formula the baby is being given in the hospital,
- a prepared bottle for the ride home,
- an extra change of baby clothes and diapers—if you are traveling very far,
- a receiving blanket and other appropriate items for the weather, and
- socks if the outfit is not already footed.

Your child will most likely be dressed in a hospital undershirt or might have on an outfit that the birthmother has purchased. Have a going home outfit with you in case the baby has only the undershirt. If the birthmother has provided an outfit, accept it graciously and keep it for your child.

The hospital's nursery staff should allow you to come in and dress the baby and give you instructions on the feeding schedule, bowel movements, and any upcoming appointments you will need to make or keep. Ask them any questions you have. Remember that every question is valid, especially if you are first-time parents. You have never done this before, and your baby comes with no instructions attached. Speak up and ask those who have been caring for him what you need to know.

I DIDN'T KNOW THAT!

In many states, local firefighters are trained in the proper installation of car seats and can show you how to install yours—if you are not sure you have gotten it right. If you can't stop at a fire station, ask hospital personnel if the car seat is strapped in properly before placing the baby in it. Car seats should be in the backseat, away from air bags, and if children are under twenty pounds, the car seat should be turned to face the seat of the car rather than facing front.

THE INTERNATIONAL CHILD

When you are adopting internationally, there are two ways that your child might come home to you. Most adoptive families call the day they receive their child the "Gotcha Day." In some countries, your Gotcha Day is in your child's native country because you travel to pick up your child and fly home with him or her. In other countries, the adoption is completed by proxy in the home country or is finalized in the United States after the baby arrives, and an escort brings the child to the United States. "Gotcha Day" occurs at the airport when the adoptive parents meet the child for the first time.

If you travel to your child's native country, be prepared to be gracious and accommodating. Beds might be harder or softer than you like, food might seem strange, and you will probably be traveling in a large group of people who might seem cumbersome and slow. Be patient, kind, and accepting. Let your agency guide be in charge, and expect delays and surprises. That way, if everything goes according to plan you will be ecstatic, and if it doesn't you won't be out of sorts. Take your Bible with you and keep your quiet time and prayer time, especially as a couple. If you are not used to praying together, there is no better time to start than on the eve of becoming parents. You can give your child a spiritual legacy that nothing else can equal.

WORDS OF WISDOM

And ye shall seek me, and find me, when ye shall search for me with all your heart.
—Jeremiah 29:13 (KJV)

As you travel, be on the lookout for ways you can help those in need, whether it is giving up a front bus seat to someone who gets carsick or sharing your baby supplies with a family who doesn't have enough. Ask God to put people in your path whom you can bless, and he will be faithful to do just that. Use your time wisely while you are on this trip. You might be fatigued or grouchy, but try not to let your emotions keep you from experiencing an overwhelming joy at the beauty of God's world. Praise him for your journey, and see all of it that you can.

GOTCHA DAY! IN YOUR CHILD'S COUNTRY

If traveling is a requirement of the country you choose, you will receive your child usually only days after arriving. Many agencies build in a day or two of sightseeing, then the parents pick up the child at the orphanage or the child is brought to them at a government office, a courthouse, or their hotel. Gotcha Day is overwhelming for everybody—the adoptive parents who have waited for this child for so long, the baby or child who is seeing so many new faces, and the childcare workers and foster parents who have interacted with your child for months or even years.

Everyone's Gotcha Day experience is different, and there is no right or wrong way to react. Some moms and dads cry; some feel as though they are going to throw up. Some look stone-faced because of all the feelings inside. Babies, too, react in all kinds of ways. Some scream bloody murder when the new mom or dad holds them, arching their backs and trying to squirm away. Others cry for a minute or two, then settle down when a parent offers a snack or toy. Some babies are sick and miserable, and it shows. Some do not cry at all but smile happily and try to win the adults' affections right away.

Adoptive families want this moment to be perfect; that's only natural. However, life is rarely perfect. Camera batteries might fail, video cameras might suddenly shut off, or nervous moms and dads might argue with each other right before the baby is brought to them. Cover yourself with the peace that the Lord can give when you ask him, and be patient with each other and your new little one.

BEST PRACTICES OF FOREVER FAMILIES

I like to look through other people's scrapbooks and life books to find poses and photograph settings that I like. For example, I saw a picture of a couple who posed in their hotel room holding hands and facing each other as though they were taking wedding vows right before they got their baby on Gotcha Day. I loved the idea of that, so we did it for our second adoption.
—Susan Fremer, adoptive mother of four

YOUR CHILD CRIES AT THE SIGHT OF YOU

Babies and toddlers often cry when they see their new mom, dad, or both for the first few days or even weeks. Do not panic; your child can and most likely will bond with you. It will just take your child some time to adjust and even mourn the loss of all that is familiar to him or her. Speak softly, allow the child to be held by whichever parent he or she seems to prefer, and try not to let your feelings be hurt if you are the other parent. Young children who have bonded with a female caregiver might reject their new mothers at first, preferring their fathers. Others might seem to be afraid of men and cling to the mother. Each child is a unique creation with specific needs, personality, and temperament. It will take time for you to learn each other's moods, expectations, likes, and dislikes.

BEST PRACTICES OF FOREVER FAMILIES

When we were in China to get my daughter Olivia, we were ready; but when they handed her to me, she was so scared and sick. She cried briefly, but she was more in shock. We took her back to our hotel room, and then it hit me—I am the mom. All of a sudden, the years and months were not enough time to be prepared. Doubt started in my heart, and fear took over. I knew God had pulled some miracles out of his hat for us during our adoption process, so how could I doubt what he had given us? But I was scared. When we returned to the government building, I thought, *Do*

I go with my gut and tell my husband I am not sure about this adoption, or do I put my hand in God's and let him lead the way? We were waiting our turn when my daughter suddenly took her first steps. I turned to watch her and said in English, "Come to Mama," and she did! She ran right into my arms. Seconds later the notary asked, "Are you happy with your daughter?" I answered a resounding, "Yes!" Give yourself permission to feel overwhelmed on Gotcha Day and even for days after. God will calm your fears.
—Susan Caruso, adoptive mom to Olivia from China

KEEP YOUR CHILD CLOSE

Keep your new child close to you. It could be easy to allow your child to cling to your interpreter or guide because hear she speaks the child's language, but this can delay the bonding with you even further. Hold your baby or young child often, and give older children as much physical affection as they will tolerate. Reassure older children through your interpreter that you love them and will never leave them. Have your guide ask older children all the questions you can think of about their preferences so that you can give them what they need once you get home and the language barrier is between you.

HELPING YOUR CHILD SLEEP

Your adopted child will most likely experience some sleep difficulties immediately after Gotcha Day that can continue for months or, in unusual cases, years. Try to determine what your child was used to in the orphanage or foster home. Did your child sleep with several other people in one bed, or with other babies in one crib? It might have been noisy all the time, or there might have always been lights on. Most adoption experts recommend rocking your child to sleep, patting your child to sleep, or even sleeping with or next to your child. This behavior is usually avoided with birthchildren, but adopted children need to know that they are safe and that they have not been abandoned.

If your child cries out in the night, do not ignore the cries. Go in and comfort your child every time, so that he or she knows you are still there. You do not have to take your child out of the crib every time or turn the light on necessarily, just make sure he or she feels safe and knows that you are there. Speak in low, soothing tones, or sing to your child. Your familiar voice will help calm the child. If sleep issues continue unabated for weeks, you might want to consult your pediatrician, who can make sure there is no medical issue going on (such as an ear infection), or a sleep specialist who understands the needs of adopted children and might be able to give you some valuable tools to try so that your entire household can get a good night's sleep!

ADDRESSING MEDICAL ISSUES

When you are adopting internationally, your child might come with some medical conditions that need to be addressed immediately. A child might have lice, impetigo, a fever, an ear infection, or a bad cold. Seek medical attention as soon as possible. Your agency guide should be able to help you alleviate your child's misery with a doctor's appointment or medicines you need. In some countries, medicines are difficult to come by, and having a supply of your own over-the-counter baby fever reducers, simethicone drops for stomachaches, and other medicines can be a big help.

BEFORE YOU COME HOME

After Gotcha Day, you might spend time visiting the area of the country your child is from, and you might spend time at his or her orphanage. Prepare yourself for the sight of potentially heartbreaking conditions your child experienced, and the tragic faces of those you are not taking home. Pray for each child you see, that God will protect them and find a family for them.

The final steps before coming home are to take care of the legal and medical appointments necessary to complete the paperwork required to take your child out of the native country and bring him or her home to the United States. You might have several appointments to finalize paperwork, appear in court for an adoption hearing, or satisfy other in-country requirements to complete the adoption.

BEST PRACTICES OF FOREVER FAMILIES
Most adoptive parents recommend bringing along a couple of pairs of plastic pants to go over diapers, as some children experience upset stomachs and diarrhea because of the food changes and stress that accompany their transition.

When all of the appointments and sightseeing are finished, it is time to fly home together. If you do not have a full-fare ticket for your child and your flight is full, you will need to be prepared to hold your child the entire time. Some families bring extra blankets to make a small pad at their feet where a toddler can play. Other parents end up walking busy toddlers and fussy babies up and down the airplane aisles. Expect a flight with lots of crying children. Be prepared with enough formula, diapers, and extra changes of clothes for your child and yourself (because upset children and babies sometimes spit up). Pack a pillow, toothbrushes, and toothpaste. Remember that even if the flight is miserable, it will soon be over and your life together at home as a family will begin.

After International Travel

When you first get home with your newly adopted child, you will likely feel either too tired to move or too exhilarated to stand still. These extremes can also occur one right after the other. You can best deal with the aftereffects of jet lag by trying to remain on a regular day-and-night schedule. If you arrive home during the day, try to put off a long sleep until night. If you must, take a short nap to get you through. Eat nutritious foods at regular intervals when you get home. Drink plenty of water, and try to get some exercise, even if you just push a stroller around the block.

GIVE YOURSELF AND YOUR BABY A BREAK

In your first days home, you and your child will need to give each other a break. That means plenty of grace is extended by you to your child, your spouse, and yourself. Do not expect to get unpacked, all the laundry done, and the e-mails caught up in the first day or two home. If you do accomplish those things all at once, you are likely to deprive yourself of sleep or your child of much-needed attention. Take it easy on yourself, and try to let as many things slide as you can. Laundry and e-mails won't go anywhere if you don't get to them right away, but these first precious days with your child can easily slip away. Get rested, and make memories. Those are your most important priorities, even if work is calling and friends are at your front door. Lighten your load by delegating as much as you can to coworkers, friends, and family. Let them drop off the dry cleaning or finish a report. Most will be glad to help.

SEE THE PEDIATRICIAN ASAP

As soon as you can, take your child to the pediatrician to assess your child's development and test for any diseases or illnesses. Your doctor should be able to tell you if your child is developmentally delayed and suggest ways to help him or her get back on track. He can advise you about the proper diet and exercises you can do with your child and give him or her the medical attention needed. If you feel that something is wrong with your child and you are not satisfied with the treatment at your pediatrician's office, ask to be referred to a specialist or contact your insurance company about changing doctors. Your pediatrician needs to be familiar with the growth charts from your child's country and be aware of common ailments in that area. He also needs to test for immunizations so that your baby does not receive too many or too few shots.

Bringing Home the Hurt Child

If your child has been hurt in the past, there are many ways he or she might express these feelings.

Babies who have not had someone to bond with typically self-soothe themselves by rocking, sucking on their clothing or arm, or rubbing against objects. Babies are stimulated tactilely, and there are many infant massage therapies you can learn to help soothe your child. Some children who have been neglected or abused might seem very withdrawn, and love and patience will be needed to draw them out of their shell. Direct eye contact should be encouraged, and praise should be given lavishly.

THIS IS TOO EASY!

A *child* who has been hurt might not show it. From reading the background information on your adopted foster child or international child, you might know some of the pain your child has experienced; yet a child might act as if nothing bad has ever happened. Very young children who instinctively feel the need to bond might always have a smile in place in order to win the affections of every adult who comes near. This child needs to learn that the primary caregivers are Mom and Dad and should not be passed around to everyone else's open arms at first. With this child, you will probably think, *This is too easy!* and it might be. Problems can occur later with a child who goes indiscriminately with any adult.

THIS IS TOO HARD!

Other children might express their inner pain by tormenting you. While you were not the cause of their pain, as they begin to feel safe you will probably bear the brunt of it. Children who have been neglected, abused, or abandoned will tend to test every limit and push every button to see if the new adults in their lives will also leave. This type of child needs reassurance and should not ever be threatened—even jokingly—with being left behind or even returned! When you are running late, never say to this child, "You had better hurry, or you are going to get left." Sending the wounded child away to an isolated room is also probably not the best form of punishment, because feelings of abandonment might be exacerbated by the isolation. On the flip side, the punishment might not have any effect at all because the child has learned to self-entertain and be alone most of his life. With some wounded children, you will inevitably think, *This is too hard!*

In those moments, take your child for a walk, drop to your knees and pray, and arrange childcare for short respites if your nerves are getting too frazzled or your temper is rising. You and your child are in a learning curve of trust. Your child must trust that you will not reject him or her, and you must trust God that he will give you the strength to parent this determined little person without feeling rejected yourself. (See chapter 11 on parenting the hurt child.)

FIGHTING YOUR FEARS

Whether you are bringing home a newborn or an older child, it is natural when you get home to have some fears. These might be fears that your baby will not thrive, that you will not bond with the baby, or that the birthmother will change her mind. Remember that fear is not of God, and that he—and those around you—will help you get adjusted in the first days home if you will reach out to him and to the fellowship of those who love you. If you are usually the one to organize and plan things, this is the time to step back and let others organize and plan for you. Ask your Bible study group or Sunday school class to prepare meals for your family for the first week or two, or let your mom stay with you and help. First-time parents, especially, should have a support system in place to help during the transition to parenthood.

LIFT YOUR SPIRITS WITH CHRISTIAN FELLOWSHIP

During this time of post-adoption, it is vitally important that you continue to stay in fellowship with other Christians. You might need to limit visitors for the sake of your baby's health or keep him or her out of a church nursery for a while, but that does not mean you should stay away from all of your spiritual connections. Take turns going to church if you must, or maintain your visits with your small group and get the Sunday sermons on tape or CD. Ask friends and family to pray for you during this key time of transition and bonding, and do not be afraid to pick up the phone and ask for help when you need it, even if you are used to doing everything yourself.

CAN SOMEONE TAKE AWAY MY CHILD?

If you are afraid that the baby will be taken away, know the legal process in your state so that you can put those fears aside. Once a child is in the home of the adoptive parents, the window of time for revocation is short (in some states, there is none), and it happens only infrequently. Usually, a birthmother who changes her mind does so before she gives birth or immediately after birth, before the baby goes home with you. Keep in touch with your agency or attorney, and leave the rest in God's hands. Worrying yourself sick over it will not change the outcome, and your anxiety might communicate itself to your baby, leaving you both stressed and cranky.

Post-Placement Blues

Even though you have not spent nine months being pregnant, you will still have many of the same experiences as any first-time mother. Your body will not be sore and healing, but your emotions will still be up and down. You will still experience sleep deprivation, and you will still no doubt be struck by the same sense of wonder that any first-time parents have when gazing down at the beautiful face of their sleeping infant. You will likely have to learn to live through the crying jags of colic, playfully argue over whose turn it is to change the stinky diaper, and feel guilty for taking naps during the day.

You will also experience some things that parents who go through a pregnancy do not live through. You might be surprised to feel a deep sadness and grief for your birthmother as you marvel at each new accomplishment of your son or daughter. You might find yourself thinking about her, wondering how she is doing, and even feel a sense of anger that she could let go of such a precious child. If you do not have ongoing contact, share these feelings with the Lord, then with another adoptive mom, a trusted friend, or your mother or sister if you are close with them. Pray with them for your birthmother and for your own heart to heal. Talk to your spouse about your feelings, and if possible, write to your birthmother, sharing news of the baby with her.

It is important, especially for new mothers, to express their feelings rather than keeping them inside. Even though you have not given birth, you still experience a huge life change with the coming of a new baby. Some adoptive moms experience post-adoption depression that is very similar to postpartum depression, usually because they feel unequipped to handle motherhood. A mom who experiences post-adoption depression might feel her baby is not familiar to her, the baby does not like her, or she is not equipped to love and take care of her new child. If the baby is very demanding, she might feel guilty when she feels resentful at the umpteenth time of being awakened in the middle of the night. She might feel trapped at home when the baby is too small to be exposed to outside germs, and she might experience a resurfacing of some grief over her infertility.

ARE YOU DEPRESSED?

In extreme cases, depression can cause an adoptive mother to be unable to function or care for the baby. Learn to recognize the signs of depression, such as loss of energy, unexplainable sadness, sudden weight loss or gain, increased or decreased appetite, sleep disturbances, inability to concentrate, irritability, and crying for no obvious reason. If you experience some of these symptoms, call your doctor or adoption agency and see if someone can recommend a counselor and some techniques to help you overcome your depression.

EVERYTHING'S OUT OF CONTROL!

Expect things to feel out of control and off balance in the first days or months after the finalization of an adoption. The child is adjusting to a new environment and new people and is learning to trust and love. The parents are also adjusting to this new presence in their home who requires much of them. Siblings need time to get used to sharing parents with another child and to bond with the new brother or sister. Even aunts, uncles, and grandparents are changed by the new arrival. For most, it is a joyous occasion to welcome any new life into the family. For some, it might take time to adjust to the issues of race, disabilities, or even just the adoption itself.

WHY AM I NOT FALLING IN LOVE?

Some people fall instantly in love with their adopted child the first time they see his or her picture or ultrasound image, and the reality of meeting and bringing their baby home further cements the bond they already feel. Others find that their emotions develop more slowly. There is nothing wrong with you if you do not feel head over heels in love with your adopted child the first time you see or hold your child or in the first few days home. You and your child might need to get to know each other's quirks, habits, and personality before the warm feelings of love grow in your heart. Do not worry that the feelings will not come for you or a spouse. Spend time interacting with your child. Notice your child's strengths and beauty, and praise God for the privilege of leading this special child back to him.

If you are worried about whether or not your spouse is falling in love with your child, keep the lines of communication open and discuss it. Pray about it together. Encourage your spouse to spend time alone with your child, and do not come running to his or her rescue the moment the child lets out the first cry. Some parents are actually afraid of parenting, especially if it is new to them or they have little experience with infants. Soon, they will get the hang of it if you step back and do not interfere too much with their attempts to bond.

OUR OTHER CHILDREN ARE ACTING UP

If you already have children, keep in mind that your adopted child is disrupting their routine, and they might become more demanding, grouchy, and hard to deal with. Involve your children in the care of their new sibling. If they traveled with you, give them ample time to recover from their jet lag before expecting them to make up mounds of schoolwork they missed. Reassure them that you will still be there for them, too, and try not to rely on older children too much to do the "dirty work" so that they do not resent their new brother or sister. They need time to bond with the new addition as well. Even if you fall in love instantly, your children might not. Extend grace and let them attach to their sibling at their own pace. If you have teens, they should pitch in and help, but remember that your teenager did not adopt this child—you did. Baby-sitting occasionally is great; expecting too much of them is not.

It's Not What I Expected

Whatever you expect from your adoption, these first days will probably be different from the image you carried in your mind for so long. Whatever you feel, give yourself permission to relax and take it slowly. You will learn your child's nuances, and your child will learn yours. It is like intricate dance steps. It takes lots of practice to look graceful.

RED LIGHT, STOP!

Questions to consider at this point in your adoption journey:

____ Do you have the necessary items needed to bring your child home?

____ Are you ready for foreign travel to pick up your child?

____ Have you discussed with anyone your fears about parenting, the revocation period, or adjusting to a new child?

____ Have you lined up help and days off for when your child first comes home?

____ Are you ready to address any medical issues your adopted child might have?

GREEN LIGHT, GO!

Action points for your adoption journey:

____ Get the car seat and other items you need to bring the baby home. Make bottles and bring extra clothes.

____ If you are traveling internationally, make copies of all your paperwork and put them in your suitcase. Leave copies of your wallet contents in a safe place or with a trusted person at home.

____ Line up friends and family to help you with meals and errands after your child comes home.

____ Spend as much time as you can together as a family after your adopted child comes home. Nothing can replace your first days together.

____ Gather all the mementos and photographs of your child and his birth family that you can. Keep them in a safe place for when he or she gets older.

____ Engage your other children in bonding with their new sibling. Also, give them extra attention and grace during the adjustment period.

♥ *My Adoption Miracle*
Love Never Fails
by Robin Pennington, wife of Paul Pennington, director of
FamilyLife's Hope for Orphans

After we had our first child, Elizabeth, twenty-five years ago, I had an ectopic pregnancy and was told that we would be able to have another baby only if we did in vitro fertilization. That turned us toward adoption to increase our family. I'd love to say that we adopted children at first because we knew how much they needed a home. Honestly, it was because we wanted a family. I wanted a baby. Still, God uses us for his plan when we let him. Little did we know how he would use adoption to change our hearts and lives.

We applied at an agency and received a baby three weeks later. We actually became second-time parents sooner than we would have if I had delivered that ectopic pregnancy, receiving Kit through domestic adoption when she was three days old. Two years later, I was being encouraged by the doctor again to consider in vitro, and instead I stopped at a new adoption agency on my way home and told them we would love to adopt an African-American baby boy. Seth came home shortly after that, when he was ten days old. After that, we had an eight-year gap in adding to our family, until my husband, Paul, and I took part in the *Experiencing God* study (by Henry Blackaby). Then Paul said, "We need to allow God to bring us more children, if that's what we are supposed to have." I was skeptical, because he had been saying no to more children for so long, so I said, "Okay, then you go find us a baby." Paul called around and told me, "Korea needs people to adopt baby boys." So we got our paperwork together, and three and a half months later, Paul went to Korea to get Ethan.

Paul called me while he was there, overwhelmed by how many kids there were in the orphanages. He said, "People don't know. They just don't know." Something in him changed from that day on. He realized he couldn't just stand by and do nothing. So the day we finalized our adoption of Ethan, we applied to adopt again. I told Paul, on the way to an adoption meeting, that I felt we were supposed to adopt a child with a heart problem, and he felt that way too. That's when we found out about Hope. She was dying of heart problems and infection and kidney problems, and we found out later that a worker who had seen Paul at the orphanage in Korea had been praying that we would adopt her.

When Hope came home, that first year was very, very hard. I practically lived at the hospital, as she required multiple surgeries. In fact, the cardiologist looked at us and said, "Are you people crazy? Did you do this to ruin your life? Why would you take on a child like this?" Paul said, "Because God called us to," and the surgeon just said, "Good luck."

184

It's hard to describe now what that time was like. When you adopt a special-needs child, Satan really doesn't like it, because that has been his territory, and he knows that God is going to be glorified. Because when you see a child adopted with special needs, the world watches and says, "Why?" Ultimately, your actions point to the Lord on a daily basis.

Still, I was totally unprepared, and at times I thought, *What have I done?* I had to learn that resistance did not mean we had done the wrong thing. After we adopted Hope, we saw pictures of a little boy from Korea who had very short arms. I said, "Paul, we know him." Paul said, "No, we don't." We tried to find a family to adopt him for about a month but couldn't. We decided to bring him home, but we were so scared. Paul was afraid he would not know how to be the right father for Noah. And I cannot even tell you what we would have missed if we hadn't. Noah is brilliant; he is so whole emotionally. He wakes up happy and goes to bed happy. He is the icing on the cake for us.

Having these kids has given me such a heart for special-needs children. It has been such a hard journey, and still is, with disappointments and adjusted expectations. I would not expect Noah, with short arms, to be a baseball player. His challenge is visible. Other kids' challenges are not visible from the outside, but they are just as real. For those kids you may have to adjust to the reality that they may not be able to go to college, learn a trade, or live on their own. When it is the most difficult, you even feel guilty that your other children are being negatively impacted by the one child with difficulties that drain all your time, energy, emotions, and resources. And yet through it all you still see the image and the grace of God. Now Paul is the director of Hope for Orphans, and we are partnering with Christians in many spheres of influence who can radically change the lives of orphans around the world in the coming years.

So would I do it again? Over and over and over. We cannot imagine life without these children. They are our adoption miracles.

Chapter Eleven

Helping Them Heal: Bonding and Other Post-Placement Concerns

F or all children, no matter what their age or prior circumstances, bonding and attaching is a crucial part of healthy development. First connections begin just after birth, when a child is given to the mother and father and the first cuddling and feeding begin. Except in the case of a newborn who goes home with adoptive parents from the hospital, all adopted children have experienced an interruption of some kind in their bonding process, so it is important for adoptive parents who have missed any significant amount of time in their child's life since birth to learn ways to promote healthy bonds and attachments.

In institutionalized children, not only is the initial bond broken, but also babies learn fast that there is no one who will quickly and reliably respond to their needs. Even as tiny infants, children with healthy attachments learn to trust others and their own feelings, while children without parents to attach to might learn not to trust. This can impact their emotional development for life. As Deborah Gray explains in *Attaching in Adoption:*

> In good relationships, babies and toddlers are learning to stretch out positive moods and signal for help when in pain or frustrated. This ability to calm down gradually gets hardwired in developing brains. Babies learn that their needs are important and worthy of attention. This opens the door to an essential life skill of being able to identify their feelings as reliable. They also learn to tolerate a typical amount of frustration. Because parental help is at hand, they do not numb themselves to feelings of frustration, loneliness, boredom, or pain. Instead, their lives are a pattern of basic needs getting met and problems getting solved.[29]

For children who have been institutionalized with little individual attention and nurturing, the idea of trusting someone might be completely foreign. In international adoptions of institutionalized children, not only might you look different, sound different, and smell different to your child, but also you might expect emotional reactions from your child that she cannot possibly comprehend or give at first. When you receive your child, your ideal image of scooping her up, covering her with kisses, and hearing her squeal with delight might be far from the reality. Your child might stiffen, pull away, or refuse to make eye contact. On the other hand, an adopted child might go easily and with smiles not only to you but also to any adult who looks her way. The child with this kind of reaction has learned to get her needs met by being charming to everyone, thereby "manipulating" adults in order to get what she needs. All of these can be signs that your child does not know how to emotionally attach. Do not panic! With time and tender care, children who are at first emotionally distant or overly friendly to everyone can form loving, healthy bonds to their adoptive families.

You can foster this healthy emotional growth by interacting with your child in ways that make her feel secure and begin to rebuild her trust. This is crucial, because these bonds of trust are essential for your child to grow into an emotionally secure adult. As Gray states:

> Secure attachment helps children learn to believe that they are lovable, that trust in parents is wise, and that others will help them when they have needs. . . Children with secure attachments have a head start in developing the positivism, self-control, and mastery skills valued in our society.[30]

GRIEF CAN BE A GOOD THING

If your adopted child has had the loving care of an orphanage worker or foster family, he or she might grieve for a time when placed with you. Your child might cry uncontrollably or completely withdraw for days. Do not panic in this case either. Signs of grieving at the time of placement and shortly after are actually a good thing, says Dr. Dana Johnson, director of the International Adoption Clinic at the University of Minnesota. Signs of grief mean that your child has formed a healthy emotional bond with someone and recognizes that it has been taken away. Children who have been able to bond are better prepared to be able to bond again than children who have been so neglected that they seem withdrawn or almost catatonic.

THROW OUT THE OLD RULE BOOK

The bottom line with adopted children who have experienced interrupted attachments is to throw out the old parenting rules and get ready to learn some new ones. Even if you have already had biological children or if your mother, sisters, cousins, and best friends have all given you volumes of parenting advice, you will need new tactics with this fragile child. You need to learn new ways to reach your child's hurting heart. This might mean bringing a child into your bed to sleep, giving an older child a bottle so that he can experience some of the closeness and holding he missed, and being consistent with boundaries and structure.

In his article "Adopting an Institutionalized Child: What Are the Risks?" Johnson writes that the chance of an institutionalized child being "completely normal" on arrival is "essentially zero."

> Kids aren't in orphanages because they come from loving, intact families with a good standard of living and ready access to good health care and nutrition. Abandonment by a destitute, single parent with poor prenatal care and inadequate diet is the most common reason why a child is available for adoption. The second most common reason is termination of parental rights because of neglect and/or physical/sexual abuse (often alcohol related). Over 50 percent of institutionalized children in Eastern Europe are low birth weight infants, many were born prematurely, and some have been exposed to alcohol in utero. Finally, children with major medical problems or physical handicaps might be placed in orphanages by their parents due to limited access to corrective treatment and rehabilitation services. These kids are a high-risk group by any standard.[31]

Johnson states that because in orphanages children usually have a lack of consistent caregivers, stimulation, and good nutrition, these institutionalized kids fall behind in "large and fine motor development, speech acquisition and attainment of necessary social skills. Many never find a specific individual with whom to complete a cycle of attachment. Physical growth is impaired. Children lose one month of linear growth for every three months in the orphanage."

Johnson does *not* state these research findings to scare people away from adopting. In fact, he adopted an international daughter. But he does think people going into adoption should be prepared for a child who will need extra from them in order to make the healthy progress in life that he or she has been denied so far. Johnson writes that formerly institutionalized children usually make great strides in growth and development during the first years with the adoptive family.

In order to form healthy bonds in hurt children, adoptive parents are going to have to establish routine, structure, and an atmosphere of living trust with their child. In Lark Eshleman's helpful book *Becoming a Family*, Eshleman explains to laypersons how attachments are formed, what damage interruptions in attachments cause, and techniques to try to re-form bonds of trust. Eshleman says, "Love alone is not enough to heal some of the types of actual neurological or physiological damage suffered in infancy and early childhood. You might need to learn new types of specialized parenting skills, some of which will seem counterintuitive. Without this knowledge, parents repeatedly and unnecessarily watch their children grow up with neurological and behavioral difficulties."[32]

Eshleman writes that when infants cry because they are afraid, wet, or hungry, meeting their needs has a positive effect on an infant's nervous system, calming the levels of hormones that are produced when people are in a state of stress. When an infant cries and his or her needs are repeatedly not met, the stress hormone levels remain higher, and an infant will eventually "stop wasting his energy and will not expect things to change."

It will take time to help infants who have reached this point by the time they are adopted to "reset their baseline," Eshleman says, to recognize that they can try again with different results. She compares it to someone who first moves to a big city recognizing how noisy it is. Over time, the noise fades into the background and becomes unnoticeable. If the city resident goes on vacation to a quiet country retreat, he might now have to adjust to the lack of noise. So it is for institutionalized children. They need time, touch, and tender loving care to make these adjustments.[33]

Eshleman and other adoption experts outline many strategies for parents to help their adopted child bond with them, from sending personal items ahead to the orphanage such as clothes, toys, photos of yourselves, audiotapes, and disposable cameras with a note asking orphanage workers to take pictures of your child, to getting your home ready with soft lights, soothing music, soft clothing (cotton), and a baby carrier that will keep the young child close to your chest. Parents can ease transition from the institution by trying to bring home whatever items they can that their child had in the institution, bringing home some of the foods they were used to eating, and trying to imagine the changes from their child's perspective.

Formerly institutionalized children need to be in a soothing environment without overstimulation at first, to get used to new faces and new sensory experiences. Eshleman is a strong proponent of adoptive parents holding their new child as much as possible at least for the first several days, stating that this closeness can form the basis for healthy attaching.

Even if a child is crying, she suggests not handing the baby off to an aunt or sister to soothe. Allowing the child to cry in your arms communicates that you will be there for the child unconditionally, Eshleman believes. While parents of healthy biological children who have been able to form bonds since birth might let a child cry him or herself to sleep on occasions to teach the baby to accept a bedtime or utilize the services of a baby-sitter while the child is still very young, parents of a formerly institutionalized child have to trade these natural parenting techniques in for new ones.

Some practical ways you can help your new child adjust include:
- wearing soft clothing,
- keeping perfumes and soaps the same so the baby begins to recognize your smell,
- carrying the baby close to you as much as possible,
- encouraging eye contact with peek-a-boo and singing,
- responding to the baby's needs promptly, and
- taking the child to the doctor as soon as possible to make sure your child is not experiencing physical discomfort from any undiagnosed illnesses.

Believe it or not, even the childhood games of peek-a-boo and hide-and-seek are necessary for healthy emotional attachment. In both games, a child learns that if he hides from his parents, the parent will always find him and be there for him. Children who do not play games like these are more likely to be unsure of their parents' commitment to them.

For toddlers and older children, in order to form healthy attachments, they might need to regress to infantile behavior to basically re-create what they missed. Some preschoolers or even early-elementary-age children might like to try a bottle while rocking on their mother's lap. You might feel completely ridiculous giving a bottle to a six-year-old, but in the long run would you rather feel silly for a few moments and have a bond that lasts a lifetime or refuse to try something harmless that might give your child a feeling of security he or she has rarely had before?

Reactive Attachment Disorder (RAD)

Children who do not make healthy bonds over time or who begin to show certain signs of withdrawing or acting out as they progress through childhood might be diagnosed with reactive attachment disorder (RAD). RAD kids do not have to be adopted kids; many children are unable to form healthy attachments if they are abused or neglected during their early stages of development.

DETECTING THE SIGNS

The symptoms of an attachment disorder often manifest themselves during

the transition to kindergarten, when a child who might have always been seemingly calm (if somewhat manipulative) for no apparent reason begins to
- act out violently,
- act overly engaging and charming,
- refuse to be affectionate on the parents' initiation,
- refuse to make eye contact,
- offer indiscriminate affection to strangers,
- destroy things,
- hurt him or herself,
- hurt animals,
- steal, or
- lie.

Other symptoms can include learning and speech disorders, a lack of conscience, food hoarding, poor relationships with peers, and a lack of impulse controls.

GETTING HELP
All kids exhibit some of these behaviors at some. Kids will also test their limits. The difference is that in RAD kids there seem to be no limits. If you think your child is exhibiting signs of reactive attachment disorder, whether it is when you first bring him or her home as an older child or years after being adopted as an infant, it would be wise to seek the help of a professional therapist familiar with RAD. Choose one who is willing to give you strategies and techniques to help your child overcome the deep, inner fears that are controlling his or her behavior.

WHAT YOU CAN DO AT HOME
At home you can promote healthy attachment in an older child who exhibits signs of an attachment disorder by being very consistent, no matter how hard you are pushed; maintaining your physical presence as much as you can to "prove" that you are not going anywhere, no matter how horrible your child acts; taking your child back to some of the things that were missed in early childhood like rocking and cuddling; and teaching your child what appropriate responses in social situations look like. Other things you can do at home to foster attachment might be as simple as giving your child a nickname, fostering the feeling that there is something special between the two of you, and telling your child repeatedly that you are a team.

In another helpful resource, *Parenting the Hurt Child: Helping Adoptive Families Heal and Grow*, authors Gregory Keck and Regina Kupecky give parents helpful hints for forming loving attachment from infancy through adulthood. In their years of research, Keck and Kupecky have developed the following list of these and other important points that every adoptive parent should keep in mind:

- Parenting hurt children requires loving patience and clear expectations for improvement.
- Parenting hurt children is frequently painful.
- Hurt children bring their pain into their new families and share it with much vigor and regularity.
- Parents who did not cause the child's trauma often suffer the consequences of it.
- Even though the child might seek to anger the parent, children will not be able to securely attach to an angry parent.
- Anger prevents healing.
- Nurturing will promote growth, development, and trust.
- Parents do not need to have a consequence for a child's every misdeed.
- Family fun should not be contingent upon the child's behavior.
- Parents should expect difficult times, as well as a reduction of them.
- A child's history isn't only in the past. It affects the present and the future.
- Parents need to determine what information is private and what can or should be shared with people outside the family. Angry parenting will keep the mean child mean, the wild child wild, the scared child scared, and the hurt child hurt.
- Reparenting is what hurt children need, regardless of their chronological age. Going back to pick up some of the pieces will be necessary before moving forward.[34]

Children who have had interruptions in their attachment and who are still in the infant or toddler stage might be easily recognizable, because either they seem to love no one, refusing eye contact and stiffening as a reaction to touch, or they seem to love everyone. Parents of adoptive children might not recognize that the good baby who will go to absolutely anybody and charm their socks off might be a child who has already learned to put on that behavior to get what he or she needs from adults, without any real attachment to one in particular. Children who do not prefer any caregiver over anyone else also need to be taught how to attach to their parents primarily, and others secondarily.

Extending Grace and Unconditional Love

While there have been countless dollars and thousands of hours spent by professionals doing research on the way infants and children attach and the things they need most, it shouldn't be surprising to Christians that the conclusions reached by the "experts" is the same advice Jesus gave two thousand years ago. The best way to help hurting children is to love them unconditionally. When Christ was asked about the greatest commandment, he said to love God with every fiber of your being, and then to love others as you love yourself. That's the best parenting advice you can receive. Extend grace and unconditional love, without anger, and you can lay a foundation for overcoming and healing a multitude of hurts.

WORDS OF WISDOM

"Love the Lord your God with all your heart and with all your soul and with all your mind." This is the first and greatest commandment. And the second is like it: "Love your neighbor as yourself."
—Matthew 22:37–39 (NIV)

Wise parents who understand that their child needs to form healthy attachments study their child intently, learning the child's limits, triggers, and the things that overload him or her. After they know these things about their child, they let the child in on the secrets to their behaviors, so that they can begin to recognize what sets them off and practice self-control. Many children are not consciously aware of the root of what is causing their outward misbehavior or inappropriate behavior.

HELP YOUR CHILD NOT TO OVERLOAD

Parents who want to help their child teach him to recognize his feelings, what is happening when he starts having those feelings, and some healthy escape routes for dealing with the feelings. Teaching your child to use words, for example, rather than kicking, stomping, throwing things, or screaming, is one way to encourage your child to recognize and address his pain. If the pressure of competing in sports causes your child to act out, you might need to adjust your expectation and take him out of the sport. If attempting a new skill he has not learned before sends him into a meltdown, know his triggers. Attempt new skills at the time of day when he is most rested and cheerful. Let something that is causing a lot of frustration go and try to learn it another day. Consistency, flexibility, and unconditional love should be the three constants in parenting your adopted child.

Telling Your Child About the Adoption

Another important milestone you will have to face in your child's journey to healing is when to tell your child he or she was adopted and what to say. It is common practice today to believe that a child should grow up with the knowledge of being adopted into a family who will love him or her forever. In past decades, adoption in America was considered a subject you didn't talk about, and some adopted adults never found out that they were adopted until their parents passed away and they discovered paperwork in their personal effects. The deception involved in keeping a secret of that magnitude communicates itself to the adopted child, and honesty is the better policy. Dr. Benjamin Spock, the world-famous doctor who was the first pediatrician to train in pediatrics and psychoanalysis, says that conversations about the child's adoption should begin early and matter-of-factly:

> The parents should, from the beginning, let the fact that she's adopted come up naturally and casually, in their conversations with each other, with the child, and with their acquaintances. This will create an atmosphere in which the child can ask questions whenever the subject begins to interest her. She will find out what adoption means bit by bit, as she gains understanding."[35]

GOD'S UNIQUE CREATION!

When your child asks how he arrived in your family, give age-appropriate information about the different ways that children become part of a family. Help your child feel good about his identity in Christ. Let your child know that he was uniquely designed by God to be part of your family and God's royal family. Remind him that God knew before your child was even born about all the things that would happen to him, and that God has a special purpose for his life. As your child enters the elementary-school years, introduce biblical stories of adopted people like Moses, Joseph, Esther, and Jesus. Talk about what important roles these people each played in saving God's people. Teach adopted children that God has a plan for them, and that their adoption is part of that plan.

WHAT TO TELL YOUR CHILD

Even when your adopted child is assured of your love and of God's love, your child might still struggle with feelings of being abandoned by the birth-arents—even if he or she doesn't tell you. There is an emotional process of self-evaluation that most adoptees go through at some point in their lives. They question why they were not *good enough* for their birthmother to keep. Consequently, adopted children might grow up to be people *pleasers*, always trying to be the perfect children so that they will not be abandoned again, or they might deal with low self-esteem. The fact that they are valued—by your family and by God—is a topic that will need to be addressed and readdressed all throughout your child's life. As children enter school and reveal their adopted status, their peers' reactions might prompt them to ask more questions and do some soul-searching. Eventually they might want to search or reconnect with their birth families. (See "Adoption Reunions", chapter 12.)

"I remember as early as third grade or fourth grade telling classmates in school that I was adopted, and they were like, 'No way. You can't be.' They just couldn't believe it," says Dave Bartlett, who was adopted by a loving Christian family a few days after his birth in 1963. "That was the first time I felt, 'Oh, wow! There is something different about me.' It was very scary. I took those doubts to my parents, and they assured me that adoption was perfectly normal. I was okay with being adopted, but I always felt a little bit different after that." (See Bartlett's "My Adoption Miracle" story, chapter 12).

Bartlett, like many adopted children, secretly wondered about his birthmother—what she looked like, if she was alive, and if she thought about him. These questions are natural and lead many children later in life to search for their birth families. In a culture where open adoptions are being encouraged more and more, domestically adopted children might have an easier time than internationally adopted children in discovering information about their birth families. In order to satisfy international adoptees' curiosity, it is especially important for adoptive families to gather as much information as they can about their child's history when they are in their child's country.

"Every child that comes into adoption comes with a history, even the ones who are adopted as newborns," says Kristine Faasse, licensed social worker and national adoption consultant for the Christian adoption agency Bethany Christian Services. "They come with genetic traits and their own personalities. Each person has their own individual history, and it is important to preserve it. Put everything you can get from their past in a big box and keep it for them, even if they do not seem interested. For foster children, especially, don't ever say, 'That's a ratty old blanket; let's get rid of it.' Keep these pieces of their past. And if you can get information or a picture of their birthparents, keep it. If you meet them, take pictures. Every child needs to know where they came from and that they were loved."

Some adopted children develop real anger toward their birthparents for not raising them, even when the adoptees grow up in loving adoptive homes. Anger creates division and causes people to act foolishly. It can divert an adopted child from fulfilling his God-given purpose—if he becomes consumed by anger at his birthparents for placing him for adoption. Wise parents will do everything they can to help their child express his anger and let go of it, by talking together, praying together, searching the Bible to see what it says about anger, looking at how other adoptees have reacted to their adoptions, seeing a Christian adoption counselor, and practicing calming techniques.

TEACHING THE HURT CHILD TO FORGIVE

Ultimately, your child has to be taught to forgive his birthparents completely in order for him to let go of his deep hurt. This will not be an easy process, and it might take years to accomplish. Remind your child that God is not wasting his pain, and that every hurt he experiences becomes part of the tapestry of his life; so he can be a witness and a testimony to God's faithfulness.

Visiting the Past

Adoptive parents can help keep anger from ever taking root in their child's heart by giving their child the freedom to be curious about his or her history.

PRESERVING YOUR CHILD'S CULTURE

Some families of international children work hard to preserve their child's knowledge of his or her native language; others take their children to cultural festivals and celebrate the country's special holidays. By teaching your child to appreciate his or her country of birth, you might be preparing your child for the work God will call him or her to do later in life.

A VISIT TO YOUR CHILD'S BIRTH COUNTRY

When an international child reaches the upper-elementary years and before the onset of adolescent hormones and mood swings, you might want to consider taking that child to visit his or her birth country. Your child at that age is old enough to cognitively understand the adoption process and be curious about his or her culture. This trip might not feel necessary to your child or possible in your individual circumstances, but it can be an important piece of the puzzle of your child's history that can help provide a secure sense of self. Amanda Levin, who was adopted from Honduras, describes her feelings about visiting her birth country in an article for *Adoptive Families* magazine. Amanda write:

> As I sat in the hot airport, kicking myself for wearing black shorts, I started thinking. I remembered all the times I had tried to picture Honduras, all the things I had imagined. It hit me that this was my birthcountry. From that moment on, everywhere we went, I watched in fascination. This was my past, my heritage. Everything seemed as if it were somehow tied to me. I distinctly remember buying a soda and the woman speaking to me in Spanish. How was she to

know I had been adopted and lived in the United States? To this woman, I was just like all the other girls who bought Cokes in her store. I was just like everyone else she saw in Honduras.

In Honduras, I felt a great connection with everything. I don't think another person can really understand that feeling of self discovery I experienced. From a trip that I had thought would be nothing more than shopping and sightseeing came so much more. I left Honduras with a greater understanding of myself as well as the country. To be able to identify with a culture on such a strong level is not something many people have the opportunity to do. I am just thankful that I was one of those people.[36]

Talk to your child about whether she would like to see where she was adopted. If you go, visit her orphanage or foster family if possible. Some international children who were adopted as toddlers or older children or who experienced a lot of trauma might not want to go back to their country. That is usually just fine, especially if the trip would bring up old hurts. If your child reacts very strongly, this might be an indication that she still needs to learn to process some of her pain. Seek a professional opinion, talk to other adoptive families and see what their experiences have been, and keep the lines of communication with your child open.

KEEPING THE SIBLING CONNECTION

If your child was adopted from foster care and has siblings, it can be very important for your child to try to maintain some kind of contact with these siblings. This can be accomplished through visits, the exchange of letters and pictures, e-mail, or phone calls. Siblings have a special bond, even if they have not lived together very much. Some research shows that siblings might have stronger bonds to each other than to their parents, especially if they have a history of parental abuse or neglect. Gloria Hochman, Ellen Feathers-Acuna, and Anna Huston of the National Adoption Center write:

The bond between brothers and sisters is unique—it is the longest lasting relationship most people have, longer than the parent/child or husband/wife relationship. While the bonds might wax and wane, a person's lifetime quest for personal identity is undeniably interwoven with his or her siblings.[37]

The authors say this is, in part, because siblings are "constant companions and playmates" during childhood and that by playing and interacting with one another, siblings learn how to interact with others. Helping your adopted son or daughter maintain sibling relationships may minimize felt losses and thus allow him or her to heal faster and more completely.

Seeking Help

Progress in life is rarely an unwavering straight line. If your adopted child has bonding difficulties, fetal alcohol syndrome, a deep-rooted lack of self-worth, or other life-affecting emotional wounds, there will be many times when you take one step forward and two steps back. Regression is a natural part of the process of growing, so expect it at times and keep praying your way in the right direction. It is important to recognize that forward progress is not always visible, because you can't see what God is doing behind the scenes in the big picture of your child's life. When on the surface your child seems to be losing ground, God might be doing important foundational work in his or her heart that will lead to visible change later.

If your situation becomes more than you or your adopted child can handle, if it becomes violent or dangerous to the adopted child or other members of your family, seeking professional help might be the way to help you get back on track. It will be most helpful to find a therapist or counselor who understands the situation from a spiritual perspective and understands the special issues that come with adoption, especially in the area of attachment.

FINDING THE RIGHT COUNSELOR

You'll need to find a qualified counselor with whom you and your family are comfortable. This will take time and research. For help with finding the right counselor, try the American Association of Christian Counselors, www.aacc.net; Christian Counselors, www.christiantherapist.com; or Christian Therapists, www.christiantherapists.us. If attachment is the main issue and the Christian therapists you consult with are not specialists in that area, take a look at Attach, www.attach.org, and try searching their list of attachment specialists. (This is not an endorsement of these organizations, but they do offer lists of therapists who identify themselves as either Christian or attachment therapists or both. You will need to do your homework.) A trial session with several different counselors might be required before you find one who connects with your child and his or her particular challenges, so do not be discouraged—and don't give up—if you do not mesh with the first counselor you see.

To help your child at home, the best place to start when your child regresses in the area of bonding and trust is to go back to some of those old bonding techniques that might range from children's games to extra cuddling to a more structured routine. It also helps to continue to raise his or his self-esteem by complimenting your child frequently, saying good things about the child to others (when the child can hear them), and finding things about him or her that you can praise.

What if My Child Never Bonds?

Some children never do bond. Their behavior never becomes acceptable, no matter how many techniques, therapists, and prayers a parent tries. Parents with the best of intentions and an abundance of love might adopt a child *or* give birth to a child who has personality disorders, a mental illness, or serious social and behavioral issues. The child might never have been neglected or abused but still demonstrate these serious difficulties. However, when an adopted child seems unreachable, parents might experience a level of guilt, anger, and disillusionment that can tear the family apart. Some marriages end in divorce, or other kids in the home are emotionally damaged or physically injured. Dissolved adoptions, in these extreme cases, are the reality for some families.

These unhappy outcomes are not the norm, and adoptive parents should not have an unhealthy amount of fear that it will happen to them. If it does, God is still in control. He still has a plan to give you "hope and a future" (Jeremiah 29:11 NIV). He still loves you, and he still has a blueprint for your lives and your child's life. You might never know on this earth the reason you have to experience this pain, but you can still trust in a God who knew you before your child was knit together in the mother's womb.

Adoptive parents in these critical situations need to keep their eyes open, their hearts and spirits engaged, and feelings of bitterness yanked out every time they try to take root. It might not be fair that their adoption did not provide a storybook happy ending, but no one promised that it would. It takes an in-the-trenches commitment not only to make the decision to adopt but also to stick to your promise to raise that child—your child—with godly principles. Like divorce for married Christians, disruption or dissolution of an adoption, no matter what the circumstances, should not be approached as an option.

In extreme cases of violence toward others or self-destruction, it might be very appropriate to remove the child from the home for a period of time to keep other family members safe, but abandonment by nullifying an adoption validates the child's deepest fears—that he or she is not worthy of love—and that is the antithesis of the very foundations of the Christian faith.

Your Adopted Child's Education

An area that hurt children often struggle with is school. Some are overcoming a language barrier, look different, are behind academically, have a learning disorder, have a physical disability, have a hard time focusing, or are fighting all of the above. Imagine yourself in a room where you feel that you have nothing in common with anyone else, where people might tease you or treat you differently, where you do not understand the unspoken social hierarchy, and where you speak a different language. Imagine that you have been so hurt by people in your past that you trust no one. Could you sit in a classroom with those feelings, in that environment, all day every day? It would be incredibly difficult, as it might be for your child.

Your child *will* learn. She was created by God to be curious about the world around her and to desire to learn how it works. She will accumulate knowledge as she grows. It is inevitable. She might not, however, acquire knowledge at the rate you expect. She might take longer to process some academic subjects, or she might not struggle at all. Each child is unique and is uniquely gifted. If your child is learning about the Lord, getting along with peers, and attempting to do her work, let academics take a backseat to love. An education is important, and your child will become educated. Staying mentally and emotionally healthy enough to use that education one day is even more important than staying at grade-level academically.

BEST PRACTICES OF FOREVER FAMILIES

When we adopted older children from the Ukraine, they did not know a word of English. We hired a college student who taught ESL (English as a Second Language), and she came over and spent time working with the kids for a few hours a day, several days a week. Within ninety days, they were speaking English pretty fluently. I can tell you that ESL really works.
—Bob Zaloba, adoptive dad to three from Ukraine .

GETTING EXTRA HELP
Don't let your pride stand in the way of getting help if you need it in any area. If household chores are eating up the time you could be spending with your child, see if you can afford someone to clean once a week, or evaluate if those chores can be done less frequently. If your child is really struggling and you don't know what to do, find professional help. If you have fears that you are not doing a good enough job, find a great prayer partner. If your child needs a special education class, ask for it. The bottom line is: do whatever it takes to get the assistance you need to keep relationships—with God and each other—your top priority.

THINK OUTSIDE THE BOX
Boost your child's self-esteem by helping him find something fun that he is good at, preferably something fun you can do together, like a game or outdoor

activity. Enroll him in extracurricular activities he'd enjoy to discover hidden talents. Your adopted child might struggle in the classroom but soar on the soccer field, might be able to paint a masterpiece, or play the piano well enough to join the symphony. You can help unlock your child's potential through your encouragement and willingness to help him work at new things.

Part of your job as a parent is to help your child discover his passions and purpose. As Christians, you have an extra-powerful weapon in your arsenal to help do that and to help your child heal: the certain knowledge that your child was loved and designed lovingly by the Creator of the universe. The fact that you can nurture your child's whole being—body, mind, heart, and spirit—because of your saving belief in Jesus Christ means that you can truly address all the needs and voids in your adopted child. Without the spiritual connection, all people at the very core of their being feel that something is "missing" in their lives. As parents armed with the knowledge of what the missing component is, you can help fill in every gap with nurture, with prayer, and through the guidance of the Holy Spirit, who is called in Scripture "the Comforter." In John 14:16, Jesus offers this promise:

> I will pray the Father, and he shall give you another Comforter, that he may abide with you for ever. (KJV)

You can teach your child what a unique creation he is, showing him verses like those in Psalm 139, which state that he is "fearfully and wonderfully made" and that God cared about him before time even began!

RED LIGHT, STOP!

Questions to consider at this point in your adoption journey:

____ Are you prepared to see your new child grieve?

____ Are you willing to try bonding techniques that might seem silly or feel foreign to you?

____ Have you spent time imagining what it must be like to be in your child's shoes, thinking of all the new sights, sounds, smells, and tastes?

____ Are you willing to step out of your comfort zone and get the professional help your child might need?

____ Have you decided how to keep your child in contact with siblings?

____ Have you decided when and how to tell your child about his or her adoption?

____ Will you walk with your child toward healing, no matter how difficult the journey might be?

GREEN LIGHT, GO!

Action points for your adoption journey:

____ Learn all about the effects of interrupted attachment and institutional-ization on children.

____ Equip yourself to know where to look for the right professionals to help your child.

____ Make some preliminary decisions about what type of schooling you think might work best for your child. Be flexible.

____ Decide when and how to talk about adoption with your child by learning what information your child can understand at what age.

____ Talk about what you will do to maintain contact if your child has siblings.

____ Honor your child's past by preserving the pieces of it.

____ Take your child back to his native country when he is old enough to understand.

____ Teach your child about his uniqueness and God-designed purpose.

My Adoption Miracle
The Miracle of Sam
by Sandi Patty, Singer

When my husband, Don, and I got married in August 1995, we had seven kids between us. We didn't think we needed any more! Yet in the first few months after we got married, Don and I talked about the fact that it would be really special to have a child together that belonged to both of us and that everyone could share. Then it would dawn on us that we already had seven kids, and people would think we were crazy to add another one!

Yet the urge wouldn't completely go away, and we started to talk about adopting a baby. Don is adopted, and we thought it would be special for him to have the experience of being an adopted son with an adopted son of his own. We would have a conversation about adoption, then put the idea away for a while, never really getting serious about it because life was full with the family we already had.

In one of our adoption conversations, Don was thinking about his adoptive dad, Sam Peslis, who had died when Don was just eleven years old. He told me, "You know, if we ever did decide to adopt a baby, it would be great to have a little boy and name him after my dad. I'd like to name him Sam."

Don's adoptive mother had also passed away when Don was in his twenties, but the couple had provided a loving home for him, and he wanted to honor them and the blessing they had been in his life. We still weren't convinced that adoption was the right path for us, but the topic just wouldn't completely go away. One day when I was thinking about it once again, I said a quick prayer to God that if he wanted us to adopt a child, he was going to have to literally drop a baby in our laps.

It wasn't very long after that that we went on a cruise with some friends of ours named Shari and Wes. Wes is an attorney who sometimes handles adoptions, and the couple's son Ryan is adopted, so adoption was a natural topic of conversation that came up on the cruise. We didn't tell Wes and Shari we were considering adopting; we just talked a lot about Ryan's adoption and Don's adoption and adoption in general.

A week after we got home from the cruise, I was working in the kitchen on a Saturday morning when the phone rang; it was Shari. She told me that a baby had been born and that the adoption plans for him had fallen through. Wes was handling the adoption and had twenty-four hours to try to find an adoptive home, or the baby would go into the foster-care system. Shari was almost apologetic for calling and said, "Sandi, I don't even know why I'm calling you, but I feel like the Lord told me to. Do you know anyone who is looking to adopt?"

I couldn't believe it, because I really hadn't told anyone about that flippant little prayer I had made about God dropping a baby in our laps. In fact, I had really forgotten it.

I told Shari, "We might be interested in adopting him." She was almost speechless, but I explained to her that Don and I had talked about adopting a little boy and naming him Sam after Don's dad.

I hung up the phone, and Don and I talked about it, wondering if we should really do it and what the kids would think. The kids thought it was a great idea, and we called Wes and Shari back and said we thought we wanted to proceed—if no one else came forward in the twenty-four-hour time limit.

No one did. On Sunday morning, Wes and Shari came over to our house, and we asked them if we could go to the hospital and see the baby. Wes arranged it, and we drove the short distance. Shari prayed for us before we went in, and she asked God to make it very clear if adopting this child was the right thing for us.

"Don't be subtle, Lord," she prayed.

Wes and Shari went down the hall to the baby nursery, while Don and I waited in a small lobby. Soon, we could hear the wheels of the baby cart as they pushed it toward us. What I didn't expect was for Shari to be sobbing as she pushed it. I thought someone else must have come forward wanting to adopt that baby or that something was wrong with him, because Shari seemed really overcome, and she was pointing toward the bassinet as they pushed it.

Then I saw what she was pointing to. The little card taped to the inside of the bassinet above this beautiful baby's tiny head read "Sam." At first, I thought Wes and Shari must have called ahead and told the nurses to make a little nametag so it would be special for us. Then Shari told me the reason for her tears. The nametag was already there. The nurses named him when he was born, and they named him Sam. God wasn't subtle, and he literally dropped baby Sam into our lives.

We went to Target that night; everybody helped set up a little nursery; and on Monday we brought Sam home. He was the most beautiful, four-pound, eleven-ounce, tawny-skinned, fuzzy-haired baby I'd ever seen. Today, Sam has been part of us for more than a decade, and he has really helped our family in the blending process. He is that little extra that we really hadn't planned on that gives us all a common bond. We are so proud to be his parents, and it has been a really neat process for Don to see adoption from the parenting side.

Adopting Sam has truly helped me understand the depth of God's love for me too. I remember standing there in the hospital, reeling at that nametag, thinking about the times in my life when I had really messed up—when Don and I had really messed up—and yet God loved us enough to entrust us with this gift of life. Sam is truly our adoption miracle.

for more on Sandi Patty, her books, and her music, visit www.SandiPatty.com.

Chapter Twelve

Adoption Reunions

Searching for Their Identity

Even if you have been the world's best adoptive parents, someday your adopted child will naturally wonder about his or her birthmother and birthfather. By the time children reach their teens and are forming their own identity and searching for their purpose, they might decide that they want to find their birthparents or, in the case of open adoption, spend more time with them. This is not true for every adoptee. Some adopted adults say they have never felt the need to search for their birth family, and they never do.

If your child expresses an interest in finding his birth family, your job as the adoptive parent is to quickly get past your initial instinctive reaction of "Why does he need to find them? Haven't we been good enough?" and recognize that this need of your child's to know his roots in no way diminishes what he feels for you.

Statistically, most adoptees who seek their birth families are women, often in their childbearing years. Many are only children and have a natural curiosity about whether they have siblings somewhere. Adult adoptees also search in order to put their curiosity to rest regarding their medical backgrounds, their looks, and their personality traits.

The important thing for adoptive parents to remember is that finding a birth family does not replace the adoptive family in the adoptee's affections. In fact, after meeting their birthparents and hearing their stories, many adoptees say they have a deeper appreciation for their adoptive parents and what they sacrificed to raise them.

"You're Not My Real Parents!"

It is typical that during adolescence, an adopted child might struggle with feelings of rootlessness and insecurity. Sometimes these natural growing-up feelings are exacerbated by unkind peers, by the way the international child looks different from his or her family or friends, or by the adolescent's rebellion against parental authority. It is during these years that the adoptive parent might hear for the first time the dreaded words: "You're not my real parents!" Uttered in anger, these words will cut an adoptive mom or dad to the quick.

Your natural response will probably be to get angry and strike back. Take a few seconds before you react to beg God for self-control, so that the damage can be minimized. Keep in mind the warning of James 3:5, which states: "So also the tongue is a small part of the body, and *yet* it boasts of great things. See how great a forest is set aflame by such a small fire!" (NASB, emphasis added). Your child is not the adult; you are. It's your job to understand that they are confused and questioning, and to try not to take it personally.

As Julie Jarrell Bailey and Lynn Giddens write in *The Adoption Reunion Survival Guide*:

> Feelings of disassociation are commonplace during adolescence, as we strike out for independence and approach adulthood. For the adopted person who has met his biological family, the feelings of disassociation dissipate over the years and closure coexists with the reality of family dynamics. However, for the adopted person not able to reunite with his birthparents, closure cannot completely exist, because there is no basis for the reality of family dynamics.[38]

When your child strikes out, allow her time to get her emotions under control. Then try to get to the heart of what prompted your child's outburst. Reassure your child that although you did not carry her in your body, you are indeed her real parents; also acknowledge that she has other, biological parents somewhere. This might be the right opportunity to talk about them more, asking your child if she has been thinking about them and then discussing those thoughts. It is common for adoptees to express anger at their birthparents for "not caring" about them enough to keep them. Again, reassure your child that her birthmother probably loved her very much to be able to part with her.

To Search or Not to Search

At this point, if you have not had an open adoption experience and do not know where your child's birthparents are, the question might be: "To search or not to search?" If your child wants to search for the birthparents, most adoption experts encourage adoptive parents to help an adult child find the biological connections. In the teen years and beyond, your child is developing the maturity to prepare for a reunion, if it should occur.

If you have little information about the birthparents, there are two places for your child to start looking first: your adoption agency and adoption registries.

I DIDN'T KNOW THAT!

Results from a five-year study in Great Britain indicate that reunions with birthparents are beneficial for adoptees and their parents. Of the adoptive families whose children sought out their birthparents, 97 percent of adoptees said that their reunion with their birth families did not change how they felt about their adoptive families; 66 percent of adoptive parents reported becoming friends with the birth family.[39]
—*Adoptive Families*

Finding the Birthparents

Finding birthparents can be a challenge, especially if the adoptee does not have the birthmother's last name. Even with a last name, the birthmother might have married or divorced and changed her name since the time of the adoption. To further complicate things, in some states adoption birth certificates are sealed, meaning that it takes a judge's order to open them. Most laws are written to ensure that the birthmother is contacted only if she wants contact, and a judge might not be willing to unseal a birth certificate. In that case, adoptees will probably need to rely on adoption registries or turn to a private investigator.

In order to find out if a birthmother wants to have contact, an adult adoptee can search adoption registries and sign up on them. An *adoption registry* is the place in each state where birthparents and adoptees can list their names and contact information with the goal of being reunited. The state registries are usually managed by the same governmental agency that oversees the adoption process in each state. If the adoptee is over age eighteen, or in some cases twenty-one, the adoptee can register to have the birthparent(s) given his or her information—if the birthparent should want to contact the child. About half of the states in the U.S. have some kind of adoption registry.

TYPES OF ADOPTION REGISTRIES

Several types of adoption information-exchange systems and registries are available:

- **Open Records:** In states that allow open records, an adoptee can request his original birth certificate with both the birthparents' names on it. This is often the easiest way to seek birthparents because the names are available.

- **Mutual Consent:** In "mutual consent" registries, if the adoptee *and* birthparent sign up, each will receive identifying information about the other. This differs from open records in that both parties have to agree.
- **Search and Consent or Confidential Intermediary:** In some states, there is a *search and consent or confidential intermediary* system, where an adoptee or birthparent seeks to find the other, and a go-between contacts the one being sought to ask for consent to give out identifying information. If the party desires to be contacted, identifying information will then be given to the searcher.

In states that have none of these methods for trying to locate a party in an adoption triad, the court must be petitioned before records will be released. This can be very difficult to do. An attorney must be hired and a motion filed asking the court to unseal a birth certificate. The adoptee must have a persuasive argument for why the record should be made available. Always wanting to know what a birthmother looked like is not going to do the trick. Usually, it is something more like documented pressing medical concerns that convinces judges to open the files.

CONDUCTING A SEARCH

Some adoptees stymied by the laws in their state hire a private investigator or search group that has means of quickly searching all adoption registries and tracking people down through a variety of methods. This can be expensive but less time-consuming. If your child decides to hire a search group, ask the group the following questions:

- How long have you been in business?
- How many reunions have you facilitated?
- How long is the average wait?
- Do you use only legal means of obtaining information? (Not only do you want your child's search to be conducted with integrity because it is the God-honoring thing to do, but if an investigator is using illegal methods to conduct searches and gets caught, your child's name will be dragged through the mud with his.)

Other ways to help your child search on her own include registering with the International Soundex Reunion Registry (ISRR www.plumsite.com/isrr/, and

Seekers of the Lost, www.seeklost.com. These sites are free and are designed to unite birthparents and adoptees who mutually sign up for the registry services. Your child might also obtain information through a search of the Internet, including online registries and adoption reunion chat groups.

Internationally adopted children should go back to their parents' adoption agency first, then contact the orphanage or foster family with whom they lived, if possible. Often, records will not be released or opened to anyone but the adoptee; so a woman adopted from South Korea might have to visit her native country in order to obtain these records. For those who truly desire a birth family connection, the trip might be worth it.

Supporting Your Child in the Search

When your adult child begins to search, ask if you can be involved in the process. Be helpful and interested. By taking part in this effort, your child knows you will stand by him through anything, that you love him more than yourself, and that he has protection and support if a reunion does not go well.

If you know that your child's birth family is not a healthy one, seek expert advice before attempting to reunite. It might not be a good idea or the right time to find her birthparents, especially if you know or suspect that they are still living a seriously unhealthy lifestyle. If your child is an adult and decides to meet them anyway, you will need to share your concerns about the birth family in a manner that is not derogatory or accusatory.

Facing Your Own Reunion Feelings

Face your own feelings about your child's desire for a reunion with the birth family. If your feelings are hurt, calm them through prayer and communication with your child. If you support your child during this time, you can be in a position to help your child handle his or her feelings about this process and its eventual outcome.

Some adoptees try to hide the search for their birthparents because they fear hurting their adoptive parents. If you can handle it, let your child know. The more you can keep information out in the open, the less room there is for hurt due to the omitting of information or outright deception.

Helping Your Child Prepare

Adoptees determined to search on their own should not get their hopes up too high. If your child finds the birthmother, he or she might not know what to do with the information. Adult adoptees need to be emotionally prepared for reunions that can span the spectrum from fairy-tale-perfect to absolutely horrible. It is important for the adoptee to consider not only the impact searching will have on his or her life but also what impact this "finding" will have on the birthparents. Some birthmothers have never told husbands or other children about the child they placed for adoption. These birthmothers might be scared and none too happy when a child resurfaces after eighteen years or more.

Cover your adopted child with prayer daily as he searches for his biological roots. Ask God to sustain your child during the search, shore him up no matter what the outcome, and prepare him for what lies ahead if the birth family is found. He will be faithful to help you and your child during this emotional time.

WORDS OF WISDOM
Cast all your anxiety on him because he cares for you.
—1 Peter 5:7 (NIV)

If you are keeping the lines of communication open with your child, you can help your child prepare for the reunion. Ask if you may accompany her, go shopping for a new outfit, and pray with your child. Help your child think through worst-case to best-case scenarios, and create a plan of words and actions for both cases. Talk together about what your child is thinking and feeling, and how your child expects to feel after first meeting the birthparent. Finally, what kind of long-term relationship does your child hope to have with the birthparent?

Your adopted child might appear to have no underlying adoption issues but is actually nursing a deep core of anger at his birthmother for choosing adoption. That doesn't mean your child is regretting the life he has with you, but that he is having difficulty processing how anyone who loved a child could place that child for adoption.

Remind your child that the birthmother had other options available but recognized that adoption was the most loving thing she could do for her child. And that God had a special plan for your child's life and knew you would adopt him before he was ever born. Your child might not understand all the reasons this side of heaven, but can rest in his loving arms knowing his identity is secure with God.

Take comfort in the fact that you were there for your child since the day you received your child, and that you will continue to be there until the day one of you dies. Reassure your adoptee that he or she is loved and valued, especially if a reunion does not provide an ongoing connection for which your child hoped.

We Found Them. What Do We Do Now?
After searching for months or even years, when an adoptee finally succeeds in finding his birthmother's or birthfather's phone number, he might be too

frightened of rejection to call. Some adoptees will just carry the phone number around, never dialing the number. Others will call as soon as they get it. Just as the responses of adoptees differ, so do responses on the part of birthparents. Some birthmothers joyfully embrace this son or daughter raised by other people. Other parents are shocked to hear the voice of the now-grown-up baby they placed for adoption and choose not to speak to them right then. Still others completely reject their birthchild, either out of pain or from a claim that they have "gotten on with their lives" and don't want to dredge up the past.

If a birthmother is glad to hear from her birthchild, there might be a joyful reunion by telephone and then in person. A birthmother might also share information about the birthfather, or she might not. If the adoptee has located the birthfather, the birthmother might not want anything to do with him. The birthfather might not want to see the birthmother either. Whatever their circumstances were in the past, the placing of a baby for adoption is an emotionally painful act, even when it is best for all involved. Adoptees will need to be cautious when bringing parties from their past together. Make sure that everyone is informed and okay before meeting.

WORDS OF WISDOM
The LORD grants wisdom! From his mouth come knowledge and understanding.
—Proverbs 2:6 (NLT)

MEETING FOR THE FIRST TIME
The initial reunion meetings might be awkward and uncomfortable at first, or they may be cloud-nine experiences. Both parties are getting to know the person they have both wondered about for so many years, and it feels good to have all those questions answered. Now the adopted adult might learn why she has a big nose or red hair. Now the birthmother can rest easy knowing that her child is safe and sound.

Reunions often come with an initial "too good to be true" phase that can be just that, because emotions will inevitably deflate some after this initial exploration.

Bailey and Giddens note that birthmothers and adoptees bring expectations to the reunion that are often not met. The birthmother might still ache for the baby she relinquished and really isn't prepared for the adult child she meets. The adoptee might have carried around fantasies that the birthmother would instantly feel familiar and fill a void in his or her heart. If these things do not occur, and they often do not, reunions can bring both elation and bitter disappointment.

Reunion, like all relationships, takes at least two consenting participants in order to make it to work. If either one of the two is unwilling or unable to contribute their fair share of the relationship, then it won't be sustainable.[40]

After the first meeting or even a few visits, the relationship will start to settle into what it might look like going forward. This might be easy, or it might present lots of challenges, loyalty struggles, and lifestyle issues. Some adoptees or birthmothers are disillusioned after the first few meetings and cut off contact again. Some feel uncomfortable with their birth family or adoptee and limit contact. Others feel comfortable from the first meeting and soon begin the process of blending their adoptive and birth families.

WHEN YOU SUDDENLY FEEL LEFT OUT

For the adoptive parents observing an initial reunion honeymoon period, it might feel like they have been replaced. Their child is suddenly on the phone all the time with her birthmother or running off to meet the birthparent, and it just hurts. Their child now has to be shared with someone the parents do not know but who has an important, foundational connection to their child. They might even feel anger toward the birthparents. If this occurs, ask God to forgive you for harboring a grudge against your child's birthparents, especially if they abandoned, neglected, or abused your child. Abusive parents are tough to forgive, but you are still called to do it.

Adopted parents can take comfort in the fact that all of these feelings are normal, even if it seems silly to have them. Adopted parents whose child is entering a reunion situation should pray not only for their child but also for themselves. They should also ask others to pray for their family.

RECOGNIZING WARNING SIGNS

After the honeymoon period, birthparents and adoptees might begin to notice more differences than similarities, especially in the areas of lifestyles and values. Disillusionment might set in and conversation run dry. It is important to recognize the warning signs of impending trouble with an adoption reunion so that it does not escalate and blow up in everyone's faces. Warning signs include an adoptee or birthparent who begins calling too frequently and showing up for visits unexpectedly. Proper boundaries need to be talked about and enforced for both parties to feel comfortable moving beyond a reunion into a long-term relationship. Some birthmothers might be compelled to act like their child's authority figure (in other words, like a mother) to try to make up for lost years, and adult adoptees might bristle at this near-stranger trying to tell them what to do.

Sometimes after reconnecting, adoptees or birthparents might come to the realization that they are just too different to have an everyday relationship. If either party is being damaged by the contact, it might be healthier to step back for a while and maintain contact from a distance through e-mail or occasional phone calls until lifestyle issues have been resolved or conflicts overcome enough to move forward. Reunions almost always come with unexpected emotions and difficulty establishing a relationship that works well for everyone, especially at first. Again, this is the blending of two families; and it can feel right and wrong at the same time.

PUTTING THE FAMILY PUZZLE TOGETHER

As you put the pieces of family together with your child, be willing to meet the birthparents on your child's schedule. Adoptive parents who work to overcome their own negative feelings can enjoy a relationship with this woman who gave them such a precious gift. She missed all of the growing-up years—the first steps, the lost teeth, the Christmas programs and Easter baskets. Let her get to know the child you love so much, and all of your lives can be richer for it. Her heart can heal, your adopted child's heart can feel complete, and you can set aside your concerns that your adopted child will love any parent more than you. Together, you can now turn the tables and adopt the birthparent into your family, demonstrating God's love and desire to adopt us into his family.

RED LIGHT, STOP!

Questions to consider at this point in your adoption journey:

____ Are you aware of how much your adopted child will wonder about his or her birthparents?

____ Are you preparing for the emotional onslaught and questioning of identity that adolescence will probably bring?

____ Are you preparing your hearts for the day when your adopted child might want to find his or her birthparents?

____ Are you going to be able to put aside any hurt feelings and help with the search?

____ Do you know how to search for a birthparent?

____ Are you willing to keep the lines of communication on this subject open with your adopted child and let him or her know that it is okay to be curious?

____ Will you help your child prepare for the emotional impact of a reunion?

____ How can you help your child move forward into a healthy relationship with his or her birthparent?

GREEN LIGHT, GO!

Action points for your adoption journey:

____ Give your adopted child extra grace through adolescence as he or she begins to form her own identity and wonder more about her biological background.

____ Forgive your adopted child for the times he or she says, "You're not my real parents!"

____ Make sure there is open communication between your child and you about any desire to search for the birthparents.

____ When old enough, if your child seeks a reunion with a birthparent, help him or her register with state and online adoption registries.

____ Pray with your child and talk about how to prepare emotionally for any outcome when meeting the birthparents.

____ Ask the Lord to help you not be jealous of your child's birthparents.

____ Expect reunions to come with a honeymoon phase, and help your child through the emotional letdown when it ends.

____ Forge appropriate boundaries with your child's birthparents, and help your child do the same.

____ Create a healthy, long-term relationship that everyone feels comfortable with, whether that means limiting contact to e-mails or phone calls or getting together on a regular basis.

♥ *My Adoption Miracle*
My Bittersweet Reunion
by Dave Bartlett

I was adopted in California shortly after my birth, and I was raised in a wonderful, loving Christian family. I knew from as far back as I can remember that I was adopted, and it was no big deal. Then came third grade, when I told some friends at school that I was adopted. I was shocked at their reaction, because they kept insisting that there was no way I could be *adopted*, as if that word made me a foreign creature all of a sudden.

From that point on, I think I wondered about my birthmother. I wanted to know what she looked like, if she thought about me, and how she was doing. I wondered if she loved me, and I had a desire to find her someday. I wanted to know why she gave me up, and if I got my sensitive nature from her. I didn't want to barge in and say, "Ta-da! Here I am." I just wanted to get a feel for who she was, and how I was connected to her. Every time my birthday would roll around, all those thoughts would come to the surface.

When I became an adult, I eventually decided to search for her. There were no Internet or state registries then, but I had been in the air force and knew it had a personnel locator service that could track people down. In 1990, I typed up a letter to my adoption caseworker to get the ball rolling, but nothing much happened. In 1992, I wrote to the air force locator service, and on August 18, I received a letter saying they had forwarded my letter to an air force captain who was my biological grandfather. Shortly afterward, I received a letter from my stepgrandmother telling me that my grandfather had passed away, but that he had told her about me and that he loved me.

She told me that my mother had gone on with her life and might not want to have contact with me. Two months later, I received an envelope in the mail with my name typed on it. It was postmarked Atlanta, and there was no return address. Inside that envelope was a single sheet of paper, a typed letter from my birthmother. What follows is a portion of her letter.

Dear David,

It seems that your efforts to trace back to some family roots have paid off. Unfortunately, my father passed away in 1987. I am enclosing an old snapshot of him so you can see the resemblance. I have to be honest and say that I put what happened in the back of my mind, and I was never even told your gender. I was a high school senior, and your father was a freshman in college. I am sad to say that he didn't own up to my condition because of shame or fear or because he had just started a college life. I don't believe my husband of twenty-seven years would need to know this or my two children would understand. The traits you have inherited from your biological family could be your musical talent and air force background. At this point, I am not ready to make contact by phone and don't know if I ever will be. I will try to write again. I hope this letter is of some comfort to you.

Sincerely,

Your Birthmom

I was twenty-nine when I received that letter, and it was a bittersweet moment for me. I do, indeed, look a lot like my biological grandfather. And my questions about whether my birthmother was alive and okay were finally answered. However, I would have loved to meet her, and the thought that I have two siblings out there somewhere who don't know about me is sad, because I would love to have a relationship with them.

Yet I am glad I searched for my birth family, even if the reunion was not Hollywood perfect. It brought things full circle for me, and knowing she is married hopefully speaks to stability in her life. It hurts deep down that I can't know my birth family, but I respect my birthmother's choice. The other side of my coin is that I was raised by a wonderful Christian mom and dad who are still with me. I just have a very blessed life.

Chapter Thirteen

Advice from Those Who Have Gone Before

If you have gotten to this point in the book, you know all about the different types of adoptions, the rules and regulations, and how to get your adoption process started and completed. You have read about many adoption miracles. Every adoption story reveals another layer of the heart of the magnificent God you serve and the way he longs to draw you in as his forever family.

This chapter gives you a chance to hear the collective wisdom of other adoptive parents and the things they wish they had known as they started and traveled along the road toward adoption. Some of their insights are practical; some are emotional. Some are common sense; some may come as a surprise. There is advice about packing and traveling, sleep disruptions and diapers. And there are helpful hints for preparing your hearts.

Preparing Hearts More Than Homes

Many adoptive families say if they had it to do again, they would spend more time preparing their hearts than they did their homes for the task that lay ahead. Most adopting families spend hours or days painting walls, setting up a bed, and creating a special space in their home for their adopted child. However, they fail to do the same kind of getting ready in their hearts and minds. They assume that it will be love at first sight and that they will feel like a family from day one. With older children, especially, this is usually not the case. There might be a honeymoon period at first when the child is amazingly compliant and gasps with wonder at the overabundance all around him; but soon the novelties wear of, and in walk issues of defiance, mistrust, and insecurity.

"For the first six months, it is rough; it can be a struggle," admits Bobby Marks, who with his wife, Jennifer, adopted a nine-year-old son from Kazakhstan in 2000. "That's what I would share. Know that it can be easier on one parent than the other, and if the child keeps testing your limits to see if you will still love him, try not to take it personally."

WORDS OF WISDOM

You have need of endurance, so that when you have done the will of God, you may receive what was promised.
—Hebrews 10:36 (NASB)

Marks discovered, as do most adoptive parents, that at some point after an adoption, the honeymoon does end. When it does, both parents and child are left wondering what happened to all the fun they were having. Some adoption experts call it "post-adoption blues." If you will prepare your heart and mind before your adoption, then you can avoid some of the disillusionment that many adoptive parents and their adopted children have experienced. Spend more time in prayer and take advantage of the wonderful resources that can help you understand your child's special needs and the enormous amount of work that lies ahead. If you do, the challenges will be the same, but you will be less likely to be blindsided by them.

Remember, God called you to do this for a reason, a divine purpose. He never promised that any part of your Christian walk would be easy. In fact, he promises that those who live for him will suffer. Why should you expect that it would be any different with adoption? No child comes with any guarantee that there will be no diseases, no rebellion, no turning his back on God, no getting in trouble at school, no wetting the bed, or even no throwing up on the new carpet. Every child has a unique genetic pattern, temperament, personality, intellect, emotional makeup, learning style, spiritual gifting, and calling. Your job in being called to be adoptive parents is to pray for him unceasingly, love him unconditionally, and guide him toward the God who adores him and has a divine purpose for him.

TIME TOGETHER IS PRECIOUS

Not just adoptive families, but most Christian American families are coming to the realization that time is their most precious commodity. It is far more valuable than money. Schedules get so filled with jobs, school, and extracurricular activities that there is hardly time to parent or sit down at the dinner table together. This can be a real detriment to the adoptive family. Many families stated that if they could do it again, they would clear their calendars to the bare minimum for several months after their new child arrived. Nothing replaces the initial time spent cuddling, rocking, playing games, laughing, tickling, telling stories, and getting to know each other. The way you start out sets the tone and teaches your child what to expect out of your relationship going forward.

IT'S OKAY TO BE NERVOUS

Adoptive parents agree that it is okay to be nervous about this whole new adventure. Give yourself permission to feel strange about the whole thing. You have not had the experience of getting to know this little person growing inside for the last nine months. You have had no ultrasound pictures and heard no heartbeats. All you have had is piles of papers. When you meet your child, it is natural to be nervous. Older children are likely to be nervous too. Infants and toddlers might not know what exactly is happening, but they will sense that something new is happening. With a newborn, you will be unsure if the birthmother will really sign those papers, and you will probably feel guilty that you want her to so badly. Adoptive parents say the wise thing is to give yourself permission to feel whatever it is that you feel, and do not condemn yourself if your feelings are not all "lovey-dovey" right off the bat. Give your emotions to the Lord. He brought you through the process, and he won't fail you now.

The Practical Stuff

HOW TO FIT THE MOST STUFF IN A SUITCASE

For international adopters, packing is always a big issue in chat boards and adoption support groups. "How can we fit all the stuff we need for weeks into one suitcase that weighs less than forty-five or fifty pounds?" is continually batted back and forth. Some families buy the vacuum packers, plastic bags that you can put clothing and other cloth items in and then suck the air out of so they are reduced to small, thin packages. The trick then can be getting all the stuff back into the suitcase overseas—if the appliance is not with you or you don't have an electrical adapter with you. Most people opted to go with more traditional packing methods, and there are plenty of helpful tips:

- Fill empty baby bottles with Cheerios for your new child. This uses the space in the bottles, and you don't have to pack the box of cereal.
- Pack clothing you do not mind discarding, and get rid of it along the way.
- Buy an extra suitcase in the foreign country to fill with your souvenirs or pack a large empty duffel inside your suitcase.
- Take only a few mix-and-match outfits, and plan to launder them in your child's country.

- Roll your shirts into tight bundles and rubber-band them to make them more compact, or make sure everything is folded, not just thrown in, to save space.
- Bring only travel-size shampoos, shaving cream, soaps, toothpaste, laundry kits, or favorite cosmetics. Hotel soaps and shampoos work well.
- Remember that many toiletries and articles of clothing can be purchased in-country rather than packing them. The prices may even be lower.
- Leave the curling irons, hair dryers, and clothes irons at home, or get connected with your traveling group ahead of time (your agency can help you with this) and each person bring one thing to share. Remember that electrical appliances can be difficult to use in foreign countries and may short out, even with the right converters. You can often buy these items inexpensively while you are there, or go without.
- Bring a week's worth of underwear and socks, and only a few mix-and-match outfits. You can always wash your clothes in the bathtub or sink if laundry services are not available.
- Wear your bulkiest items of clothing on the plane to save luggage space. Carry your coat, if one is needed.
- Bring only one pair of very comfortable walking shoes.

BEST PRACTICES OF FOREVER FAMILIES
New suitcases that are built of lighter materials can help you stay under your weight limit—so a new set of luggage might be worth the expense. Many families recommend rolling duffle bags that can be purchased at Wal-Mart for around $20.

WHAT ELSE YOU SHOULD BRING
If you are adopting an infant or a toddler, you will need to make room in your suitcase for these:

- one or two bottles (those with plastic liners are easiest to keep clean)
- sippy cups for toddlers
- powdered formula (soy might be a good choice in case a child is allergic to milk)
- diapers and wipes (six or more diapers per day)
- infant carrier
- stuffed animal or blanket for security
- umbrella stroller (if you can't buy one in the country)
- nail clippers or files
- finger puppets or a musical toy

- small garbage bags for dirty clothes
- lotion
- snacks
- diaper rash ointment
- antibiotic powder and sterilized water to reconstitute it
- liquid Benadryl for allergies
- hydrocortisone cream
- infant acetaminophen drops
- liquid electrolyte supplements such as Pedialyte
- thermometer

For older children, you might want to pack some of these:

- snacks (they are also a good way to break the ice)
- colored pencils and paper
- a stuffed animal
- Etch-a-Sketch
- backpack
- shoes
- clothes
- photo album with pictures of your family and home
- activities for the plane ride

Here are some other items you may want to pack:

- latex gloves to be used when changing diapers (some children have parasites)
- melatonin or a preferred sleep aid
- U-shaped travel pillows and head support for adults and baby
- prunes (many children become constipated due to stress and diet changes)
- books you can give to your guide after reading.
- laundry detergent
- toilet paper (for some countries—check with your agency)
- travel alarm clock
- sturdy flashlight (can be given away as a gift later)
- batteries for all of your electronic items.
- one pouch to wear around the neck for passports
- different sizes of ziploc bags
- envelopes for organizing your money in
- bilingual dictionary (preferably phonetically based)

- bug repellent
- photocopies of all travelers' passports and visas
- coffee singles (especially if you want decaf) and tea bags
- electric travel converter

I DIDN'T KNOW THAT!

A Polaroid camera or inexpensive digital camera is a great way to give your adoptive child a feeling of control over his situation. Show him how to use it and allow him to take pictures of his friends, the workers, and the orphanage or foster home. Take plenty of film, as Polaroid pictures are always a big hit (and every child will want a picture to keep).

OTHER TRAVELING TIPS

Parents and agencies warn adopting travelers that they should take a hard look at the image they portray and be careful not to look too rich. Keep your money in a pouch that is worn unobtrusively on your body or under your clothing—even when you take a shower. Leave most jewelry at home, and remember that fancy suitcases stand out in poor countries and can label you as an easy target to rob.

Try to travel with as few suitcases and separate items as possible, and opt for carry-on only on the way over. The more bags you have, the better the chance that some will be lost in transit, be stolen, or simply slow your group down. If you are in a large group, there may not be enough room for all the luggage in the vehicle that transports you once you arrive.

One great idea for older children, courtesy of Adopting from Russia, www.adoptingfromrussia.com, is to find someone before you leave home who speaks your child's language. Have the translator help you record facts about yourself, your family, and what you want your adopted child to know on a digital voice recorder or mini-audiocassette. Take the player with you and let your child listen to it. You can even read stories on it or sing a lullaby. The point is to give your child as much information about you as possible before you are home and facing the language barrier. If you have any specific instructions your child needs to know about your home (how to lock the front door or turn on the microwave, for example), have your translator make an additional recording for after you return home that you can play with your child as you tour the house. The advantage of having it all in recorded form is that your child is going to be overwhelmed with sensory overload, new sights and sounds, and lots of new information all at once and will not be able to process it all. With a recording, your child can hear your words of instruction and reassurance again and again.

Medical Care

The prescription medicines so easily obtained in the United States can be very difficult to find overseas. If you can, take with you a commonly prescribed antibiotic that treats a variety of infections, especially respiratory and ear infections (such as amoxicillin), and has a low allergic rate and few side effects.

Ask your pediatrician what antibiotic he would prescribe and, what symptoms to look for before you administer it, and use it only if absolutely necessary if your child has not been seen by a physician. If you are traveling with a group, ask if there is a nurse or a doctor, or ask veteran moms if your child's symptoms are serious enough to need medical evaluation or an antibiotic. Ask your pediatrician how to reach him while you are away, and put a call in to describe the symptoms if you can.

Bringing Gifts

Parents who have adopted from an orphanage say they wish they had known to bring lots of gifts. Most adoptive families are instructed to bring a few items for orphanage directors and their guides for the trip, but there are many others you will encounter on your trip that you might want to bless—from hotel maids to the other orphans remaining behind. Find out what the customs are for your country (so that you do not offend), and pack gifts accordingly. Some examples of gifts that adoptive parents have taken for guides, workers, and other adults include the following:

Ukraine
- AM/FM Radio
- assorted tea sets
- CDs (only if you are sure they have a CD player) or cassette tapes of Christian music
- gold jewelry
- good-quality perfume
- nice matching clothes sets
- sweaters, gloves, and scarves
- Disney-themed clothes
- purse sets (wallet and purse)
- Avon Skin-So-Soft
- calculators
- candy, especially almond M&Ms
- car-cleaning items
- flashlights
- reading glasses (from the drugstore)

- manual can openers
- gourmet instant coffees
- cosmetics
- men's dark-colored (black or navy) socks
- Polaroid cameras and film
- state (Florida, Texas, New York, California, etc.) T-shirts

RUSSIA

Gifts to be taken to Russia vary widely between orphanages and areas of the country. Some agencies and facilitators give adoptive families detailed instructions on what to bring, ranging from cosmetics to fax machines and leather briefcases. Some take care of the gifts themselves, and some recommend that you buy gifts in Russia. Adopters going to Russia are expected to bring gifts for their orphanage and a "donation," the amount of which your agency or facilitator will explain. Adoptive families are told not to bring anything that is labeled "Made in China." Here are some gifts that might be given in Russia:

- cosmetics
- money
- bath towels
- postcards from your home town or state
- clothes
- baby bottles
- baby wipes
- diapers
- hair accessories (barrettes, clips)
- Band-Aids
- children's cough syrup
- bottle nipples designed for babies with cleft lips/palates
- pencils
- shoes
- toothbrushes (ask your dentist for these)
- lollipops
- toys
- stickers
- washable markers or crayons

CHINA

In China, the custom is that recipients never open their gifts in front of the gift giver, because it would be considered rude. Gifts are accepted and then tucked away, so do not feel as though they are not well-received. Gift recipients are pleased to have been included, but they probably will not show it. Adoptive families should take items that are gender neutral or for both sexes, as many orphanage directors and other workers are men. Do not take items made in China. Gifts taken to China might include the following:

- cosmetics (these are expensive there, so they are popular gifts)
- Bath & Body Works lotions and other items
- fine chocolates
- state-and university-themed items (team sweatshirts, T-shirts, state postcards, etc.)
- baseball caps
- watches
- jewelry boxes
- silver or gold jewelry
- scarves
- postage stamps from the U.S.
- cassette tapes or CDs

The First Days Together
DOCUMENT EVERY MOMENT
Parents often say their biggest regret when they look back on their first days together is that they did not document it well enough. They might have plenty of pictures or videotape, but many parents wish they had written down their thoughts, prayers, and feelings in the moment. Memories are frail and finicky, and those things that seem vivid and unforgettable in the moment are often a blur later. Besides the camera and video camera, keep a daily journal on your laptop or the old-fashioned way with paper and pen. Years from now it will amaze you to go back and remember how God worked in your life then.

PREPARE MEALS AHEAD
On the practical side of bringing home a newborn baby from the hospital, an international child, or a child from foster care, having meals fixed ahead of time helps tremendously. Prepare and freeze meals, especially of you are going away for weeks. Stock the pantry with easy-to-fix items like macaroni and cheese, oriental noodles, and tuna fish. Pull out the pizza coupons and delivery phone number and put them by the phone too. When you are recovering from sleepless nights or jet lag, having meals on hand is one less thing to have to worry about.

KEEP VISITORS TO A MINIMUM

In the first days together, families say they wish they had known not to over-whelm their child with meeting too many aunts, uncles, cousins, and friends. Yes, family and friends have been waiting anxiously with you, supporting you through the process and helping you get to this point, but your child needs to be able to adjust to this whole new world. Newborns need to be protected from germs and viruses they might be exposed to if passed around to too many peo-ple. International infants and toddlers are taking in new sights, sounds, smells, tastes, textures, and caregivers. Absolutely everything in their world is brand-new, and they need time to get to know their parents from other adults. Ask family and friends to give you some time, whether it takes a few days or a few weeks.

TAKE PLENTY OF TIME OFF

Be there for your child's first days home. Don't miss them by thinking you need to rush back to work. Projects might be waiting, and finances might be tight after all the adoption fees; but you can always make money. Again, it's a matter of trust. Let God come through for you, and he will. You can't get time back—ever. If you miss the bonding time in the beginning, it can affect your relationship with your child for the rest of your lives.

WORDS OF WISDOM

If God is for us, who can be against us? He who did not spare his own Son, but gave him up for us all—how will he not also, along with him, graciously give us all things?
—Romans 8:31–32 (NIV)

TAKE CARE OF YOURSELF

In the midst of focusing energy, time, and emotions on your new child, take vitamins, drink lots of water, eat nutritious foods, and keep up your exercise routine. If your body remains healthy, you are much better prepared to handle all the changes and adjustments. Sleep whenever you can, just as any new par-ent would. Your motto should be: when the baby sleeps, you sleep.

During Childhood

As your child grows, relationship building and memory making should be two of your top priorities. Make his or her childhood one filled with fun, laughter, and lots of time together.

YOU CAN'T HOLD YOUR CHILD TOO MUCH

Touch provides a level of security and trust that nothing can replace. If your child lacked nurturing touch as an infant or a toddler, then it is more important than ever that you hold your child often—even if your child thinks he or she has outgrown hugs.

GOOD CHARACTER IS MORE IMPORTANT THAN GOOD GRADES

Your adopted child might have developmental delays, language barriers, and so much going on inside that focusing on academics will be just too much. Children need to be educated, but they first need to heal and be assured of their parents' love and God's love. Unconditional love and overly high expectations do not go hand in hand. Academics will come easier when the heart and spirit are well nurtured.

SOME HURTS TAKE A LONG TIME TO HEAL

If they had it to do again, many families of older adopted children and any adopted child who develops signs of attachment issues would not wait to get help, thinking the issues would resolve themselves. Most advise turning for expert assistance as soon as trouble begins, so the child can be given insight into her own behavior and tools to manage her feelings appropriately.

PRESERVE MEMORIES

Scrapbooks are worth the time and effort to document childhood. Invest in a good camera and video camera, and use them frequently. The families who felt the closest say one thing that drew them together was eating meals together at a table. Passing the food, praying together, and sharing what happened during the day kept adoptive families connected.

During the Teen Years

TEENS NEED HUGS

Even in times of conflict, don't forget the hugs. Even if they pull away or shrug them off, teenagers need physical contact from their parents. Quick hugs, side-arm hugs, cuddling while watching television, pats on the back, and back rubs are all appropriate and needed forms of physical contact.

GRACE IS MORE IMPORTANT THAN AUTHORITY

When adopted teens are struggling with their identity, their desire to fit in, their beliefs, and their longing for independence, remember that grace is more important than laying down the law in most cases, adoptive families say. Even when we are disobedient, God still has the grace to forgive us and love us. Yes, your kids need boundaries; but in these years of experimenting, rebelling, and testing, they also need to know they are loved and accepted, flaws and all.

REMEMBER UNCONDITIONAL LOVE

That's where the unconditional love comes in. You might have hoped for a football player and gotten a violinist. Maybe you wanted a child who would share your love of shopping and you got a daughter who wants to go hunting in the woods with her dad. Try not to make your love seem based on performance, expectations, or any other conditions, parents say. Just love your kids, period.

QUESTIONING IDENTITY AND AUTHORITY IS NORMAL

Teens will question their beliefs, their identity, and your authority. Be loving but firm, forgiving and full of grace, but do not let go of structure and routine, especially for teens who have previously been institutionalized. The goal in the teen years is to find the middle ground of nonconflict where you can come together and enjoy each other, while providing gentle guidance toward the path of mature adulthood.

RECOGNIZE WHAT IS NOT NORMAL

Adoptive families of adult children say when they look back on their parenting experience, they realize for the most part how naive they were in the beginning. Most agree that they would have learned more, sought help more quickly, and asked more questions about what they should and should not be expecting and experiencing in each season of their child's growth. They say they would have played more and argued less, listened more and lectured less, and tried harder to remember that God does not measure their child's success on the same scale of grades, jobs, and productivity that we do. Nor does he see the child's outcome as the success or failure of the parents (you).

The Blessings

GOD REALLY IS FAITHFUL

Even in the worst of circumstances, adoptive families say one thing that got them through every crisis was the knowledge that God is always faithful. He called them to adopt to begin with, he guided them through every step of the miracle journey that brought their child home, and they rest assured that he will not let them fall now. A child might get in trouble or leave home, drop out of school, or never attach the way his parents hoped he would. Still, God is faithful; and adoptive parents without fail said they would do it all again.

"I spent my retirement, put one child in rehab, dealt with unexpected medical issues, and still face teen crises one after the other," one adoptive father of three older children from Ukraine shared. "But I know without a doubt that I was called by God to do this. And these were supposed to be my children. I might not know his purpose in all this, but I know I am obeying him."

You Can Trust Him with All Your Children
Some adoptive parents, moms in particular, said they had to come to a realization that God can be trusted with their precious children, and that their control over any situation was just an illusion. They are God's children that he entrusted to your care. They were his design, and they are created to fulfill a unique purpose that he planned before the beginning of time. Wise adoptive parents say they had to give their child back to God and let him run the show.

Adoption Blessed Us More Than We Blessed a Child
Adoptive parents, without fail, stated that each adopted child blessed the parents' lives more than the parents blessed the child. Even if the child is difficult, the entire orchestration of the adoption process brings a deeper understanding of God's love and commitment to them. They thought they were going into adoption to bless a child in need and ended up being the recipients of the greatest blessing they had ever known.

Adoption Opened Our Eyes to Others' Needs
The adoption process also opens adoptive families' eyes to the needs around them. Before seeing a child with no family, adoptive families might have been content to live mostly for themselves, to surround themselves with comfortable things, not stretching much out of their comfort zone. Adoption changes that permanently. No longer will you be able to ignore the needs around you.

Adoption Helped Us Love Better and Deepened Our Walk with God
Finally, adoptive families say that before their adoption experience, they did not fully understand the love of God. Adoption led them to a deeper faith, a more intimate relationship with him, and a dependence that keeps them relying on his grace today. By learning to love God's way, through the spirit of adoption, they were able to give love more fully and receive it in a whole new way.

RED LIGHT, STOP!
Questions to consider at this point in your adoption journey:

____ Has learning about adoption helped you understand God's love in a new way?

____ Can you extend grace ahead of authority?

___ Can you provide structure and unconditional love?

___ Do you have a realistic understanding that adoption will bring some tough times?

___ Will you trust God during your times of suffering?

GREEN LIGHT, GO!

Action points for your adoption journey:

___ Ask adoptive families you know about what they wish they had known during each stage of the adoption journey.

___ Ask God to give you a deeper knowledge of him through your adoption.

___ Study the Scriptures and write down verses or passages that show you what God's love looks like.

___ Apply this type of unconditional love to your relationships, especially with your adopted child, who might not have known love at all.

___ Pray that God will help you hand over your child to him, as Hannah did with Samuel.

___ Extend grace to your child when he fails and falters. Reach out your hand and help him to his feet again.

___ Remember that academics are less important than character.

___ Know that the best thing you can do for your child is lead him or her to the personal love of Christ.

My Adoption Miracle
Our Precious Jem
by Traci DePree, Christian fiction author

When I was pregnant with my fourth daughter—seven years after my third daughter was born—God really had to show me that I was not done having kids yet. My first three were becoming pretty self-sufficient, and when I found out we were expecting our fourth, I just wasn't sure about it. When she was born, I realized how much I love children and wondered why I thought I was not okay with having her. This opened up my heart, I think, to having even more children.

Then my sister and brother-in-law went to work in China with the Philip Hayden Foundation to do outreach to orphans. They showed us a slide show of children who were waiting for homes, and that night I asked my husband, "What is keeping us from adopting?" He said, "Nothing." From that point, we knew we felt called to adopt.

We chose an agency and decided to adopt a child from Korea. We took classes to prepare for the adoption, and we learned to think not just about the adoption of a baby, but also what her life would look like growing up. It felt like such a long wait from the time we put in our first application until we got her. After several months, we received a referral. The baby had been premature and had some serious medical issues. Our hearts were saddened when we realized we would not be able to give that baby the care she needed. It wouldn't be fair to her or to our family, but it was so hard to say no. We had to wait five or six months for a second referral, this time for our beautiful Jem.

When they called and told us our new referral would be here in two days, we got really excited. Then they told us that the government wasn't letting any babies out of Korea, and it would be another five months before we could get her. She was six weeks old when we got the call about her. Five months later, we got a call on a Saturday that she would be here on Monday.

We got Jem when she was seven months old. We met her escort at the airport, and now my four-year-old thinks that babies come from airports! All I could think of was the questions I would have liked to ask her foster mother about what she liked and didn't like. With a pregnancy, you have nine months to get used to each other and can even learn a lot about their personality by the way they act in utero. Being Jem's mother didn't come as naturally. We had to learn about each other first.

Even at her tender age, you could tell that Jem missed Korea when we first brought her home. When she woke up and saw me, her face would fall and I knew she was missing her foster mother. A year later, she has adjusted so well, but she still doesn't like going to bed. She was used to sleeping with her foster mom, and when the lights go out she starts breathing faster.

She has stolen our hearts. She is such a sweet child, and she is so different from her loud and boisterous sisters. She is so quiet that I have to remember to go in and check on her when nap time should be over, because she will not cry or call out to let me know she is awake. She will just quietly play in her crib.

One thing about adoption I did not expect is the sadness I feel for her birthparents. I mourn for them and what they are missing all the time, because I get the privilege of raising this beautiful girl. From what we know, her birthmother was not married, and there is still great social stigma against unwed mothers in Korea. There was no way she could keep her baby, but she named her before she left the hospital, which makes me think she really did want to keep her. Adopting Jem has been such a blessing for us. So many people think we are doing this wonderful thing to have adopted this child. We are not wonderful; it's just what God wanted us to do. She has given us the blessing, and she is our adoption miracle.

Part Five

Adoption as a Ministry:
How Can You Help?

Pure and undefiled religion before God and the Father is this: to visit
orphans and widows in their trouble, and to keep oneself
unspotted from the world.
—James 1:27 (NJKV)

There are always those who take it upon themselves to defend God, as if
Ultimate Reality, as if the sustaining frame of existence, was something
weak and helpless. These people will walk by a widow deformed by leprosy
begging for a *paise*, walk by children dressed in rags living in the street, and
they think, "Business as usual." But if they perceive a slight against
God, it is a different story. Their faces go red, their chests heave mightily,
they sputter angry words. The degree of their indignation is astonishing.
Their resolve is frightening.
These people fail to realize that it is on the inside that God must be
defended, not on the outside. They should direct their anger at themselves.
For evil in the open is but evil from within that has been let out. The main
battlefield for good is not the open ground of the public arena but the small
clearing of each heart. Meanwhile, the lot of widows and homeless
children is very hard, and it is to their defence, not God's,
that the self-righteous should rush.
–Yann Martel, *Life of Pi*

Chapter Fourteen

Adoption and Orphan Care as a Worldwide Ministry

If you know the blessings of adoption firsthand, either as an adoptee or as adoptive parents, you are in a great position for adoption and orphan-care ministry everywhere you go.

SHARE YOUR STORY

You can help others know the blessing adoption has been in your life by simply sharing your story. Pray about whether you are to go beyond telling your adoption story with friends and family by sharing your family's testimony at church, telling about your adoption experience to prospective adopters at adoption workshops, or writing up your story to be submitted to local newspapers and magazines. If an interview with you is published or broadcasted, you might inspire other families to travel the path of adoption.

WORDS OF WISDOM
Speak up for those who cannot speak for themselves; defend the rights of all those who have nothing.
—Proverbs 31:8 (NCV)

Writing your story should be done in a way that will encourage and enlighten, in an article format so that smaller papers can run it as is—or contact you for more information. Be sure your contact information is clearly stated at the top of the press release or story you send, and follow up after a week or so with a phone call to see if the publication or television stations are considering it. Be polite and to the point, and if they are not planning to use it, ask how you could make your story more newsworthy and if you could check back with them at a later date. Adding adoption statistics and information that makes the story pertinent to the local audience served by the news outlet will help make your story more likely to be heard. Also, write your story around a hook that keeps a reader interested, such as a surprise ending, a shocking statistic, or an upcoming event.

ADOPTION WORKSHOPS

Nothing pulls prospective adopters' heartstrings when they are considering adoption like seeing all the little faces of Chinese girls whose parents bring them to an agency's informational seminar. Their families' testimonies are so moving that there is usually not a dry eye left in the place, and many families have felt a clear calling after witnessing the joy adoption brings.

You can show people the blessing of adoption by attending your agency's workshops, or take it a step further by teaching an adoption information workshop at your local church, library, or recreation center. You can make a presentation for your agency (with their permission and training), or remain nonaffiliated and simply show up to answer questions from people who might want to adopt.

Create a multimedia presentation and gather adoption fliers from the Dave Thomas Foundation, Shaohannah's Hope, Hope for Orphans, or agencies you could support. Offer some refreshments, keep the workshop to about an hour or ninety minutes tops, and afterward answer questions one-on-one. Prepare ahead of time for the event by listing your workshop in the calendar pages of the newspaper. These listings are usually free, but most papers need several weeks' notice. Hand out fliers at your church or business, ask to place them in the local libraries, businesses, other churches, etc.

We Are Not Adopting—How Can We Help?

If you know the heart of God for the people he has created, then you know he wants his children all over the world to be safe, healthy, nurtured, loved, and led to him. He calls on those who know him and believe in his name to be the ones to reach out to the millions of orphans who will lose their lives or grow up never knowing what a healthy relationship looks like because they have never experienced one. There are hundreds of ways for you to get help, and God expects you to do so.

Even if you do not feel called to adopt, you are still called to get involved in orphan-care or adoption ministry. Christians are expected to take care of the widows and orphans. It is not optional for those who believe in Christ and his Word, the Bible.

The first thing you can accomplish (and you are doing it already) is to become educated. Get the numbers, learn the statistics, and know what is really happening with children worldwide. Talk to others who have seen overseas orphanages and war-torn countries. Visit UNICEF's Web site, www.unicef.org, and read their reports. Once you are knowledgeable, you can share that knowledge with others by finding a way to volunteer. Be the hands and feet of Jesus for children in need. Your own adoption miracle is waiting right around the corner. Do not let it go by.

Volunteer, Volunteer, Volunteer!

Whether God has called you to adopt or not, there are a multitude of ways you can help children find forever families. God can use you to touch a child's life in a mighty way, even in a short amount of time.

VOLUNTEER AT LOCAL CHILDREN'S HOMES

Pray about whether you would be willing to answer phone calls and e-mails from those mired in the paper chase, frustrated about delays, or on the fence about whether they are being called to adopt. Consider:

- being a reference family, if you've adopted;
- being a mentor family, if you've adopted and can guide someone through the adoption process;
- lending your support and experience to get documents properly notarized, certified, and authenticated;
- helping in the office, at presentations, etc.;
- helping families create their photo album and résumé for the birthmother; or
- working with a family as they get licensed to foster-to-adopt.

One of the most daunting tasks in adoption is the paperwork. If you've already been through it, you know how it is done. Just showing others what your dossier looks like (and that it really can be finished) will be an encouragement to those beginning the process.

While you might think of orphanages as being far away in other countries, there are children's homes where kids without families live in every state. Find the ones in your area and see how you can help. A group of teens in my area volunteer at the local children's home to sort through the donated items each Christmas season and organize them into separate piles for boys, girls, infants, and toddlers.

Send donations of clothing, shoes, and toys to the children's home. Do not just send your old cast-offs. Remember that these are children who already feel different and who want to fit in just like everyone else their age.

Do not add to their differences by donating items that are stained, worn out, or terribly out of style.

If you do not know the names of any orphanages in your area, call the local office of the state department of children's services and ask them where you can help. They might need you to help fix a building, do clerical work, or sign up to be a mentor or tutor to a child who needs a positive example and good role model in his or her life.

GIVE FINANCIALLY

If you just cannot help in any way that requires your time right now, you can still give money. Pray about whether the Lord would have you sponsor an orphan or donate to an orphanage, either local or overseas. Your gift will make a difference in a child's life.

Sponsor a child by sending some money each month (usually in the $25–$35 range) to help them get the things they need before they are adopted and, in some cases, to help finance their adoptions. Many more families would probably adopt if they could just afford it, and organizations like Shaohannah's Hope are trying to bridge that gap. Your sponsorship can help unite a child with is forever family.

You can also help care for orphans around the world who will never be adoptable by supporting charitable organizations that care for them.

JOIN MISSION TRIPS

It is difficult to really understand the worldwide plight of children until you see it firsthand. It may never feel personal to you unless you go and experience the need. One way to really get tuned in to the needs of children in other countries is to sign up for a missions trip to a poverty-stricken nation. Ask to visit and tour the inside of an orphanage there. Really get to see what the living conditions are like for many, many people around the world who live with no running water, electricity, or reliable shelter. Nothing will move your heart like seeing, hearing, tasting, and smelling real poverty.

Take a short-term trip, a summer abroad, or take a year to teach English in a foreign country. You can give love and personal attention to children who might have never experienced it.

If there is a children's home in your area, they might need tutors and mentors available to spend time with kids. Maybe you could be a handyman to hang window curtains, do some painting, or otherwise help improve the appearance of the home.

Your life will never be the same, and God will kindle in you a passion to help those he loves.

If you can't travel to a foreign country, get your friends or church body together and "adopt" a whole orphanage. Develop a personal relationship with a local or foreign children's home through a missionary, people who have adopted, or your department of human services. Find out what the home's biggest needs are and pull people together to meet those needs.

BEST PRACTICES OF FOREVER FAMILIES

In 2000, Steven Curtis Chapman and his wife, Mary Beth, brought home their first adopted daughter from China. The couple was so moved by the plight of orphans that they founded Shaohannah's Hope, which has since given adoption grants to hundreds of adoptive families, and has worked to help orphans around the world. Steven has also written two adoption songs, while Mary Beth has created the *Shaoey and Dot* book series about an adopted girl and her ladybug friend. Both Chapmans continue to travel on goodwill missions to many countries to help improve the lot of orphans. They are just one family, and they are impacting the world.

Volunteers are also needed for Shaohannah's Hope and FamilyLife's Hope for Orphans. When their presentations come to town via a concert or the Hope for Orphans "If You Were Mine" workshop, they need volunteers to man the tables as well as adoptive families to share their stories and bring their beautiful adopted children for people to see. Contact these organizations to volunteer.

BECOME A GUARDIAN AD LITEM

Find out what is happening with the foster-care system in your city, county, or state and get involved. Train to become a guardian ad litem, which is a trained volunteer or paid professional who becomes knowledgeable about a child's situation (through the case file, observations, visits, and interviews) and becomes the child's advocate in court. The guardian ad litem can make recommendations to the court about placement, counseling, and custody issues. The guardian ad litem does not take care of the child but appears as an advocate in the courtroom for the child. Guardian ad litem classes are usually free or might involve a small fee, but they are needed in virtually every community.

BECOME A FOSTER PARENT

Foster parents are also desperately needed. There simply are not enough licensed homes to go around for the estimated 800,000 children currently in state care (120,000 of whom are eligible to be adopted).

START LISTENING

Sometimes the best way to lend a hand to someone in the middle of adoption is to listen. Listen to the prospective parents' fears about adopting a child who will not look like them or may not act like them. Listen to their complaints about the endless piles of paperwork, then be there to hear their frustration at the even more endless wait for a referral or a birthmother to choose them. Give a hurting mom-or dad-to-be permission to express the pain that results from arms left empty and a heart aching to love a child.

THROW A SHOWER

During the wait, you can bring joy (and diapers!) to prospective adoptive families by throwing them a baby shower (or adoption shower if the child is older). Ask them what supplies they need, and invite friends to hold a party and bring some of those needed items. If you do not know any adoptive families, hold a baby shower anyway, and donate the items to a local crisis pregnancy center for a child in need.

Helping Birth Families Heal

Birthparent ministries can run the gamut from holding a support group for birthmothers to counseling them about their ongoing pain. Volunteers can also learn from them about their side of the adoption picture. Too often, birthmothers feel they were an active part of the adoption triangle until their child was born, then, as one birthmother told me, "My services were no longer needed."

Sometimes birthmothers need a shoulder to cry on, even if it has been many years since they relinquished a child. Your sympathy might help uproot seeds of bitterness and resentment that have taken hold in their lives. Birthmothers often carry a load of guilt, worry, and sorrow that feels too heavy to bear. Some birthfathers, especially if they did not get to be an active part in placing their child, also grieve.

If you know a birthparent who has placed a baby recently (or years ago) and is still openly grieving, be bold and ask how you can help. No one should live in isolation with their pain, but birthparents often do. A common complaint is that no one is willing to talk about their child with them, but rather people are afraid to bring up the subject. Ask a birthmother how you can stand by her side. Birthfathers certainly are not exempt from feeling pain at the loss of a child, even if they are not as open about it. If you know a birthfather, ask him if he wants to share his experience. Love him, and you might be the tool God uses to help an old wound begin healing.

Birthgrandparent ministry is another avenue you can pursue. Many grandparents of children who were placed for adoption wonder and worry about their grandchildren. Christian Adoption Services in Matthews, North Carolina, recently held a birthgrandmothers' luncheon near Mother's Day. It was a chance for these women to openly talk about their relinquished grandchildren, show pictures, celebrate, and grieve together.

VOLUNTEER AT A CRISIS PREGNANCY CENTER

Crisis pregnancy centers are usually Christian-based support services for women and their partners facing unplanned pregnancies. They exist to offer an alternative to abortion by helping women create a safe home environment where they can keep their children or stand by them if they make the heart-wrenching decision to place their child for adoption. These centers often need volunteers to help in their offices, to train to be counselors, and to offer other support via coordinating fund-raisers and just spreading the word.

Mentoring Adoptive Families

A birthparent ministry can be as personal as coordinating and hosting a get-together of adopted adults and birthparents and having them share their stories. This can often be a time of healing for all. Remember that there is a lot of pain in some of these stories, and that support groups and sharing groups are apt to become very emotional, even heated at times. The best practice is to have someone attend who has experience in counseling and can facilitate healthy communication and diffuse difficult situations.

If you are a birthparent, why not pray for the strength to share your story? If it has been the hidden secret that haunts you, let God free you from your past. Ask him how he wants to use your pain. He will use you in amazing ways to reach out to other birthparents, birthmoms currently facing the decision to raise or relinquish a child, or prospective adoptive families who need to be aware of the feelings of the birthmother.

Another birthparent ministry can be to help birthparents make memories. They might need to express their love for their absent child through art, journaling, holding a symbolic service to let them go, or creating a scrapbook they would love to give to their birthchild. Offer to facilitate a Making Memories class of this kind. Even if they never have an opportunity to share their creations with the child they relinquished, these creations can give them a place to express their emotions.

RED LIGHT, STOP!

Questions to consider at this point in your adoption journey:

____ Are you willing to create an adoption ministry locally or get plugged into an existing one?

____ Are you willing to share your story as an adoptive family so that others will see that they, too, can adopt?

____ If you do not feel called to adopt, have you prayed about where God would have me meet the needs of orphans?

____ Do you know where the local children's homes are in your area and what needs they have?

____ Have you considered training to become a guardian ad litem or foster-care parent?

GREEN LIGHT, GO!

Action points for your adoption journey:

____ If you have adopted a child, share your story of the miracle in your life with those around you.

____ Participate in an adoption workshop or lead one yourself.

____ Become a mentor family to an adoptive family in the process.

____ Gather a support team to help volunteer at a local children's home.

____ Go on mission trips and work in an orphanage.

____ Volunteer with an orphan-support ministry such as Shaohannah's Hope.

____ Send donations to a specific orphanage regularly and develop a relationship with those who work there.

____ Reach out to birthparents.

♥ *My Adoption Miracle*
Mothering the Motherless
By Rita Springer, Modern Worship Leader

I was thirty-seven years old, and my whole life I had dreamed of being a soccer mom. But here I was, still single. I was faithfully praying and waiting on the Lord. I even had dreams about my husband. I had pictured adopting a child someday, but I never pictured myself doing it alone. I thought my husband and I would adopt a child from Africa together.

Then I visited a Romanian hospital and saw all these babies who were just dying right there in their cribs, and I felt the Lord start talking to me about adoption.

I didn't know what to do. I really wasn't sure I was prepared to be a single mom. I had doubts and fears. I was raised in a loving, Christian home, but I also knew what it was like to lose parental figures at a young age. I was nine when my dad died of cancer, and my grandfather died six months later. My mother died nine years after that. I knew what it was like not to have a dad, and I didn't feel it would be fair to raise a child without one.

That's when God told me, "Your dad died when you were nine, and I did a good job with [fathering] you. You and I have done all these things together. Let's go raise a warrior together."

Wow! I knew then that I was being called to go down that road and adopt. I thought I was supposed to adopt in the United States, even though I had such a heart for the nation of Africa. I called a woman at an agency in Florida, and she said she did not adopt to singles. Then she said that she felt the Lord was telling her to make an exception for me. I felt I should adopt a newborn, and I just told her I would adopt the first baby she needed a home for. I didn't care about race or if the baby had Down syndrome. I just figured God would give me the grace. Just a couple of weeks after I filled out the agency application, the director called and said, "I have the woman sitting right here who wants you to raise her baby."

The amazing thing was, my baby would be African. His mother and father, from Zimbabwe, were in the United States on visas. When the father found out about the pregnancy, he returned to Africa. The mother felt she could not care for this baby, and she chose me. I was there at his birth, and his name is Justice. He is so amazing, and it is wonderful what God is doing with us.

I have a very black baby, I am white, and I live in the South—it's amazing the looks men give me and what women will say to me going through the airport. I think God is doing something in bringing all the races together, even trying to make a point to the church. There was a man who came up to me at a church and said that God had just totally convicted him that he had a prejudiced heart.

When Justice was a year old, we had a birthday party for him. That had been the toughest, most challenging year of my life in many ways, but one that I wouldn't change for anything. God has allowed me to struggle financially, but more than 40 percent of single parents live below the poverty line, so I think he is allowing me to feel what they feel. I have struggled with balance and my music in just about every area. But Justice—he is a true joy. He travels like a champ; he never cries. I've had dreams of my son, Justice, someday evangelizing in Zimbabwe. With God, I want to raise that warrior.

Chapter Fifteen

Starting an Adoption or Orphan-Care Ministry

In the National Adoption Attitudes Survey by the Dave Thomas Foundation for Adoption, nearly half of the survey respondents said the first place they would turn for information about adoption was to their place of worship. Yet very few churches in the United States have adoption ministries in place. The needs of orphans cannot be met until the church becomes actively involved.

As new adoption ministries and grant-giving foundations form, local churches should step up and become actively involved with meeting the needs of orphans around the world. Many indirectly help orphans through their support of missionaries who work in orphanages overseas or in making donations to children's homes in the United States. But by taking adoption ministry through the local church to a whole new level, many orphans worldwide could be united with forever families and grow up in homes instead of on the streets or in institutions.

Whether you are an adoptive parent, are a prospective adoptive parent, or have no plans to adopt but feel the need to help children, you might be the one God is calling to stir people to action in your church home and local community.

DISCOVER LOCAL NEEDS
One thing you can easily do as a church body is to ask your local government caseworkers and nonprofit organizations that work with children what the needs are in your county. Find out how many children are in need of foster homes and adoptive homes. Your fellow church members might be willing to help kids if they are made aware of the need and know specifically what they can do to make a difference.

In Colorado, Project 1.27 works to connect kids in the state foster-care system with Christian families who will adopt them by facilitating paperwork and helping families get through the bureaucratic red tape. Project 1.27 was founded in 2003 by Pastor Robert Gelinas of Colorado Community Church, a parent of three adopted children. He wanted to see children placed in families rather than remaining in state care. In its first six months, Project 1.27 saw nearly five hundred people attend orientation classes, with nineteen cities and fifteen churches represented and thirty-five families committed to adopting through the Project 1.27 process. (For more information, see appendix F.)

OFFER CLASSES

Find out if members of the congregation would be interested in attending foster-care or guardian ad litem training. The classes are generally free, and the local department of human services might even hold them at your church if there is enough interest.

If you decide to invite an agency to make an adoption presentation or to host an adoption information seminar on your own, get the word out to the community. Those who have never set foot in the door might discover your church by attending a meeting there. Be gracious hosts, and offer snacks and drinks if appropriate, so that people can get to know one another during breaks and after the meeting has concluded. Create a flier that can be posted at businesses in town and included in your weekly church bulletins, and send a press release of any events to the local newspapers. Send the release to the calendar section and to the news department, as you might get a story in one section and a calendar listing of your event in another.

BEST PRACTICES OF FOREVER FAMILIES

Many adoptive families help spread the word about adoption by working with their church to host an adoption seminar or support group.

Adoption information seminars can be held for foster-care adoptions, domestic adoptions, or international adoptions. If you want to host a meeting independently of an agency, make sure you are knowledgeable to answer questions, or have local experts on hand to provide more information or speak one-on-one with those who are interested. Invite adoptive families and their children to come as well. Every adoption story is a miracle, and having families share their personal testimonies stirs hearts every time. You have no idea of the miracles God can birth in your congregation if you are willing to open the door.

As a beginning step to adoption ministry, you can also offer parenting workshops for the community and invite first-time adoptive parents or prospective adoptive parents to attend for free. It is important for adoptive families to be connected with a close community of friends who will surround them with support through the process. Your church can be that support team.

NATIONAL ADOPTION AWARENESS MONTH

Every November is National Adoption Awareness Month, when adoption advocates make it their goal to help adoptions be finalized, celebrate adoptive families, and draw attention to adoption so that others will be more aware of the needs of children who need forever families. It is the perfect time to begin your adoption-ministry events.

The National Adoption Day organization, www.nationaladoptionday.org, offers a free online tool kit to help you get started on your planning and give you ideas so you can be part of this special time for adoptive families everywhere. The tool kit is very comprehensive and guides you step-by-step through the process of planning and executing an event. It teaches you how to send press releases to the media and includes templates and media contact information. The kit also shows you how to get local and state politicians involved in your event and includes proclamations they can read. It comes complete with fliers, logos, and sample phone scripts to solicit the help of local businesses. Here are all the items included in the tool kit:

- Tips for Getting Organized
- Core Components to Every National Adoption Day Event
- Timeline for Planning a Successful National Adoption Day
- Invitation Letter (Template)
- Confirmation of Participation Letter (Template)
- Donation Letter (Template)
- Sample Phone Script for Business Outreach (Template)
- Governor Proclamation (Template)
- State Legislator Proclamation (Template)
- Mayoral Proclamation (Template)
- Ideas for How to Stage a Media Event
- Timeline for Media Outreach
- Dos and Don'ts for Media Pitching
- Getting Your Event in Daybooks
- Associated Press (AP) State-by-State Listing
- National Adoption Day Q&A
- National Adoption Day Core Talking Points
- News Release (Template)

- News Advisory (Template)
- Letter-to-Editor (Template)
- Letter to Place a Community Calendar Listing (Template)
- Community Calendar Listing (Template)
- Drop-In Article (Template)
- Public Service Announcement Cover Letter and Scripts (Template)
- Tips for Utilizing Spokespeople
- Finding Families to Talk
- Helpful Hints for Family Spokespeople
- Personal Release Form
- Helpful Hints for All Spokespeople
- Banner
- Flier
- Podium Sign
- T-shirt Design
- Certificate of Family Membership with National Adoption Day Logo
- Certificate of Family Membership without National Adoption Day
- Thank-You Letter (Template)
- National Adoption Statistics Fact Sheet
- About National Adoption Day
- Myths & Facts About Adoption
- Logos

If you are willing to start or support an adoption ministry but don't have a clue where to begin, check out the adoption foundation Shaohannah's Hope at www.shaohannahshope.org. One of Shaohannah's Hope's goals is to help local churches plug into adoption ministry. The Web site has resources that range from sermons to inspirational song suggestions in its "Building Bridges of H.O.P.E." section.

Another prominent Christian ministry, FamilyLife (www.familylife.com), has also developed an adoption ministry, Hope for Orphans. Hope for Orphans has ministry components for prospective adopters and for the local church, including planning tools for church adoption events, a DVD available for purchase of founder Dennis Rainey speaking about adoption, and an "If You Were Mine" adoption workshop that travels throughout the country.

SUPPORT AN ORPHANAGE

There are many orphanages around the world struggling to provide food, clothing, clean water, and medical assistance to the children in their care. Many of the children in these orphanages may never be eligible for adoption into families in the United States, but your congregation can "adopt" them by sponsoring their orphanage and forming a partnership with their caregivers to meet their needs.

PARTNER WITH ADOPTIVE FAMILIES

Adoptive families can use the support of their local church body in a variety of ways. Perhaps your congregation can raise some of the financial assistance needed to meet adoption expenses. Maybe your church is willing to open its doors and provide meeting space for local adoptive families who want to form a support group. Your church can help adoptive families in the church body by offering to bring meals, run errands, or provide child-care during the first months when an adopted child comes home.

BECOME RESPITE CAREGIVERS

Church members who want to help local children can take classes to become licensed as "respite caregivers" for foster parents. A respite care provider is a licensed foster home that cares for foster children when their foster parents need a break or must take a vacation. Respite care providers help foster-care kids and foster parents too.

How to Get Going

To begin adoption ministry in your church, you need to get organized, consult the correct church authorities, decide what projects you want to try, and get others lined up to help.

MEET WITH YOUR PASTOR

The first thing to do is to pull together a cohesive presentation and present it to your pastor. Schedule a meeting with him, because he needs to be included before you make any plans to launch a ministry. Tell him of your desire to see the church help more children, and tell him how you want to go about doing it. Let him know whether you would just need his encouragement, his endorsement from the pulpit, his permission to form a committee, funds, or all of the above.

Do not expect an answer right away. You might have been thinking about this for some time, but he will need time to think, pray, and perhaps take it to the board, the deacons, or a committee before he can give you a green light to get started. Have your plan well thought out, including what you would like to accomplish immediately, in the next six months, over the next year, and over the next five years.

Discuss the various possibilities that might be the best fit for your church body, including whether you would want to help kids in the state foster-care system, help couples facing infertility choose adoption and find birthmothers, support birthparents in crisis pregnancies, build connections with foreign orphanages, provide support for adoptive families who need financial assistance, or do some combination of the above.

WORDS OF WISDOM

I was hungry and you gave me something to eat, I was thirsty and you gave me something to drink, I was a stranger and you invited me in.
—Matthew 25:35 (NIV)

ESTABLISH YOUR BOOKKEEPING

After you meet with the pastor, you need to set up a bookkeeping system that has accountability. You will need to decide who can write checks, where and by whom the money will be deposited, who keeps the books, and whether the person or persons handling the money should be bonded, and then you should begin to strategize where you want the funds to go. Start small, but don't be afraid to dream big. Most ministries began with just a few people, a great idea, and limited resources. Once the dream is planted and the work of tending it begins, then it can grow.

CREATE A COMMITTEE

Ask friends to work with you, or you cancreate a formal core committee. Decide where and at what times to meet, and create an agenda to discuss. Together, you can do great things for children in need and help families in your own community who want to expand their families through adoption, and your church can set a community-wide example of how to serve.

WRITE LETTERS OF REFERENCE

An immediate thing your church members can do is to write letters of reference for couples they know who are beginning the adoption process. You can even write a sample letter that can be printed or e-mailed as a point of reference.

ORGANIZE FUND-RAISERS

Begin planning fund-raisers—and be creative. Maybe your youth group will want to sell soda at the next church dinner and donate the proceeds to your effort. Perhaps you can hold a bake sale before and after church, or organize a silent auction, a spaghetti dinner, or an old-fashioned carnival. Decide whether the monies will be used right away to help a family financially in their adoption, to sponsor an adoption workshop, or to print fliers and back more fund-raisers—wherever they can best be used to help you get started.

Churches Making a Difference for Orphans

BRENHAM FIRST BAPTIST, BRENHAM, TEXAS

When adoptive parents Jay and Suzanne Faske became aware of the needs of orphans, they began adopting children. Then, they approached the mission board of their small church and asked for their support in starting an orphan ministry.

"The mission board was very receptive and gave us some ideas of how to get started," Michelle shares. "They felt that we needed to start by raising awareness in our church. They gave us permission to use a portion of a wall in the hallway entering the sanctuary. On this wall, we put photos of waiting domestic and international children, scripture, and statistics about orphans."

After that, the church helped bring in twenty-nine orphans from Kazakhstan for summer visits with families who might eventually adopt them. In August and September 2003, these children stayed in the United States with host families for four weeks. The program was so successful that all of the children were adopted.

Today, this ministry hosts a support group for more than seventy adoptive families, organizes mission trips, and educates other churches about the call to care for orphans.

"It has really changed our church," Michelle says.

WEST ANGELES CHURCH OF GOD IN CHRIST, LOS ANGELES, CALIFORNIA

Bishop Charles Blake has called his congregation of twenty-two thousand to put their hands and feet to work caring for orphans through a program he started in 2001 called Save Africa's Children. He wanted to help the millions of African children orphaned due to the AIDS epidemic. Donors have now given more than $4 million to 320 orphan-care facilities in Africa, and Blake and forty church members toured some of the ministries in Zambia, South Africa, and Kenya.

IRVING BIBLE CHURCH, IRVING, TEXAS

In 1999, several women at Irving Bible Church felt a calling to provide a support group for families who had adopted or were considering adoption of older kids from Russia. Since then, the church's Tapestry ministry has grown to include an educational arm and community involvement. Church members offer adoption and foster-care education to those seeking adoption information, continue to offer support groups for adoptive families, and work to serve and support children in the local foster-care system.

JUST GET INVOLVED

There are countless ways your church can become involved in adoption ministry and the care of orphans, from sponsoring birthparent support meetings to adopting an orphanage in your area or overseas and improving the lives of the children there by donating supplies, time, and money. If you choose to support or build an orphanage in another country, your church members can organize teams to visit, help with the building, play with the children, and help with their care. Caring for kids makes for a mission trip that no one will ever forget, and as your church members' lives are impacted, they will come home and spread the word. It is impossible to visit the poorest of the poor and not see how God works in mighty ways, how much he has blessed you, and how much work there is to be done to help "the least of these."

RED LIGHT, STOP!

Questions to consider at this point in your adoption journey:

____ Have you talked with your pastor about his heart for adoption ministry and where it can fit into your church?

____ Have you begun assembling a core team to help and started brainstorming your first projects?

____ Can you begin planning an event during National Adoption Awareness Month (November)?

____ Have you set short-term and longer-term goals for your adoption ministry?

____ Can you plan an adoption workshop and get local adoption experts to help, plus adoptive families to give their testimonies?

____ Are you ready to support adoptive families through the adoption process?

____ Have you begun to support an orphanage, plan mission trips, or help local orphans in your community?

GREEN LIGHT, GO!

Action points for your adoption journey:

____ Become educated about orphans—how many there are, what they need, and how your church can help get the word out.

____ Discuss starting an adoption ministry with your pastor.

____ Assemble your adoption ministry team.

____ Plan your short-term and long-term strategies. Consider your strengths and weaknesses.

____ Launch a media campaign to get the word out for your upcoming events.

____ Write letters of reference for adopting families you know.

____ Hold an Adoption Sunday and have adoptive families share their miracle adoption stories.

My Adoption Miracle
A New Home, a Grateful Heart
by Robert and Jennifer Marks

Our adoption journey started when we went with other church members on a mission trip to Honduras. I had been on two prior trips, but on this one my wife went. We don't agree over who brought it up first, but we came home from the trip agreeing that we should adopt. We did not have any children because we had been working hard to pay off student loans and establish our careers, but now we felt that we wanted to give a child a home. We wanted a school-age child so that we could continue to work while he was in school and be home with him around the school schedule. My sister worked with Congress at the time as an adoption advocate, so I called her and told her my wife and I wanted to adopt an older child and asked her if she could put us in touch with someone to talk to.

At first, she thought I was kidding. She basically ignored me for three months. Then I called her a second time, and she was in the process of reviewing a program where kids had come to the United States from Kazakhstan for the summer to stay with families who might be interested in adopting them. Out of many children who came that summer, only three did not find homes. One was a little boy who had been moved three times during the summer and had not been chosen. We believe that's because God already had him picked out for us.

One family had told the program director that he was really unresponsive. When we got T. R. home, we discovered he had a hearing loss that kept him from being able to respond. When the summer was over, the children went back to Kazakhstan, most with the knowledge that they would soon be returning to their forever families. We ended up calling everyone who had met T. R. over the summer and getting all these good reports on him, so we called Kazakhstan on the day after Thanksgiving five years ago. Because my sister speaks Russian, she was able to ask him for us if he wanted to be adopted. He said, "Yes!"

Once we got off the phone, nervous and excited, it hit us: how were we going to pay for it all? My wife worked at the time as a pharmacy sales rep, and the next day someone sent the company a thank-you e-mail for helping with their adoption expenses. Jennifer went in to human resources and discovered that the company would reimburse us for $10,000 of our adoption expenses! We took the letter from the company stating this to the credit union and were able to get a loan to have the money up front.

T. R. had been abandoned at birth and raised in the preschool orphanage all his life. At the age of eight, most children are moved from this young children's home to an older children's home. We had heard that sexual abuse and other problems ran rampant in the homes for older children. Although T. R.

was now over the age limit for the preschool orphanage, God protected him and he was able to stay there until we came to adopt him.

We were thirty-one and thirty-two when our son came home. The first six months were a struggle and harder on Jennifer than me, I think. T. R. didn't want to upset me, and I had an easier time, not taking his testing personally. We just had to show him that we were going to love him no matter what. Today, he has certainly grown comfortable with us and knows that no matter what he does, we'll love him.

He has such a grateful heart, and he works harder than most kids. He struggles some in reading, so last summer he went to a reading camp. Every child who read a certain number of books or pages was entered into a drawing for a new bike. We had already given T.R. a bike, so he was worried about what he would do with it if he won. "Don't worry," I told him. "You won't win." But he did.

Later that day, the camp director called to tell me there was a problem. "Your son won the bike, but he won't take it. He says he doesn't need it," the director said. I picked T. R. up and explained to him that he could take the bike and give it to a child who didn't have one. He wanted to give it to somebody poor, and I said, "Okay."

That's when he looked at me and said, "Okay, now how do we get it to Kazakhstan?"

It's funny, because my wife and I now talk about whether we are ever going to have kids or adopt again. We think we are supposed to adopt again. T. R. will tell you he wants to adopt a lot of kids. He knows what it is like to have nothing, and he has such appreciation for what he has now. He is our adoption miracle.

Part Six

Where to Go from Here: Continuing the Journey

"For I know the plans I have for you," declares the LORD, *"plans to prosper you and not to harm you, plans to give you hope and a future."*
—Jeremiah 29:11 (NIV)

How wonderful it is that nobody need wait a single moment before starting to improve the world.
—*Anne Frank*

APPENDIX

Appendix A

Glossary of Adoption Terms and Common Adoption Acronyms

Glossary of Adoption Terms

active adoption registry: An adoption registry that allows one party (adoptee or birthparent) to register to seek information on the other. Once one party is registered, "a designated individual (often an agency or court representative) is assigned to contact those persons being sought and determine their wishes for the release of information."[i] (See also adoption registry; passive adoption registry; voluntary adoption registry.)

adoptee: A child or an adult who was added to a family through the legal adoption process. Adoptees can be infants, children, or adults who are adopted by relatives, stepparents, or nonrelatives. Other terms include "adopted child" and "adopted adult."

adoption: To take a person into a family by legal means, entitling them to full rights as a member of that family in the eyes of the law. It is a complete transfer of rights from birthparents to the adoptive parents.

adoption agency: A state-licensed business that connects children with adoptive parents and families. An agency may specialize in domestic adoptions, international adoptions, or both and may work with families and couples in their state only, in many states, or in all fifty states. An agency may be secular or religious and for-profit or nonprofit.

adoption assistance: Monthly subsidy payments to help adoptive parents raise children with special needs. These payments were first made possible by the enactment of the Adoption Assistance and Child Welfare Act of 1980, which provided federal funding for children eligible under Title IV-E of the Social Security Act. The term also refers to any help adoptive parents receive.[ii]

adoption attorney: A lawyer who specializes in arranging adoptive placements. An attorney can be used with or without an agency. Some attorneys work with families from the beginning until after placement. Some assist only in certain tasks (such as filing readoption paperwork).

adoption circle: Recent adoption language that aims to be more inclusive than the term "adoption triad," recognizing that there are other parties involved in addition to the adoption triad of birthmother, child, and adoptive parents. These may include social workers, foster-care parents, grandparents, siblings, and others.

adoption decree or decree of adoption: The formal legal order that states an adoption has been finalized.

adoption facilitators or adoption consultants: People who help locate birthmothers for singles, couples, and families who wish to adopt. Facilitators and consultants might be licensed social workers or may not hold any kind of license. Some states do not allow adoption consultants to facilitate adoptions.

adoption petition: The document prospective parents file to request the court's permission to adopt a child.

adoption plan or placing a child for adoption: A birthmother's or birthparents' plan to place their child for adoption.

adoption registry: A place where birthparents and adoptees can list their names and contact information with the goal of being reunited. (See also active adoption registry; passive adoption registry; voluntary adoption registry.)

adoption subsidy: Federal or state adoption benefits designed to help offset the short and long-term costs associated with adopting children who need special services. There are certain criteria children must meet, as well as different types of benefits including monthly cash payments, medical assistance, social services, and adoption expenses.

adoption tax credit: A federal program that allows adopting families a credit or reduction of taxes as reimbursement for adoption expenses. Some states also have these tax credits. For tax year 2005, the adoption tax credit on federal income taxes was $10,630 for families whose income was less than $155,860. For higher incomes, the amount is reduced until it is eliminated for incomes above $195,860.[iii]

adoption tax exclusions: IRS provisions that allow adoptive families to exclude from their taxable income certain private-sector employer cash contributions toward their adoption expenses or other employer-sponsored adoption benefits.

adoption taxpayer identification number: A temporary taxpayer identification number assigned to the child in a pending domestic adoption where the adopting taxpayers do not have and/or are unable to obtain the child's Social Security number (SSN). The ATIN, which can be applied for through the IRS, is to be used by the adopting taxpayers on their federal income tax return to claim the child as their dependent and also claim the child and dependent care credit.[iv]

adoption triad or adoption triangle: This term refers to the three major parties involved in an adoption: the birthparents, the adoptive parents, and the adoptee.

adoptive families: Families who have added or are in the process of adding at least one member to the family through legal adoption.

agency adoption: This kind of adoption occurs when workers at a licensed adoption agency arrange an adoption, whether it is domestic or international. Most "agency adoptions" refer to private adoption agencies, not "public" (state or county) agencies.

amended birth certificate: A birth certificate where the identifying information for the parents has been changed from the birthparents to the adoptive parents.

apostille: A form of document certification used in countries that participate in the Hague Convention. This form has numbered fields that make it understandable to all participating countries. If the foreign country in an international adoption participates in the convention, adoption documents will require an attached apostil (rather than authentication forms).[v]

attachment or bonding: The deep and enduring emotional connection a child feels for his or her parents or caregivers in the first few years of life.

attachment disorder: See reactive attachment disorder.

authentication: A process of verifying original paperwork included in a dossier for international adoption. Authentication is performed in different regions of the country by consulates for different nations.

biological family, birth family, or family of origin: A family that has members who conceived a child, gave birth to that child, and placed that child for adoption.

biracial: A term that refers to a child who has biological parents of two different races, such as Chinese and Caucasian. It is commonly used to refer to a child who has one white parent and one African-American parent.

birthfather or biological father: A man who conceives a child with a woman, and that child is later placed with another family for adoption.

birthfathers registry or putative father registry: A place where a man who thinks he conceived a child with a woman can register his alleged paternity of the child. By registering, in many states the birthfather preserves his right to challenge any adoption plans the mother may have for his child.

birthmother or biological mother: A woman who gives birth to a child and places that child for permanent adoption. Sometimes the term is used to describe a pregnant woman who plans to place her child for adoption.

black-market adoption: An adoption that occurs outside the auspices of the law. It is often referred to as "buying" a baby and may involve very large sums of money paid to an attorney, an adoption agency worker, or an other party.

certification: The process by which the Department of State in the adoptive parent(s)' home state verifies that adoption dossier documents have been notarized by a currently licensed notary public in that state.

Child Citizenship Act of 2000: This act, which was signed and became effective in 2001, automatically grants United States citizenship to certain foreign-born children—including adopted children—currently residing permanently in the United States.

confidential or "closed" adoption: An adoption where no contact or identifying information is exchanged between the birthmother or birthparents and the adoptive family.

confidential intermediary: A state employee or trained volunteer sanctioned by the courts who is given access to sealed adoption files for the purpose of conducting a search.

consent, surrender, or relinquishment: The legal process by which the birthmother or birthparents voluntarily agree to allow their child to be adopted.

cooperative adoption or adoption with contact: Arrangements that allow some kind of contact between members of a birth family and a child's adopters after the adoption has been finalized. The arrangements may be formal or informal, verbal or written down.

courier services: People, often adopters themselves, who specialize in hand-carrying—for a fee—adoption dossier documents to the appropriate state departments and foreign consulates for certification and/or authentication. The couriers then send the documents back to the adopters.

disclosure: Information formerly hidden that is now released or transmitted.

disruption: An adoption that fails before the time of finalization, for any number of reasons.

dissolution: An adoption that fails or is reversed after finalization.

dossier: A group of legal documents that must be collected and presented to the appropriate entities in order to adopt a child from another country.

dossier preparation services: People, often adopters themselves, who—for a fee—will collect the legal documents necessary for adoptive parents to adopt a child.

employer assistance or adoption benefits: Monies paid toward adoption costs by an adoptive family's employer or employers or other employer-offered adoption benefits such as parental or family leave.

finalization: The legal procedure that finishes an adoption. Finalization may take place in front of a judge in the United States or in a court or government office in a foreign country.

financial affidavit: A notarized (sworn) statement, filled out by the adopting parents, which discloses their personal finances in order to show that they are financially capable of providing for an adopted child.

forever family: A loving term used to describe what the adoptive family is for the adoptee.

foster child: A child in the legal custody of a state, county, or private adoption agency. Foster placements may be short-term or long-term, and a foster child may not be legally adopted unless the rights of the biological parents are voluntarily or legally terminated.

foster parents or foster family: People who have been approved or licensed to care for foster children in their homes, either short-term or long-term. Some foster parents go on to adopt their foster children. In other countries, foster parents may be called "nannies."

foster to adopt or foster adoption: A public agency adoption program where a potential parent or parents who are licensed to foster the child or multiple children in their care plan to adopt said child(ren) when the birthparents' rights are terminated.

genetic predisposition: The fact that a child has received certain inherited genes from birthparents that increase the likelihood of the child's developing certain traits, features, or even diseases.

Gotcha Day: A familiar term for the day that an adoptive family receives their adopted child. In international adoption, it is the day that the child is first handed over to the adopting family.

guardian ad litem: A person, paid or volunteer, sometimes an attorney, who represents the best interests of a child, a ward, or an unborn infant in a particular court case. The guardian ad litem is appointed by the court.

Hague Convention on Intercountry Adoption: This treaty, which was signed by sixty-six countries in 1993 and by the United States in 1994, covers provisions and safeguards for adoption between countries. The U.S. passed the Intercountry Adoption Act of 2000, a bill that implemented the convention, and expects to ratify it in 2007.[vi]

home study: Before a potential adopting family can be approved, a home study is conducted by a licensed social worker that includes in-person interviews, reference checks, background checks, home viewing, and other pertinent information.

I-171H: Form I-171H, "Notice of Favorable Determination Concerning Application for Advance Processing of Orphan Petition," is sent to the prospective adoptive parent(s) if they appear to qualify for further processing. This form, which is the approval notice of the I-600 or I-600A visa petitions, allows a child from a foreign country to enter the United States in order to be adopted or after having been adopted.[vii]

I-600A petitions: This form is titled "Application for Advance Processing of Orphan Petition," and is an application to the United States Immigration and Naturalization Service (INS) by adopting parents to classify an orphan as an immediate relative. This provides for expedited processing and issuance of a visa to allow the child to enter the United States after having been adopted abroad or in order to be adopted in the United States.[viii]

independent adoption or parent-initiated adoption: An adoption that is arranged without the services or assistance of a public or private adoption agency.

institutionalization: The placement of children in hospitals, institutions, or orphanages, which, if done during early critical-developmental periods and for lengthy periods of time, is often associated with developmental delays due to environmental deprivation, poor staff-child ratios, or lack of early stimulation.

institutionalized child: A child who lives in an orphanage, especially used to refer to those in foreign countries.[ix]

intercountry or international adoption: Adoption in which the birthparents and adoptee are citizens of different countries.

Interstate Compact on the Placement of Children: This is an agreement between states that allows for and governs the process of adoptive placement of children across state lines.

kinship placement: See relative adoption.

legal guardian: A person who can make legal decisions for a child but cannot adopt the child unless the biological parents, the state, or whoever has custody of the child agrees.

legally free: A child whose birthparents' rights have been terminated and who is free to be adopted.

lifebook or life book: A book filled with pictures and writings that represent a child's life and is designed to help the child understand and have a record of his unique history. The lifebook may include birthparents, other relatives, orphanage caregivers, etc. It may be put together by social workers, foster parents, and/or adoptive parents.

log-in date: The calendar date when a dossier is logged in to the China Center of Adoption Affairs (CCAA) in Beijing, China. This date begins the official "countdown" for adopters waiting for a referral.

matching: The process by which a legally free child is paired with an approved adoptive family suited to meet the needs of a waiting child. In some foreign countries, such as China, adoption officials "match" a child with adopting parents based on information and pictures found in the parents' dossier.

Multiethnic Placement Act of 1994, amended in 1996: This act, known as MEPA or MEPA-IEP, was enacted to promote the best interests of children by prohibiting the use of a child's or a prospective parent's race, color, or national origin to delay or deny the child's placement and by requiring diligent efforts to expand the number of racially and ethnically diverse foster and adoptive parents. The Interethnic Adoption Provisions amendment (IEP) underscores the prohibition against delaying or denying the placement of a child for adoption or foster care on the basis of race, color, or national origin of the foster or adoptive parents or of the child involved.[x]

multiracial, multiethnic: A child with a heritage that includes more than two races.

nonrecurring adoption expenses: These one-time adoption expenses, such as the cost of a home study or attorney fees, may be at least partially reimbursable by certain states under the Adoption Assistance and Child Welfare Act of 1980, with a maximum limit of $2,000 to families adopting children with special needs.

nonrelative adoption: This term refers to the adoption of a child by someone who is not biologically related to the child.

notary public: A notary public is an officer commissioned by a secretary of state to serve as an unbiased and impartial witness. In the case of adoption, a notary public affixes his or her signature and seal to verify that documents were signed by the adopters.

open adoption: An adoption that includes ongoing contact between birth families and adoptive families after the finalization of the adoption, usually including visits.

orphan: A child whose parents have died, relinquished their parental rights, or whose parental rights have been terminated by a court. In international adoption, it can refer to a child with no parents or only one parent who cannot care for the child.

passive adoption registry: An adoption registry that requires a birthparent or birthparents and adoptee to register their consent for release of information before an adoption reunion can occur. Both parties are notified once a match is made. (See also active adoption registry; adoption registry; voluntary adoption registry.)

post-placement: A term that refers to things that happen after a child has been adopted.

reactive attachment disorder: Also known as "attachment disorder," this term refers to a disorder that develops when a child fails to attach to a loving, protective caregiver. The child learns not to trust adults and to depend only on himself. Success in overcoming RAD varies, but it does happen.

readoption: The act of applying with a court of jurisdiction to finalize an adoption in a state when the adoption was already finalized in the foreign country where the adoption took place. After an international adoption, readoption is required in some states but not in others.

referral: The notification by a foreign country that a waiting child has been matched with adopters. The referral may include the child's name, age, location, height, weight, medical information, and other details.

relative adoption: Also known as "kinship placement," this is the formal adoption of a child by a blood relative such as an aunt, grandparent, or sibling.

reunion: The meeting for the first time of an adult adoptee and the birthparent, birthparents, or other relatives.

sealed adoption records: A court ruling that prevents any information about an adoption, including the original birth certificate, records of court proceedings, agency reports, and other documents from being disclosed without a court order to protect the confidentiality of the parties. Release of information is governed by state law in the United States.

sealing of a birth certificate: A ruling by a court of jurisdiction that prevents information on an adoptee's birth certificate from being disclosed. A court order is required to "unseal" a sealed document.

semi-open adoption: A type of adoption where certain information about the adoptee is exchanged between the birth family and adoptive family after finalization, usually through an intermediary. Some identifying information remains private.

simple adoption: Simple adoption takes place when there is a nonjudicial type of adoption that is still considered legal. This occurs in some African cultures.

social worker or caseworker: A person licensed by a state to conduct home studies of potential adoptive parents. A social worker or caseworker may also be an employee of the state who oversees foster-care placements and public adoption cases.

special needs: This is a broad term that refers to disabilities and challenges classified as mental, social, physical, emotional, or educational. The term also refers to some placement factors, such as race or age, that can make finding an adoptive home more challenging.

stepparent adoption: The legal adoption of a child by a stepparent.

termination of parental rights: The process by which a court of jurisdiction severs a parent's rights to parent his or her child. The termination may take place voluntarily or involuntarily (after abuse, neglect, or abandonment).

transracial adoption: An adoption that takes place between adoptive parents and a child of differing races.

voluntary adoption registry: A reunion registry system that allows adoptees, birthparents, and biological siblings to locate one another if they wish by maintaining a voluntary list of adoptees and birth relatives. (See also active adoption registry; adoption registry; passive adoption registry.)

waiting children: Children in the United States and other countries who are legally free to be adopted and who are waiting for forever families. Sometimes this term refers to children in the foster-care system for whom adoption is desired.

wrongful adoption: When an agency or a worker in an adoption fails to disclose known information, or information that should be known, about an adoptee to the prospective adoptive parents.

Common Adoption Acronyms[xi]

AA	Adult Adoptee
ABC	Amended Birth Certificate
AD	Adoptee
ADAD	Adoptive Dad, Adoptive Father
AMOM	Adoptive Mom, Adoptive Mother
APARS	Adoptive Parents
ASIB	Adoptive Sibling
ASIS/ABRO	Adoptive Sister, Adoptive Brother
BC	Birth Certificate
BD	Birth Daughter
BDAD	Birthdad, Birthfather
BFAM	Birth Family
BMA	Black Market Adoption
BMOM	Birthmom, Birthmother
BPARS	Birthparents
BS	Birth Son
BSIB	Birth Sibling
BSIS/BBRO	Birth Sister, Birth Brother
CI	Confidential Intermediary
CPS	Child Protective Services
DD	Dear (or Devoted) Daughter
DH	Dear Husband
DNR	Do Not Remember
DOB	Date of Birth
DS	Dear Son
DSS	Department of Social Services
DTC	Dossier to China, the day a potential adoptive family's documents are sent to China
EMOM	Expectant Mom
FCC	Families with Children from China, a support group
INS	Immigration & Naturalization Service
ISO	In Search Of

ISRR   International Soundex Reunion Registry

LID   Log-in Date, the date a dossier is logged in by the China Center of Adoption Affairs

NON-ID   Non-Identifying Information

OBC   Original Birth Certificate

PA   Private Adoption

PAPS   Prospective Adoptive Parents

PI   Private Investigator

POB   Place of Birth

RAD   Reactive Attachment Disorder

SS   Social Services/Social Security

SW   Social Worker

TA   Travel Approval, the date an adoptive family will travel to a foreign country to get their adopted child

VS/DVS   Vital Statistics/Department of Vital Statistics

Appendix B

Selected Private Adoption Agencies, Legal Links, and Adoption Information Sites

Resources

The resources included in these pages are a springboard for adopting families—and those who are considering adoption—to become educated about the various issues surrounding adoption. These resources/listings are not intended to be all-encompassing; nor are they an exhaustive list of available resources; nor does the listing of these resources constitute an endorsement of any individual or organization by the author or publisher; nor can any resource listing be construed as offering legal advice.

Selected Christian Adoption Agencies and Directories

This list contains agencies whose philosophy centers on biblically based Christian principles. This does not mean that any agency will be perfect or will be exempt from any unscrupulous practices; however, these agencies have, in most cases, taken extra steps to show their accountability, such as meeting accreditation standards and/or openly posting their annual reports and tax reports. This list is far from exhaustive, and there are hundreds of other reputable agencies around the country.

Remember, the key to finding the right agency is to ask friends and family, do your own research, ask lots of the right questions, pray about your decision, and choose an agency that feels right for you.

NATIONAL ADOPTION INFORMATION CLEARINGHOUSE'S NATIONAL ADOPTION DIRECTORY SEARCH

Web site: http://naic.acf.hhs.gov/general/nad/index.cfm
The NAIC is an umbrella site that offers this directory page, which allows information seekers to look by state for the existing toll-free, state-sponsored adoption information lines, and foster-care information lines, licensed private adoption agencies for domestic adoptions, licensed private adoption agencies for intercountry adoptions, local/regional offices of the state (public) adoption agency, adoptive/foster family support groups, support groups for birth families and adoptees, contact information for the state adoption specialist/manager, state foster-care specialist/manager, state licensing specialist, state Interstate Compact on Adoption and Medical Assistance (ICAMA) administrator, state

Interstate Compact on the Placement of Children (ICPC) administrator, state medical assistance specialist, state post-adoption services contact, state adoption assistance specialist, state reunion registry, state confidential intermediary service, state adoption exchange, state photo listing of children waiting for adoption, and an attorney referral service. The site also includes definitions for each of these categories.

Individual Agencies

Adoption—A Gift of Love (AGOL)
Phone: 940-243-0749
Web site: www.adoption-agol.org
International Only
AGOL is a 501(c)(3), licensed child-placement agency for the countries of China and Mexico. It is committed to offering education, emotional support, referrals, and guidance to international adoptive families. Additionally, AGOL has dedicated itself to help improve the quality of lives and futures for children who remain in orphanages in third-world countries through humanitarian aid to orphanages, sponsorship of medically needy children to come to the U.S. for medical care, and funding of medical care for children in their country of origin.

Adoption Associates, Inc.
Phone: 800-677-2367
Web site: www.adoptassoc.com
International Only
Adoption Associates is a 501(c)(3), nonprofit agency headquartered in Jenison, Michigan, that has placed 2,895 children since it opened its doors in 1990. In 2004, AAI placed 140 children domestically and 245 international children. It has six offices—four in Michigan, one China coordinator in Connecticut, and an office in St. Petersburg, Russia.

All God's Children International
Phone: 800-214-6719
Web site: www.allgodschildren.org
International Only
All God's Children International is a 501(c)(3), nonprofit agency head-quartered in Portland, Oregon, with satellite offices in Michigan and Ohio. The agency was started in 1991 and has since served more than 1,500 families.

America World Adoption Association

Phone: 888-ONE-CHILD (888-663-2445)

Web site: www.awaa.org

International Only

America World is a 501(c)(3), nonprofit agency headquartered in McLean, Virginia, with a West Coast office in Tucson, Arizona, and regional offices and associates throughout the country. It has adoption programs for China, Ukraine, Vietnam, and Russia and has placed "thousands" of children. America World requests that at least one parent agree to the following statement: "As adoptive parent(s) with America World I/we have confessed Christ as my/our Lord and Savior and believe the following chapters from the Bible: Deuteronomy 6, John 3 & 14, Romans 10, and Ephesians 2. I/We will teach my/our children by adoption the same."

Antioch Adoptions

Phone: 425-558-0921

Web site: www.antiochadoptions.org

Domestic Only

Antioch Adoptions is a Christian adoption agency that is a ministry of Antioch Bible Church. It raises funds through donations to place children in Christian adoptive families in western Washington State. The agency does not charge the adoptive families any fees, but adoptive families must undergo a series of adoption and parenting classes to qualify and must donate time, materials, and/or financial resources throughout the process. The church program also is involved in recruiting and developing families to consider adoption of older or minority children in foster care, reaching out to women facing a pregnancy for which they are unprepared, and educating the community about adoption.

Bethany Christian Services

Phone: 800-BETHANY (800-238-4269)

Web site: www.bethany.org

Domestic and International

Bethany Christian Services is a 501(c)(3), nonprofit agency headquartered in Grand Rapids, Michigan. It offers domestic programs and international adoption programs for Albania, China, Colombia, Guatemala, Hong Kong, India, Lithuania, Philippines, Russia, South Korea, and Ukraine. Bethany is one of the largest adoption agencies in the United States and was started in 1944. With more than seventy-five locations nationwide, Bethany touches the lives of more than thirty thousand people each year.

Buckner International Adoption
Phone: 866-236-7823
Web site: www.bucknerinternationaladoption.org
Domestic and International
Buckner International Adoption is a part of Buckner, a 125-year-old social services ministry headquartered in Dallas and dedicated to ministering to the most vulnerable in society, providing services for families, seniors, and children. Buckner is the largest faith-based, nonprofit family service agency in the country and offers international programs in China, Ukraine, Guatemala, Russia, Romania, and Bulgaria.

Celebrate Children
Phone: 407-977-2810
Web site: www.celebratechildren.org
International Only
Celebrate Children International, Inc., is a Florida-based 501(c)(3), nonprofit agency, whose mission states: "As disciples of Jesus Christ, we are committed to going into the world to serve others. We are committed to helping the children of the International community find loving and qualified families through adoption." They have programs in China, Guatemala, Ukraine, Vietnam, Russia, Bulgaria, Taiwan, and Kazakhstan.

Children's Hope International
Phone: 888-899-2349
Web site: www.childrenshopeint.org
International Only
Children's Hope International is a 501(c)(3), nonprofit agency headquartered in St. Louis, Missouri, with offices in eleven other cities around the country and twelve offices in foreign countries. It began in 1992 and was one of the first agencies to handle adoptions in China. Today, it has programs in China, Russia, Kazakhstan, Colombia, Guatemala, Nepal, Vietnam, and India and assists families in all states. CHI places approximately eight hundred children each year and posts its annual report and tax reports on its Web site.

Christian Adoption Services, Inc.
Phone: 704-847-0038
Web site: www.christianadopt.org
Domestic and International
Christian Adoption Services, Inc., was founded in 1979 as a private, nonprofit organization headquartered in Matthews, North Carolina. Today, it coordinates

adoptions in Korea, China, Philippines, Russia, Kazakhstan, Poland, and Guatemala. CAS also provides domestic adoptions of infants, supports relative adoptions, and collaborates with parent-initiated, independent adoptions. CAS has a foster-care program and serves single mothers by providing short-term respite for children whose parents may be having a difficult time parenting and are considering adoption.

Christian Family Services, Inc.
Phones: 314-968-2216 (MO) and 618-397-7678 (IL)
Web site: www.cfserve.org
Domestic Only
Christian Family Services, Inc., is a nonprofit child welfare agency, licensed in the states of Missouri and Illinois since 1973, that seeks to find homes for children in that bistate area through adoption and foster care. It also helps families find solutions through professional counseling services.

Christian World Adoption
Phone: 888-97-ADOPT (888-972-3678)
Web site: www.cwa.org
International Only
Christian World Adoption is a nonprofit adoption agency with headquarters in Charleston, South Carolina, and Flat Rock, North Carolina. It has placed thousands of children from fifteen countries since 1991. Currently, CWA has programs in China, Ethiopia, Guatemala, Kazakhstan, Russia, and Ukraine.

Dillon International, Inc.
Phone: 918-749-4600
Web site: www.dillonadopt.com
International Only
Dillon is a licensed, not-for-profit child-placement agency that has specialized in international adoption since its beginning in 1972. It is headquartered in Tulsa, Oklahoma, with offices in St. Louis, Missouri; Little Rock, Arkansas; Richmond, Indiana; and Wichita, Kansas. Dillon has placed more than five thousand children since 1972 and currently has programs in China, Haiti, Guatemala, India, Kazakhstan, Korea, Ukraine, and Vietnam.

Families Thru International Adoption, Inc.
Phone: 888-797-9900
Web site: www.ftia.org
International Only

Families Thru International Adoption, Inc., is a nonprofit, state-licensed child-placement agency specializing in international adoptions from Brazil, India, Russia, China, Guatemala, and Vietnam. It was founded in the early 1990s by an adoption attorney who had previously helped place many children from China.

The Family Network, Inc.
Phone: 831-462-8954
Web site: www.rainbowkids.com or www.adopt-familynetwork.com
International Only
The Family Network, Inc., is a California-licensed, nonprofit child-placement agency. Since 1979, The Family Network, Inc., has placed hundreds of children with loving families through its international adoption programs in China, Guatemala, and Ukraine. The Family Network also provides additional adoption-related services to families and individuals residing in its licensed counties in California.

Gladney Center for Adoption
Phone: 817-922-6000
Web site: www.adoptionsbygladney.com
Domestic and International
The Gladney Center was founded in 1904 as the Texas Children's Home and Aid Society. It was renamed the Edna Gladney Home in 1950. Since it was founded, it has assisted more than thirty-six thousand birthmothers. The adoption agency also has international programs for adoptions from China, Colombia, Ethiopia, Guatemala, Kazakhstan, Mexico, Russia, Ukraine, and Vietnam. The nonprofit agency has international humanitarian aid projects in Guatemala, Russia, China, Ethiopia, and Mexico that include rebuilding orphanages, camp experiences for orphans, and other programs.

A Helping Hand
Phone: 800-525-0871
Web site: www.worldadoptions.org
Domestic and International
A Helping Hand is a 501(c)(3), nonprofit agency headquartered in Lexington, Kentucky, that specializes in international adoptions in China and Guatemala and has worked with "thousands of families" in thirty-three states since it began in 1994. It also has an office in Dallas and claims to have one of the lowest-priced China programs in the country.

Holt International Children Services
Phone: 888-355-4658
Web site: www.holtintl.org
Domestic for Oregon Residents Only and International
Holt is a nonprofit, licensed agency that has programs in Bulgaria, China, Guatemala, Haiti, India, Korea, Mongolia, Philippines, Thailand, and Vietnam, as well as a domestic program for Oregon residents. It was founded in 1956 and is headquartered in Eugene, Oregon, with satellite offices in six other states. Holt has placed nearly forty thousand children with adoptive families and provides relief efforts to orphanages in foreign countries, child sponsorships, and other ministry efforts.

Hope's Promise
Phone: 303-660-0277
Web site: www.hopespromise.com
Domestic and International
Hope's Promise is a nonprofit, licensed child-placement agency committed to serving women and children within the United States and abroad as well as equipping and strengthening adoptive and biological families to successfully parent their children. It is involved in child placement, education, international sponsorship programs, participating in international child-welfare services, networking with existing agencies, and advocating for families in the policy-making arena.

International Christian Adoptions
Phone: 909-695-3336
Web site: www.4achild.com
International Only
ICA is a nonprofit, licensed adoption and foster-family agency that provides the adoptive triad (birthparents, adoptive parents, and children) with compassionate and caring service.

Lifeline Children's Services
Phone: 205-967-0811
Web site: www.lifelineadoption.org
Domestic and International
Since its founding by two businessmen in 1981, Lifeline has domestically placed more than 800 babies into Christian homes and ministered to more than 2,500 women in crisis. Lifeline seeks to make an investment in the lives of

children, mothers in the wake of crisis, families wanting the blessing of a child, and orphans around the globe needing a home in which they can see and hear the gospel. Lifeline operates Lifeline Village, a home for mothers in crisis pregnancies, and also places children from China, Ukraine, and Guatemala.

Lifeline of Hope
Phone: 406-257-0868
Web site: www.lifelineofhope.org
International Only
Lifeline of Hope is a nonprofit agency started by two Christian couples that operates from its headquarters in Kalispell, Montana, as well as its Russian headquarters in Khabarovsk. It has adoption programs for Russia, Kazakhstan, and Bulgaria and provides relief aid to orphans in Uganda, India, Pakistan, and Kyrgyzstan.

Love Basket, Inc.
Phone: 636-797-4100
Web site: www.lovebasket.org
Domestic and International
Love Basket is a nonprofit, licensed adoption agency, with headquarters in Missouri and offices in Wisconsin and Minnesota, that was founded in 1979 by two missionary families. Its domestic adoptive placement began in 1985, and its international programs include India, Ukraine, Romania, and Guatemala.

New Horizons Adoption Agency (NHAA)
Phone: 507-878-3200
Web site: www.nhadoptionagency.com
Domestic, expanding to include international
New Horizons Adoption Agency Inc. is an independent, nonprofit Christian agency licensed by the Department of Human Services in the states of Iowa, Minnesota, and South Dakota. Founded in 1987 with the support of caring individuals and families, NHAA places an emphasis on finding Christian homes for children. Its board of directors consists of adoptive parents and interested individuals who guide the growth of New Horizons. NHAA facilitates sixty-five to eighty placements each year.

New Life Children's Services
Phone: 800-432-9124
Web site: www.newlifeadopt.com

Domestic Only for Residents of Texas (some exceptions for special needs)
New Life Children's Services was birthed in 1983 out of a heart to minister God's love to pregnant women. Dr. A. B. "Bo" Henderson was the associate pastor at Houston Northwest Baptist Church, and as he counseled women who were pregnant, he realized there needed to be an agency that would place babies in two-parent Christian adoptive homes. New Life has placed more than three hundred infants in Christian homes.

Nightlight Christian Adoptions
Phone: 714-278-1020
Web site: www.nightlight.org
Domestic, International, and Embryo Adoption
Nightlight is a nonprofit adoption agency licensed by the state of California to provide adoption services. Nightlight has been providing adoption and counseling services to the community since 1959. Nightlight has international programs for adoption from Belarus, Bulgaria, China, Russia, and Ukraine. Nightlight also offers couples the opportunity to adopt embryos for in vitro fertilization in hopes of carrying a pregnancy to term and giving these embryos life.

Reaching Arms International
Phone: 763-591-9701
Web site: www.reachingarms.org
International Only
Reaching Arms is a nonprofit adoption agency headquartered in New Hope, Minnesota, that has placed more than eight hundred children since 1992. It currently has programs in Ukraine, Poland, Russia, Guatemala, and Armenia and has established children's homes in Ukraine, Kenya, and Guatemala.

Ventures for Children International (VCI)
Phone: 479-582-0305
Web site: www.venturesforchildren.org
International Only
Ventures for Children is a Christian international adoption agency and humanitarian aid organization committed to outreach to children in need. VCI has comprehensive aid and adoption programs in Vietnam, Kazakhstan, Russia, China, Cambodia, Haiti, and Nepal with programs constantly under development worldwide. VCI has donated more than a half million dollars in compassionate aid to provide relief to disadvantaged children.

Selected Links to Adoption Attorneys and Adoption Laws

These links provide information on adoption laws and contact information for attorneys throughout the country who specialize in adoption. These links do not specify the attorney's faith, so if having a Christian attorney is important to you, ask the attorneys you are considering whether they are Christians. Ask friends and family for recommendations, and shop around for the attorney whose rates and philosophy are the best fits for you.

Adoption Legislation, sponsored by the Independent Adoption Center
Web site: www.adoptionlegislation.org
A running list of past and current adoption legislation, including information on the IRS tax credit.

Adoption Media, LLC, Adoption Laws
Web site: www.laws.adoption.com
The Adoption Laws section of this site includes summaries and full text of state laws, federal statutes concerning adopting and placing and the adoption process, and the international Hague Convention on Protection of Children.

American Academy of Adoption Attorneys
Phone: 202-832-2222
Web site: www.adoptionattorneys.org
The American Academy of Adoption Attorneys is headquartered in Washington, DC, and lists members in all fifty states who are experienced in domestic and international adoption issues. Members must agree to abide by the organization's ethics code and bylaws.

LegalMatch
Web site: www.legalmatch.com
LegalMatch is a national attorney/client matching service of attorneys, rather than a straight referral service. When a consumer presents an issue to LegalMatch, the software matches the consumer's case to the appropriate local lawyer(s) based on the specifics of the need and the lawyer's location and area of legal practice.

National Adoption Information Clearinghouse, Legal Issues and Laws
Web site: http://naic.acf.hhs.gov/general/legal/index.cfm

These pages from the NAIC include links to the state laws on adoption (which includes information on who can adopt and be adopted, consent to adoption, rights of presumed fathers, termination of parental rights, access to family information, and more), a state statutes search (search for issues related to child abuse and neglect, child welfare, and adoption), and federal laws publications and resources that provide the overarching standards and guidelines for state laws related to child abuse and neglect, child welfare, and adoption.

Selected Adoption Accreditation and Advocacy Organizations and Research Institutes

American Adoption Congress
Phone: 202-483-3399
Web site: www.americanadoptioncongress.org
The American Adoption Congress works to raise public awareness about the realities of adopted life for birth and adoptive families, and to change public policies related to adoption practices to acknowledge adoption as an extension of family. It also works to promote legislation in all states guaranteeing access to identifying information for all adopted persons and their birth and adoptive families through records access and preservation of open adoption agreements.

Center for Adoption Research
Phone: 508-856-5397
Web site: www.centerforadoptionresearch.org
The Center for Adoption Research is dedicated to assisting families and professionals by providing independent research, evaluation, and education to improve the lives of children in adoptive and foster families.

Children's Action Network (CAN)
Phone: 800-525-6789
Web site: www.childrensactionnetwork.org
CAN uses the power of the entertainment community to bring awareness to children's issues from immunization campaigns to the National Adoption Campaign. Through its efforts, CAN helps develop an annual one-hour television special on CBS, *A Home for the Holidays*, which features celebrities, musicians, adoptive families, and waiting children who share their personal stories.

The Collaboration to AdoptUSKids
Phone: 888-200-4005
E-mail: info@adoptuskids.org
Web site: www.adoptuskids.org
AdoptUSKids is a project of The Children's Bureau, part of the Federal Department of Health and Human Services. In October 2002, The Children's Bureau contracted with The Adoption Exchange Association and its partners (The Collaboration to AdoptUSKids) to devise and implement a national adoptive-family recruitment and retention strategy, operate the AdoptUSKids.org Web site, encourage and enhance adoptive-family support organizations, and conduct a variety of adoption research projects. The Web site provides a central photo listing of the nation's waiting children.

Congressional Coalition on Adoption Institute
Phone: 703-288-9700
E-mail: info@ccainstitute.org
Web site: www.ccainstitute.org
The Congressional Coalition on Adoption Institute's mission statement says that it is "a nonprofit, nonpartisan organization dedicated to raising awareness about the tens of thousands of foster children in this country and the millions of orphans around the world in need of permanent, safe, and loving homes; and to eliminating the barriers that hinder these children from realizing their basic need of a family." To that end, the CCAI is formed of a caucus of members of Congress dedicated to improving adoption policy and practice, and to focusing public attention on the advantages of adoption. The group serves as an informational and educational resource to policymakers as they seek to draft positive adoption, foster-care, and other adoption-related legislation and to meet their constituents' needs. CCAI also hosts several public-awareness events each year, including the annual Angels in Adoption awards.

Council on Accreditation Services for Children and Families (COA)
Phone: 866-262-8088
Web site: www.coanet.org
The Council on Accreditation Services for Children and Families, which was founded by the Child Welfare League of America and Family Services of America, is a child and family service and behavioral health-care organization. COA promotes best-practice standards; quality services for children, youth, and families; and advocates for the value of accreditation.

Dave Thomas Foundation for Adoption
Phone: 800-ASK-DTFA (800-275-3832)
Web site: www.davethomasfoundationforadoption.org
Dave Thomas, the founder of the fast-food chain Wendy's, was adopted as a child and created a foundation for adoption to help children find permanent homes. The Dave Thomas Foundation for Adoption focuses on increasing adoption awareness while supporting model adoption-service programs. This site gives away free pamphlets on the adoption process for prospective adopters, National Adoption Month promotion kits, and other resources.

Ethica
Phone: 301-650-0649
Web site: www.ethicanet.org
Ethica is a nonprofit corporation that says it "seeks to be an impartial voice for ethical adoption practices worldwide and provides education, assistance, and advocacy to the adoption and foster-care communities." Ethica does not accept donations from adoption agencies or other entities that place children for adoption. Ethica's goal is to educate and inform the adoption community about global issues impacting adoptions.

Evan B. Donaldson Adoption Institute
Phone: 212-925-4089
Web site: www.adoptioninstitute.org
The Evan B. Donaldson Adoption Institute aims to improve the lives of people touched by adoption in many ways, including offering lawmakers reliable information and practical perspectives to improve adoption laws; providing the media with a trusted source of information; encouraging employer support for adoption; reducing barriers that impede adoption of children who need permanent families; researching policies and practices that affect adoption; educating policymakers and the public about the importance of giving adopted people access to information about their origins; developing a legal framework to ensure access to genetic information and a clear delineation of parental responsibility for children born through reproductive technology; and promoting ethical standards for adoption professionals.

The International Resource Centre for the Protection of Children in Adoption
Web site: http://iss-ssi.org/Resource_Centre/Resource_Center_EN/resource_center_en.html

This is a resource center run by the International Social Service (ISS) in Canada to facilitate the implementation of the 1989 UN Convention on the Rights of the Child and the 1993 Hague Convention on the Protection of Children and Cooperation in Respect of Intercountry Adoption.

Joint Council on International Children's Services (JCICS)

Phone: 703-535-8045

Web site: www.jcics.org

The Joint Council on International Children's Services is an affiliation of licensed, nonprofit international adoption agencies. JCICS membership includes parent groups, advocacy organizations, and individuals who have an interest in intercountry adoption. JCICS member agencies subscribe to established standards of practice designed to protect the rights of children, birthparents, and adoptive parents.

National Council for Adoption (NCFA)

Phone: 703-299-6633

Web site: www.adoptioncouncil.org or www.ncfa-usa.org

NCFA is a research, education, and advocacy organization whose mission is to promote the well-being of children, birthparents, and adoptive families by advocating for the positive option of adoption. Adoption agencies can become members of NCFA if they meet specific requirements.

National Council for Single Adoptive Parents (NCSAP)

Phone: 888-490-4600

Web site: www.ncsap.org

The National Council for Single Adoptive Parents (formerly the Committee for Single Adoptive Parents) was founded to inform and assist single people in the United States who want to adopt children. The council supports the right of adoptable children to have loving families, regardless of differences in race, creed, color, national origin, or disability. The National Council for Single Adoptive Parents is a member of the Joint Council on International Children's Services and the North American Council on Adoptable Children.

North American Council on Adoptable Children

Phone: 651-644-3036

Web site: www.nacac.org

Founded in 1974 by adoptive parents, the North American Council on Adoptable Children is committed to meeting the needs of waiting children and the families who adopt them by offering adoption training conferences; providing adoption professionals with information about innovative ways to recruit and retain adoptive parents; conducting training sessions and workshops on adoption subsidy, child welfare reform, and other issues related to foster care and special-needs adoption; and developing and empowering hundreds of adoptive parent groups through leadership training and other support services.

U.S. Department of State, Children & Family Section
Web site: http://travel.state.gov/family/family_1732.html
The Office of Children's Issues provides information about and assistance in the adoption process in more than sixty countries, including: information about visa requirements and other U.S. requirements for international adoption; information about the Hague Intercountry Adoption Convention, and coordination with other countries about the treaty and related matters; help with individual inquiries on the status of adoption cases; and ensuring that U.S. citizens are not discriminated against by foreign authorities or courts.

Selected Adoption Research, Information, and Resources Web Sites

The following Web sites provide information on a variety of subjects related to adoption, with many sponsored links to agencies, attorneys, and further resources. They may also offer chat groups, forums, and links to support and reunion groups. Most are comprehensive adoption information sites. However, not all adoption information posted on the Internet is accurate. Please check and double-check information before relying on it to make your adoption decisions.

About Adoption, www.adoption.about.com
This resource site is sponsored by the popular About.com and offers articles, general information, poems, personal stories, adoption news, foster-care news, and more.

Adoption Media LLC is the sponsor of the following sites: Adopting.org, www.adopting.org; Adoption.com, www.adoption.com; Adoption.org, www.adoption.org; 123 Adoption, www.123adoption.com

Adoption101.com, www.adoption101.com
Adoption 101 dubs itself a free "Adoption School" on the Internet. There are online seminars, updates on legislation, and other information with the site's goal of promoting safe, ethical, and affordable adoptions through education.

Adoptive Families, www.adoptivefamilies.com, is the online site of the print publication of the same name. The Web site offers additional articles, links, adoption search tools, and more. It can help you find an attorney or agency in your area, give you the right questions to ask before you sign on the dotted line, and navigate adoptive families through the adoption process.

FamilyLife, www.familylife.com, offers lots of good adoption resources from a Christian perspective, including a downloadable adoption guide, which can be found at http://www.familylife.com/hopefororphans/AdoptionGuide.pdf. FamilyLife's Hope for Orphans program also sponsors adoption information workshops called "If You Were Mine" and offers links to Christian adoption agencies, waiting children photo listings, and adoption ministry resources.

Focus on the Family, www.focusonyourchild.com/hottopics/a0001283.cfm (or call 800-232-6459 and ask for adoption services)
The Christian-based organization Focus on the Family offers articles on adoption, a forum, and other resources on its Focus on Your Child Web site.

How to Adopt, www.howtoadopt.org, is an informational site developed by Shaohannah's Hope to walk prospective adoptive families through the steps to adoption. It offers links to other resources and connects families to the grant application page of Shaohannah's Hope.

Rainbow Kids, www.rainbowkids.com, is a huge online site dedicated to helping adoptive families with their international and transracial adoptions, from preadoption to post-placement issues. The online publication features tons of articles, links, and resources, and helps connect parents to waiting children around the world with a photo listing and agency information.

Appendix C

Public Adoption Agencies by State
This list includes government agencies that handle placement of waiting children in the foster-care system and state-run children's homes and orphanages.

Alabama
Alabama Foster and Adoptive Parent Association (AFAPA)
Phone: 888-545-2372
Click link to send e-mail: brebunch@bellsouth.net
Web site: http://www.afapa.org

Alabama Post Adoption Connections (APAC)
Phone: 866-803-2722
Click link to send e-mail: info@casapac.org
Web site: http://www.casapac.org

Families 4 Alabama's Kids-Become a Foster/Adoptive Parent
Phone: 866-4AL-KIDS (866-425-5437)
(under the auspices of the Alabama Department of Human Resources)

Alaska
Alaska Adoption Exchange
Phone: 907-465-3631; 907-465-3286; or 800-704-9133
Web site: www.akae.org

Arizona
Arizona Foster and Adoption Offices, under the auspices of the Arizona Department of Economic Security—Children, Youth, and Families Division
Phone: 877-KIDS-NEEDU (877-543-7633)
Web site: www.de.state.az.us/dcyf/adoption/information.asp

Arkansas
Arkansas Department of Health and Human Services, Arkansas Adoption Resource Exchange
Phone: 888-736-2820; (local) 501-682-8462
Web site: https://dhhs.arkansas.gov/wa_FC_adoption/FCA_Inquiry.asp.

California

California Department of Social Services, Child and Youth Permanency Branch
Sacramento, CA 95814
Phone: 800-KIDS-4-US (800-543-7487); (local) 916-651-7465
Web site: http://www.dss.cahwnet.gov/cdssweb/Adoptions_166.htm

Colorado

Colorado Department of Human Services
Phone: 303-866-5700
Web site: www.changealifeforever.org/contact.asp

Connecticut

Connecticut Department of Children and Families
Office of Foster Care and Adoption Services
Phone: 888-KID-HERO (888-543-4376)
Web site: www.state.ct.us/dcf/FASU/FASU_FAQs.htm

Delaware

Delaware Department of Services for Children, Youth, and Their Families (DSCYF)
Phone: 800-464-4357 (Delaware Statewide Adoption Recruitment Line)
Web site: http://www.state.de.us/kids/information/adoption.shtml

Florida

Department of Children and Families
Florida's Adoption Program
Phone: 800-96-ADOPT (800-962-3678)
Web site: www.dcf.state.fl.us/adoption

Georgia

Georgia Department of Human Resources
Division of Family and Children Services
Phone: Georgia Statewide Adoption Recruitment Line 877-210-kids (877-210-5437)
Web site: www.wednesdayschildga.com

Hawaii

Hawaii Department of Human Services
Phone: Hawaii Statewide Adoption Recruitment Line 808-441-0999
Web site: www.hawaii.gov/dhs

Idaho
Idaho Department of Health and Welfare
Division of Children and Family Services
Phone: 208-334-5697
Web site: www.healthandwelfare.idaho.gov/portal/alias__Rainbow/lang__en-US/tabID__3334/DesktopDefault.aspx

Illinois
Department of Children and Family Services
Division of Foster Care and Permanency Services
Phone: Adoption Hotline 800-572-2390
Web site: www.state.il.us/dcfs/adoption/index.shtml

Indiana
Indiana Division of Family and Children
Bureau of Family Protection and Preservation
Phone: 888-25-ADOPT (888-252-3678)
Web site: www.in.gov/fssa/adoption

Iowa
Iowa Department of Human Services
Division of Adult, Children & Family Services
Phone: KidSake 800-243-0756
Web site: www.dhs.state.ia.us/dhs2005/dhs_homepage/children_family/adoption/index.html

Kansas
Kansas Department of Social and Rehabilitation Services
Children and Family Policy Division
Phone: Coming Home Kansas 877-530-5275
Web site: www.srskansas.org/services/adoption.htm

Kentucky
Kentucky Department for Community Based Services (DCBS)
Cabinet for Families and Children
Phone: 800-232-5437
Web site: http://chfs.ky.gov/dcbs/dpp/permanency+services+branch.htm

Louisiana
Louisiana Department of Social Services

Office of Community Services
Phone: 225-342-4086
Web site: www.dss.state.la.us/departments/ocs/Adoption_Services.html

Maine
Maine Department of Health and Human Services
Bureau of Child and Family Services (DHHS-BCFS)
Phone: 877-505-0545
Web site: www.afamilyforme.org/adopt.html

Maryland
Maryland Department of Human Resources
Phone: 800-39-ADOPT (800-392-3678)
Web site: www.dhr.state.md.us/ssa/adopt.htm

Massachusetts
Massachusetts Department of Social Services
Phone: 800-KIDS-508 (800-543-7508)
Web site:
www.mass.gov/portal/index.jsp?pageID=eohhs2subtopic&L=4&sid=Eeohhs
2&L0=Home&L1=Consumer&L2=Family+Services&L3=Adoption

Michigan
Michigan Department of Human Services
Child and Family Services Administration
Phone: 517-373-3513
Web site: http://www.michigan.gov/dhs/0,1607,7-124-5452_7116---,00.html

Minnesota
Minnesota Department of Human Services
Phone: Minnesota Statewide Adoption Recruitment Line 866-665-4378
Web site: www.dhs.state.mn.us/main/groups/children/documents

Mississippi
Mississippi Department of Human Services
Division of Family and Child Services
Phone: Adoption Resource Exchange 800-821-9157
Web site: www.mdhs.state.ms.us/fcs_adopt.html

Missouri
Missouri Department of Social Services
Phone: Foster-Adoptline 800-554-2222
Web site: www.dss.mo.gov/cd/adopt.htm

Montana
Montana Department of Public Health and Human Services (DPHHS)
Phone: 406-444-5919
Web site: www.dphhs.mt.gov/aboutus/divisions/childfamilyservices/adoption/adoptioninmontana.shtml

Nebraska
Nebraska Department of Health and Human Services
Office of Protection and Safety/Child and Family Services Division
Phone: 800-7PARENT (800-772-7368) or 402-471-9331
Web site: www.hhs.state.ne.us/chs/adp/adpindex.htm

Nevada
Nevada Department of Human Resources
Division of Child and Family Services
Phone: 702-486-7633
Web site: http://dcfs.state.nv.us/DCFS_Adoption.htm

New Hampshire
New Hampshire Department of Health and Human Services
Division for Children, Youth, and Families
Phone: 800-852-3345
Web site: www.dhhs.state.nh.us/DHHS/FCADOPTION/default.htm

New Jersey
New Jersey Department of Human Services
Office of Resource Families and Adoption Support
Phone: 800-99-ADOPT (800-992-3678)
Web site: www.state.nj.us/humanservices/adoption/adopt.html

New Mexico
New Mexico Department of Children, Youth, and Families
Phone: 800-432-2075
Web site: www.cyfd.org/index.htm

New York
New York State Office of Children and Family Services / Adoption Service (OCFS/NYSAS)
Phone: 800-345-5437
Web site: www.ocfs.state.ny.us/adopt

North Carolina
North Carolina Department of Health and Human Services / Division of Social Services
Phone: 919-733-9464
Web site: www.dhhs.state.nc.us/dss/adopt

North Dakota
North Dakota Department of Human Services (NDDHS)
Children and Family Services Division
Phone: 800-472-2622
Web site: www.state.nd.us/humanservices/services/childfamily/adoption

Ohio
Ohio Department of Job and Family Services / Office of Family and Child Services
Phone: 800-755-4769 or 614-466- 9274
Web site: http://jfs.ohio.gov/oapl/index.htm

Oklahoma
Oklahoma Department of Human Services
Phone: 877-OKSWIFT (877-657-9438)
Web site: www.okdhs.org/adopt

Oregon
Oregon Department of Human Services
Office of Permanency for Children and of Training
Phone: 800-331-0503 or 503-945-5651
Web site: www.oregon.gov/DHS/children/adoption

Pennsylvania
Pennsylvania Department of Public Welfare / Office of Children, Youth, and Families
Statewide Adoption Network (SWAN)
Phone: 800-585-SWAN (800-585-7926)
Web site: www.dpw.state.pa.us/Child/AdoptionFosterCare/003670363.htm

Rhode Island
Rhode Island Department of Children, Youth, and Families (RIDCYF)
Adoption & Foster Care Preparation & Support
Phone: 401-724-1910
Web site: www.dcyf.ri.gov/adoption.htm or www.adoptionri.org

South Carolina
South Carolina Department of Social Services
Phone: 803-898-7318 or Adoption and Birthparent Services 800-922-2504
Web site: www.state.sc.us/dss/adoption/index.html

South Dakota
South Dakota Department of Social Services / Department of Child Protective Services
Phone: 605-773-3227
Web site: www.state.sd.us/social/cps/adoption/index.htm

Tennessee
Tennessee Department of Children's Services
Phone: 800-807-3228
Web site: www.state.tn.us/youth/adoption/index.htm

Texas
Texas Department of Family and Protective Services
Phone: 800-233-3405
Web site:
www.tdprs.state.tx.us/Adoption_and_Foster_Care/About_Adoption/default.asp

Utah
Utah Department of Human Services
Phone: 801-538-4437
Web site: www.hsdcfs.utah.gov/adoption.htm

Vermont
Vermont Department of Social and Rehabilitation Services
Phone: 800-746-7000
Web site: www.projectfamily.state.vt.us

Virginia
Virginia Department of Social Services / Family Services-Adoption Unit

Phone: 888-821-HOPE (888-821-4673)
Web site: www.dss.virginia.gov/family/ap/index.html

Washington

Washington Department of Social and Health Services (DSHS)
Division of Children and Family Services
Phone: 888-794-1794
Web site: www1.dshs.wa.gov/ca/adopt/intro.asp

Washington, DC

District of Columbia Child and Family Services Agency
Phone: 202-671-LOVE (202-671-5683)
Web site: http://dhs.dc.gov/dhs/cwp/view,a,3,q,492397,dhsNav,|30989|.asp

West Virginia

West Virginia Department of Health and Human Resources
Office of Social Services, Children and Adult Services
Phone: 304-558-4303
Web site: www.wvdhhr.org/oss/adoption

Wisconsin

Wisconsin Department of Health and Family Services
Phone: 608-266-3595
Web site: www.dhfs.state.wi.us/children/adoption/index.htm

Wyoming

Wyoming Department of Family Services
Phone: 307-777-3570
Web site: http://dfsweb.state.wy.us/adoption.html

Appendix D

Select Country-Specific Adoption Information

The information in this appendix is public information compiled and provided by the U.S. State Department. Adoption information for foreign countries is subject to change without notice, and each country provides different information. Some countries include the specific requirements that must be met to adopt. Others include the names and addresses of agencies that can be used to facilitate adoptions. Some discourage adoption inquiries by stating that none or very few intercountry adoptions have taken place in recent years. Some provide the ages of children available and the wait time to adopt; others do not. Therefore, check to make sure that information is up-to-date before making any adoption decisions. Up-to-date country-specific adoption information can be found at www.travel.state.gov under "Children & Family," then "International Adoption."

For general information about countries, you can also check out the CIA World Fact Book at http://www.cia.gov/cia/publications/factbook.

Albania

All adoptions must be processed by an adoption agency accredited by the Albanian Adoption Committee. Currently, two U.S. adoption agencies have been accredited: Bethany Christian Services, Phone: 616-459-6273; Fax: 616-459-0343; and International Children's Alliance, Phone: 202-463-6874; Fax: 202-463-6880.
Children Available: Healthy and special needs, ranging from two to fifteen years of age
Parents: Must be ages twenty-five to fifty for children ages two to five; older parents accepted for school-age children. Single women may adopt.
Time Frame for Referral: Approximately twelve to twenty-four months
Waiting Time After Referral: Approximately two to four months
Travel: One trip, four to five weeks in country; both parents must travel for first week.
Country Fees: $9,500 plus travel and accommodations
Post-Placement Reports: Required on arrival and at three, six, twelve, eighteen, and twenty-four months

Armenia

There are currently no licensed adoption agencies in Armenia. The U.S.

Embassy in Yerevan has a list of lawyers who may be able to help adopting parents in pursuing adoptions.

Adoption Fees: Approximately $45 in fees to Armenian governmental agencies. Attorneys assisting families to adopt may charge additional fees for services rendered.

Adoption Procedures in Armenia: A dossier (including tax returns for the last three years and family photos) must be submitted to the Adoption Department of the Prime Minister's Office of Armenia. The Armenian government wants to see that the prospective adoptive parents have some connection to Armenian culture. This can include an extended stay in the country or Armenian heritage on at least one side of the family.

Once the general permission to adopt is obtained, the parents must register with the Ministry of Social Security data bank. The parents may then start looking for a child. The adoptive parents or their representative should contact orphanages in Yerevan or in other districts of Armenia to locate a child for adoption.

Once the child is identified for adoption, the parents must inform the Ministry of Social Security. The ministry then transfers the case to the Adoption Department of the Prime Minister's Office for final approval. A special working group comprising deputy ministers of several ministries will review the case during one of their scheduled sessions, which take place every second week. After receiving a final approval from the Prime Minister's Office, the case is then transferred to the District Municipal Office of the child's residence. The municipality will provide the adoptive parents, or their legal representative, with all necessary documents in order to get the new birth certificate, the adoption certificate, and the Armenian passport.

An authorized representative of the adoptive parents can do all of the above steps. Authorization can be provided by a notarized power of attorney authorizing the representative to arrange the adoption. Prospective adoptive parents can expect travel to Armenia to sign adoption papers and attend the I-604 orphan investigation interview at the U.S. Embassy in Yerevan.

Azerbaijan

Azerbaijan suspended adoptions in April 2004, in order to conduct an investigation into adoption practices; however, in 2005 it began accepting dossiers and registering adoption applications. As we went to press in 2006, only three American families had completed adoptions. Many families report that they continue to face bureaucratic delays. Although the Azerbaijani Parliament is considering a new law on international adoption, there are no drafts of the law available, nor has the U.S. Embassy in Baku received any information on this new law. The embassy continues to seek clarification from the Azerbaijani government about the future of adoptions and encourage international adoption as a viable option when domestic adoption is not possible for an Azerbaijani child. In spring 2006, the Department of State urged all U.S. citizens considering adopting in Azerbaijan to carefully research the difficulties and uncertainties of adopting from this country. (Although adoptions are technically open, a number of U.S. adoption service providers have decided the situation is in too much a state of flux for them to operate comfortably. There are no guarantees that adoptions will be achieved on a regular basis and in a transparent manner.)

Barbados
Since 2000, only four visas have been issued for international adoption from Barbados.
Adoption Agency: The adoption agency for all of Barbados is the Child Care Board, located at: Fred Edghill Building, Cheapside, Fontabelle, Barbados. The phone number is 1-246-426-2577. There are no private adoption agencies operating in Barbados.

Belarus
In 2005, the Belarusian government put intercountry adoptions on hold. The government has not provided information on the reason for the apparent suspension, the possible duration of the suspension, or possible provisions for pending adoptions.

Belize
U.S. citizens who wish to adopt in Belize can adopt in two different ways. In order to obtain a full adoption in Belize and for the child to receive an IR-3 visa, adoptive parents are expected to reside in Belize for twelve months before a final adoption is granted. Adoptive parents who are U.S. citizens may also obtain provisional adoption that will allow a parent to take a Belizean orphan abroad to be adopted; children adopted in this manner receive an IR-4 visa. From 2000 to 2004, forty-two visas were issued to orphans from Belize.
Adoption Authority: Prospective adoptive parents interested in general information on adopting from Belize may also contact Belize Human Services Department, Fax: 011-501-227-1276.
Parents: One must be at least twenty-five years old and at least twelve years older than the child. Singles can adopt, but single men cannot adopt female children.
Time Frame: Adoptions in Belize generally take between twelve and twenty-four months.

Adoption Agencies and Attorneys: There are no accredited adoption agencies in Belize. Before sending a first payment to a lawyer or representative, adoptive parents should make sure that costs are inclusive and not subject to change. English is the official language of Belize, so all attorneys in Belize speak English.

International adoptions occur before a Supreme Court judge and require the services of a local attorney authorized to present cases to the Supreme Court. Adoptive parents who wish to obtain information about forms and detailed adoption requirements should contact a Belizean attorney. A list of attorneys can be found at http://belize.usembassy.gov/list_of_lawyers.html.

Adoption Fees: Attorney fees for adoption services in Belize range from $3,000 to $5,000 (U.S. dollars). U.S. citizens adopting a child in Belize should report any exorbitant fees to the American Embassy or to the Department of State.

Bolivia

Bolivia does not allow intercountry adoptions to countries that are not ratified through the Hague Convention on Intercountry Adoption. Currently, the United States has signed but not yet ratified this convention. (The United States is expected to ratify the convention by 2007.) U.S. citizens who are not resident in Bolivia are not permitted to adopt children from Bolivia. Americans interested in Bolivian adoption issues are encouraged to contact the Consular Section at the American Embassy in La Paz via e-mail at consularlapaz@state.gov. Between 2000 and 2004, 125 adoption visas were issued.

Adoption Authority: The governmental authority responsible for adoption matters in Bolivia is the Vice-Ministry of Youth, Children, and the Elderly (Viceministerio de La Juventud, Niñez y Tercera Edad), which may be reached via the following contact information: Viceministerio de La Juventud, Niñez y Tercera Edad

Phone: 591-2-215-0090 (direct line)

There are currently no licensed adoption agencies in Bolivia handling the adoption of Bolivian children by U.S. citizens. The U.S. Embassy in La Paz maintains a list of attorneys who may be able to help U.S. Citizens who are legal residents of Bolivia or U.S.-Bolivian dual nationals pursuing adoptions.

Parents: Married or unmarried U.S. citizens must be at least twenty-five years of age to adopt a child in Bolivia.

Time Frame: Recent experience suggests that the total time required (i.e., from initial consultation with an approved adoption agency until the child arrives in the U.S.) will be several months to over one year. Both adoptive parents do not need to be present in Bolivia during the entire process, but both adoptive parents must be present for the provisional placement, the evaluation, and the ratification of the adoption by the court. The child must be present for the visa interview, attended by at least one U.S. citizen adoptive parent. Adoptive parents should plan to stay in Bolivia for approximately four to six weeks. Adoptive parents are advised not to make travel plans for an adoptive child until they have the child's U.S. visa. The Immigrant Visa Unit at the U.S. Embassy in La Paz will do its best to process adoption visa paperwork quickly; however, unexpected delays in the adoption process are possible. The U.S. Citizenship and Immigration Service and consular officials have no authority to intervene in any Bolivian legal process.

Bosnia and Herzegovina

While there is nothing in Bosnian law that specifically prohibits foreigners from applying to adopt a Bosnian child, the law stresses that there must be overwhelming justification and exceptionally compelling reasons for a foreigner to be permitted to adopt a Bosnian child. It is extremely difficult to obtain this approval. Furthermore, in a country that is still recovering from a long and brutal conflict, it can be extremely difficult to determine if the whereabouts of a parent are simply unknown or if the child is truly an orphan. From 2000 to 2003, seven adoption visas were issued.

Brazil

Brazilian adoption law gives preference to Brazilian citizens and citizens of countries that have implemented the 1993 Hague Convention on International Adoption. Without Brazilian citizenship, it is unlikely that a U.S. citizen will be able to adopt a healthy, single child under the age of five years. From 2001 to 2005, 223 adoption visas were issued.

Children: Single, healthy children, ages five and older; sibling groups of any number and of all ages; and special-needs children of all ages

Parents: Must be over age twenty-one and at least sixteen years older than the child. Singles can adopt.

Time Frame: Brazilian law requires prospective parents to live in Brazil with the child for a cohabitation period of at least fifteen days for children under two years and at least thirty days for older children. The average time to complete an intercountry adoption case in Brazil varies from three months to one year.

Adoption Authority: The division of government responsible for international adoption in Brazil is the State Judiciary Commission of Adoption (CEJA). Each state maintains a CEJA that acts as the central adoption authority and sole organization authorized to approve foreign adopting parents. The following CEJAs are known to work with American citizens:

Alagoas
Avenida Durval de Goes Monteiro, 6001
Phone: 55-82-3328-9006; Fax: 55-82-3328-9010
Web site: www.tj.al.gov.br
Minas Gerais
Phone: 55-31-3330-2833; Fax: 55-31-3330-2391
E-mail: ceja@tjmg.gov.br; Web site: www.tjmg.gov.br
Paraná
Phone: 55-41-3233-3518; Fax: 55-41-3225-6044
E-mail: adoção@tj.pv.br; Web site: www.tj.pr.gov.br
Rio de Janeiro
Phone: 55-21-2588-3295; Fax: 55-21-2588-2657
E-mail: ceja@tj.rj.gov.br; Web site: www.tj.rj.gov.br
Santa Catarina
Phone: 55-48-221-1224/1226; Fax: 55-48-221-1100
E-mail: ceja@tj.gov.br; Web site: www.tj.sc.gov.br
São Paulo
Phone/Fax: 55-11-3242-3465
E-mail: cejaisp@tj.sp.gov.br; Web site: www.tj.sp.gov.br
Adoption Agencies and Attorneys: The CEJAs maintain lists of attorneys throughout Brazil, some of whom specialize in adoption cases. The U.S. consulate general in Rio de Janeiro can provide interested parties with a list of CEJA addresses and phone numbers.

Bulgaria
Adoption Authority: Phone: 359-2-923-7303 (Bulgarian only)
Web site: http://www.mjeli.government.bg (Bulgarian only)
Parents: Married or single, at least fifteen years older than their adoptive children, but no more than forty-five years older. There are no Bulgarian age minimums or maximums; prospective adoptive parents are expected to comply with their home government's age requirements (for the U.S., prospective adoptive parents must be at least twenty-five years old; there are no age maximums).
Time Frame: It normally takes at least several months to complete an intercountry adoption in Bulgaria; however, some adoptions have taken over a year to complete.
Adoption Agencies and Attorneys: Prospective adoptive parents must use a Bulgarian-licensed U.S. adoption agency or a Bulgarian adoption agency accredited by the Bulgarian Ministry of Justice. The Ministry of Justice is currently reviewing license applications for several U.S.-based adoption

agencies. For a complete list of adoption agencies accredited by the Bulgarian Ministry of Justice, visit http://www.usembassy.bg/consular/adoptagency.html.

Canada

Adoption Authority: In Canada, the provinces are responsible for setting and administering adoption policies and procedures. From 2000 to 2004, eleven orphan visas were issued. The following is contact information for federal and provincial adoption authorities who can provide specific information on adoption in Canada:

Government of Canada

Human Resources Development Canada
Phone: 819-997-1562; Fax: 819-953-1115
Web site: http://www.hrdc-drhc.gc.ca/hrib/sdd-dds/cfc/content
/interAdopt.shtml

Alberta

Alberta Children's Services / Program Manager, Adoption Services
Phone: 780-422-5641; Fax: 780-427-2048
Web site: http://www.child.gov.ab.ca/whatwedo/adoption

British Columbia

Ministry for Children and Families / Adoption Branch
Phone: 250-387-3660; Fax: 250-356-1864
Web site: http://www.mcf.gov.bc.ca/adoption

Manitoba

Manitoba Family Services / Child and Family Services / Intercountry
Adoptions Specialist
Phone: 204-945-6964; Fax: 204-945-6717
Web site: http://www.gov.mb.ca

New Brunswick

Family and Community Services / Adoption Consultant
Phone: 506-444-5970; Fax: 506-453-2082
Web site: http://www.gov.nb.ca

Newfoundland

Department of Health and Community Services / Director of Child, Youth
Policy and Programs Services Branch

Phone: 709-729-6721; Fax: 709-729-6382
Web site: http://www.gov.nf.ca/health

Northwest Territories
Department of Health and Social Services / Coordinator, Child and Family
Services Unit
Phone: 867-873-7943; Fax: 867-873-7706
Web site: http://www.gov.nt.ca

Nova Scotia
Department of Community Services / Manager of Adoption and Foster Care
Phone: 902-424-3205; Fax: 902-424-0708
Web site: http://www.gov.ns.ca/coms/families/adoption.html

Nunavut
Department of Health and Social Services
Phone: 867-975-5700; Fax: 867-975-5705
Web site: http://www.gov.nu.ca

Ontario
Ministry of Community, Family and Children's Services / Adoption Unit,
Central Services
Phone: 416-327-4742; Fax: 416-212-6799
Web site: http://www.cfcs.gov.on.ca

Prince Edward Island
Department of Health and Social Services / Child, Family and Community
Services
Phone: 902-368-6514; Fax: 902-368-6136
Web site: http://www.gov.pe.ca

Quebec
Ministère de la Santé et des Services sociaux/Secrétariat à l'adoption interna-
tionale
Phone: 514-873-4747 or 800-561-0246; Fax: 514-873-1709
Web site: http://www.msss.gouv.qc.ca

Saskatchewan
Saskatchewan Social Services/Adoption Program Consultant
Phone: 306-787-5698; Fax: 306-787-0925
Web site: http://www.gov.sk.ca

Yukon
Family and Children's Services / Placement and Support Services
Phone: 867-667-3473; Fax: 867-393-6204
Web site: http://www.gov.yk.ca

China
Adoption Authority: The government office responsible for adoptions in China is the Ministry of Civil Affairs, specifically the China Center of Adoption Affairs.
China Center for Adoption Affairs (CCAA)
Phone: 86-10-6522-3102
An approved adoption agency may submit adoption applications directly to the CCAA for consideration. Once the application is approved, the CCAA will send a referral of a child to the agency. To finalize the adoption, the prospective adoptive parent(s) needs to travel to China for a stay of approximately ten to fourteen days to complete the process.
Time Frame: Approximately one year from the time the dossier is submitted to the CCAA until finalization.

Chile
Priority is given to Chilean families over non-Chilean families who wish to adopt. From 2000 to 2004, thirty-five orphan visas were issued.
Adoption Authority: SENAME (Servicio Nacional de Menores) is the clearinghouse for adoptions and approves parents who wish to adopt. Couples interested in adopting in Chile must contact SENAME first before beginning any adoption proceedings.
Servicio Nacional de Menores de Chile (SENAME)
Phone: 56-2-398-4447
Web site: www.sename.cl
Children: Most of the children available for international adoption are age four and older. Not all children eligible for adoption in Chile meet U.S. immigration requirements to receive an orphan visa.
Under Chilean law, children to be adopted may not leave the country until the adoption is complete.
Parents: Married couples between the ages of twenty-five and sixty, and at least twenty-five years older than the child.
Fees: Adoptive parents should expect to spend no more than $3,000. Adoptive parents should report exorbitant fees to the American Embassy, the Department of State, or SENAME.
Time Frame: International adoptions in Chile normally take about two years from start to finish.

Adoption Agencies and Attorneys: The new Chilean adoption law provides for SENAME to oversee the adoption process from the request to terminate parental rights to the issuance of the final adoption decree. Only SENAME and the following accredited agencies are able to sponsor petitions for international adoptions:

Fundation Chileana de la Adopcion (Phone: 665-2139; 665-2150)

Fundacion San Jose para la Adopcion Familiar Cristiana (Phone: 399-9600)

Instituto Chileano de Colonias y Campamentos y Hogares de Menores (Phone: 72-541-271)

Colombia

Adoption Authority: The government office responsible for adoptions in Colombia is the Colombian Family Welfare Institute (ICBF).

BIENESTAR FAMILIAR (ICBF)

Phone: 011-57-1-437-7630 (Ext. 3158 or 3157)

Web sites: www.icbf.gov.co (Spanish);

http://www.icbf.gov.co/ingles/home.asp (English)

From 2000 to 2004, 1,405 orphan visas were issued.

Colombian law does not allow for private adoptions. Children may be adopted only through the Colombian Family Welfare Institute (ICBF) and approved adoption agencies. Every adopted child must have a final adoption decree in order to leave Colombia.

Parents: Married couples over age twenty-five only. Babies are assigned to younger couples; older children to older couples.

Time Frame: Colombian law requires that both adopting parents be physically present when the adoption is presented to a "family judge." No exceptions are made for this requirement, and the process takes two to four weeks, sometimes more. After both parents have appeared before the court, one of the parents may return to the United States, but the other parent must remain in Colombia until the adoption/immigrant visa process is completed. The entire process may take eighteen to thirty months.

Fees: Parents receiving visas for their adopted children have reported spending between $12,000 and $20,000 (U.S. dollars) from start to finish.

Dominican Republic

Adoption Authority: The Oversight Agency of the System for the Protection of Children and Adolescents is the government agency responsible for overseeing adoptions in the Dominican Republic. Their main office is located at Calle Moises Garcia No.7 esq. Calle Galvan, Ensanche Gazcue, Santo Domingo, Dominican Republic, phone: 809-685-9257. Inquiries should be in the Spanish language. Upon arrival in the Dominican Republic to try to arrange an adoption, U.S. citizens should register at the American Citizens Services unit of the Consular Section. The American Citizens Services unit provides information concerning current travel advisories and other information about the Dominican Republic, including lists of physicians and attorneys. The Consular Section's American Citizens Services unit is at the corner of Calle Cesar Nicolas Penson and Maximo Gomez, phone: 809-221-2171.

Adoption Agencies and Attorneys: Adoptions can be arranged through private adoption agencies working with Dominican attorneys or directly with Dominican attorneys. If a private attorney is retained, the cost can be as high as $5,000, but this includes locating the child and providing a caretaker and room and board until the child is turned over to the adopting parent(s).

Parents: Under Dominican law, a single individual, a married couple, or an unmarried couple may adopt a child. A single individual must be at least twenty-five years old and at least fifteen years older than the child. A married couple may adopt a child if one of the spouses is at least twenty-five years old.

Time Frame: The entire adoption process in the Dominican Republic, from the original release of the child for adoption to the final adoption decree, may take six months or more.

Ecuador

All Ecuadorian adoptions by U.S. citizens must be processed through U.S.-based adoption agencies legally authorized to deal with Ecuadorian adoption agencies or private attorneys. From 2000 to 2004, 209 orphan visas were issued.

Adoption Authority: The Technical Adoptions Unit and the Family Assignment Committee (Unidad Tecnica de Adopciones y el Comite de Asignacion Familiar) oversees adoptions in Ecuador. The courts in Ecuador issue adoption decrees. The Childhood and Adolescence Court (Juzgado de la Ninez y Adolescencia) must grant permission for the child to depart the country if living with only one of the parents. This permission is valid for only one year.

Parents: Married couples over age twenty-five and at least fourteen years older than the child and singles over age twenty-five may adopt. Singles may adopt only a child of the same sex.

Time Frame: Prospective adoptive parent(s) must come to Ecuador and expect to remain for three to four weeks to finalize the adoption as stated below. Once an adoption decree is issued, only one parent needs to remain in Ecuador, usually an additional week. The adoption process in Ecuador generally takes between nine to sixteen months from beginning to end.

Adoption Agencies and Attorneys: The government of Ecuador requires that you must work through a private agency that has signed an agreement with the government of Ecuador. The agency can give you an estimate of the cost of an adoption in Ecuador. Following is a list of those agencies, which may grow as more agencies qualify:

The Alliance for Children
Phone: 617-431-7148; Fax: 617-431-7474
FAFECOPR (Ecuador)
Phone: 022-259-556; 022-254-832; 022-466-963
Bethany Christian Services / National Office
Phone: 616-224-7585
E-mail: bwm@bethany.org
Children's Home Society of Minnesota
Phone: 651-255-2265; Fax: 651-646-0436
E-mail: jlarson@chsfs.org
Ecuador
Phone: 72-822-562
E-mail: ximegon@etapaonline.net.ec
Children's House International
Phone: 801-756-0587
E-mail: TrudyCHI@aol.com
Los Ninos / International Adoption Center
Phone: 713-363-2892; Fax: 713-363-2896
The Open Door Adoptions
Phone: 229-228-6339
E-mail: walter@opendooradoption.com
Rainbow House International
Phone: 505-861-1234
E-mail: donna@rhi.org
Ecuador
Phone: 593-2-255-1526; cellular 099-738378
E-mail: mrizzo@andinanet.net
Spence-Chapin
Phone: 212-369-0300; Fax: 212-722-0675
Ecuador
Phone: 593-2-504893; Fax: 593-2-504893
Villa Hope
Phone: 205-870-7359; Fax: 205-871-6629
Ecuador
Phone: 593-4-2650605/6/7

El Salvador
Adoption Authority: There are several Salvadoran governmental bodies involved in the adoption process. These include the Family Courts and the Procuraduria General de la Republica (PGR). The Procuraduria is responsible for family welfare law in El Salvador. The Instituto Salvadoreño Para el Desarrollo Integral de la Niñez Adolescencia (ISNA) is responsible for the care of orphans and other children in government custody. Representatives from ISNA and the PGR oversee international adoptions in El Salvador's adoption central authority called the Oficina Para Adopciones (OPA). Information regarding Salvadoran laws and procedures for the purposes of adoption may be obtained by contacting Oficina Para Adopciones, Phone: 503-222-4444 or 503-222-4133.

From 2000 to 2004, forty-eight orphan visas were issued.

Time Frame: The local adoption process typically takes between eighteen and thirty-six months to complete, not including the time necessary for the U.S. Embassy to complete its own investigation, as required by immigration regulations due to the high incidence of fraud in adoption cases in El Salvador. Under Article 176 of the Family Code, adoptive parents who wish to adopt a particular child who is not related to them must be prepared to reside with the child in El Salvador for at least one year prior to finalization of the adoption.

Parents: Adopting parents must be twenty-five years of age and married for five years. There must be a minimum of fifteen years' age difference between the adopting parents and child. Parents adopting a child under one year of age cannot be older than forty-five. Single individuals may adopt in El Salvador.

Ethiopia
Adoption Authority: The government office responsible for adoptions in Ethiopia is the Adoption Team in the Children and Youth Affairs Office (CYAO), which is under the Ministry of Labour and Social Affairs (MOLSA). The head of the adoption team can be reached at 011-251-1-505-358. Prospective adoptive parents may contact the head of the adoption team to request information about approved orphanages caring for children in need of permanent family placements through international adoption.

Note: Prospective adoptive parents who have worked with unscrupulous adoption facilitators have reported problems, some of them serious, including learning after the adoption has been finalized that the child is infected with HIV/AIDS; that a prospective adoptive child does not exist, is missing, or has already been adopted by another family; that the children they anticipated adopting do not meet the U.S. definition of orphans; that fraudulent documents have been submitted to the court on their behalf; and facing unanticipated extended stays in Ethiopia and higher than expected costs.

From 2000 to 2004, 782 orphan visas were issued.

The following U.S. adoption agencies are licensed to facilitate adoptions in Ethiopia. Private independent adoptions can take place only with the approval of MOLSA.

Adoptions Advocates International
Phone: 360-452-4777
E-mail: merrily@adoptionadvocates.org; Web site: http://www.adoptionadvocates.org

Americans for African Adoptions, Inc.
Phone: 317-271-4567; Fax: 317-271-8739
E-mail: amfaa@aol.com; Web site: http://www.africanadoptions.org

Children's Home Society & Family Services
Phone: 651-646-6393; Fax: 651-646-0436
E-mail: info@chsm.com; Web site: http://www.chsm.com

Christian World Adoption
Phone: 843-722-6343; Fax: 843-722-1616
E-mail: hardingt@cwa.org; Web site: http://www.cwa.org

Dove Adoptions International, Inc.
Phone: 503-324-9010; Fax: 503-324-9080
Web site: http://www.adoptions.net

Wide Horizons for Children, Inc.
Phone: 781-894-5330; Fax: 781-899-2769
E-mail: info@whfc.org; Web site: http://www.whfc.org

Parents: Married couples and single women may adopt if at least twenty-five years old. Some single men have been allowed to adopt on a case-by-case basis. There is no statutory maximum age limit on the adoptive parent; however, Ethiopian practice is to limit the age of the parent to no more than forty years greater than that of the adopted child.

Time Frame: Adoption agencies will advise adoptive parents approximately how long an adoption will take. Recent private adoptions have taken between six and twenty-four months.

Guatemala

Adoption Authority: Adoptions by U.S. citizen parents in Guatemala are processed under a "notarial system." Guatemalan attorneys receive and refer potential orphans to parents desiring to adopt a child. If the parents accept the referral, they will provide the attorney with a power of attorney to act on their behalf to complete an adoption. In most cases the attorney represents the birthparent(s), the adopting parents, and the child(ren) in the Guatemalan govern-ment proceedings. After obtaining clearance from a social worker under the supervision of a family court to proceed with a potential adoption case, and upon receipt of "preapproval" from the Department of Homeland Security Office (DHS) in Guatemala, the attorney submits the case for review by the Guatemalan Solicitor General's Office (Procuradoria General de la Nacion, PGN). The PGN scrutinizes the adoption case for signs of fraud or irregulari-ties before providing its approval of the adoption. Upon receiving PGN approval, the adoptive parents in the U.S. are legally responsible for their child(ren). The attorney obtains final approval from the Guatemalan birth-mother and then requests a birth certificate listing the adoptive parents as the parents of the adopted child. With these final documents, the attorney submits the complete case file, including the I-600 orphan visa petition, to DHS in Guatemala. DHS reviews the case and either approves the I-600 or notifies the attorney in writing if any further problems prevent approval of the case. Once DHS approves the I-600, the case is sent to the embassy's Consular Section and a visa interview is scheduled, usually within a few days. Note that the PGN does not charge fees for adoptions.

The U.S. Embassy in Guatemala issued more than 3,500 immigrant visas in fiscal year 2004 to Guatemalan children adopted by U.S. citizens.

Haiti

Adoption Authority: The Haitian courts issue adoption decrees and other legal documents, and the Institut du Bien Etre Social et de Research (IBESR) provides authorization to adopt. The IBESR is also responsible for accrediting adoption agents and orphanages in Haiti. Documentation from both the Haitian courts and from the IBESR is essential if you are planning to adopt a child in Haiti. Successful and speedier adoptions generally require the services of a Haitian attorney. Lists of Haitian attorneys are available from the U.S. Embassy or the Department of State, Office of American Citizen Services.

Parents: Must be older than age thirty-five; for married couples, one prospec-tive parent may be under age thirty-five, provided the couple have been married for ten years and have no children together.

Time Frame: The adoption process can require an average of two to six months' time, primarily because of Haitian legal intricacies. Adoption applica-tions can take more than one year in certain cases.

Honduras

Adoption Authority: All adoptions must go through the Instituto Hondureño del Niño y la Familia, also known as "IHNFA," a social welfare agency charged by the Honduran government with overseeing local and international adoptions. The government of Honduras is strict in its application of adoption law. There are no private adoptions in Honduras. Adoptions in Honduras usually take from six months up to one year. Please be cautious in dealing with individuals who offer to facilitate or short cut the adoption procedure; they cannot legally short circuit the process. Adoption agencies are required to register with IHNFA. If they are not registered, IHNFA cannot assist the agencies in the adoption process.

Adoption Agencies and Attorneys: You will need to hire a Honduran attorney since only an attorney may present the adoption petition to the courts. Most adoption agencies in the United States that are registered with the IHNFA have contracts with designated attorneys in Honduras. However, in most cases, you can choose to work with a different attorney. The embassy has a list of attorneys who are bilingual. The consulate maintains a notebook of letters from parents who have adopted in Honduras available for review that may be useful in selecting an attorney. The list of adoption agencies has been provided by the IHNFA for information only.

Adoptions International, Inc.

Phone: 215-627-6313; Fax: 215-592-7881; Honduran representative: 011-504-32-9626

Brightside for Families and Children

Phone: 413-788-7366; Honduran representative: 011-504-37-5096

Children's Home Society of Minnesota

Phone: 651-646-7771 or 800-952-9302; Honduran Representative: 011-504-36-6290

Children's Hope

Phone: 517-828-5842; Fax: 517-828-5799; Honduran representative: 011-504-35-8070

Concern

One West Main Street

Fleetwood, PA 19522

Concern for Children

Web site: www.concernforchildren.org

Honduran representative: 011-504-32-9626

(Note: Contact Concern for Children through a form on its Web site or its Honduran representative. No phone number in Ohio has been provided.)

Crossroads

Phone: 952-831-5707; Fax: 952-831-5129

The Family Network Inc.

Phone: 800-888-0242; 408-655-5077; Honduran Representative: 504-38-4087

Fax: 408-655-3811

Family Partners Worldwide, Inc.

Phone: 404-872-6787; Fax: 404-874-9362; Honduran representative: 011-504-36-9739

Los Niños (The Children) International Adoption Center

Phone: 713-363-2896; Fax: 713-363-2892; Honduran representative: 011-504-31-1965

New Family Foundation, Inc.

Honduran representative: 011-504-33-3538

Pearl S. Buck Foundation, Inc.

Phone: 215-249-1516; Fax: 215-249-9657; Honduran representative: 504-31-2193

Voice for International and Domestic Adoptions

Phone: 518-828-4527

Hong Kong

Adoption Authority: The government office responsible for adoptions in Hong Kong is the Adoption Unit, Social Welfare Department, 38 Pier Road, Harbor Building 4/F., Central, Hong Kong (Phone: 852-2852-3107; fax: 852-2851-9189; e-mail: grau@swd.gov.hk; Web site:http://www.info.gov.hk/swd).

The adoption process in Hong Kong begins with the prospective adoptive parents in Hong Kong submitting an application to the director of the Social Welfare Department. The Social Welfare Department then compiles a "home study" and requires a medical examination of the couple. If, based on the findings of the home study, the application is approved, the Social Welfare Department attempts to match the couple with a child. If a match is made, the department gives written consent to release the child into the applicants' home for a period of at least six months. An adoption worker will make periodic visits to the applicants' home to determine whether adoption by the applicants would be in the best interests of the child. Meanwhile, the applicants submit the required applications to the director of the Social Welfare Department and to the Hong Kong District Court for an Adoption Order. Upon receipt of the recommendation from the director of the Social Welfare Department, the District Court sets a hearing date for the adoption to take place. From 1996 to 2000, 135 orphan visas were issued.

As an alternative, U.S. citizens in the United States may apply to bring a Hong Kong child to the United States for adoption through the International Social Service (ISS) in Hong Kong under the Intercountry Adoption Program. ISS works closely with Hong Kong's Social Welfare Department in placing children overseas. ISS has an office in the United States at 700 Light Street,

Baltimore, MD 21230 (phone: 410-230-2734; fax: 410-230-2741). ISS Baltimore may be able to provide general information on adoptions. For specific information about Hong Kong adoption procedures, write to:
International Social Service Hong Kong Branch
Phone: 852-2834-6863; Fax: 852-2834-7627
E-mail: isshkbr@netvigator.com

Children: Under Hong Kong law, children between six months and eighteen years of age can be adopted.

Parents: Married couples who are at least twenty-five years old, are in good physical and mental health, and have adequate resources to parent an adopted child are more likely to succeed in adoption applications. Preferred married couples are those who have been married for at least three years (five years if it is the second marriage for either parent), and can provide the child a stable home. Persons over age forty-five are considered for adopting a child if they are willing to accept older children or children with special needs.

Hungary

Adoption Authority: The government office responsible for adoptions in Hungary is the National Child and Youth Protection Institute (GYIVI).
Phone: 3202-200 (Ext. 118)

There is less demand by Hungarian families for older children or those of nonethnic Hungarian background. Generally these children are entered on the national register and available for adoption by foreigners. From 1999 to 2003, eighty-nine orphan visas were issued.

Parents: Hungarian law does not specify an age limit for adoptive parents, but Hungarian authorities require that one of the adoptive parents be under age forty-five. Single people may adopt; however, an adoption may be denied based on the strongly held opinion that a child be raised in a family.

Time Frame: The adoption authorities have fifteen days to notify adoptive parents they have been approved to adopt in Hungary. Parents then have sixty days to submit required documents. After prospective adoptive parents arrive to meet their child, it takes four to six weeks to complete the adoption.

Adoption Agencies and Attorneys: There are no accredited international adoption agencies in Hungary. Adoptive parents must work directly with GYIVI. The embassy usually advises adoptive parents to seek the assistance of a U.S. adoption agency or a lawyer with experience in Hungarian international adoptions if no friends or relatives are available to help in Hungary with the complex adoption process.

India

Indian law has no provisions for foreigners to adopt Indian children, but under the Guardian and Wards Act of 1890, foreigners may petition an Indian District Court for legal custody of a child to be taken abroad for adoption. Following a 1984 Indian Supreme Court decision, non-Indians are required to work through an adoption agency in their home country that is licensed in accordance with local law and appears on a list of agencies approved by the Indian government. Only an Indian agency recognized and listed by the Indian government may make children available for adoption by foreigners. You may wish to contact an Indian attorney to assist you in obtaining custody. Specific questions regarding adoption in India may be addressed to the Consular Section of the U.S. Embassy or Consulate in India.

Israel

Adoptions are strictly controlled by the Ministry of Social Welfare and the District Courts. Few children are available to foreigners. The adoptive parent(s) must be of the same religion as the child and work through a licensed adoption agency.

Jamaica

Adoption Authority: The government office responsible for adoptions in Jamaica is the Jamaican Adoption Board. The Adoption Board is the only agency legally authorized to provide adoption services in Jamaica.
Oceana Complex
Phone: 876-948-2841/ 876-948-2842; Fax: 876-924-9401
From 2000 to 2004, 216 orphan visas were issued.
Adoptions through an Adoption Order may take place in Jamaica or through an Adoption License in a "scheduled country," such as the United States, and adopted there.
Parents: Single individuals or married couples may adopt children in Jamaica if they are age twenty-five or older.
Time Frame: For parents seeking an Adoption License, there is no residential requirement. The parents will likely have to travel to Jamaica at least twice (once to meet with the Adoption Board and again to apply for a visa), however. For parents seeking an Adoption Order, the parents must reside in Jamaica during the preadoption placement and until the case appears before a Jamaican court. This typically takes at least four months.

Japan

Adoption Authority: The Family Court and the Child Guidance Center (CGC) (often located in the City or Ward Office) are the government offices responsible for adoption in Japan. They have jurisdiction over the placement of children, home studies, and adoptions. From 1996 to 2000, 220 orphan visas were issued. Prospective adoptive parents may find children available for adoption through either the CGC or private parties such as missionaries, social welfare organizations, or adoption agencies. It is important to remember that the CGC will issue a certificate identifying a "child who requires protection" only if the adoption is arranged through them. If the adoption is arranged privately, the adoptive parents must present the appropriate statement of release for emigration and adoption to prove the child is adoptable. Even if the Japanese government certifies a child as requiring protection or considers a child legally adoptable, however, it is possible that the child may still not meet the U.S. definition of an orphan.

All adoption agencies in Japan are privately operated. There are attorneys; however, they aren't necessarily recommended and aren't required for processing adoptions. As far as adoption agencies, they are not necessary; however, they are used if recommended/required by the host county government. If prospective adoptive parents would like to obtain a list of adoption agencies, they can contact the embassy of Tokyo.

Time Frame: The court will not consider adoption applications of those prospective parents who are in Japan on temporary visitor visas. At least one prospective parent must show evidence of long-term residence in Japan. When the adoption is finalized, at least one adoptive parent must appear before the court. Japanese law does not permit proxy adoptions.

Kazakhstan

Adoption Authority: Immigrant visas for Kazakhstan residents, including adoptive children, are administered at the U.S. Embassy in Almaty. Since August 1, 2003, immigrant visas for residents of the Kyrgyz Republic, Uzbekistan, and Tajikistan, including adoptive children, are also processed at the U.S. Embassy in Almaty.

Ministry of Education Committee on Guardianship and Care
83 Kenesary Street
Astana, Kazakhstan 010000

Under Kazakhstani law, adoptive parents may work with any agency they choose. However, adoption agencies are encouraged to contact the Ministry of Education to notify the ministry of their intention to provide adoption services.

From 2000 to 2005, 4,397 orphan visas were issued.

Time Frame: Prospective adoptive parents must reside with the child for a minimum of two weeks at the child's habitual place of residence in Kazakhstan prior to the adoption ("the Bonding Period"). The preadoption bonding period cannot be waived. Kazakhstani law also provides for a fifteen-day waiting period ("the Appeal Period") after the court hearing before the adoption becomes final. A judge can waive this period at his or her discretion, but this has become an increasingly rare occurrence. The court decision, adoption certificate, post-adoption birth certificate, and child's Kazakhstani passport cannot be obtained until the judge finalizes the adoption. Prospective adoptive parents can expect to stay in Kazakhstan anywhere from forty to sixty days, and occasionally longer, to complete Kazakhstani adoption requirements.

Kenya

Adoption Authority: The government office responsible for adoptions in Kenya is the civil court system. When adopting a child, many steps must be taken before a child can be placed in the care of the adoptive parent. If anyone other than an adoption agency places a child with prospective adoptive parents, the chief inspector of children must be notified of the placement. The adoption society or a legal guardian must make inquiries and obtain reports on the personal circumstances of the applicant, child, and child's parents or guardians. Foreigners interested in adopting a child in Kenya may wish to employ legal representation that is familiar with the practices of Kenya's legal system, as the court's interpretation of adoption laws can vary widely depending on the case. From 1998 to 2000, thirty-one orphan visas were issued.

Parents: Kenyan law specifically states that an adoption order shall not be made in favor of a sole applicant who is male or an applicant who is of a different race than the child unless there are extenuating circumstances. Although it still remains an issue, the courts are beginning to take a more liberal view of racial differences between potential adopters and the child.

Korea (South)

Adoption Authority: The government office responsible for adoptions is the Ministry of Health and Social Welfare. There are a large number of U.S. adoption agencies authorized and affiliated with the Korean government to facilitate adoptions. From 2001 to 2005, 8,785 orphan visas were issued.

Parents: Couples married for at least three years who are between ages twenty-five and forty-four.

Time Frame: Children are usually escorted to the United States after a successful home study and dossier approval process.

Lativa

Adoption Authority: The Ministry for Family and Children's Rights is responsible for administering intercountry adoptions. Foreigners interested in adopting a Latvian child should express their interest in writing to the ministry at the following address:

Ministry for Family and Children's Rights
Phone: 371-735-6497; Fax: 371-735-6464
E-mail: pasts@bm.gov.lv; Web site: http://www.bm.gov.lv

There is some popular opposition in Latvia to the adoption of Latvian children by foreigners. This has contributed to a reluctance to reform international adoption procedures, which entail several extended trips by adoptive parents to Latvia to complete all requirements. From 2000 to 2004, 116 orphan visas were issued.

Time Frame: The time needed to complete an adoption in Latvia from beginning to end varies depending on the age of the adoptive child. There are very few newborn and younger children in need of a permanent family placement who are available for international adoption. Some parents wait several years to adopt an eligible child. Adoptions involving children between five and ten years of age can take less than a year, as there currently are many more older children eligible for international adoption.

Lebanon

Adoption Authority: Since adoption is overseen by religious institutions in Lebanon, the adoptions must be supervised by authorized church authorities and must be approved by these authorities as well as the Christian Court. This also applies to children who are adopted through non-Christian denominations. There are no adoption agencies in Lebanon. Churches and church officials care for abandoned children but may not always have the legal expertise to process an adoption. Attorneys who specialize in family law usually handle adoption cases.

Parents: The prospective adoptive parent(s) must be at least forty years old, and the age difference between the prospective adoptive parent(s) and the child must be at least eighteen years (fifteen years for Armenian Orthodox adoption). Singles are permitted to adopt.

Liberia

Adoption Authority: The government office responsible for adoptions in Liberia is the Ministry of Justice. All petitions for adoption are filed in the Probate Court, which issues a decree of adoption if all legal requirements are met. All adoptive parents usually go through an adoption agency in the U.S.

prior to going through the adoption process. From 1996 to 2000, eighty-three orphan visas were issued. The Liberian Ministry of Health informed the U.S. Embassy in Monrovia that effective October 15, 2004, adoptive families must obtain a letter from the Ministry of Health approving the adoption of a specific child. This is in addition to obtaining a Relinquishment (from the guardian or the caretaker of the child being adopted) and Adoption Decree (Liberian Court).

Parents: Any adult may adopt children. There are no marriage requirements or specific age requirements. Any minor child present within Liberia may be adopted. The place of birth and residence are irrelevant of the adoptive parent.

Lithuania

Adoption Authority: The Adoption Agency (Ivaikinimo Agentura)/Ministry of Social Security and Labor

Phone: 370-5-231-0928; Fax: 370-5-231-0927

Web site: http://www.ivaikinimas.lt

From 2000 to 2004, 124 orphan visas were issued. Prospective adoptive parents may contact the U.S. Embassy in Lithuania to obtain a list of local attorneys active in Lithuanian adoption.

Parents: There must be a minimum of eighteen years between the ages of the adoptive parents and the child. Adoptive parents cannot be over the age of fifty. In addition, international adoption of Lithuanian children is generally restricted to married couples. A single parent may be considered in exceptional cases when (1) the individual has been the foster parent of the particular child to be adopted, (2) the child has extremely serious health problems, or (3) the child is older and unable to be placed with another family.

Time Frame: Once a family is approved to adopt, it can take several years for a child eligible for international adoption to be matched with prospective adoptive parents' preferences.

Mexico

Adoption Authority: The State System for the Full Development of the Family (Desarrollo Integral de la Familia, or DIF) is a government institution in each Mexican state dealing with family matters. It acts as the legal representative for abandoned children and provides foster care for abused or orphaned minors. Children who are abandoned or orphaned can be given up for adoption by the DIF. In cases of abandoned children, the local office of the Ministerio Publico (the investigatory arm of the courts) will be contacted regarding the circumstances of the child's abandonment The Ministerio Publico will initiate the appropriate investigation to determine the identity of the child. If there are no leads, an adoption of the child may be processed.

There is no central office (i.e., Mexican federal government) for adoptions. Every state has its own Procuraduria de la Defensa del Minor, which is a branch of the DIF.

The DIF is assigned responsibility to study each child's eligibility for adoption and arrange adoptions. The DIF determines whether a family would be suitable for a particular child by ensuring that a home study has been done. The DIF makes every effort to place children with relatives or Mexican citizens. From 1996 to 2000, 665 orphan visas were issued.

Parents: Married or single, male or female. They must be over twenty-five years of age and seventeen years older than the child.

Time Frame: Mexican adoption procedure includes a six-month trial period during which the child lives with the adoptive parents to assure mutual benefit. The adoption is not final until after this time, and the child cannot leave Mexico before it is complete. However, in the case of a foreign adoption, the trial period may be waived at the judge's discretion. If the judge does not approve a waiver, the adoptive parents must live in Mexico for six months to care for the child. In the event of a waiver, the entire adoption process is shortened to approximately one year. Because of the large amount of paperwork, the adoptive parents should be prepared to spend at least ten working days in Mexico.

Moldova

International adoptions are permitted in exceptional cases, when no relatives or other Moldovan families are able to adopt orphans or become their guardians. Children who have health or developmental problems that Moldovan families cannot afford to treat are also considered exceptional cases.

Adoption Authority: Phone: 373-22-232-255 Information about children eligible for adoption is published in the Monitorul Official, the Moldovan government's official register. After publication, an adoptable child is available for domestic adoption by Moldovans for six months. After six months, an adoptable child is available for international adoption. Prospective adoptive parents from Moldova are required to use an accredited adoption agency when adopting in Moldova. There are seven U.S.-based adoption agencies accredited by the Moldovan Adoption Committee:

Adoption Associates Inc.

Phone: 616-667-0677; Fax: 616-667-0920

E-mail: adopt@adoptassoc.com; Web site: http://www.adoptassoc.com

Carolina Adoption Services

Phone: 336-275-9660, 800-632-9312 (in-state callers); Fax: 336-273-9804

E-mail : info@carolinaadoption.org; Web site:
http://www.carolinaadoption.org
East West Adoptions, Inc.
Phone: 510-644-3996; Fax: 603-908-8473
E-mail: info@eastwestadopt.com; Web site: http://users.lmi.net/ewadopt
Special Additions
Phone: 913-681-9604; Fax: 913-681-0748
E-mail: specialadd@aol.com; Web site: http://www.specialad.org
Spence Chapin Services
Phone: 212-369-0300; Fax: 212-722-0675
Web site: http://www.spence-chapin.org
Wasatch International Adoptions
Phone: 801-334-8683; Fax: 801-732-8905
E-mail: mailto:info@wiaa.org; Web site: http://www.wiaa.org
Wide Horizons for Children, Inc.
Phone: 781-894-5330; Fax: 781-899-2769
Web site: http://www.whfc.org
Parents: Minimum age requirement for adopting parents is twenty-five, and
maximum is fifty, unless one parent of a married couple is under the age of
fifty. Married couples and single people may adopt.
Time Frame: An adoption can take six to nine months to complete, from the
time a child is matched with prospective adoptive parents to the completion of
the adoption.

Nicaragua
Adoption Authority: The government office responsible for adoptions in
Nicaragua is the Ministry of Family. You may contact Mi Familia (Ministry of
the Family) at the following address:
De ENEL Central
Phone: 505-278-1837; 505-278-5637 (Ext. 220 or 233)
Mi Familia is responsible for vetting and approving the adoption of
Nicaraguan children.
From 2000 to 2004, forty-nine orphan visas were issued.
The adoptive parents must work directly with the Ministry of Family until the
final stage of the adoption. Once the Ministry of Family authorizes the adop-
tion, the adopting parents may hire a lawyer to complete the adoption proce-
dures. Because it can be difficult to navigate the Nicaraguan legal system, you
may want to consider hiring an adoption attorney to assist you. Lists of attorneys are available from the American Embassy.
Parents: Single or married parents should be between the ages of twenty-five

and forty. However, Mi Familia has been flexible on the age requirement on a case-by-case basis.

Time Frame: The actual adoption process can take anywhere from six months to a year and in some cases longer.

Niger

In the last five years, no orphan visas have been issued to Nigerien children by the Department of State.

Nigeria

Adoption Authority: The government office responsible for adoptions in Nigeria is the Civil Court of the state where the child is located. In general, foreigners who intend to adopt a specific child must first obtain temporary custody of the child (i.e., foster care). Foster-care requirements differ from Nigerian state to state, and it can be as long as one year before an adoption will be granted. Other states have citizenship or other requirements to adopt. Prospective adoptive parents are advised to obtain more information on adopting in individual states through their Nigerian attorneys or Social Welfare offices for the state where the adoption will take place. The U.S. Consulate in Lagos is not aware of any legally recognized agencies in Nigeria that assist adopting parents, or of any licensed Nigerian adoption agencies. However, there are orphanages, hospitals, and other institutions that are relatively more experienced with international adoption. Check with the U.S. Consulate in Lagos for information on these institutions. Adoptive parents should plan on residing in Nigeria for at least a three-month period. From 1999 to 2005, 285 orphan visas were issued.

Time Frame: Adoption procedures can take from a few months to a few years, depending on the state of origin of the child.

Panama

Adoption Authority: The government offices responsible for adoptions in Panama are the two major courts, the "Juzgado de la Niñez y Adolescencia" (Children and Minors' Court) and "Juzgados Seccionales de Familia" (Family Courts). There are twelve District Courts throughout Panama. The Juzgado de la Niñez y Adolescencia is the legal system for orphan adoptions in Panama. You may contact the Ministerio de la Familia by phone at 279-0667 or 279-0101; or fax at 279-0713. Panama allows adoptions through private agencies and will work through any licensed United States adoption agency.

Parents: Panamanian courts allow United States citizens to adopt; however, the courts will first try to place children with citizens of Panama. Most adoptions of Panamanian children by U.S. parents take place in Panama.

Peru
Adoption Authority: The government office responsible for adoptions in Peru is the Ministry for Women and Social Development (Ministerio de la Mujer y Desarrollo Social) or MIMDES. MIMDES is responsible for identifying possible orphans for assignment to prospective adoptive parents, assisting the court's investigation of the child's background, contracting and coordinating with the approved U.S. adoption agencies, and certifying the court-issued adoption decree.

All international adoptions in Peru must be processed through a Peruvian-approved U.S. adoption agency. As of April 2001, there were fourteen approved agencies. There is a different process for domestic adoptions, which may be requested by Peruvian nationals, some blood relatives, or non-Peruvians who have lived in Peru for more than two years. From 1998 to 2002, 151 orphan visas were issued.

A Peruvian child must be abandoned in order to be eligible for international adoption. A Peruvian court must make a legal finding of abandonment before the child is assigned to prospective parents. In effect, this provision prohibits so-called "direct" adoptions, in which the birthparent gives a child directly (or via an intermediary) to prospective parents for adoption, and prohibits adoptive parents from searching for and locating a child on their own. At the current time, there is a scarcity of infants available for adoption and a large number of prospective adoptive parents wishing to adopt infants.

Parents: An adopting parent must be at least eighteen years older than the child to be adopted. In some cases, the prospective parents may not be more than fifty-five years old. Both married and single persons may adopt in Peru.

Time Frame: Recent experience suggests the total time required (from the initial inquiry with an approved adoption agency until the child arrives in the U.S.) can range from several months to often over one year. Although both adoptive parents do not need to be present in Peru for the entire time, both must be present for the provisional placement, evaluation, and ratification of the adoption through the court. Adoptive parents should plan to stay in Peru for approximately eight weeks, and sometimes longer.

Specific questions regarding adoption in Peru may be addressed to the Bureau of Citizenship and Immigration Services or the Immigrant Visa Unit at the U.S. Embassy in Lima, Peru (Avenida La Encalada, Cuadra 17 s/n, Monterrico, Surco, Lima 33, Peru (phone: 51-1-434-3000; fax: 51-1-434-3065).

Philippines

Adoption Authority: The government offices responsible for domestic adoptions in the Philippines are the Regional Trial Courts, which issue the adoption decrees, and the Department of Social Welfare and Development (DSWD), which is also involved in the legal proceedings. For the intercountry adoptions, the offices responsible for adoption are the Department of Social Welfare and Development and the Intercountry Adoption Board (ICAB).

In general, custody of the child is granted to the prospective adoptive parents, who then bring the child to their home country. The adoption is filed with a court in the adoptive parents' home country. The following is a list of authorized adoption agencies in the U.S. that handle intercountry adoptions (in alphabetical order by state):

Bay Area Adoption Services
Phone: 650-964-3800; Fax: 650-964-6467
E-mail: baas@baas.org
Catholic Charities
Phone: 415-406-2387; Fax: 415-406-2386
Chrysalis House
Phone: 559-229-9862; Fax: 559-229-9863
E-mail: chi11@pacbell.net
Vista Del Mar Family & Child Service
Phone: 310-836-1223; Fax: 310-836-3863
International Alliance for Children
Phone: 860-354-4451; Fax: 860-355-2265
Department of Public Health & Social Services
Phone: 671-735-7399; 671-735-7171; 671-735-7173; Fax: 671-734-5910
Government of Guam
P.O. Box 2816
Agana, Guam 96932
Catholic Charities
200 North Vineyard Boulevard
Suite 200
Honolulu, HI 96817-3938
Child & Family Service
Phone: 808-543-8436; 808-681-6353; Fax: 808-599-5711
E-mail: VNAFARRETEBRAGA@cfshawaii.org
Lifelink/Bensenville Home Society
Phone: 630-766-3570; Fax: 630-860-5130
E-mail: alladopt@psinet.com

New Life Social Services
Phone: 773-478-4773 or 773-478-4734; Fax: 773-478-7646
E-mail: nlss@aol.com
Hand in Hand International Adoption
Phone: 219-636-3566; Fax: 219-636-2554
E-mail: indiana@hihiadopt.org
Associated Catholic Charities
Fax: 410-659-4060
International Social Service American Branch, Inc.
Phone: 410-230-2734; Fax: 410-230-2741
E-mail: info@issab.org
Wide Horizons for Children, Inc.
Phone: 781-894-5330; Fax: 781-899-2769
E-mail: marylou@whfc.org
Web site: http://www. whfc.org
Bethany Christian Services
Phone: 616-224-7466; Fax: 616-224-7585
Evergreen Children's Services
Phone: 313-862-1000; Fax: 313-862-6464
Crossroads Adoption Service
Phone: 612-831-5707; Fax: 612-831-5129
E-mail: kids@crossroadsadoption.com; Aslnnot@ix.netcom.com
Hope Adoption & Family Services International, Inc.
Phone: 651-439-2446; Fax: 651-439-2071
E-mail: hope@mtn.org
Nebraska Children's Home Society
Phone: 402-451-0787; Fax: 402-451-0360
E-mail: Kruegerca@hotmail.com; Web site: http://www. nchs.org
Voice of International & Domestic Adoptions
Phone: 518-828-4527 or 518-828-0688
E-mail: VIDAADOPT@aol.com or Vida@berk.com
Christian Adoption Services
Phone: 704-847-0038; Fax: 704-841-1538
E-mail: cas@perigee.net
Family Adoption Consultants
Phone: 330-468-0673; Fax: 330-468-0678
Holt International Children's Services
Phone: 541-687-2202; Fax: 541-683-6175
E-mail: info@holtintl.org
The Pearl S. Buck Foundation

Phone: 215-249-0100; Fax: 215-249-9657

Holston United Methodist Home for Children

Phone: 423-638-4171 or 423-638-4909; Fax: 423-638-7171 or 423-675-4915

E-mail: Mpromise@aol.com; Carlanderson@holstonhome.org

Lutheran Social Services of Wisconsin & Upper Michigan, Inc.

Phone: 715-833-0992; Fax: 715-833-9466

E-mail: chakala@lsswiss.org

Parents: Singles and married couples must be at least twenty-seven years old, and sixteen years older than the child to be adopted.

Poland

Adoption Authority: Evaluation of children for foreign adoption can be done only by the adoption centers authorized to do so by the Minister of Economy, Labor, and Social Welfare. At present, only the Public Adoptive-Guardian Center (Publiczny Osrodek Adopcyjno-Opiekunczy) has such authorization. The center maintains a list of all children residing in orphanages who are available for international adoption because their parents have died, have relinquished all rights to them, or have had them relinquished by a court.

Publiczny Osrodek Adopcyjno-Opiekunczy

Phone: 011- (if calling from the U.S.), 48- (from Poland), or 22- (from Warsaw) 622-0370 to -0372

There are three adoption centers that are also authorized to qualify foreign prospective parents for adoption in Poland. The parents or duly licensed American adoption agencies may submit documents of candidates for adoption only to these centers:

Public Adoptive-Guardian Center (address above)

National Adoptive-Guardian Center of the Children's Friends Society (Towarzystwo Przyjaciol Dzieci—TPD)

Phone: 435-4677 through 435-4688; Fax: 011/48/22/827-7813

E-mail: koao-tpd@wp.pl

Catholic Adoptive-Guardian Center (Katolicki Osrodek Adopcyjno-Opiekunczy)

Phone: 011-48-22-610-5149; Fax: 011-48-22-610-6123

From 2000 to 2005, 936 orphan visas were issued. An adoption attorney can help with the process. For U.S.-based agency adoptions, it is suggested that prospective adoptive parents contact the Better Business Bureau and licensing office of the Department of Health and Family Services in the state where the agency is located. The U.S. Embassy in Warsaw has a list of attorneys known to work in Poland.

Parents: Nothing in Polish law states the age requirements of adoptive parents. In practice, however, mothers may be up to forty years older than the child, and fathers up to forty-five years older. Singles may adopt.

Time Frame: There is a twenty-one-day appeal period between the time of the final adoption hearing and the time the court's decision goes into legal force. The judge may shorten the appeal period to fourteen days. Prospective adoptive parents can expect to stay in Poland at least three to four weeks before they can obtain all proper documentation and a new passport for the child. The entire process may take a year or more.

Portugal

Adoption Authority: The government office responsible for adoptions in Portugal is the Directorate-General of Solidarity and Social Security in the Ministry of Labor and Solidarity and the Ministry's offices of the Seguranca Social.

Phone: 351-21-792-01-00; Fax: 351-21-793-47-39

E-mail: dgas@seg-social.pt

The Portuguese Central Authority for international adoptions advised the U.S. Embassy in Lisbon that for purposes of handling adoption requests, it will accept cases only from licensed U.S. adoption organizations, submitted through a competent government authority. Adoption of a Portuguese child by American citizens is a complex process that is likely to be lengthy. From 1996 to 2000, seventeen orphan visas were issued.

Parents: Couples must have been married or living together for at least four years. Singles and couples must be at least age thirty. The maximum age allowed for adopting a child is fifty.

Russia

Please plan to stay a minimum of three business days in Moscow to obtain documents and complete the medical exams necessary for the immigrant visa interview. Parents should calculate a five-day "cushion time" in the validity dates they request when applying for a Russian visa. The U.S. Embassy recommends that flight arrangements for departing Russia not be finalized until the immigrant visa is issued.

Adoption Authority: The government office responsible for international adoptions in Russia is the Ministry of Education and Science of the Russian Federation.

Phone: 011-7-095-229-6610

From 1999 to 2003, 34,813 orphan visas were issued.

Adoption Agencies and Attorneys: Russia requires adoptive parents to use an adoption agency that is accredited by the Russian government to provide adoption services. Adoption agencies that do not have Russian accreditation must work under the auspices of an accredited adoption agency. The U.S. Embassy in Russia has a list of agencies accredited by the Russian authorities to provide adoption services. A list of accredited adoption agencies is available at the adoptions page of the U.S. Embassy's Web site and on the Web site for the Embassy of the Russian Federation.

Parents: Singles and married couples may adopt. Single parents must be at least sixteen years older than the child. Russia also has medical requirements for adoptive parents. Anyone considering adoption in Russia should consult their adoption agency about medical conditions that may disqualify them from adopting in Russia.

Time Frame: The average time for the adoption process is five months from the time US CIS approves the I-600A petition to the issuance of the immigrant visa.

Rwanda

Adoption Authority: Ministry of Local Administration and Social Affairs
Phone: 011-250-87741 or 011-250-83595; Fax: 011-250-82228
There are no known adoption agencies that provide adoption services in Rwanda. Upon request, the U.S. Embassy can provide a list of attorneys. Immigrant visas for Rwandan citizens, including adopted orphans, are issued at the U.S. Embassy in Nairobi, Kenya. Please visit the Immigrant Visa Section on the Web site of the U.S. Embassy in Nairobi for information on immigrant visa services: http://nairobi.usembassy.gov/wwwhins1.html.

Prospective adoptive parents must petition the local court having jurisdiction over the prospective adoptive child's residence. Once the adoption is approved, the adoption decree is filed at the local vital records registry for the child's place of residence.

Papers are filed with the Ministry of Local Administration and Social Affairs. A travel letter from the Ministry of Family and Gender is required for the child to exit Rwanda. Documents from the government of Rwanda are in French. The U.S. Embassy Kigali will provide English translations of these documents for use in Nairobi. Prospective adoptive parents will need English translations of the birth certificates and death certificates (if applicable) of the adopted child's birthparents to complete immigrant visa processing in Nairobi. The U.S. Embassy in Rwanda can assist in locating translation services, but no U.S. government resources are available for translating birth or death certificates.

Only two immigrant visas were issued to Rwandan orphans in the last five years.

Parents: Adoptive parents must be under the age of fifty. However, a judge can waive the age requirement.

Time Frame: Allow one to two months to complete the Rwandan adoption and subsequent immigration procedures. Allow for a stay of two weeks in Africa (four working days in Rwanda and ten days in Kenya).

Sierra Leone

Adoption Authority: The government office responsible for adoptions in Sierra Leone is the Ministry of Social Welfare, Gender and Children's Affairs. All petitions for adoptions are filed in the High Court, which issues an adoption court order (a document granting adoption if all legal requirements are met).

Due to a high rate of document and adoption fraud in Sierra Leone, the U.S. Embassy in Dakar, Senegal, carefully scrutinizes all immigrant visa petitions. The U.S. Embassy in Freetown, Sierra Leone, will conduct field investigations into the circumstances surrounding the adoption as warranted. Adoptive parents are required to travel to Sierra Leone to attend the court hearing for the adoption. From 2000 to 2004, 158 orphan visas were issued.

Adoption Agencies and Attorneys: The U.S. Embassy in Freetown maintains a list of local solicitors (attorneys). There are no registered adoption agencies in Sierra Leone. There are organizations registered as nongovernmental organizations (NGO) or private voluntary organizations (PVO) that provide assistance to children and facilitate international adoptions.

Parents: Any adult may adopt children. There are no marriage requirements or specific age requirements. The place of birth and residence of the adoptive parent are not determining factors.

Time frame: There are no fixed time lines or constraints on the court's processing of adoptions.

Slovak Republic

Slovakia ratified the Hague Convention on Intercountry Adoption in October 2001. The government of Slovakia will approve international adoptions only when the prospective adopting parent(s) reside in countries that have ratified this convention. Prospective parents who are legal residents of Slovakia may adopt orphans under Slovak law. The United States has signed but not yet ratified the Adoption Convention.

South Africa

Adoption Authority: The government offices responsible for adoptions in South Africa are the following:
Commissioner of Child Welfare
Phone: 012-328-4026
Department of Social Development

Phone: 012-312-7592 Fax: 012-312-7837

South African law requires in adoption cases that one of the parents be a South African citizen. Previously, intercountry adoption was not allowed, but this was declared unconstitutional in a recent court ruling. However, the law has not yet formally been changed. Interested U.S. citizens are strongly encouraged to contact U.S. consular officials in South Africa before formalizing an adoption agreement to ensure that appropriate procedures have been followed. This will make it possible for the embassy to issue a U.S. immigrant visa for the child. From 1997 to 2001, twenty-three orphan visas were issued.

There are no host-government-approved agencies or attorneys. Applicants usually complete the adoption process through a U.S. adoption agency or directly through the South African government.

Sri Lanka

Adoption Authority: The government office responsible for adoptions in Sri Lanka is the Department of Probation and Child Care Services, 95 Sir Chittampalam Gardiner Mawtha, P.O. Box 546, Colombo 02, Sri Lanka. Phone: 94-1-327600 or 94-1-448577; fax: 94-1-327600.

The Sri Lankan Department of Probation and Sri Lankan Child Care Services may, as the need arises, amend the adoption procedures. Specific questions regarding adoptions in Sri Lanka should be addressed either directly to the Department of Probation and Child Care Services, to the Sri Lankan Embassy in Washington, or to the Consular Section of the U.S. Embassy in Sri Lanka. From 1997 to 2001, twenty-one orphan visas were issued.

The District Court of Colombo and the District Court of Colombo South that have the appropriate jurisdiction are empowered to make orders of adoption of Sri Lankan children by persons not resident and domiciled in Sri Lanka. Foreign applicants cannot find children for adoption privately. Allocation of children can be made only from the Sri Lankan State Receiving Homes and Voluntary Children's Homes that have been registered by the Department of Probation and Child Care Services for more than five years and only by specific authorization of the Commissioner of Probation.

Children: Children under three months old will not be permitted to be adopted by foreign nationals.

Parents: Married couples must be over age twenty-five and at least twenty-one years older than the child. Sri Lankan law does not permit a single parent to adopt a child.

Time Frame: Expect to stay at least four to five weeks, since court action for an adoption must take place in Sri Lanka.

St. Lucia

Adoption Authority: The adoption authority responsible for adoptions in St. Lucia is the Ministry of Health in the Division of Human Services and Gender Affairs (the Division), which can be contacted by phone at 1-758-452-7204.

There are no official adoption agencies in St. Lucia; however, the Division of Human Services and Family affairs facilitates and oversees many adoptions, local and international. The adoption legislation does not require intervention by the division; therefore, some adoptions are processed privately by various attorneys.

There are no specialized adoption attorneys. If there is an international request regarding adoption, the division will be asked for assistance. All adoptions must be finalized through the Office of the Attorney General and by the High Court. In order to adopt St. Lucian children, persons who are not citizens of St. Lucia must reside in St. Lucia for at least six continuous months immediately prior to the adoption.

Parents: You must be at least twenty-five years old and be at least twenty-one years older than the minor. Singles can adopt.

Time Frame: The adoption process takes approximately six months, but can take longer.

St. Vincent and the Grenadines

Adoption Authority: The authority responsible for adoptions in St. Vincent and the Grenadines phone number is 1-784-456-1111

Contact the St. Vincent and the Grenadines Adoption Board. The Adoption Board of St. Vincent and the Grenadines handles many international adoptions and will "walk you through" the adoption on a case-by-case basis.

From 2000 to 2004, nine orphan visas were issued.

Parents: You must be twenty-one years old or older to adopt; you do not have to be married.

Time Frame: The process takes about three to six months on average.

Sudan

Adoption Authority: There is no central government office responsible for adoptions in Sudan. Each case is handled by the local Social Services supervisor of the Governate for the Province.

Adoption in Sudan is governed by the Child Care Act of 1971. Adoption is not allowed for Muslim children but may be allowed for non-Muslim children, insofar as the religious laws of the child's denomination allow. A child whose religion is unknown is automatically considered to be Muslim.

Sudanese law also allows for a court-appointed "caretaker" (similar to a legal guardian in the United States) to oversee the welfare and upbringing of a child until he or she reaches legal majority (twenty-one years of age). Caretakers may be assigned for both Muslim and non-Muslim children, but they must be of the same religion as the child. Applications for "caretaker" or adoptive parent status must be initiated with the Social Services supervisor of the Governate for the Province where the child lives. If it decides to support the application, the Governate will then refer the application to Civil Court.

Once custody is granted, there is a probationary period of one year wherein the Social Services supervisor must conduct regular visits. After the year is over, the caretaker or adoptive parent may return to the court to request permanent custody of the child until he or she reaches the age of majority. In certain exceptional circumstances, it is possible to reduce the probationary period with the approval of the governor of the Province where the child resides. From 1996 to 2000, two orphan visas were issued.

Parents: To qualify as a caretaker or adoptive parent, the applicant must be between thirty and fifty years of age, with a good reputation and behavior. Unmarried men are not eligible. Children over fourteen years of age may not be placed in the custody of a caretaker or adoptive parent.

Suriname

Adoption Authority: The government office responsible for adoptions in Suriname is the Bureau of Family Rights and Affairs. Phone: 597-478759 or 597-475763

From 2000 to 2004, three orphan visas were issued.

Parents: Prospective adoptive parents who are married must be at least eighteen years older than the child. Married prospective adoptive parents must be married for at least three years to adopt. Single prospective adoptive parents must be at least twenty-five years of age. The age difference between the parents and the child may not be more than fifty years for the father and forty years for the mother.

Time Frame: The time frame for adoption processing varies. The local adoption authority states that processing will take anywhere from two to five months. Visa processing time at the U.S. Embassy in Paramaribo should also be considered. Filing an I-600A petition prior to arrival in Suriname will expedite processing time.

Taiwan

Adoption Authority: Children's Bureau, Ministry of Interior. The articles of law relating to adoption in Taiwan are found in the Civil Code (Family and

Children Welfare Act in Book VI), Articles 1072 through 1083.

An application for adoption is first submitted to the Taiwan Supreme Court, which designates an office of the Taiwan District Court to process the adoption. This step takes four to eight weeks. After two to three months, the adoptive parent(s) or a designated representative will receive a notice to appear before the District Court. During this waiting period, a Taiwan social worker from the local bureau of social affairs or a designated agency will interview the prospective adoptive parent(s) or review the home study. The court will rule on the adoption within two or three months and publish a final ruling one week later.

The following is a list of welfare agencies in Taiwan:

Catholic Welfare Services
Phone: 02-2311-0223 or 02-2311-7642; Fax: 02-2371-0338
E-mail: Rosa0125@ms22.hinet.net; Web site: http://www.cc.org.tw
Christian Salvation Service
Phone: 02-2729-0265
E-mail: csstte@ms14.hinet.net
The Home of God's Love
Phone: 039-514-652
E-mail: teskales@ms6.hinet.net or Bevanna@ms15.hinet.net
The Pearl Buck Foundation
Fax: 02-2331-8690

Parents: A single parent may adopt a child in Taiwan. The adoptive parent must be at least twenty years older than the person being adopted. If there are two adoptive parents, both must be at least twenty years older than the person being adopted.

Thailand

Adoption Authority: All adoptions in Thailand must be processed through the Child Adoption Center of the Department of Public Welfare (DPW), which is the sole governmental social welfare agency responsible for adoption of Thai children. Four nongovernmental organizations (NGOs) are licensed to deal with DPW's Child Adoption Center in cases where a child is to be placed abroad, but only three of these NGOs process cases for prospective adoptive parents who reside in the United States. These are:

Holt Sahathai Foundation
Phone: 66-2-381-8834
Pattaya Orphanage
Phone: 66-38-422-7451.
Thai Red Cross Foundation

Phone: 66-2-252-8181 or 66-2-256-4178

For complete information and application forms, prospective adoptive parents should contact one of the above agencies or DPW directly at Child Adoption Center, Phone: 66-2-246-8651

From 1994 to 1998, 302 orphan visas were issued.

Children: It is rare for a child under two to be available. Only one child may be adopted, unless they are sibling groups.

Parents: Parents must be married, at least twenty-five years of age, and at least fifteen years older than the child to be adopted.

Trinidad and Tobago

Adoption Authority: To adopt a child in Trinidad and Tobago, prospective adoptive parents must contact the Adoption Board. It is the only organization authorized to adjudicate the adoption application and make recommendations to the courts for legal adoptions, phone: 868-627-4447.

The Adoption Board is not responsible for legal custody/guardianship cases. To seek legal custody/guardianship, the prospective custodians/guardians need to contact the Clerk of the Peace through the courts in Trinidad and Tobago, phone: 868-623-8180.

Note: There are two ways of adopting a child from Trinidad and Tobago. The first option is to go through the adoption process in Trinidad and Tobago. However, foreigners are prohibited from adopting Trinidadian children unless they are domiciled and residing in Trinidad and Tobago.

The second option is to seek custody/legal guardianship of a child from the courts in Trinidad and Tobago for the purpose of adopting the child in the United States. Custody or legal guardianship does not provide full parental rights given to adopting parents and is vulnerable to revocation by the courts if the biological parents or other relatives subsequently petition the courts for change of custody/guardianship. For U.S. citizens residing in the U.S., however, obtaining legal custody/guardianship is often the only viable option. From 2000 to 2004, twenty orphan visas were issued.

Parents: Single parents and married couples are allowed to adopt or gain legal custody/guardianship in Trinidad and Tobago. The adoptive parents must be at least twenty-five years of age and twenty-one years older than the child they are adopting. To gain custody/legal guardianship, the prospective custodian/guardian must be at least twenty-one years old.

Time Frame: The local adoption process takes more than six months due to the Adoption Board's six-month probation period. Securing custody/legal guardianship can take anywhere from one week to several months.

Fees: Adoption in Trinidad is free. Payment to anyone, including the parents, is illegal.

Turkey

Adoption Authority: The government office responsible for adoptions in Turkey is the T.C. Basbakanlik Sosyal Hizmetler ve Cocuk Esirgeme Kurumu Genel Mudurlugu.

Phone: 90-312-231-9665; Fax: 90-312-231-0650

There are two ways to adopt a child in Turkey: (1) reach an agreement between biological parent(s) and adoptive parent(s), follow up the legal procedures, and sign a contract in front of a notary public, or (2) through the adoption authority, from the orphanage.

(*Note:* The adoptive parents should be careful when making arrangements with third persons.) Only private attorneys, no agencies, may assist with adoptions. Under Turkish adoption law, a prospective adoptive parent is given provisional custody of an orphan to care for him or her for one year. This is called a Care Contract. Although a child may reside outside Turkey for the Care Contact period, he or she must return to Turkey in order for Turkish authorities to legally approve the adoption and for a judge to issue the adoption decree.

Ukraine

Adoption Authority: Adoption Center in Kiev, Ukraine, Phone: 380-44-246-54-31/32/37/49; Fax: 380-44-246-5452/62

The Adoption Center, a part of the Ministry of Education, is the only legal Ukrainian authority for adoptions. It maintains the database of adoptable children available for both domestic and international adoptions. The Adoption Center is involved in the international adoption process from the moment prospective parents apply for registration until an adoption hearing is held in court. The National Adoption Center has a policy of direct contact with prospective adopting parents. Adopting parents must send their documents directly to the National Adoption Center. The Adoption Center will communicate with facilitators after an application is filed. Translators or interpreters are not available on the staff of the Adoption Center. Callers or visitors have to speak either Russian or Ukrainian, or have their own interpreters.

Ukraine does not allow adoption agencies to operate or locate a child for adoption in Ukraine. However, facilitators are allowed to assist with translation and interpretation services. Prospective adopting parents can protect themselves by openly discussing all fees and expenses in great detail before hiring a facilitator or interpreter. Discuss recommendations with adoption agencies and with other families who have hired these individuals in the past.

From 1999 to 2005, 1,548 orphan visas were issued.

Parents: Married and single people may adopt from Ukraine. Prospective adopting parents have to be at least eighteen years old, and the difference between the age of the adopting parent and adopted child must be at least fifteen years, although this can be waived if circumstances warrant.

Time Frame: It takes two to six months to be matched with a Ukrainian orphan after adopting parents submit their dossier with the National Adoption Center. Parents can also expect a three- to four-week wait between the initial filing of the adoption in the local court and issuance of the final adoption decree.

United Kingdom

Adoption Authority: The Department for Education & Skills is responsible for Children's Social Services, including adoption policy. While the following address is the Central Authority for the Hague Convention on International Adoption, each adoption case will be handled by the relevant social services department in the area where the adoptive child is located. Anyone who wishes to contact the Adoption Team should write to the following:

Placement, Permanence & Child Protection Division

Wellington House

E-mail: info@dfes.gsi.gov.uk

From 2000 to 2004, twenty-eight orphan visas were issued.

Parents: Anyone over the age of twenty-one can legally adopt a child.

Time Frame: There is no standard time frame.

Uzbekistan

Adoption Authority: The government office responsible for adoptions in Uzbekistan is the Ministry of Education and the local mayor's office. Prospective parents submit all documentation to the Guardianship and Trusteeship Organ of the Khokimiate of the region. The Organ passes the documents to the Khokim for approval. Based on the Khokim's approval, the local vital records office issues a certificate of adoption, as well as a new birth certificate with the adopted parents' names. With the Khokim's permission and the vital record office, the administration for entry, exit, and citizenship issues a passport and exit permission to the child. This process takes at least a month. From 1998 to 2000, three orphan visas were issued.

Parents: With the new family code, parents from a country with a diplomatic representation in Uzbekistan are allowed to adopt. The age difference between the adoptive child and the prospective adoptive parents must not be less than fifteen years. Single parents may adopt as well.

Vietnam

From 1995 to 2000, 3,091 orphan visas were issued. On June 21, 2005, the United States and Vietnam signed a bilateral agreement that laid the groundwork for intercountry adoptions between the two countries to recommence after a thirty-month hiatus. The agreement entered into force on September 1, 2005, and on January 25, 2006, the U.S. Embassy in Hanoi issued the first orphan immigrant visa to a Vietnamese child adopted by an American family under the agreement framework. As part of its implementation of the new agreement, the government of Vietnam is requiring all U.S. adoption service providers (ASPs) desiring to operate in Vietnam to be licensed by the Vietnamese Ministry of Justice's Department of International Adoptions (DIA). The DIA has indicated that, with extremely rare exceptions, it will accept adoption applications ("dossiers") ONLY through ASPs that have received such licenses. Prospective adoptive parents considering adopting from Vietnam should consult the adoption page of the Web site of the U.S. Embassy in Hanoi, http://vietnam.usembassy.gov/orphan_visa.html, where the embassy is posting the names of American ASPs that have received DIA licenses.

Zimbabwe

In the past eight years, a U.S. citizen has adopted one Zimbabwean child. There is no central registry for identifying children for adoption.

Appendix E

Selected Adoption Financial Resources Web Sites

Abba Fund, www.abbafund.org, provides no-interest adoption loans to qualifying adopting families.

Adoption-Friendly Workplace, www.adoptionfriendlyworkplace.org, offers information and advice for seeking adoption benefits from employers and offering resources to companies to start adoption benefit programs.

Adoption Policy Resource Center, www.fpsol.com/adoption/advocates.html, offers a checklist of questions to help families adopting from the foster-care system understand that they can negotiate for adoption subsidies to help with the post-adoption care of their child.

Affording Adoption, www.affordingadoption.com, is an informational site for adoptive families that offers links to grant, loan, and fund-raising Web sites. It was developed by a mother of three adopted children and also includes links for discounted travel and a partial list of employers that offer adoption benefits.

Antioch Adoptions, www.antiochadoptions.org, is an adoption agency that charges no fees for its services, but adoptive parents must live in the western portion of Washington State.

Building Families Fund, www.topekacommunityfoundation.org, is a donor-advised fund of the Topeka Community Foundation that provides grant monies of up to half the "reasonable cost" of an adoption for Kansas residents who are Christians and are adopting domestically or internationally. For more information, call 785-272-4804.

Caroline's Promise, www.carolinespromise4u.org, tries to provide grants to Christian couples residing in North Carolina who are adopting domestically or internationally. The number of individual $3,000 to $5,000 grants provided to couples each year is dependent on fund-raising.

A Child Waits Foundation, www.achildwaits.org, offers low-interest loans to qualified adoptive families involved in international adoption of up to half their adoption costs or a maximum of $10,000. The loans are given based on financial need.

Financing Adoption, www.financingadoption.org, is a site that aims to make adoption, especially international adoption, more affordable and easier for families to undertake. It is designed primarily to educate and advocate for adoption despite its costs by providing information and the means to seek financial adoption assistance and fund-raising ideas.

Gift of Adoption Fund, www.giftofadoption.org, each month awards grants of $2,000 to $5,000 to adopting parents experiencing extraordinary hardship. This includes low-income families and families adopting children with special medical needs. Home study approval and a $20 application fee are required.

His Kids, Too!, www.hiskidstoo.org, offers a limited number of grants to families who have completed a home study, have INS approval, and are adopting internationally. The grants are up to $2,000 for one child or up to $4,000 for two children. Grants are awarded up to three times a year.

Ibsen Adoption Network, www.angelfire.com/home/ibsen, currently awards adoption grants to Washington State residents only who are adopting older and special-needs children. Grants are awarded twice a year and average $1,500 per family. Contact Marilyn Brisbane at 360-866-7036 or download an application form from the site.

International Children's Adoption Resource Effort (iCare), www.intlcare.org, has partnered with the Florida-based Christian adoption agency Celebrate Children, www.celebratechildren.org, to give partial adoption grants. Families must be adopting through Celebrate Children, as grant funds are sent directly to the agency.

Kingdom Kids Adoption Ministries, www.kingdomkidsadoption.org, offers a fund-raising opportunity for adopting families to receive grants from funds raised. The program works like this: Families agree to the Kingdom Kids guidelines and apply for a needs-based grant. Kingdom Kids tells a family what grant they can receive (based in part on funds raised). Families then send out a letter with a Kingdom Kids brochure to fifty to one hundred friends and family, with the donors sending any contributions to Kingdom Kids. The donations are tax-deductible. Note: Not all funds sent in by a family's donor list are guaranteed to go to that family. Kingdom Kids retains full discretion over how all funds are disbursed.

Life International, www.lifeintl.org, offers adoption grants for qualifying families that match dollar-for-dollar monies given toward a family's adoption by their local church. Life International wants to see local churches become involved in raising support for orphans and connecting to the children they have helped. LI also works with fifteen orphanages primarily in the Ukraine, providing a Christian presence, improving living conditions, and offering job training and other support.

MN☆

Micah Fund, www.bbcmpls.org/childsministries/MicahFund.htm, provides financial assistance to qualified Christian adoptive parents who live in Minnesota for use toward payment of fees to those agencies committed to providing quality services to birthparents, their children, and the prospective parents. Since 1989, the Micah Fund has helped place more than 225 children in loving Christian homes.

A Mother's Love, www.amotherslovefundraising.com, is a unique site started by an adoptive mom to help others raise adoption funds by fund-raising. Founder Valerie Gagnon sends out a packet of catalogs for adoptive families to sell the products they choose, then the family sends the orders in to Valerie to be processed. A Mother's Love then issues a profit check. A Mother's Love also sells "scratch-off cards" that adoptive families can take to family and friends, asking them to scratch off one or more "donation squares" to determine how much they will donate to your adoption fund. The amounts uncovered range from 50 cents to $3.00, and each card when fully scratched off nets a $100 profit.

The National Adoption Foundation, www.nafadopt.org/NafGrants.htm, has a National Adoption Program that makes quarterly grants ranging from $500 to $4,000 to adopting parents. There is no income requirement. They can be contacted at 203-791-3811.

The National Endowment for Financial Education, www.nefe.org/adoption/default.htm, offers an online brochure that walks adoptive couples through the process of finding and raising funds for their adoption, as well as the avenues to pursue for adoption reimbursement, tax credits, and subsidies.

Open Arms Children's Charities, www.open-arms.org, typically awards one grant per quarter to an adopting family with a completed home study. There is a $15 application fee required. Adoption grants are funded solely through application fees, donations, and fund-raisers, so the number and amount of grants vary each quarter.

Shaohannah's Hope, www.shaohannahshope.org. Created by singer Steven Curtis Chapman, an adoptive father of three girls from China, Shaohannah's Hope offers partial grants to qualifying adoptive families.

United Way International, www.unitedway.org, provides assistance for costs of travel for adopted children with illnesses needing immediate medical attention. Applications are selectively considered and must be supported with a doctor's statement. Please contact: Melissa Guerra at 703-519-0092.

Appendix F

Selected Adoption Support Groups and Organizations

Adoption Learning Partners

Phone: 800-566-3995

Web site: www.adoptionlearningpartners.org

Adoption Learning Partners provides educational resources via the Internet for adoptive parents, adoptees, and birthparents. Their e-learning courses help prepare adoptive parents for the arrival of their adopted child, and they also help adoptive families with growing children gain new skills to help them talk about adoption. Or, when an adopted person or birthparent is contemplating a search, they can turn to Adoption Learning Partners for guidance.

Older Child Adoption

Phone: 828-778-0862

Web site: www.olderchildadoption.com

Older Child Adoption offers online articles and a discussion forum, bookstore, and links about older child adoption, adoptive parenting, international adoption, and special-needs adoptions.

Project 1.27

Phone: 303-256-1225

Web site: www.project127.com

Project 1.27 seeks to unite families in churches with waiting children in Colorado's foster-care program by facilitating the adoption process for a fee of under $400. While families in Colorado can adopt from the foster-care program through the state directly, Project 1.27 helps with the paperwork, subsidies, background checks, training, and other requirements.

Dossier Support

Couriers to Foreign Consulates

There are many foreign consulates throughout the U.S. where dossier documentation must be sent to be authenticated or apostilled. The following couriers are all adoptive moms who started their services to help other adopting families process their paperwork. Here is information on courier services for some consulates:

Chicago:
There's Always Hope
Phone: 815-741-4700
E-mail: info@theres-always-hope.com;
Web site: www.theres-always-hope.com
Denise Hope provides visa and dossier services to the Chinese consulate in Chicago. She checks dossier documents for the proper signatures and seals, then hand carries dossier documents to the consulate for authentication, rechecks the documents, and overnights the documents back to the adoptive family or to their adoption agency. The Chicago Chinese consulate authenticates documents from Colorado, Illinois, Indiana, Iowa, Kansas, Michigan, Minnesota, Missouri, and Wisconsin.

Denise also provides visa and dossier services for Guatemala and Haiti. The Chicago Guatemalan consulate covers Illinois, Indiana, Iowa, Michigan, Minnesota, Missouri, North Dakota, Ohio, and Wisconsin. The Haitian consulate covers Alabama, Alaska, Arizona, Arkansas, California, Colorado, Georgia, Hawaii, Idaho, Illinois, Indiana, Iowa, Kansas, Kentucky, Louisiana, Michigan, Minnesota, Mississippi, Missouri, Montana, Nebraska, Nevada, New Mexico, North Carolina, North Dakota, Ohio, Oklahoma, Oregon, South Carolina, South Dakota, Tennessee, Texas, Utah, Virginia, Virgin Islands, Washington, Wisconsin, and Wyoming.

Houston:
My China Docs Adoption Document and Visa Service
E-mail: cmarut@earthlink.net; Web site: www.mychinadocs.com
Courier Cindy Marut checks dossier documents for the proper signatures and seals, then hand carries dossier documents to the Chinese and Guatemalan consulates in Houston for authentication, rechecks the documents, and overnights the documents back to the adoptive family or to their adoption agency. The Houston Guatemalan consulate authenticates documents from Arkansas, Louisiana, Oklahoma, and Texas. The Chinese consulate in Houston authenticates documents from Alabama, Arkansas, Florida, Georgia, Louisiana, Mississippi, Oklahoma, and Texas. Cindy also helps adopting families apply for their Chinese entry visas.

Los Angeles:
Red Tape Solution
Phone: 951-805-3008
Web site: www.redtapesolution.com
Red Tape Solution provides visa and dossier services to the Chinese and

Guatemalan consulates in Los Angeles. Janice Moore checks dossier documents for the proper signatures and seals, then hand carries dossier documents to the consulate for authentication, rechecks the documents, and overnights the documents back to the adoptive family or to their adoption agency. The Los Angeles Chinese consulate covers Southern California, Arizona, New Mexico, Hawaii, and the Pacific Islands.

New York City:
Legal-Eaze
Phone: 203-458-6007
Web site: www.legal-eaze.com
Patti Urban at Legal-Eaze provides dossier and visa services to the Chinese, Guatemalan, and Kazakhstan consulates in New York City. The Chinese consulate covers Connecticut, Maine, Massachusetts, New Hampshire, New Jersey, New York, Ohio, Pennsylvania, Rhode Island, and Vermont. The Guatemalan consulate covers Connecticut, Maine, Massachusetts, New Hampshire, New Jersey, New York, Pennsylvania, Rhode Island, and Vermont. Legal-Eaze can process any independent Kazakhstan adoption dossier regardless of where the client lives. Legal-Eaze also offers dossier preparation services and other pre- and post-adoption support services.

San Francisco:
The Paper Midwife International Adoption Dossier Services
Phone: 650-465-0137
Web site: www.papermidwife.com
Jill S. Touloukian provides dossier authentication services to the Chinese, Vietnamese, and Guatemalan consulates in San Francisco. She also offers dossier preparation services and consultation services to adopting families. The San Francisco Chinese consulate covers northern California, Oregon, Washington, Nevada, and Alaska. The Vietnamese consulate will authenticate documents that originated anywhere in the United States.

Washington, DC:
The Assistant Stork
Phone: 540-659-6845
Web site: www.asststork.com
Laura Morrison provides courier services to the consulates for Bolivia, Brazil, China, Ecuador, Ethiopia, Georgia, Guatemala, Haiti, India, Indonesia, Jamaica, Kazakhstan, Kuwait, Moldova, Nepal, Nicaragua, Oman, Philippines, Russia, Thailand, Turkmenistan, Ukraine, United Arab Emirates, Uzbekistan,

and Vietnam (although some of these countries are not currently open to adoption by Americans). She also offers dossier preparation services and visa application services to all countries.

Selected Adoption Story and Blog Sites

Adopt Share, www.adoptshare.com, is a site where adoptive families can share their stories, ideas, and experiences.

Adoption Blogs, www.adoptionblogs.com, is an online site that posts links to many adoption and adoption-related blogs, including a Christian blogs page at http://christian.adoptionblogs.com.

Adoption Web sites, www.adoptionwebsites.net, is a site where adoptive families can create their own Web sites and blogs before, during, and after their adoption journeys. All fees paid for the service (minus the cost of maintaining the domain) are donated to orphan charities, according to the site.

Hannah and Her Mama: Our Story, www.hannahandhermama.com, is a personal journal site about older-child adoption. It contains the journals of adolescent Hannah, who was adopted at age six from Russia and experienced severe attachment issues, and her mother, Susan. The site includes Hannah's own words on how it felt to be adopted and her adoptive mother's efforts to help her bond. It also provides plenty of links and information on reactive attachment disorder (RAD) and bonding.

Appendix G

Selected Adoption Ministries: Where You Can Get Involved

The following organizations are just a few of those that support relief efforts for underprivileged children and orphans around the world:

ACTION International Ministries

Phone: 800-755-6918

Web site: www.actionintl.org/action

ACTION is an evangelical, nondenominational missionary-sending agency that works in major urban centers of Asia, Latin America, and Africa. ACTION missionaries reveal the gospel and love of Christ to neglected and abused children and their families through practical ministries that specialize in reaching the urban poor. The mission currently has more than 160 missionaries (and many other team members) in thirteen countries. ACTION's prayer target is for 221 additional missionaries to join them in the vital task of world missions, for the glory of God!

Acts of Mercy

Phone: 949-609-8552

Web site: www.acts-of-mercy.com

Rick Warren is the founding pastor of Saddleback Church in Lake Forest, California, and author of several books including *The Purpose-Driven Life* series. He and his wife, Kay, founded Acts of Mercy to offer church-to-church relief, aid, and training to help the local church make an impact on HIV/AIDS, poverty, and the training of pastors and church leaders. Acts of Mercy wants to help equip churches to be the instrument to accomplish Christ's ministry in the world.

Ambassadors for Children

Phone: 317-536-0250

Web site: www.ambassadorsforchildren.com

Ambassadors for Children partners with orphanages, schools, at-risk youth programs, and international humanitarian organizations to provide basic necessities, medical and dental care, educational support, and constructive cognitive and social development for disadvantaged, abused, and abandoned children.

Care Net
Phone: 703-478-5661

Web site: www.care-net.org

Care Net has been promoting, equipping, and developing pregnancy centers for more than twenty-five years and supports nine hundred pregnancy centers across the United States and Canada. Care Net pregnancy centers offer free pregnancy tests, ultrasounds, peer counseling services, post-abortion support, and other practical, emotional, and spiritual help to empower women and men facing pregnancy-related concerns. You can support Care Net financially or by volunteering at a local pregnancy center. To find a pregnancy center in your area, visit www.pregnancycenters.org/advantage.asp.

Children of Zion Village
Phone: 410-942-0550

Web site: www.cofz.org

The Children of Zion Village is an orphanage and children's home in Namibia, Africa. It also has a ministry that links missionaries with churches wanting to help establish orphanages. Volunteers are needed to adopt existing orphanages that need financial and prayer support, sponsor children, teach, help build, and repair facilities, and do much more.

Children's HopeChest
Phone: 719-487-7800

Web site: www.hopechest.org

Children's HopeChest works with ten thousand orphans in Russia and Ukraine to aid them in their journey toward independent living. Some orphans are connected with a sponsor who prays for them, writes them letters, and releases financial resources into their lives. Other orphans will experience family in the context of a Family Center or within a foster family. Some older orphans will benefit from the programming of a Ministry Center that provides life skills training, mentorship, role modeling, and recreational activities. Others will learn how to live on their own through an Independent Living Program. Volunteers are needed to support Children's HopeChest financially and through trips to the orphanages.

Child SHARE
Phone: 877-KID-SHARE (877-543-7427)

Web site: www.childshare.org

Child SHARE was established in 1985 by the Westwood Presbyterian Church as a challenge to congregants to respond to the foster-care crisis in Los Angeles.

Today, the organization has a foster and adoption support network of more than four hundred churches in Southern California. The program has found homes for more than twenty-five hundred foster-care children, many of whom have been adopted.

Compassion International
Phone: 800-336-7676
Web site: www.compassion.com
Compassion works in many countries around the world to connect sponsors and children. Compassion operates feeding centers and learning programs through churches and ministries in the countries.

Doctors Without Borders
Phone: 212-679-6800
Web site: www.doctorswithoutborders.org
Each year, Doctors Without Borders / Médecins Sans Frontières (MSF) volunteer doctors, nurses, logisticians, water-and-sanitation experts, administrators, and other medical and nonmedical professionals depart on more than 3,800 aid missions. They work alongside more than 22,500 locally hired staff to provide medical care. In emergencies and their aftermath, MSF provides health care, rehabilitates and runs hospitals and clinics, performs surgery, battles epidemics, carries out vaccination campaigns, operates feeding centers for malnourished children, and offers mental health care.

GAiN (Global Aid Network)
Phone: 972-234-0800
Web site: www.gainusa.org
The Global Aid Network is a humanitarian effort by Campus Crusade for Christ that demonstrates the love of God in word and deed to provide hope for hurting and needy people around the world through relief and development projects. Volunteers can go on trips to work on development projects, fill CarePacks, volunteer at the organization's warehouse, donate finances and materials, and pray.

Half the Sky Foundation
Phone: 510-525-3377
Web site: www.halfthesky.org
Half the Sky was created by adoptive parents of orphaned Chinese children to enrich the lives and enhance the prospects for the babies and children in China who still wait to be adopted, and for those who will spend their childhoods in

orphanages. The nonprofit organization establishes early childhood education, personalized learning and infant nurture programs in Chinese welfare institutions to provide the children stimulation, individual attention, and an active learning environment. Volunteers can get involved by donating finances, sponsoring a child, spreading the word at home, or joining a China crew to help build, expand, and improve orphanages.

Harvest Hands Ministries
Phone: 915-764-4201
Web site: www.harvesthandsministries.org
Garry and Terry Mathewson founded Harvest Hands Ministries in 1999 in order to preach and teach the gospel of Jesus Christ, feed the hungry, and give relief to the oppressed in Mexico. Harvest Hands feeds impoverished children, constructs local churches, sponsors children to attend school, provides medical care, and is building an orphanage. Their work also includes providing Sunday school materials and pastoral support, clothing, Bibles, personal care items, school supplies, and wheelchairs. Visiting church groups help Harvest Hands Ministries accomplish these many tasks.

Here I Am Orphan Ministries (Forever Families)
Phone: 979-289-5104
Web site: www.foreverfamilies.org
Here I Am Orphan Ministries and Forever Families were founded by Jay and Suzanne Faske, the parents of fourteen children, twelve of whom are adopted. The Faskes sought to involve their church in adoption ministry, and now these charitable organizations educate prospective parents about adoption, find homes for orphaned children, and support orphan care around the world.

Hope for Orphans
Phone: 800-FL-TODAY (800-358-6329)
Web site: www.familylife.com/hopefororphans
Hope for Orphans aims to encourage the body of Christ to help solve the needs of orphans around the world by adopting and providing orphan care. Hope for Orphans holds "If You Were Mine" educational adoption seminars, offers educational resources, and helps churches develop adoption ministries.

Hopegivers International
Phone: 866-373-4673
Hopegivers is a ministry founded by the Archbishop M. A. Thomas and known worldwide for its efforts over the past forty years to end the suffering of

orphaned and abandoned children. During its ministry, Hopegivers has been responsible for the establishment of more than 90 orphanages that house almost 9,000 children; 53 medical clinics throughout India; 190 schools with 88,000 students; a hospital and a nursing school; and an outreach program to more than 500 leper colonies.

International Justice Mission (IJM)
Phone: 703-465-5495
Web site: www.ijm.org
Founded in 1997, IJM began operations after a group of human rights professionals, lawyers, and public officials launched an extensive study of the injustices witnessed by overseas missionaries and relief and development workers. This study, surveying more than sixty-five organizations and representing forty thousand overseas workers, uncovered a nearly unanimous awareness of abuses of power by police and other authorities in the communities they served. Accordingly, IJM was established to help fill this void, acting as an organization that stands in the gap for victims when they are left without an advocate. IJM staff members (human rights experts, attorneys, and law enforcement professionals) receive case referrals from, and work in conjunction with, other nongovernmental organizations and casework alliances abroad. Volunteers can work with IJM through financial donations, internships, employment, prayer partnerships, and more.

Kingdom Kids Adoption Ministries
Phone: 509-465-3520
Web site: www.kingdomkidsadoption.org
Kingdom Kids was founded by adoptive parents Steve and Michelle Gardner to help meet the needs of orphans around the world. The Gardners hold adoption workshops in churches around the country, help find replacement homes for disrupted adoptions, and help adoptive families fund-raise for their adoption finances.

Northwest Medical Missions Team
Phone: 800-959-HEAL (4325)
Web site: www.nwmedicalteams.org
Immediately following a disaster, Northwest Medical Teams mobilizes and deploys volunteer disaster-response teams to meet emergency medical and other relief needs. It also implements curative and preventive health-care programs, including medical, dental and surgical clinics and training, primary health care (PHC), and water and other health-related construction projects.

The organization seeks to prevent the spread of HIV through education and to respond to the needs of people affected by AIDS, and it also meets other needs around the world.

Shaohannah's Hope
Phone: 800-784-5361
Web site: www.shaohannahshope.org
Shaohannah's Hope is dedicated to helping prospective adoptive parents overcome the financial barriers associated with adoption by awarding financial grants to qualified families already in the process of adopting. Partners with Shaohannah's Hope can help other families adopt by signing up for a monthly sponsorship, giving a one-time gift, or volunteering.

VisionTrust International
Phone: 719-268-2943
Web site: www.visiontrust.org
VisonTrust International is dedicated to the care and development of abused, orphaned, and extremely poor children living in third-world countries by providing daily food and addressing critical health problems; fulfilling the need for purpose through consistent Bible teaching; and investing in children's education through school enrollment and supplemental tutoring. VisionTrust partners can sponsor one or more children, start an orphan-care ministry in their church, or serve children on a short-term mission team.

Warm Blankets
Phone: 877-33-BLANKET (877-332-5265)
Web site: www.warmblankets.org
The mission of Warm Blankets Orphan Care International is to restore the lives of orphans in partnership with churches, corporations, organizations, and individuals who have a passion to help needy, parentless children. They build awareness of the despair faced by children around the world and the ways in which their needs can be addressed, provide resources that meet sustained spiritual, physical, social, and emotional needs of children, and share the message of the transforming power of Christ's love through words and action to each child.

World Orphans
Phone: 888-ORPHANS (888-677-4267)
Web site: www.worldorphans.org
World Orphans works to rescue orphaned and abandoned children in under-

developed countries by funding construction of orphan homes required for local Christian churches to meet the spiritual, physical, and educational needs of children.

World Vision
Phone: 888-511-6414
Web site: www.Worldvision.org
World Vision helps transform the lives of the world's poorest children and families in nearly one hundred countries, including the United States. Our nonprofit work extends assistance to all people, regardless of their religious beliefs, gender, race, or ethnic background.

This is a list of web links to organizations that serve orphans and needy children in specific regions:

Africa
Africa International Christian mission: www.aicmission.org
Children of Zion: www.cofz.org
Far Reaching Ministries: www.farreachingministries.org
Invisible Children: www.invisiblechildren.com
Watoto Children Ministries: www.watoto.com

Asia
Cambodia/Tabitha: www.tabithausa.org
CCBN China: www.cbnchina.org
Children of Promise: www.promise.org
Children's Hope International Foundation: www.chifoundation.org
Gospel Mission of India: www.ebenezermission.org
Home for Good: www.hfgf.org/about.html
Hope Foster Home: www.hopefosterhome.com
Love Without Boundaries: www.lovewithoutboundaries.com
The Miracle Foundation: www.miraclefoundation.org
Phillip Hayden: www.philiphayden.org

Central/South America
Love Links in El Salvador: www.love-link.org

Eastern Europe
Children's Hope Chest: www.hopechest.org
The CoMission for Children at Risk:

www.comissionforchildren.com/profiles/aom.php
Firefly Children's Network: www.fireflykids.org
Life International: www.lifeintl.org

United States
Becoming a Foster Parent: www.acf.hhs.gov/acf_services.html
Orphan Foundation of America: www.orphan.org
U.S. Orphanages (directory): www.legends.ca/orphanages

List of region-specific organizations courtesy of How to Adopt,
www.howtoadopt.org.

Appendix H

Sample Letters and Documents

The following section provides only examples of letters and documents. Your forms might or might not look different from the forms shown in this section, depending on the type of adoption you opt for and the area in which you reside.

#1—Letter to a Birthmother

This letter is an example of one that potential adoptive parents would write to a mother relinquishing a child. Note that the greeting does not use the word birthmother. *A woman is not a birthmother until after she has relinquished a child. Before then, she is just the mother and may be put off by any other title. The wording in a birthmother letter is important. It should not be preachy, but empathetic. It should* never *claim to know how a birthmother feels, and should not sound desperate. It should include pictures.*

Hello!

We are Steve and Caroline, and we're so glad you are reading our letter! We invite you to get to know us, and hope that you will feel the love we have for each other and the love we have to share with any little one who comes into our lives through the loving gift of adoption.

(A simple greeting introduces the reader to the fact that you hope to adopt.)

We are a married Christian couple who are so very grateful that you seek a loving family to raise and nurture your child. While we could never imagine how difficult this time in your life must be as you consider adoption, we are praying that God will give you some peace as you make this decision.

(This paragraph praises and encourages the mother for choosing adoption, without claiming to know how she feels or being preachy.)

As her loving husband of ten years, let me tell you about Caroline. She makes every day fun, and I never get tired of being around her. She reads great books to me that I would never get around to reading and enjoys spontaneous adventures like a picnic at the park or a hiking trip in the mountains. She loves to shop and cook, and life is never dull around her. I love her more every day that we spend together, and I can't wait to see her focus her time, her energies, and all that love on a precious baby.

(Birthmothers like to hear one spouse describe the other, rather than a husband and wife bragging on themselves.)

As his best friend for the past decade, let me tell you about Steve. Steve lights up any room he walks into with his infectious laugh and easygoing nature. He keeps me on my toes with his zest for life, and I love being with him—whether it's in the car to get groceries or heading off on a ski trip to Colorado. Steve fixes everything around the house, joins me in the kitchen to cook and clean, and spends time with kids as a volunteer with Big Brothers, Big Sisters. His heart is with the kids he serves, and he will be the most awesome dad! He is also so generous and always a gentleman. He still opens my car door and tucks his arm around me if I'm chilly. He is my hero.

(Give specific examples of your spouse's best attributes, and use active verbs as much as possible.)

We love to hit the beaches here in Florida, searching the shore for seashells and sticking our toes in the warm sand. We look forward to the day when we can introduce our son or daughter to wiggling fiddler crabs, delicate purple and pink coquina shells, and the amazing waves that break on the shore.

(Describe scenes in detail, rather than using generalities such as "We love the beach." Help the mother picture her child's activities with you.)

We promise to raise any child we adopt with love, values, faith, and a love of life. We hope that you will consider us, and if we can provide any additional information, you may contact us at 800-555-1212.

(End with contact information, and you may also want to include the type of adoption you desire. If you want to have an open adoption, your letter should state that and should let the mother know that you look forward to getting to know her.)

Steve and Caroline

#2—Prospective Adopter's Profile Questionnaire

Office of Linda J. Barnby, P.A.
ATTORNEY AT LAW

1681 MAITLAND AVENUE, MAITLAND, FLORIDA 32751
TELEPHONE: (407) 831-4944 FAX: (407) 331-7663

PROFILE QUESTIONNAIRE *

With no input from your spouse, you will carefully write or type your answers to each of the following questions on a separate sheet of paper. Please wait to share your answers with your spouse until you have each independently completed your separate profiles. The information provided here will be reviewed by Linda Barnby.

PART ONE
Personal & Background Information

1. Describe your physical appearance (e.g., hair, eyes, height, weight, complexion, etc.).

2. Describe your family (e.g., date and place of your birth, born to or adopted by your parents/stepparents, etc.). Describe your parents as a couple, including their marriage, areas of disagreement, and major issues (e.g., money, sex, discipline, communication, etc.). Whom did you feel closest to? Describe your brothers and sisters, if any.

3. Describe your life growing up. Tell me about school (e.g., academics, social activities, relationships with peers, rewarding and disappointing experiences, etc.). Also describe your life outside school (e.g., jobs, hobbies, life as a teenager, dating, etc.). What kinds of things made you happy and angry during these years?

4. Is religion important to you? Briefly tell me your thoughts about religion and its place in your life.

5. What experience have you had with children?

6. Describe the most fulfilling personal experience in your life.

7. What makes you happiest? Saddest?

8. What has caused you the most disappointment in your life?

9. What does security mean to you? How do you achieve it?

10. Describe your children, if any (e.g., sex, personality traits, health, etc.). If they do not live with you, with whom do they live, and why?

PART TWO
Marriage

11. Describe how you met, courted, and married your spouse. Describe your relationship with your parents and your spouse's parents now. What are some of the similarities and differences between your families (e.g., culture, religion, economics, education, approach to life, etc.). Describe any previous marriages, including dates and reasons for divorce.

12. Describe your spouse's personality.

13. What are your spouse's good and bad qualities?

14. What qualities do you most appreciate in your spouse?

15. What does your spouse do that makes you feel special?

16. What has been your most rewarding experience as a couple?

17. What do you see as the happiest times of your marriage?

18. What would you like to achieve in the future, not including this adoption plan?

19. What goals do you work toward in your marriage?

20. What are the areas of disagreement between you and your spouse? How do you resolve them? Describe some of the problems in your marriage that have been overcome, and how you worked them out.

21. What areas of your marriage have room for improvement?

22. Describe your role in your marriage (e.g., decision maker, caregiver, etc.). Who is the money manager in your family? How are major purchases, investments, or expenditures decided upon?

23. How are the household duties shared?

24. What activities do you enjoy sharing with your spouse? What activities do you enjoy separately from your spouse?

25. What, if any, community activities are you and your spouse involved in, either separately or together?

26. How do you expect the adoption to affect your marriage?

27. What adjustments to your lifestyle will you need to make to accommodate the addition of a child to your family?

28. Please describe your past efforts to conceive, your current plan to attempt conception now and in the future, and the likelihood of success.

PART THREE
Career & Home Life

29. How do you feel about your job? What are your future job goals?

30. In what ways is your job satisfying? Unsatisfying?

31. Describe the activities and functions you perform on your job.

32. How would you characterize the level of stability in your employment?

33. Describe your home (e.g., single or multiple family, owned or rented, number of rooms, square footage, yard size, etc.).

34. How would you describe the atmosphere in your home?

35. What kinds of pets do you have, if any? What role do they play in your life?

36. Describe your neighborhood (e.g., families, single persons, retired, racial diversity, etc.).

37. What in your home could be potentially hazardous for a child (e.g., lead-based paint, unfenced yard, weapons, guns, balcony, workshop with tools, stacked lumber, un-railed porch, power tools, waterfront yards, swimming pool, unvented gas heaters, etc.)?

38. Do you have firearms? Where do you keep them? Are they loaded? Are they locked up? For what purpose do you have them (e.g., safety, hunting, etc.)?

39. How will you provide for your child's safety?

40. Do you drive? Do you have a car separate from your spouse's?

PART FOUR
Child-Rearing

41. Why do you want a child?

42. What do you expect to gain by having a child?

43. What do you see yourself offering a child?

44. What is your philosophy on child rearing?

45. How are your ideas on child rearing different from your spouse's?

46. How does or will your style of parenting compare to your parents'?

47. If both of you are working outside the home, what will your child-care plan be?

48. Who will help out when you need extra parenting help (e.g., baby-sitting, advice, temporary relief, etc.)?

49. Please describe the discipline approach you plan to use to control your child's behavior. Does your discipline plan for your child include spanking or physical punishment? For what offenses?

50. Would you be willing to attend a parenting / child behavior modification class?

PART FIVE
Adoption

51. How do you feel about the prospective birthparents?

52. What will you tell your child about his or her birthparents? About the reasons his or her birthparents made their adoption plan?

53. What information about your child's adoption do you plan to share with your child, and when and how do you anticipate such discussions will occur?

54. How do your children feel about adoption and having an adopted brother or sister?

55. What are the reactions of your family members and friends to your adoption plan?

*Used with permission of Linda J. Barnby

#3—Adoption Agency Contract

Adoption Application

Home Office:
11780 Borman Dr.   www.ChildrensHope.net
St. Louis, MO 63146   Adoption@ChildrensHope.net
314.890.0086 Phone   314.427.4288 Fax

(Rev. 3/29/06)

SECTION 1 – FIRST STEP ON A JOURNEY OF LOVE

- Type or Print CLEARLY in ink.
- If a question does not apply to your family, use "N/A".
- If you need additional space, please attach a separate sheet of paper.
- This application is confidential and used for *internal* purposes only.
- Please allow 2 weeks for review of this application.
- You must allow 1 year after a life changing event before applying (marriage, divorce, birth, death, adoption)
- Please include the following with your completed application:
    1. *$100 check* (non-refundable) to *Children's Hope International* for application fee.
    2. **Photos**: No larger than 4 x 6 photos: 2 – Non-professional, close-up (head and shoulders) photos of adoptive parent(s); 1 – Other children in home; 1 – Exterior photo of house; 3 – Interior photos of house – choose three different rooms. Please write family name on back of pictures.

SECTION 2 – CONTACT INFORMATION

□ Ms. □ Mrs. _____ _____ _____
             Legal First Name   Legal Middle Name   Legal Last Name

□ Mr. _____ _____ _____
             Legal First Name   Legal Middle Name   Legal Last Name

_____   _____
Mother's Preferred or Nick Name   Father's Preferred or Nick Name

_____   _____
Street   Apt/Unit No.

_____   _____   _____
City   State   Zip Code

(____) ____-_____   (____) ____-_____   (____) ____-_____
Home Number   Work Number - Mother   Work Number – Father

(____) ____-_____   (____) ____-_____   (____) ____-_____
Fax Number   Mobile Number - Mother   Mobile Number – Father

_____
Primary E-mail Address (□ Mom □ Dad □ Both □ Hm □ Wk)   Secondary E-mail Address (□ Mom □ Dad □ Both □ Hm □ Wk)

FOR OFFICE USE ONLY

Country_____   Processed By_____   Date_____

Regional Office_____   Reviewed By _____   Date_____

Check No. _____   Approved By _____   Date_____

SECTION 3 – GENERAL INFORMATION

	Mother	Father
SSN		
Passport #	(if available)	(if available)
Birth Date:		
	(MM/DD/YY) Age	(MM/DD/YY) Age
Citizenship:		
Race: (optional)		
Religion:		
Education:		
Maiden Name:		N/A
Country Born in		

SECTION 4 – MARITAL INFORMATION

☐ Married   ☐ Divorced   ☐ Single (Never Married)   ☐ Widowed

1. If married, date of marriage:_____(*must be married at least 1 year before application can be accepted*)

2. Are there previous marriages? _____ If yes, see below. Divorces?_____ *(no more than 2 divorces per parent)*

Mother		Father	
1. Marriage date:	Divorce date:	1. Marriage date:	Divorce date:
2. Marriage date:	Divorce date:	2. Marriage date:	Divorce date:

3. Do you have children? _____

4. Are there children from previous marriages? _____

Child's Name	Age	Biological / Adopted	Living Arrangements/Date Adopted	Is he/she from previous marriage?
1.				
2.				
3.				
4.				
5.				
6.				

5. Have you ever terminated your parental rights of a biological or adopted child? _____
If yes, please explain on a separate sheet.

6. Are there other people living in your home? _____ If yes, please list their names and ages:_____

7. What is their relationship to you?
_____

SECTION 5 – ADOPTION INFORMATION

1. Are you Infertile? _____

2. Are you pregnant? _____

3. Are you currently working on another adoption besides this application? _____

4. Have you ever been turned down for adoption by another agency? _____

5. Please state what country you have chosen to adopt in _____ and why?
   _____
   _____
   _____

6. Why do you want to adopt? _____

7. What is your preference regarding the child you want to adopt? (*please check all that apply*)

   Age: _____ ☐ Months ☐ Years

   Sex: ☐ Male   ☐ Female   ☐ Either   ☐ Siblings

   Comments: _____

8. If adopting trans-racially, do you have any concerns you would like to discuss? _____
   _____
   _____

9. Are you applying to adopt a child with special needs? _____

10. If you have been pre-approved for a Waiting Child, please provide:
    Child's Name: _____   Reference # _____

SECTION 6 – HOME STUDY / AND / IMMIGRATION AND NATURALIZATION

(IF YOU LIVE IN MO, IL, KS, NY, TN, OR, or WA, CHI WILL DO YOUR HOMESTUDY)

1. Do you have a social worker connected with an agency to do your home study?   ☐ Yes ☐ No

   If yes, Name of Agency: _____

City:	State:	Zip:
Contact:	Tel: ( )	Fax: ( )
Completed?	In Progress?	Expected completion?

SECTION 7 – HEALTH INFORMATION

Mother's Health: ☐ Excellent ☐ Good ☐ Fair ☐ Poor   **Father's Health:** ☐ Excellent ☐ Good ☐ Fair ☐ Poor
(If you answer **yes** to any of the below, please provide <u>full details & dates</u>. Please use another sheet if needed.) **IF YOU LIST ANY MENTAL HEALTH ISSUES, PLEASE PROVIDE A LETTER FROM DOCTOR**

	Mother	Father
Tuberculosis	☐ Yes ☐ No	☐ Yes ☐ No
Tumor (non-cancerous)	☐ Yes ☐ No	☐ Yes ☐ No
Cancer	☐ Yes ☐ No	☐ Yes ☐ No
Heart Disease	☐ Yes ☐ No	☐ Yes ☐ No
Liver Disease	☐ Yes ☐ No	☐ Yes ☐ No
Neuropathy	☐ Yes ☐ No	☐ Yes ☐ No
Genetic Disease	☐ Yes ☐ No	☐ Yes ☐ No
Any Operations*	☐ Yes ☐ No	☐ Yes ☐ No
Diabetes:		
Type I	☐ Yes ☐ No	☐ Yes ☐ No
Type II	☐ Yes ☐ No	☐ Yes ☐ No
Alcoholism	☐ Yes ☐ No	☐ Yes ☐ No
Substance Abuse	☐ Yes ☐ No	☐ Yes ☐ No
Seizures	☐ Yes ☐ No	☐ Yes ☐ No
Impairments:		
Vision	☐ Yes ☐ No	☐ Yes ☐ No
Hearing	☐ Yes ☐ No	☐ Yes ☐ No
Mobility	☐ Yes ☐ No	☐ Yes ☐ No
Communicable Diseases:		
Herpes	☐ Yes ☐ No	☐ Yes ☐ No
HIV	☐ Yes ☐ No	☐ Yes ☐ No
Hepatitis A	☐ Yes ☐ No	☐ Yes ☐ No
Hepatitis B	☐ Yes ☐ No	☐ Yes ☐ No
Hepatitis C	☐ Yes ☐ No	☐ Yes ☐ No
Other_____	☐ Yes ☐ No	☐ Yes ☐ No
Mental Illness:		
Bi-Polar Disorder	☐ Yes ☐ No	☐ Yes ☐ No
Eating Disorder	☐ Yes ☐ No	☐ Yes ☐ No
Depression	☐ Yes ☐ No	☐ Yes ☐ No
Anxiety	☐ Yes ☐ No	☐ Yes ☐ No
Other_____	☐ Yes ☐ No	☐ Yes ☐ No

Medical Issue 1   ☐ Mother ☐ Father
Condition_____
Date of Diagnosis _____
Treatment Received _____
Prognosis/Outcome_____
Ongoing Treatment, if any _____
Medication, if any_____

Medical Issue 2   ☐ Mother ☐ Father
Condition_____
Date of Diagnosis _____
Treatment Received _____
Prognosis/Outcome_____
Ongoing Treatment, if any _____
Medication, if any_____

Medical Issue 3   ☐ Mother ☐ Father
Condition_____
Date of Diagnosis _____
Treatment Received _____
Prognosis/Outcome_____
Ongoing Treatment, if any _____
Medication, if any_____

Other than tonsils, appendix, dental, joints, vision, cosmetic, pregnancy, etc.

1. Mother – Ht. _____Weight_____   Father – Ht. _____Weight_____

2. Are you taking any medications? _____If yes, see below.

    1. Medicine:_____   Reason:_____   ☐ Mother ☐ Father
    2. Medicine:_____   Reason:_____   ☐ Mother ☐ Father
    3. Medicine:_____   Reason:_____   ☐ Mother ☐ Father
    4. Medicine:_____   Reason:_____   ☐ Mother ☐ Father
    5. Medicine:_____   Reason:_____   ☐ Mother ☐ Father

3. Does the health insurance cover the adopted child? _____

SECTION 8 - POLICE RECORD

1. Have you ever been arrested or convicted of any crimes, including but not limited to, shoplifting, fraud, theft, prostitution, solicitation, DUI, DWI, domestic violence, child abuse, assault, or possession of a controlled substance?

    Mother_____   **Father**_____

4. Have you ever been arrested or convicted of crimes other than those listed above, not including minor traffic violations?

    Mother_____   **Father**_____

If you answered "yes" to any of the questions above, please provide additional information: **Also state whether it is a _misdemeanor_ or _felony_.**

	Arrest/Conviction 1 ☐ Mother ☐ Father	Arrest/Conviction 2 ☐ Mother ☐ Father	Arrest/Conviction 3 ☐ Mother ☐ Father
Charge			
Year it occurred			
Dismissed/Guilty/ Probation/Not Guilty, etc			
Fine/Probation/Jail, etc.			
Time spent in jail, if any			
Type & length of probation			

Please provide additional information, use separate sheet if needed:

_____
_____
_____
_____
_____

SECTION 9 - FINANCIAL INFORMATION

	Mother	Father
Employer:		
Position:		
Annual Income:	$	$
Other Annual Income:	$	$

1. Total Assets(*vehicles, personal property, value of home, stocks/bonds, checking/savings, etc.*) $_____

2. Indebtedness (*including mortgage, credit cards auto payments & other*) $_____

5. Do you own or rent your home/apartment? _____

SECTION 10 – COMMENTS / HOW DID YOU HEAR ABOUT CHILDREN'S HOPE?

1. Please tell us why you chose CHI: _____
   _____
   _____

2. How did you hear about our agency? (*check all that apply*)

Word of Mouth:
   □ CHI Adoptive Family   □ Other Adoptive Family   □ Friend   □ Relative   □ Co-Worker   □ Other

Internet search: □ Google   □ Yahoo   □ MSN   □ Adoption.com   □ Other _____

   □ Television: □ News Story   Yellow Pages □

Newspaper: □ Ad   □ News Story

Magazine: □ Ad   □ Article

□ Radio
□ Flyer / Church Bulletin
□ Social Worker / Home Study Agency _____
□ Infertility or Adoption Support Group _____
□ Adoption Conference _____
□ Other _____

3. Have you met with staff of a CHI Regional Office?
   □ Workshop _____   □ Individual Meeting _____   □ Did not meet

4. Aside from workshops and individual meetings, the Regional Office contacted/assisted me by:
   □ Phone   □ E-mail   □ Letter   □ Information Meeting

5. Assistance provided by the Regional Office influenced my decision to choose CHI?   □ Yes   □ No

6. Location of Regional Office that assisted me: _____

SECTION 11 – EMERGENCY CONTACT INFORMATION

	Emergency Contact 1	Emergency Contact 2
Name	_____	_____
Relationship	_____	_____
Phone Number	_____	_____
Email Address	_____	_____

SECTION 12 – STATEMENT OF AGREEMENT AND SIGNATURE

I/We understand:
- That there are risks in adoption and realize that a target country has the power and authority to close its doors to adoption if they should so decide.
- That information on health and all other matters on the adoptive child received through CHI is limited, and based on all available data sent by adoption officials in the foreign country.
- Should I/We travel to the foreign country and decide not to continue with the adoption after making final agreement to do so, CHI will not be held responsible for the ultimate decision of the officials in the adoptive country or for financial loss that you may have incurred to that point.
- **That you agree not to pursue another adoption or plan a pregnancy. If an unplanned pregnancy should occur, you will inform CHI immediately and CHI will determine how to proceed.**

I/WE HEREBY CERTIFY BY SIGNING BELOW, GIVE CONSENT AND AGREEMENT TO THE ABOVE AND THAT ALL INFORMATION GIVEN IN THIS APPLICATION IS CORRECT TO THE BEST OF MY/OUR KNOWLEDGE AND ABILITY.

X _____ Date: _____

X _____ Date: _____

PLEASE RETURN THIS APPLICATION TO

CHILDREN'S HOPE INTERNATIONAL
11780 BORMAN DRIVE
ST. LOUIS, MO 63146

Tel: (314) 890-0086	Fax: (314) 427-4288
Web site: www.ChildrensHope.net	E-mail: Adoption@ChildrensHope.net

OR
THE CHILDREN'S HOPE REGIONAL OFFICE IN YOUR AREA

#4—Financial Statement

FINANCIAL DECLARATION FOR ADOPTION

First and Last Name(s) of Applicant(s)

1._____

2._____

This Year's Annual Salary: (Male)_____

(Female)_____

Last Year's Annual Salary: (Male)_____

(Female)_____

Other Income: (Male)_____

(Female)_____

Life Insurance: (Male)_____

(Female)_____

ASSETS: (VALUE)

Vehicles $_____

Personal Property $_____

Real Estate Residence $_____

Other $_____

Savings Accounts $_____

Checking Accounts $_____

Other Investments $_____

TOTAL ASSETS $_____

LIABILITIES: Mo. Payments / Total Owed

Credit Cards $_____

Bank Loans $_____

Home Mortgage $_____

Other Liabilities $_____

TOTAL LIABILITIES $_____

NET WORTH: $_____

I / we do hereby attest that the contents of the above declaration are true and correct, no part of it is false, and nothing material has been concealed there-from.

_____

Adoptive Parent

_____

Adoptive Parent

Subscribed and sworn to before me this _____ **day of**

_____ **20**_____ **.**

Term Expires_____

Notary Public in and for the State of _____ County

of_____.

#5—Medical Report
(Filled out by physician and notarized.)

MEDICAL DECLARATION FOR ADOPTION

Applicant's Name:

_____

Date of Birth:

_____

Address:

_____

Medical History	NO	YES	Date	Result
Have you ever had: Tuberculosis?				
Tumor?				
Heart disease?				
Liver disease?				
Sexual disease?				
Neuropathy?				
Mental disease?				
Other communicable disease?				
Alcoholism or substance abuse?				
Any genetic disease?				
Any surgical operations?				

If the answer is yes to any of the above, please explain the outcome on the other side of the form and state whether or not it will affect the patient's ability to parent.

Physical Examination

Date of Exam: _____

Height: _____ Weight: _____

Blood Pressure:_____

Vision: _____Hearing: _____

Heart: _____

Lungs: _____

Lymphatic System: _____

Thyroid:_____

Nervous System: _____

Urinalysis: _____

Blood Test: _____

HIV (pos/neg): _____

Is the patient taking any medication? _____

Physician's Statement

Signature of MD: _____ Date: _____

Name (print clearly):

_____

License number:

_____

Address:

_____

#6—Completed Home Study

Adoption Home Study Services, Inc.
3818 Dogtrot Street
New Port Richey, Florida 34655
727-375-2996

Adoptive Family Home Study: Adam and Natalie Gillespie

IDENTIFYING DATA:

Name — Adam Daniel Gillespie
DOB — XX/XX/XX (city, state)
SSN — XXX-XX-XXXX
Passport — Number Here
Occupation — Business owner

Name — Natalie Kent (Nichols) Gillespie
DOB — XX/XX/XX (city, state)
SSN — XXX-XX-XXXX
Passport Number Here
Occupation — Author

Address
Telephone

Date of Marriage 6/1/96

Children in the home: Justin Gillespie (DOB), Lydia Gillespie (DOB), Jessica Woolbright (DOB), Joshua Woolbright (DOB)

PREPARED BY

Donna Bradley, MSW, who is a social worker for Adoption Home Study Services, Inc., prepared the home study. Adoption Home Study Services, Inc., is a non profit agency, licensed by the State of Florida Department of Children and Families as a Child Placing Agency and as such is licensed to conduct home studies for adoption. Adoption Home Study Services, Inc., has experience preparing home studies for people adopting from China.

AGENCY CONTACTS

Adam and Natalie Gillespie desire to adopt a female child, under the age of twelve months, from the People's Republic of China. The Gillespies were seen for four face-to-face contacts in their home and in public locations in Florida. The first meeting on February 2, 2005, was to discuss the adoption process from the People's Republic of China. Adam was interviewed individually on February 9, 2005. Natalie was interviewed individually on February 9, 2005. They were interviewed together on February 9, 2005. All of the interviews on February 9, 2005, took place in their home. The meeting in their home included discussions of parenting issues and issues relating to the adjustment and parenting of an adopted child. Adam and Natalie Gillespie were interviewed on March 5, 2005, to review the home study. Numerous phone calls and e-mails have also been exchanged. The entire home study process lasted approximately six hours. Adam and Natalie Gillespie were present at all four interviews. Their children who are living in the home were also interviewed during the home visit. Adam and Natalie Gillespie are both eligible to adopt a child from the People's Republic of China.

Adam and Natalie Gillespie have met the preadoption requirements for the state of Florida. Criminal checks such as Florida Department of Law Enforcement, verified on February 3, 2005, and Department of Children and Family Services, verified on January 27, 2005, have confirmed that there has never been a founded report of child abuse or neglect against Adam or Natalie Gillespie. Law enforcement checks confirmed locally on January 27, 2005, and on the state level on February 3, 2005, that neither of them has ever had a criminal record. Fingerprints have been submitted to the FBI for clearance. Both Adam and Natalie state they have never been arrested. Both Adam and Natalie state they have never been rejected or had an unfavorable home study for any reason. In response to a direct question, they both denied any history of alcoholism, mental illness, substance abuse, sexual or child abuse, pilferage, or domestic violence, even if it did not result in an arrest or conviction. Adam and Natalie state that they do not use drugs of any type.

Adam and Natalie Gillespie were counseled on the process, expenses, potential difficulties, and possible delays associated with international adoption. The Gillespies have thought about the possibility that they may receive little or no information on the child's history. Adam and Natalie Gillespie are aware of the possibility of their child's developing a previously undiagnosed medical condition following the placement. They were counseled on issues dealing with developmental delays, attachment and bonding, and institutionalization. Adam and Natalie are accepting of this and willing to take that risk. They will assume full responsibility for the medical and financial needs of their child after placement. They are knowledgeable of the laws of the state of Florida pertaining to international adoption, the requirements of the CIS, and the adoption process in general.

MOTIVATION IN ADOPTION

Adam has three children from a previous marriage. Natalie has two children from a previous marriage. They have one biological son together. Adam's oldest daughter is now an adult; his second-born daughter is living away from home, and she is a college student. The Gillespies are successfully raising their four children in their blended family. They enjoy parenting and know that they have much love and joy to share with an adopted child. The children are all supportive of the adoption, and the Gillespies are now looking forward to the day that they can travel to China to meet their new daughter. They know their child will be accepted and nurtured in their community. They both desire another child and view adoption as a way of expanding their family. Adam and Natalie are comfortable with adoption and do not view it as second best. They state this child will have the same love and advantages that any biological child would have. This includes education and rights of inheritance.

ADOPTIVE FAMILY DESCRIPTION

Author's Note: This section contains a paragraph on each child and his or her likes and dislikes, hobbies, and academic achievements.

ADOPTIVE FATHER

Adam Daniel Gillespie presents as friendly, calm, and outgoing. Throughout the interviewing process, Adam was open and direct in discussing his family of origin, his marriage, family, and personal beliefs. All of Adam's siblings and his father are very supportive of Adam and Natalie's adoption plan. Adam remains close to his family. They see one another as often as is possible and they speak by phone and e-mail frequently.

ADOPTIVE MOTHER

Natalie Gillespie presents as friendly, outgoing, and nurturing. Throughout the interview process, Natalie was open and comfortable discussing her family of origin, her marriage, and her personal beliefs. Natalie stated that she enjoys a close relationship with her sisters. She said they see each other often and speak by phone daily. Natalie stated, "They are my best friends." All of Natalie's siblings and their families are supportive of Adam and Natalie's decision to adopt.

MARITAL

Adam and Natalie met at church. They became close friends and enjoyed talking and getting to know each other. They dated for a year and were married on June 1, 1996, in Largo, Florida, as verified by their marriage license. Adam and Natalie enjoy a strong and happy marriage of eight and a half years. They have a common value system and goals. They solve disagreements by discussion and are willing to compromise when necessary. They rarely have an argument; however, when they do disagree they resolve it through discussion and compromise. They feel that they both have excellent communication skills. They both value honesty and respect in their relationship. They work together as a team and their personalities balance each other. Adam describes Natalie as an intelligent person, a loving wife, and a nurturing mother. He stated that she gives her all to everyone that she knows. Natalie describes Adam as a supportive and nurturing father. Natalie stated that Adam is a man of integrity and an awesome father.

Adam and Natalie share many common interests. They spend much of their free time enjoying their children. The family places a high value on servicing others who may be less fortunate. The entire family has spent time in Mexico helping with the homeless. They spend much of their free time with their church community. The children are all active in the youth programs of the church. They also enjoy family dinners, walks to the park, movies, and boating.

RELIGION

Adam and Natalie state they are Christians. They are active members of a local church.

OCCUPATION

Adam Gillespie is the sole shareholder in the corporation ADG Consulting Group, Inc. Adam is the president of the corporation. Adam has been employed in the automobile industry for more than twenty-five years, and his potential for future earnings in this field is excellent, as verified by a letter from his accountant.

Natalie Gillespie has been employed as a journalist, a freelance writer, and an author for the past eleven years. Natalie is the sole shareholder in the corporation Natalie Nichols Gillespie, Inc. She is the president of the corporation. Natalie has been a successful writer for more than eleven years, and her potential for future earnings in this field is strong. Natalie works from home part-time; therefore, child-care will not be necessary.

Adam and Natalie state they are committed to providing their children with an education. It is their desire that their children earn a four-year college degree or attend a specialized trade school. They feel an education is essential in today's world and are committed to providing this opportunity for their children.

FINANCES

Author's Note: This section of the home study contains a breakdown of our family's assets and liabilities, salaries, and medical and life insurance.

HOME AND COMMUNITY

Adam and Natalie have resided in their home in Florida for the past two and a half years. They have smoke alarms throughout the house and one fire extinguisher in their home. The Gillespies have installed safety locks on their kitchen cabinets and safety plugs in their electrical outlets. The Gillespies' home meets all standards of the state of Florida for child placement. The community of Weeki Wachee, Florida, has a diverse ethnic population due to tourism, the immigration of persons from other countries, and the many international corporations based in the area. A child of different ethnic background will be easily accepted. Their home is conveniently located near medical facilities, shopping, recreational areas, and schools. This is a beautiful place to raise children.

HEALTH

A. Kamara, MD, examined Adam and Natalie Gillespie on February 7, 2005. Their physician stated that there is no medical reason to prevent either of them from adopting. Laboratory tests confirm both Adam and Natalie are free of contagious disease, including tuberculosis and HIV. Based on the medical reports provided, Adam and Natalie Gillespie are in excellent health and are physically and mentally capable of parenting an additional adopted child.

DISCUSSION OF CHILD REARING AND ADOPTION ISSUES

Adam and Natalie are very involved and active in their children's lives. They are supportive and nurturing parents who encourage their children to pursue their individual interests. They know the importance of educating their daughter about her Chinese culture and heritage.

Adam and Natalie desire to provide an environment that supports open communication and higher education. Adam and Natalie will strive to teach their children to be kind and generous to other people. They will look for ways to teach their children strong values that include tolerance and empathy for others. Adam and Natalie are active members of a church where the children are taught and encouraged to learn the values that are important to the family.

Adam and Natalie believe it is best to discipline in an age-appropriate way, using positive reinforcement as much as possible. They believe in setting realistic limits with children, and they use natural and logical consequences to teach their children responsibility as needed. They both look forward to hearing the laughter of another child in their home and being given the opportunity to share in her life. Adam and Natalie are committed to providing their children with all the opportunities afforded a biological child. These include a sense of family, love, respect, education, and rights of inheritance. The Gillespies' nurture plan is appropriate for raising an adopted child.

They have made arrangements with Natalie's sister and her husband, Noelle (age 35) and Jason (age 36) Hall, to be guardians in the event something unforeseen would happen to them. Based on the information provided, Jason and Noelle Hall appear to be qualified candidates to be the guardians for an adopted child.

RECOMMENDATION

Adam and Natalie appear to be a family-oriented couple excited about the opportunity to adopt a child from China. They are doing an excellent job of raising their children. The couple is interested in adopting a female child under twelve months of age from the People's Republic of China. Their lifestyle is such that the arrival of another child would be handled well and with care. They have agreed to post-placement reports at six months and twelve months to be provided by Adoption Home Study Services, Inc., as required by the People's Republic of China. Five references describe the Gillespies as having a strong marriage and stable home. They have been described as being very loving and nurturing with their children.

Based on observation, interviews, references, and legal clearance, Adam and Natalie Gillespie present as having the stamina, emotional stability, good judgment, and solid marriage needed for parenting. It is therefore recommended that Adam and Natalie Gillespie be considered qualified candidates to **adopt a female child under the age of twelve months** from the People's Republic of China.

Respectively Submitted by:

_____

Donna Bradley, MSW
Adoption Home Study Services, Inc.

Adoption Home Study Services, Inc., is a licensed nonprofit child-placement agency in the state of Florida.

Florida Certificate number 0904-041-0000

Licensed to perform adoption home studies by Florida statute 63.092 (2)

STATE OF FLORIDA

County of Pasco

The foregoing instrument was acknowledged before me on this _____of

_____ 2005,

By Donna Bradley, MSW, who has produced a license as identification and

who did take an oath.

_____

Name of Notary Public

My commission expires,_____, 20_____.

#7—USCIS I-171H

U.S. Department of Justice
Immigration and Naturalization Service
5524 West Cypress Street
Tampa, Florida 33607-1708

Name and Address of Prospective Petitioner	Name of prospective petitioner
ADAM D. GILLESPIE 9490 WHISPER RIDGE TRAIL WEEKI WACHEE, FLORIDA 34613	ADAM D. GILLESPIE

	Name of Spouse, if married
NOTICE TO PROSPECTIVE ADOPTIVE PARENTS IS ENCLOSED. PLEASE BE SURE THAT YOU READ AND UNDERSTAND IT BEFORE YOU ADOPT A FOREIGN BORN CHILD.	NATALIE NICHOLS GILLESPIE

Date application Filed	Date of completion of Advance processing
JAN. 26, 2005	APRIL 18, 2005

NOTICE OF FAVORABLE DETERMINATION CONCERNING APPLICATION
FOR ADVANCE PROCESSING OF ORPHAN PETITION

IT HAS BEEN DETERMINED THAT YOU ARE ABLE TO FURNISH PROPER CARE TO AN ORPHAN OR ORPHANS AS DEFINED BY SECTION 101(B)(1)(F) OF THE IMMIGRATION AND NATURALIZATION ACT. A SEPARATE ORPHAN PETITION, FORM I-600, MUST BE FILED IN BEHALF OF EACH CHILD WITH DOCUMENTARY EVIDENCE AS DESCRIBED IN INSTRUCTIONS 2c, 2d, 2e, 2f, 2G, AND 2h OF THAT FORM. A FORM OR FORMS FOR YOUR USE ARE ENCLOSED. NO FEE WILL BE REQUIRED WITH FORM I-600 IF YOU FILE FORM I-600 WITHIN EIGHTEEN MONTHS FROM THE DATE OF COMPLETION OF ALL ADVANCE PROCESSING. IF YOU DO NOT FILE FORM I-600 WITHIN EIGHTEEN MONTHS FROM THE DATE OF COMPLETION OF ALL ADVANCE PROCESSING APPLICATION. YOUR APPLICATION SHALL BE CONSIDERED ABANDONED. ANY FURTHER PROCESSINGS WILL REQUIRE THE FILLING OF A NEW ADVANCE PROCESSING APPLICATION OR AN ORPHAN PETITION.

Form I-600 should be filed at the Service office or American consulate or embassy where your advance processing application is being retained or has been forwarded as dincated by an "X" mark below:

1. ☐   YOUR ADVANCE PROCESSING APPLICATION IS BEING RETAINED AT THIS OFFICE.

2. ☐   YOUR ADVANCE PROCESSING APPLICATION HAS BEEN FORWARDED TO OUR SERVICE OFFICE AT

3. ☒   YOUR ADVANCE PROCESSING APPLICATION HAS BEEN FORWARDED TO THE AMERICAN CONSULATE OR EMBASSY AT: **GUANGZHOU, CHINA VIA THE**   **National Visa Center (NVC)**
         32 Rochester Avenue
         Portsmouth, New Hampshire 03801

In addition, please note the following:

☐   Any original documents submitted in support of your application are returned to your.

☐   Your homestudy is returned to you.

☒   Fingerprint expiration date   **May 15, 2006**   _____

☒   Approved to adopt   ☐ 1   Child/Children.

THIS DETERMINATION DOES NOT GUARANTEE THAT THE ORPHAN PETITION(S) WHICH YOU FILE WILL BE APPROVED. AN ORPHAN PETITION MAY BE DENIED BECAUSE THE CHILD DOES NOT QUALIFY FOR CLASSIFICATION AS AN ORPHAN OR FOR OTHER PROPER CAUSE. DENIAL OF AN ORPHAN PETITION, HOWEVER MAY BE APPEALED.

cc: CHILDREN'S HOPE INTERNATIONAL
       9229 LACKLAND RD.
       ST. LOUIS, MO 63114-5412

VERY TRULY YOURS,

Patricia Dwyer

for   **John M. Bulger**
      District Director

Form I-171H
(12-15-82)

#8—USCIS I-600A

OMB No. 1615-0028; Expires 08/31/08

Department of Homeland Security
U.S. Citizenship and Immigration Services

**I-600A, Application for Advance
Processing of Orphan Petition**

Do not write in this block.   **For USCIS Use Only.**

It has been determined that the:

☐ Married   ☐ Unmarried

prospective adoptive parent will furnish proper care to
a beneficiary orphan if admitted to the United States.

There:

☐ are   ☐ are not

preadoptive requirements in the State of the child's proposed
residence.

The following is a description of the preadoption requirements, if any,
of the State of the child's proposed residence:

_____

_____

The preadoption requirements, if any,:

☐ have been met.   ☐ have not been met.

Fee Stamp	

DATE OF FAVORABLE
DETERMINATION

DD

DISTRICT

File number of applicant, if applicable.

Please type or print legibly in black ink.

This application is made by the named prospective adoptive parent for advance processing of an orphan petition.

BLOCK I - Information about the prospective adoptive parent.

1. My name is: (Last)   (First)   (Middle)

2. Other names used (including maiden name if appropriate):

3. I reside in the U.S. at: (C/O if appropriate)   (Apt. No.)

(Number and Street)   (Town or City)   (State)   (Zip Code)

4. Address abroad (If any):   (Number and Street)   (Apt. No.)

(Town or City)   (Province)   (Country)

5. I was born on: *(mm/dd/yyyy)*

In: (Town or City)   (State or Province)   (Country)

6. My telephone number is: (Include Area Code)

7. My marital status is:

☐ Married
☐ Widowed
☐ Divorced
☐ Single
 ☐ I have never been married.
 ☐ I have been previously married _____ time(s).

8. If you are now married, give the following information:

Date and place of present marriage *(mm/dd/yyyy)*

Name of present spouse (include maiden name of wife)

Date of birth of spouse *(mm/dd/yyyy)*   Place of birth of spouse

Number of prior marriages of spouse

My spouse resides ☐ With me   ☐ Apart from me
                                         (provide address below)

(Apt. No.)   (No. and Street)   (City)   (State)   (Country)

9. I am a citizen of the United States through:
☐ Birth   ☐ Parents   ☐ Naturalization

If acquired through naturalization, give name under which naturalized,
number of naturalization certificate, and date and place of naturalization.

If not, submit evidence of citizenship. See Instruction 2.a(2).

If acquired through parentage, have you obtained a certificate in your
own name based on that acquisition?
☐ No   ☐ Yes

Have you or any person through whom you claimed citizenship ever lost
United States citizenship?
☐ No   ☐ Yes (If Yes, attach detailed explanation.)

Received	Trans. In	Ret'd Trans. Out	Completed

Form I-600A (Rev. 10/26/05) Y

OMB No. 1615-0028; Expires 08/31/08

Department of Homeland Security
U.S. Citizenship and Immigration Services

I-600A, Application for Advance Processing of Orphan Petition

| **Do not write in this block.** | **For USCIS Use Only.** |

It has been determined that the:

☐ Married   ☐ Unmarried

prospective adoptive parent will furnish proper care to a beneficiary orphan if admitted to the United States.

There:

☐ are   ☐ are not

preadoptive requirements in the State of the child's proposed residence.

The following is a description of the preadoption requirements, if any, of the State of the child's proposed residence:

_____

_____

The preadoption requirements, if any,:

☐ have been met.   ☐ have not been met.

Fee Stamp

DATE OF FAVORABLE DETERMINATION

DD

DISTRICT

File number of applicant, if applicable.

Please type or print legibly in black ink.

This application is made by the named prospective adoptive parent for advance processing of an orphan petition.

BLOCK 1 - Information about the prospective adoptive parent.

1. My name is: (Last)   (First)   (Middle)

2. Other names used (including maiden name if appropriate):

3. I reside in the U.S. at: (C/O if appropriate)   (Apt. No.)

(Number and Street)   (Town or City)   (State)   (Zip Code)

4. Address abroad (If any):   (Number and Street)   (Apt. No.)

(Town or City)   (Province)   (Country)

5. I was born on: *(mm/dd/yyyy)*

In: (Town or City)   (State or Province)   (Country)

6. My telephone number is: (Include Area Code)

7. My marital status is:

☐ Married
☐ Widowed
☐ Divorced
☐ Single
   ☐ I have never been married.
   ☐ I have been previously married _____ time(s).

8. If you are now married, give the following information:

Date and place of present marriage *(mm/dd/yyyy)*

Name of present spouse (include maiden name of wife)

Date of birth of spouse *(mm/dd/yyyy)*   Place of birth of spouse

Number of prior marriages of spouse

My spouse resides   ☐ With me   ☐ Apart from me (provide address below)

(Apt. No.)   (No. and Street)   (City)   (State)   (Country)

9. I am a citizen of the United States through:

☐ Birth   ☐ Parents   ☐ Naturalization

If acquired through naturalization, give name under which naturalized, number of naturalization certificate, and date and place of naturalization.

_____

If not, submit evidence of citizenship. See Instruction 2.a(2).

If acquired through parentage, have you obtained a certificate in your own name based on that acquisition?

☐ No   ☐ Yes

Have you or any person through whom you claimed citizenship ever lost United States citizenship?

☐ No   ☐ Yes (If Yes, attach detailed explanation.)

Received	Trans. In	Ret'd Trans. Out	Completed

Form I-600A (Rev. 10/26/05) Y

#9—Request for Processing of I-600A

To: U.S. Citizenship and Immigration Services
        (Insert address of local office)

From: Adam and Natalie Gillespie
        (Insert your address and phone numbers)

January 24, 2005

RE: Enclosed Form I-600A and Supporting Documentation

Dear USCIS,

Enclosed you will find our I-600A, all the required supporting documents, and a money order for the filing fee in the amount of _____.

We are in the process of completing our Home Study, which will be forwarded to your office upon completion. The Home Study is being conducted by licensed social worker *(insert social worker name, company, and address here)*.

May we respectfully request that your office begin processing our fingerprints while waiting for our Home Study?

Thank you for your hard work on our behalf!

Sincerely,

Adam and Natalie Gillespie

Attached:

#10—Request for State Certification

February 8, 2005

To: Secretary of State
        Commission Division
        600 W. Main, Room 367
        Jefferson City, MO 65101
        573-751-2336

Dear Secretary of State,

I am writing to request that you state-certify my birth certificate, as my husband and I are in the process of adopting a little girl from China. My complete name is Natalie Kent (maiden name Nichols) Gillespie. My husband's name is Adam Daniel Gillespie.

The birth certificate should be returned as soon as possible to our home address: *(insert address here).* Enclosed is the certification fee of $10.00, check #178.

Thank you for your assistance, and if you have any questions or concerns, please contact me at XXX-XXX-XXXX.

Sincerely,

Natalie Kent (Nichols) Gillespie

Attached: check #178 in the amount of $10

#11—Letter of Reference

Bill and Karen Smith
2134 Jones Street
Clearwater, Florida 33765
kb@aol.com
727-555-1212

May 8, 2005

To: *(adoption agency name, social worker, or attorney and the foreign government processing the international adoption, if applicable)*

(Example:) Dear CHI and Officials of the China Center for Adoption Affairs,

It is our pleasure to write this letter of reference for our friends, Mike and Anna Williams. We have known Mike and Anna for approximately five and a half years. We met through a church group and have become friends as well as serving in activities in the community together.

Mike and Anna have worked very hard to be good parents to their children. They have taken an active role in the raising of their children in areas of education and in teaching them moral and spiritual values and are involved in every part of their children's lives. Mike and Anna have retained a strong marriage through tests and trials and have an even stronger relationship today because of those tests. They are both generous and caring individuals, and their love of their children is obvious to all who know them.

We believe they would make wonderful adoptive parents. They have demonstrated love for others in many circumstances and would provide a loving home to any child who would be placed in their care.

We have seen no signs of substance abuse of any kind in either Mike or Anna and would highly recommend them as candidates to be the parents of an adopted child. A child of a different race would be especially welcome in their family. We have no reservations about their abilities to adopt, raise, and especially love another child.

If you have any further questions or we can be of assistance, please feel free to contact us via either e-mail, U.S. Postal Service, or by phone.

Sincerely,
Bill Smith
Karen Smith

#12—Support Letter for Family and Friends

Alan and Cindy Johnson
1234 My Own Street
Anytown, FL 11111
H: 212-123-5555
Cell: 212-123-5556
E-mail: adoptingparent@aol.com

Dear Friends, Family, and Colleagues,

We are writing you today with a special request on our hearts. We are in the process of adopting a precious baby to add to our wonderful family. We feel that God is calling us to take care of the orphan, and we are humbly asking if you will join with us in this call to bring our little one home.

(Tell a little bit about your child here: what country he or she is from, where your child is located if he or she is in foster care, or how you were matched with a birthmother. Give the details about why this adoption is the right thing for this child and explain how it fulfills the call from God to care for others.)

Will you join us in prayer for the protection of our little one until we bring *(him or her)* home, and prayerfully consider contributing financially to help us meet the high costs of the adoption process? We are working with a Christian adoption agency, *(insert name and Web site here)*, to bring our child home and expect to complete our adoption by *(insert month here)*. Donations can be made to *(name the fund-raising organization or bank account you are using here. If donations are tax deductible, be sure to say that)*.

If you can help us financially and with your prayer support, we would be so grateful. If we can answer any questions, feel free to contact us at 212-123-5555 or e-mail us at adoptingparent@aol.com.

Thank you for loving and helping us, and God bless you!

Alan and Cindy Johnson

On May 25, 2006, our family finally got the call from our adoption agency. "It's a girl!" they said. You Fu Shuang, born July 30, 2005, was waiting for us in the Youyang Children's Welfare Institute in Chongqing, China. Our baby, to be named Amberlie Joy FuShuang Gillespie, spent her first ten months in an orphanage. She will finally get to experience a mommy and daddy's love, and she will someday understand her heavenly father's love-a love that would compel this family from Florida to travel around the world to find her. A love that will be hers forever-just like God welcomes us into his forever family. Welcome, home, Amberlie Joy FuShuang Gillespie. We love you.

To see a photo of Amberlie Joy, read the whole miracle story of Amberlie's adoption, or to find out how you can help children in need, visit our Web page at www.successfuladoption.com.

#13—Adoption Announcement

*Please join with
Adam and Natalie Gillespie and family
as we praise God and
proudly announce the adoption of*

Amberlie Joy FuShuang Gillespie

*"Fu" means "Blessed,"
"Shuang" means "Clear, Bright, and Outspoken"*

*from the province of Chongqing,
People's Republic of China.*

*Born: July 30, 2005
Adopted: July, 2006*

*Pure and lasting religion in the sight of God our Father
means that we must care for orphans and widows in their
troubles, and refuse to let the world corrupt us.
—James 1:27 (NLT)*

*To read the whole miracle story of Amberlie's adoption
and to find out how you can help children in need, visit our
Web-page at www.successfuladoption.com.*

Notes

CHAPTER ONE

1. A. Chandra, J. Abma, P. Maza, and C. Bachrach. (1999). Adoption, adoption seeking, and relinquishment for adoption in the United States. Advance Data (No. 306) from Vital and Health Statistics of the Centers for Disease Control and Prevention, National Center for Health Statistics, U.S. Department of Health and Human Services. Retrieved October 24, 2005, from http://www.cdc.gov/nchs/data/ad/ad306.pdf. This publication includes data from the National Surveys of Family Growth through 1995, using data on nationally representative samples of more than 10,000 women.

2. Kerry Hasenbalg, Excerpt from Keynote Speech given at the Orphan Summit II presented by FamilyLife's Hope for Orphans, Little Rock, AK, March 22, 2006.

3. U.S. Census Bureau, "Adopted Children and Stepchildren: 2000," a Census 2000 Special Report by Rose Kreider, p. 2, Table 1. Accessed May 24, 2005, http://www.census.gov/prod/2003pubs/censr6.pdf#search=' 2000%20census%20adoption.

4. U.S. Department of Health and Human Services, Administration for Children and Families, "The AFCARS Report: Preliminary FY 2003 Estimates as of April 2005," p. 1. Accessed April 10, 2005. http://www.acf.hhs.gov/ programs/cb/publications/afcars/report10.pdf.

5. The National Adoption Attitudes Survey was fully commissioned by the Dave Thomas Foundation for Adoption in cooperation with Evan B. Donaldson Adoption Institute in New York. The survey was conducted by Harris Interactive, publisher of The Harris Poll ®, by telephone from January 10 to January 31, 2002, polling 1,416 Americans age eighteen and older.

6. National Adoption Day Media Center, "Adoption Statistics," http://www.nationaladoptionday.org/2005/media/materials/Background/Ad option%20Statistics%20Factsheet.doc (accessed November 24, 2005).

CHAPTER TWO

7. For more on Kingsbury, see Natalie Nichols Gillespie, "Faith, Fiction, Family and a lot of fun," *mtl* magazine (Nov/Dec 2005): 27.

8. Luwis, Brian, "The Spirit of Adoption." America World Adoption Association, http://www.america-china.org/stories/spiritofadoption.aspx (accessed March 15, 2006).

9. Ibid.

10. National Adoption Day Media Center, "National Adoption Day 2005," http://www.nationaladoptionday.org/2005/media/materials/Background/Adoption%20Statistics%20Factsheet.doc (accessed November 24, 2005).

11. "Cooperative Adoptions: Contact Between Adoptive and Birth Families After Finalization," National Adoption Information Clearinghouse, http://naic.acf.hhs.gov/general/legal/statutes/cooperative.cfm#note6 (accessed Oct. 25, 2005).

CHAPTER THREE

12. Corkydawn Mason, "Adoption Agency Study" for FamilyLife's Hope for Orphans, presented at Orphan Summit II, March 24, 2006.

13. Speech from John Brown III, ECFA chairman of the board, given at the FamilyLife Orphan Summit II, March 23, 2006, in Little Rock, AK.

14. Taken from the IRS, "Adoption Taxpayer Identification Number," http://www.irs.gov/individuals/article/0,,id=96452,00.html#QA4 (accessed September 14, 2005).

15. Adapted from the North American Council on Adoptable Children, "How to Adopt," http://www.nacac.org/howtoadopt.html (accessed November 1, 2005).

CHAPTER FOUR

16. U.S. Department of State, "Immigrant Visas Issued to Orphans Coming to the U.S," http://travel.state.gov/family/adoption/stats/stats_451.html (accessed November 13, 2005).

17. Jean Nelson-Erichsen and Heino Erichsen, "Meeting Your Child," chap. 11 in *How to Adopt Internationally* (Ft. Worth: Mesa House, 1997), pp. 106-7.

18. Dana Johnson, M.D., "Adopting an Institutionalized Child: What Are the Risks?" Association for Research in International Adoption, http://www.adoption-research.org/risks.html (accessed March 16, 2006).

19. U.S. Department of State, "International Adoption" page, http://travel.state.gov/family/adoption/notices/notices_473.html (accessed May 14, 2005).

20. Nelson-Erichsen and Erichsen, "Meeting Your Child," p. 21.

CHAPTER FIVE

21. Peter Gibbs and Martha J. Henry, "Adoption in Massachusetts: Private and Public Agency Placements and Practices in 2001-2002"(Center for Adoption Research, University of Massachusetts, May, 2004), pp. 14-26.

22. Sandra Lennington, "Networking," an article that first appeared in the now defunct *Adoptnet Magazine*, 1990, http://www.adopting.org/network.html (accessed August 5, 2005).

23. National Adoption Information Clearinghouse State Statute Series 2005: "State Regulation of Adoption Expenses": 2, http://naic.acf.hhs.gov/general/legal/statutes/expenses.pdf (accessed November 1, 2005).

24. Corkydawn Mason, "Adoption Agency Study," FamilyLife's Hope for Orphans, presented at Orphan Summit II, Little Rock, AK, March 24, 2006.

25. For more information on the Federal Income Tax Credit, visit www.irs.gov. This information was taken from the Internal Revenue Service, "Topic 607-Adoption Credit," http://www.irs.gov/taxtopics/tc607.html (accessed July 3, 2005).

26. Details can be found on the National Military Family Association's "DoD Adoption Reimbursement" Fact Sheet. November 2005, http://www.nmfa.org/site/DocServer/DoD_Adoption_Reimbursement_11-05.pdf?docID=3561 (accessed November 22, 2005).

27. Information provided by the National Adoption Information Clearinghouse, "Adoption Assistance for Children Adopted from Foster Care: A Factsheet for Families," published in 2004, http://naic.acf.hhs.gov/pubs/f_subsid.cfm (accessed August 18, 2005).

CHAPTER SEVEN

28. Mark Lino, *Expenditures on Children by Families*, 2004. U.S. Department of Agriculture, Center for Nutrition Policy and Promotion. Miscellaneous Publication No. 1528-2004, http://www.cnpp.usda.gov/Crc/crc2004.pdf (accessed November 4, 2005).

CHAPTER ELEVEN

29. Deborah Gray, *Attaching in Adoption* (Indianapolis: Perspectives Press, 2002), 16.

30. Ibid., 18–19.

31. Dana Johnson, "Adopting an Institutionalized Child: What Are the Risks?" Taken from the Association for Research in International Adoption, http://www.adoption-research.org/risks.htm (accessed October 21, 2005).

32. Lark Eshleman, *Becoming a Family* (Lanham, MD: Taylor Trade, 2003), 5.

33. Ibid., 29.

34. Gregory Keck and Regina Kupecky, *Parenting the Hurt Child: Helping Adoptive Families Heal and Grow* (Colorado Springs: Pinon Press, 2002).

35. Benjamin Spock, "When to Tell a Child She Is Adopted," adapted from Dr. Spock's Baby and Child Care, August 15, 2004, http://www.drspock.com/article/0,1510,4017,00.html (accessed October 13, 2005).

36. Amanda Levin, "My Homeland Visit," First published in *Adoptive Families*, 2000. Excerpted from Adoptive Families Web site, http://www.adoptivefamilies.com/articles.php?aid=143 (accessed March 24, 2006).

37. Gloria Hochman, Ellen Feathers-Acuna, and Anna Huston of the National Adoption Center in "The Sibling Bond," written for the National Adoption Information Clearinghouse, 1992. http://naic.acf.hhs.gov/pubs/f_siblin.cfm (accessed March 26, 2006).

CHAPTER TWELVE

38. Julie Jarrell Bailey and Lynn N. Giddens, *The Adoption Reunion Survival Guide* (Oakland, CA: New Harbinger Publications), p. 12.

39. "News & Notes" Nov./Dec. 2005, *Adoptive Families* web site. http://www.adoptivefamilies.com/articles.php?aid=536 (accessed December 1, 2005).

40. Julie Jarrell Bailey and Lynn N. Giddens, *The Adoption Reunion Survival Guide* (Oakland, CA: New Harbinger Publicationa), p. 141.

APPENDIX A

i. Adopting.org, sponsored by Families.com, "Adoption and Foster Care Glossary," http://www.adopting.org/adoptions/adoption-and-foster-care-glossary-active-registry.html (accessed October 23, 2005).

ii. Ibid., http://www.adopting.org/adoptions/adoption-and-foster-care-glosary-adoption-assistance.html.

iii. Internal Revenue Service, "Topic 607-Adoption Credit," http://www.irs.gov/taxtopics/tc607.html (accessed October 10, 2005).

iv. Ibid., "Adoption Taxpayer Identification Number." http://www.irs.gov/individuals/article/0,,id=96452,00.html#QA1.

v. NYS Department of State, "Frequently Asked Questions," http://www.dos.state.ny.us/corp/msrfaq.html (accessed September 20, 2005).

vi. U.S. Department of State, "Hague Convention on Intercountry Adoption," http://travel.state.gov/family/adoption/convention/convention_462.html (accessed September 10, 2005).

vii. U.S. Citizenship and Immigration Services, "Forms and Fees," http://uscis.gov/graphics/formsfee/forms/index.htm (accessed June 12, 2005).

viii. U.S. Citizenship and Immigration Services, "IV. Basic Orphan Petition Procedures," http://uscis.gov/graphics/services/bopproc.htm (accessed October 23, 2005).

ix. Adopting.org, sponsored by Families.com, "Adoption and Foster Care Glossary," http://www.adopting.org/adoptions/adoption-and-foster-care-glossary-institutionalization.html (accessed October 10, 2005).

x. U.S. Department of Health and Human Services, Administration for Children & Families, "A Guide to the Multiethnic Placement Act of 1994 as Amended by the Interethnic Adoption Provisions of 1996," http://www.acf.hhs.gov/programs/cb/pubs/mepa94/index.htm (accessed October 23, 2005).

xi. Some of these terms adopted from Adopting.org, sponsored by Families.com, "Adoption Lingo List," http://www.adopting.org/adoptions/adoption-lingo-list.html (accessed September 9, 2005).